Writing and Race

Edited by Tim Youngs

Longman
London and New York

Addison Wesley Longman
Edinburgh Gate
Harlow
Essex CM20 2JE
England
and Associated Companies throughout the world.

Published in the United States of America
by Addison Wesley Longman Inc., New York.

First published 1997

ISBN 0 582 27374 9 CSD
ISBN 0 582 27375 7 PPR

British Library Cataloguing-in-Publication Data
A catalogue record of this book is available
from the British Library

Library of Congress Cataloging-in-Publication Data
A catalog entry for this title is available
from the Library of Congress

Set by 35 in 10/12 pt Sabon
Produced by Longman Singapore Publishers (Pte) Ltd.
Printed in Singapore

Contents

Notes on contributors

Christopher Gair is Lecturer in English at the University College of St Mark and St John, Plymouth. He has published numerous essays on Jack London, and on North American Realism and Naturalism, and is currently working on a study of ethnic detectives. He is co-editor of *Symbiosis: A Journal of Anglo-American Literary Relations* and author of *Complicity and Resistance in Jack London's Novels: From Naturalism to Nature* (1997).

Simon Gikandi is a professor of English language and literature, specialising in modern and postcolonial literature, at the University of Michigan, Ann Arbor. His most recent publications include *Writing in Limbo: Modernism and Caribbean Literature* (Cornell University Press, 1992) and *Maps of Englishness: Writing Identity in the Culture of Colonialism* (Columbia University Press, 1996). He is associate editor of *The Cambridge History of African Literature* (forthcoming).

Michael K. Green has a PhD in philosophy from the University of Chicago and teaches philosophy at the State University of New York, Oneonta. His essays have appeared in *Political Theory, The Journal of Business Ethics, Social Theory and Practice, Kant Studien,* and elsewhere. He has recently edited a book on *Issues in Native American Cultural Identity* for Peter Lang publishers.

Sam Haigh is a lecturer in the Department of French Studies at the University of Warwick, where she teaches courses on Francophone Caribbean literature and the history of French colonialism. She is currently editing a book entitled *Caribbean Francophone Writing: An Introduction.*

Liam Kennedy is a lecturer in American Studies at the University of Birmingham. He is the author of *Susan Sontag: Mind as Passion* (Manchester University Press) and is currently researching representations of race and ethnicity in contemporary American culture.

Richard H. King is Professor of American Studies at the University of Nottingham. His most recent book is *Civil Rights and the Idea of Freedom* (1992). He is currently working on an intellectual history of post-World War II analyses of racism in Germany, the United States, Britain and France.

Gesa Mackenthun is assistant Professor of American Studies at Greifswald University. She is the author of several essays on discovery narratives and theories of empire. Her book *Metaphors of Dispossession. American Beginnings and the Translation of Empire, 1492–1637* is forthcoming from the University of Oklahoma Press. She is currently working on a book about 'postcolonial' conceptualisations of the colonial past.

David Murray teaches American Studies at the University of Nottingham. He has written extensively on Native Americans and on American literature. His publications include *Modern Indians* (1982) and *Forked Tongues* (1992). He is currently working on a book about early Indian–white exchanges.

Lynnette Turner is Senior Lecturer in Literature at the University of Hertfordshire. She has published articles on late nineteenth-century anthropology, on gender and ethnography, and is currently working (with co-editor Syed Manzural Islam) on an anthology of ethnographic writings for Oxford University Press.

Chris White is a lecturer in literature at Bolton Institute of Higher Education, and also teaches on the Gender and Women's Studies degree programme. She has published a number of essays on nineteenth-century homosexual writing and on Michael Field's poetry, and is the co-editor with Elaine Hobby of *What Lesbians Do in Books* (Women's Press).

Tim Youngs teaches in the Department of English and Media Studies at the Nottingham Trent University. He is the author of *Travellers in Africa: British Travelogues 1850–1900* (Manchester University Press, 1994) and edits the journal *Studies in Travel Writing*.

General editors' preface

Crosscurrents is an interdisciplinary series which explores simultaneously the new terrain revealed by recently developed methodologies
while offering fresh insights into more familiar and established
subject areas. In order to foster the cross-fertilisation of ideas and
methods the topic broached by each volume is rich and substantial
and ranges from issues developed in culture and gender studies to
the re-examination of aspects of English studies, history and politics.
Within each of the volumes, however, the sharpness of focus is provided by a series of essays which is directed to examining that topic
from a variety of perspectives. There is no intention that these essays,
either individually or collectively, should offer the last word on
the subject – on the contrary. They are intended to be stimulating
rather than definitive, open-ended rather than conclusive, and it is
hoped that each of them will be pithy, and thought-provoking.

Each volume has a general introduction setting out the scope of
the topic, the various modes in which it has been developed and
which places the volume as a whole in the context of other work in
the field. Everywhere, from the introduction to the bibliographies,
pointers will be given on how and where the ideas suggested in the
volumes might be developed in different ways and different directions, and how the insights and methods of various disciplines might
be brought to bear to yield new approaches to questions in hand.
The stress throughout the books will be on crossing traditional
boundaries, linking ideas and bringing together concepts in ways
which offer a challenge to previously compartmentalised modes of
thinking.

Some of the essays will deal with literary or visual texts which
are well-known and in general circulation. Many touch on primary material which is not easily accessible outside major library
collections, and where appropriate, that material has been placed

in a portfolio of documents collected at the end of each volume. Here again, it is hoped that this will provide a stimulus to discussion; it will give readers who are curious to explore further the implications of the arguments an opportunity to develop their own initiatives and to broaden the spectrum of their reading.

The authors of these essays range from international writers who are established in their respective fields to younger scholars who are bringing fresh ideas to the subjects. This means that the styles of the chapters are as various as their approaches, but in each case the essays have been selected by the general editors for their high level of critical acumen.

Professor Barrie Bullen
Dr Paul Hyland
Dr Neil Sammells

Acknowledgments

I am very grateful to Neil Sammells and Addison Wesley Longman for contracting this volume and for their patience in awaiting its completion; to John Lucas, who first suggested the *Crosscurrents* series as a home for the project; and to all the contributors for their participation and hard work. Uncomplaining co-operation from everyone has made editing a pleasure.

Ideas for my 'white ape' paper were first tried out as conference papers at The College of William and Mary in Virginia in 1994 and at Leiden University in the same year. My thanks to the organisers of the INCS Ninth Annual Colloquium for the former and to Wim Tigges for the latter.

Besides giving support for conference attendance, the Faculty of Humanities at the Nottingham Trent University awarded me a sabbatical during which – among other things – the bulk of the editing was done and my own essays drafted. Without this help the book would have taken a lot longer.

I would like to thank Dick Ellis for his support of my teaching and research; John Tomlinson for always smiling while giving out money from his research fund; Bob Ashley for helping me to set up my 'Narratives and Cultures' course; Keith Fairless for teaching it with me and for making me think again about material I thought I knew well; and the students who have taken the course, in particular the first cohort, who showed enthusiastically – even at 9 o'clock on Monday mornings – that it had a future.

Without Gurminder Sikand this book would not have been possible. Without Nathaniel Rajinder it would have been completed much sooner, but much less happily. *Writing and Race* is for him.

Tim Youngs

For
Natty

1 *Introduction: Context and Motif*

Tim Youngs

Context and motif

The aim of *Writing and Race* is to present in reasonably accessible language multidisciplinary reflections on the critical analysis
of race.[1] Contributors to this volume are drawn from American
Studies, French Studies, Philosophy, Intellectual History, Cultural
Studies, English, and Gender Studies, and we hope that the essays
will be read by students and scholars in yet more disciplines. (I
shall discuss anthropology in a moment.) One advantage of having
a subject, like race, that is studied and taught across disciplines lies
in the illuminating approaches that may result from the sharing
of ideas, methods and information. A disadvantage, however, lies
in the impossibility of keeping up with developments in all the
relevant fields.

The present collection is designed to give an introduction to
concepts in each contributor's discipline while showing, through
case-studies, how these may be applied and extended. Each essay
has its own integrity. But the volume does reveal common preoccupations, and many connections can be made between the essays
(though repetition has been avoided). For example, several of the
contributions look at images of the barbarian, the savage, the
monstrous, the primitive, and the bestial, posing the question of
how far constructions of race are determined by a psychological
need, regardless of particular epochs and places, to distinguish
self and Other. On the other hand, taken individually, each case-
study will test any assumption that specific perceptions and uses
of race can be attributed or subordinated to this basic need. The
volume can be read, then, as engaging in a continuing dialogue
between context and motif.

That dialogue is made possible here through the discussion of a broad geographical and historical range: from Europe to the Caribbean, North America, and the South Pacific, stretching from the sixteenth to the twentieth century; through a variety of topics and genres, including ethnography, North American autobiography and fiction, modernism, gender and sexuality, popular adventure tales, philosophy, and the Holocaust; and through differences in critical approach.

For the remainder of this Introduction I want to outline some of the work that has influenced many of the contributors. I shall not spend much time discussing theories of colonial discourse or of postcolonialism because many helpful introductions to and commentaries on these already exist.[2] Rather, I want to focus on ideas which, though still important, have been much less widely circulated. These are mostly from or about anthropology and its written practice, ethnography. Since these debate, often with a great deal of sophistication, matters of the textual representation of other cultures, their usefulness to a collection on *Writing and Race* cannot be overstressed.[3] The problems they address are pertinent to all that is in this volume.

Race, anthropology, and ethnography

Since the professionalisation of anthropology – the discipline that formalised racial thinking – coincided with the outward movement of nineteenth-century European colonialism and imperialism, there is a neat symmetry in the fact that the critical reassessment of it has coincided with the introspective retreat that marked decolonisation. In the last thirty years or so, more and more scholars have questioned the assumptions that earlier seemed fundamental to the discipline. Their objections centre on the right to represent the Other, and on the purposes and accuracy of representations. George Marcus and Michael Fischer, noting that these objections have coincided with conceptual revision in other disciplines, have written of a 'crisis in representation' which 'arises from uncertainty about adequate means of describing social reality'.[4]

The fact of *written* representation is crucial: writing inscribes the unequal power relationship between the observer and the observed that has so marked the discipline. As one anthropologist has put it, 'Anthropology is the study of nonliterate societies and their cultures'; it 'emerged in the nineteenth century as the discipline devoted to peoples considered by evolutionists of that time as "primitive" and "inferior"', and is distinguished from sociology, which is the study of ' "advanced", "complex", industrial, literate, large-scale societies'.[5]

Recent criticism, impelled by developments in literary and cultural theory, has directed attention to the images and structures of representation. Encouraged by Edward Said's assertion in *Orientalism* that the things to look for in representations of the Other are 'style, figures of speech, setting, narrative devices, historical and social circumstances, not the correctness of the representation nor its fidelity to some great original',[6] some critics have set out to undermine ethnographers' traditional claims to objectivity and authority. This revision of received ideas has focused mainly on the relationship between the ethnographic subject and object and on the language which conveys (or obscures) it. There may be an unspoken assumption that the values of the ethnographer's society are those of the civilised norm against which other peoples should be measured and are usually found wanting. Figures and images employed in the writing may themselves reinforce this process. As Anthony Fothergill has clearly explained:

> Definitions tend to proceed by negation: 'they' is 'not us'. The means by which we come to know the unknown Other will always be determined by our own terms of reference, our own horizon of understanding. Even the absolutely alien is always our alien, the negation of *our* normality. In this sense any writing of the Other, whether it acknowledges it or not, is a writing from within, a re-inscribing, via negation, of the writer.[7]

Fothergill's argument is an important one: the terms with which one can describe the strange can only be familiar ones. The Other cannot enter one's consciousness unmediated. To ignore the procedures by which one introduces the Other, and to overlook the effects of one's role in this, is, in the view of many current ethnographers and cultural critics, to perpetuate the inequalities of power associated with nineteenth-century racial ideologies.

These inequalities are apparent in the evolutionists' conviction that different cultures had reached different stages of development. E.B. Tylor wrote in *Anthropology* (1881) of three stages of culture:

(1) a 'savage' stage, characterized by subsistence on wild plants and animals and the utilization of stone age implements; (2) a 'barbaric' stage characterized by agriculture, metal work, and some form of community life in villages and towns; and (3) a 'civilized' stage which began when men acquired the art of writing.[8]

Thus, as one critic of anthropology has remarked with brilliant clarity, the evolutionists spatialised time.[9] In other words, the positioning of peoples at various levels of human progress meant that the regions they occupied were deemed to embody this temporal significance. Thus came to be widely circulated the motif of the European travelling 'back in time' through primeval landscapes. The effects of so labelling these regions are still felt by those who now 'write back' from the countries designated primitive or savage.

Criticising the temporal inequalities of anthropology, Fabian, in *Time and the Other*, asserts that:

Anthropology contributed above all to the intellectual justification of the colonial enterprise. It gave to politics and economics – both concerned with human Time – a firm belief in 'natural', i.e. evolutionary Time. It promoted a scheme in terms of which not only past cultures, but all living societies were irrevocably placed on a temporal slope, a stream of Time – some upstream, others downstream. Civilization, evolution, development, acculturation, modernization (and their cousins, industrialization, urbanization) are all terms whose conceptual content derives, in ways that can be specified, from evolutionary Time. (p. 17)

Fabian's observations lead him to the conclusion that in anthropology Time is used 'for the purpose of distancing those who are observed from the Time of the observer' (p. 25). This he calls 'the denial of coevalness' (p. 31), and it usually assigns to the observed a condition associated with the observer's past. The suggestion of the observed inhabiting an unchanging, unprogressive society is furthered by the use of the 'ethnographic present', the tense adopted by ethnographers to describe a people and their environment as if they were perpetually the same. Fabian is quick to remind his readers of the material conditions of anthropology. His discussion is not of discourse in the abstract, but proceeds from the assumption that 'all anthropological knowledge is political in nature' (p. 28); political because of its implication in colonialism and because of the unequal relations of power evident in the contrast between the societies of the observer and the observed. Fabian's discussion supplies a useful pointer for critics who look to examine the language and images employed by anthropologists in relation to the material conditions of their discipline. The following quotation from *Time and the Other* should clarify this:

> Figures of speech – the use of possessive pronouns, first person singular or plural, in reports on informants, groups, or tribes – are the signs in anthropological discourse of relations that ultimately belong to political economy, not to psychology or ethics . . . Temporalizations expressed as passage from savagery to civilization, from peasant to industrial society, have long served an ideology whose ultimate purpose has been to justify the procurement of commodities for our markets. (p. 95)

Fabian's phrase 'our markets', with its presumption that his readers all hail from the colonial powers, might be taken to prove his point.

If other cultures are made known through terms that are already familiar to those who describe them, and if the values of observation entail a temporal inequality, there is another prominent feature of ethnography which also renders the other culture secondary. This is its instrumental use in what James Clifford has called 'ethnographic allegory'.[10] Clifford argues that 'Ethnographic texts are inescapably allegorical' (p. 99). Ethnographies use other places and other peoples to tell stories that are really about the storyteller's own society, though Clifford does emphasise that 'Ethnographic texts are not only, or predominantly, allegories' (p. 109). The 'we' of ethnography use others for self-knowledge or for self-affirmation.

According to Clifford, the kind of historical, temporal allegory referred to by Fabian has largely (but not exclusively) been replaced in the twentieth century by humanist allegories which have 'eschewed a search for origins in favor of seeking human similarities and cultural differences', but in which 'the representational process itself has not essentially changed' (p. 102). Of course, taken to its logical extreme, the contention that ethnography is allegory may amount to little more than admitting that self-knowledge must proceed from perception of and interaction with the Other. But Clifford's point is a vital one in its correction of the misapprehension that ethnography is *only* about the Other.

Clifford believes that an awareness of the allegorical character of ethnography will lead its producers and audience to 'struggle to confront and take responsibility for our systematic constructions of others and of ourselves through others' (p. 121). One of the stories ethnography tells to and about 'ourselves' is of our nostalgia for a pastoral condition which criticises the post-industrial, technological present while ultimately reconciling ourselves to it precisely because the alternative resides in an unrecoverable past or in a distant 'primitive' society that is physically remote and, because 'pre-modern', temporally distinct also. The positive depiction of other societies need not mean an accurate, fair or objective representation at all; rather, it may be the result of an urge to comment negatively on particular features of our own society.[11]

Relevant here is Henrika Kuklick's observation that descriptions of the rural village and narratives of the origins of the state figure prominently in anthropological accounts of other societies and in mythologised versions of British history. The village and state are linked because the former is often held to exhibit on a small scale an 'optimal pattern of habitual relationships among individuals that should be extrapolated from the rural microcosm to the state macrocosm'.[12] Acknowledging, like Clifford, her debt to Raymond Williams's *The Country and the City*,[13] Kuklick notes that the rise in British popular consciousness of the image of the countryside as a repository of the desirable characteristics of Britishness coincided with the decline of and irreversible changes to the village caused by the industrial revolution. The significance of this for anthropology is, she says, obvious:

> the remote societies described by anthropologists could be vehicles for projective fantasy just as vanished British rural communities could; and primitives abroad and at home both supposedly enjoyed the benefits of existence close to nature.[14]

The fact that the increasing popularity of nostalgic evocations of the countryside occurred alongside the disappearance of much that comprised it confirms that perceptions are culturally and historically grounded. Structural anthropologist Lévi-Strauss noticed in the 1950s that a similar phenomenon occurs once modernism has imposed on 'primitive' societies. 'Our' society 'pretends to itself that it is investing them with nobility at the very time when it is completing their destruction, whereas it viewed them with terror and disgust when they were genuine adversaries'. In telling phrases, Lévi-Strauss decides that 'Not content with having eliminated savage life, and unaware even of having done so, it feels the need feverishly to appease the nostalgic cannibalism of history with the shadows of those that history has already destroyed'.[15] Of course, Lévi-Strauss's diagnosis itself reveals a kind of nostalgia for an uncorrupted state of primitivism, but he is well aware of the urge to escapism that lies behind such yearnings and of the paradox that 'while I complain of being able to glimpse no more than the shadow of the past, I may be insensitive to reality as it is taking shape at this very moment, since I have not reached the stage of development at which I would be capable of perceiving it'.[16]

A few cultural critics have recently rejected the idea of a one-way gaze; of the literate observer objectively recording the life of another people. Henrika Kuklick has challenged the notion that anthropological subjects have been passive. She maintains instead that 'In varying degrees at various times they have themselves shaped Westerners' perceptions of their cultures', and that 'on the colonial frontier, relationships between Europeans and indigenous peoples were as egalitarian as they would ever be' (p. 280), with British traders, for example, becoming integral members of societies in regions they did not control. Nor were the people who were observed unaffected by the presence of the anthropologist. Colonial rule 'shaped the societies anthropologists studied' (p. 291), and it is now generally admitted by practitioners and theorists of the discipline that the immediate presence of the anthropologist does have an effect on the people who are being watched and questioned.

A notable development in the criticism of ethnography is the ever louder recommendation that in their writings ethnographers should be self-reflexive and more accommodating of the Other's voice. Edward Said has written in a wider context that the two necessary conditions for knowing another culture are 'uncoercive contact with an alien culture through real exchange, and self-consciousness about the interpretative project itself'.[17] The ideal of real exchange is a difficult one to achieve or measure but the call for self-consciousness is one that has been readily heeded, though Said's criterion was already being observed by many: James Clifford, for example, had stated that 'while ethnographic writing cannot entirely escape the reductionist use of dichotomies and essences, it can at least struggle self-consciously to avoid portraying abstract, a-historical "others" '.[18] In keeping, then, with 'postcolonial' desires to make amends for the previous inequalities of power in ethnographic representations, there has been much reflection on ethnography as textual construction and on the ethnographer's role in creating what some have called 'fictions'.[19] Clifford insists that because of the omission of certain voices and inconsistencies and of facts about the author's own background and presence, because of the authority assumed by the ethnographer to speak for the Other, and because of the rhetoric and figures employed in the writing, 'Ethnographic truths are thus inherently *partial* – committed and incomplete'.[20] This being so, some attention has been directed to the material factors that influence the construction of these 'partial truths'. According to James Clifford, these factors include: the social context; the rhetoric; the institutional conventions; the genre; the politics of representation (and the authority behind these); and the history of all these criteria.[21]

The recognition of these constraints has coincided with attempts by fieldworkers to produce ethnographies that will avoid some of the problems caused by the colonial inheritance of anthropology. Foremost among the strategies adopted are self-reflexivity and dialogism. The former may involve extensive use of the first person; a constant reminder of the ethnographer's presence amongst his or her informants, with reflections on how interaction with them may affect their responses; and explicit attention to the construction of the text as well as to the conditions in which the fieldwork was carried out so as not to give the illusion of a smooth, narrative order to events and lives that may in fact be not nearly so coherent as suggested in traditional ethnography.

Dennis Tedlock has distinguished dialogical anthropology, which 'is a continuing process and itself illustrates process and change', from analogical anthropology, which 'is a product, a result', and in which it seems that 'the ethnographer and the native must never be articulate between the same two covers'.[22] The introduction of dialogism sees the ethnographer trying to present as accurately as possible the voice of the informant. This may consist of comments on the actual processes of being questioned. One result of this method is to highlight what Clifford might call the fictionality of the text. The pretence of a one-way stream of questions from the ethnographer met with revealing answers from an uninquisitive 'native' disappears, and with it the illusion of an objective, impersonal figure penetrating a passive culture to give readers an authoritative view and claiming to speak universal truths. A prerequisite for any attempt to convey fairly the 'creative nature of the field interaction' is, in the words of one scholar, 'an attentiveness to the dialogical and temporal character of the event, and a refusal to reduce it to monological, atemporal form'.[23] Steven Webster urges that

> the authentic ground of ethnographic truth in dialogue be retained in ethnography through the conscious use of fictional devices of narrative which intimate transparency to truth without giving in to the positivist illusion of an objective or predictable state of affairs. Ethnography must remain as hesitant and open to contingency and interpretation as is the concrete social experience upon which it is based.[24]

Of course, the fact remains that unless the ethnographic subject has an equal part in the production of a text, the ethnographer, however well-intentioned, is only offering readers an incorporated voice. And at least one anthropologist has countered such arguments by announcing that 'Introspection and self-awareness provide poor and unreliable protection against cultural bias'.[25] In this view, scientific measurement must be replicable and it is doubtful whether self-knowledge is 'a sufficient condition of replicability in investigating a society different from our own'.[26] Gross's conclusion is that 'ethnographers must overcome the bias which teaches that the *only* valid way [to] intercultural understanding lies in the empathic and introspective approach'.[27] Another objection has been that the self-conscious admission of problems in the field provides the benefit of catharsis since 'such writings can be seen as guilt-relieving mechanisms for returned field workers'.[28] Indeed, on a larger scale, it might be said that a good deal of the introspection in anthropology over the past few decades marks a similar atonement for guilt over the past association of anthropology with imperialism. Marcus and Cushman, meanwhile, concluded in the early 1980s that experimental ethnographies had yet to resolve the question of whether '*reflection* on understanding and an understanding itself' can be balanced 'in a single text'.[29]

Summing up and recommending ideas for an anthropology which will redefine traditional roles, one of the developments Diane Lewis called for in the early 1970s was the idea of a 'native ethnography' – i.e. 'the study of culture from the inside, by the insider, as a dominant approach in the discipline'.[30] One of the difficulties with this is that the involvement of the subject inevitably changes the situation to be recorded, and this has to be taken into account.

Of course, there is a deep irony in the way that Western academics have pronounced so authoritatively on the lack of authority and have busied themselves trying to find fairer, more accurate means of representation. The intense preoccupation with the task of cleansing past sins from present productions gives the misleading impression that ethnography is now freed from the taint of its colonial past and lacks the institutional will or power to effect harmful misrepresentations. Edward Said has quite rightly complained that in all the writings he has read on anthropology and Otherness 'there is an almost total absence of any reference to American imperial intervention as a factor affecting the theoretical discussion'.[31] Scholars should not, in his view, so fetishise the textual that they end up ignoring the physical manifestations of, or opposition to, imperialism; nor should those in the United States so celebrate their analytic penetration of texts that they forget their own implication in – and therefore possibilities for influencing – the activities of what has replaced earlier empires as 'the dominant outside force' in other parts of the world.[32] Ethnography nowadays may be bound up with the research conducted by intelligence agencies, multinational corporations and government agencies (for one should not forget either domestic ethnography). All this tends to be ignored in the rush to declare a weakening of power. Clifford Geertz, for example, has contrasted older anthropological certainties with the newer 'grave inner uncertainties . . . loss of confidence, and the crisis in ethnographic writing that goes with it'.[33]

Within the body of ethnographic criticism – and sometimes running counter to it – has been a growing concern with feminist ethnography. This has been motivated in no small part by the feeling that discussions of ethnographic authority have overlooked the importance of gender. Henrietta Moore has insisted that 'Feminist anthropology is not . . . about "adding" women into the discipline, but is instead about confronting the conceptual and analytical inadequacies of disciplinary theory'.[34] She continues:

It is the study of gender, of the interrelations between women and men, and of the role of gender in structuring human societies, their histories, ideologies, economic systems and political structures.[35]

In the words of Lynnette Turner, 'introducing the issue of gender into analyses of ethnography brings to light ambivalences and contradictions at each stage of the ethnographic process, from fieldwork and fieldwork notes, to the later negotiation of formal monograph requirements'.[36] An examination of gender will, in this view, further erode patriarchal claims to speak with universal authority.

One trend has been to assert an underlying empathy between colonial and colonised women, or even between Western women and anthropological subjects, whether male or female. At one extreme it has been maintained by some that this bond is actually the result of a strong identification such that 'feminists speak from the position of the "other"'.[37] This particular position has been criticised by Turner for its uncritical essentialism and its 'unproblematic conception of common marginality'.[38] Henrietta Moore has underlined the cultural construction of women, arguing that the 'inevitable fact of biological difference between the sexes tells us nothing about the general social significance of that difference',[39] and warning that 'the power relations in the ethnographic encounter are not necessarily ones which are erased simply by commonalities of sex'.[40] The call by some feminists for an empathetic relationship between the female anthropologist and subject has not found favour with Judith Stacey, who contends that

ethnographic method exposes subjects to far greater danger and exploitation than do more positivist, abstract, and 'masculinist' research methods. The greater the intimacy, the apparent mutuality of the researcher/researched relationship, the greater is the danger.[41]

Inderpal Grewal, writing not specifically on feminist ethnography, but on some of the ideas that have shaped it, has spoken out strongly against the notion of a shared agenda for white Western and black women, complaining that:

For many Euro-American feminist critics the need to see Western feminism as anti-imperialist in the face of much evidence to the contrary comes out of the denial of such collaborations [with United States 'ideologies of democracy and freedom'] and the desire to see feminism as wholly oppositional and existing outside particular ideological formations.[42]

Lynnette Turner summarises Marilyn Strathern as warning that anthropological analyses of gender relations in other societies should recognise the different conceptions within these societies, so that – perhaps contrary to some feminist procedures – the social anthropological study of male–female relations in other societies cannot be used to understand Western experience. Thus, 'Feminist notions of society will necessarily resonate with specific assumptions that may well not be applicable to the group being studied.'[43]

The debates and issues in ethnography that I have outlined above all underlie the essays in the present volume. It would be as well to remember, having seen how these arguments are far from closed, that the verb in *Writing and Race* is an active one.

Colonial discourse

Much of the impetus for studies of race produced in the 1980s and 1990s has come from the work of colonial discourse theorists.[44] Peter Hulme, whose *Colonial Encounters* has been one of the most influential of these texts, has defined colonial discourse as:

> an ensemble of linguistically-based practices unified by their common deployment in the management of colonial relationships, an ensemble that could combine the most formulaic and bureaucratic of official documents ... with the most non-functional and unprepossessing of romantic novels.[45]

This useful definition evidently broadens the range of writing to be studied by those interested in the workings of colonial discourse. (This goes for textual representations of race in other than colonial contexts too.) Something of that range is apparent in the present volume, with essays on, among other topics and genres, exploration and travel narratives, philosophical and sexual treatises, anthropological writings (including questionnaires and letters), Irish-American and African-American novels, and popular fiction of the late nineteenth century.

In many ways the developments in colonial discourse theory parallel those in critiques of ethnography. For example, Hulme, like Clifford, underlines the subjectivity and incompleteness of writing on race:

> One of the ways in which ideologies work is by passing off partial accounts as the whole story. They often achieve this by representing their partiality as what can be taken for granted, 'common sense', 'the natural', even 'reality itself'.[46]

But it must be remembered that the academic discourse of self and Other locates the centre in the West. Barbara Christian's complaint about this binary model can be expressed quite succinctly: 'many of us have never conceived of ourselves only as somebody's *other*'.[47]

Whereas, for obvious reasons, it is rarely that the people who are the objects of anthropology can make their voices heard from within the academy (their experiences and position would remove them from the site of study and so make them no longer part of the group to be observed), it has been easier for those from former colonies to give their own perspectives on the discourses of colonialism. Even then, however, the question arises of how far their involvement in the European or North American university system has them reproducing the voices of Western academia.

The dominance of intellectuals from the United States and Western Europe has been powerfully criticised by Neil Lazarus, who has complained that 'the globalism of postmodernist social theory amounts to an unwarranted generalisation from the specific experience of a class fraction of the western (or western-centred) bourgeoisie'.[48] A similar point about the pressure exerted by the metropolitan university has been made more trenchantly by Aijaz Ahmad, who attacks what he calls the 'imperial dominance' of the universities in India (where he works) by those of Europe and the United States.[49] Ahmad's book *In Theory* marks one of the most intellectually rigorous and persuasive contributions to studies of what might be called colonial discourse,[50] though Ahmad himself strongly rejects that term, arguing that its concentration on images and representations is a distraction from the material conditions that actually affect people's lives. Although the distinction Ahmad makes between the material and ideas is not always easy to uphold,[51] and his objections to a focus on discourse risk obscuring the very means by which material states are rationalised, naturalised or opposed, his argument constitutes a compelling corrective to the privileging of discourse by many theorists.[52]

The passage from *Orientalism* that I have quoted above, on the importance of looking at 'style, figures of speech, setting, narrative devices, historical and social circumstances', has been heavily criticised by Ahmad, who believes it is 'unimaginably difficult, if not altogether pointless' to refer to the setting and circumstances of a representation without 'raising, in some fundamental way', those issues of fidelity and correctness that Said claims need not be looked at, for, in Ahmad's words, 'it is usually with reference to "historical and social circumstances" that worthwhile distinctions between a representation and misrepresentation are customarily made'.[53] Theorists and philosophers might well counter that no such distinction is possible, but Ahmad is unyielding in his opposition to this 'image of language as the enemy of experience, this assertion that representation is always-already a misrepresentation, this shallow pathos about the impossibility of truthful human communication' (p. 194). Ahmad's anger – this seems not too strong a word to use – is directed at those who, in his view, have substituted for serious study of the material world, in which power is actually exercised and real struggles take place, the spurious radicalism of literary theory, which makes of everything a text.[54] By this means, complains Ahmad, the inhabitants of the 'third world' are denied agency. They are posited as the victims of colonial exploitation and misrepresentation. The political structures within the 'third world', Ahmad continues, are ignored in this insistent attention to the West's misconstruction of its others. The violence of Partition is Ahmad's example of the kind of event for which blame should attach to those in the 'third world' but which is overlooked or downplayed by those who emphasise instead this 'other Power [Orientalism] which has victimized us and inferiorized us for two thousand five hundred years or more' (p. 195).

Ahmad argues that in what he terms the 'cognate subdisciplines of "Third World Literature" and "Colonial Discourse Analysis"', there seems to be 'far greater interest in the colonialism of the past than in the imperialism of the present' and in '"fictions" of representation and cultural artefact' rather than in 'the "facts" of imperialist wars and political economies of exploitation'. The consequence, or perhaps the intention, is that 'one is hearing, as these subdisciplines now function in the United States, a lot less about the United States itself and a lot more about Britain and France' (p. 93).

Ahmad is as critical of postcolonial theory as he is of colonial discourse studies.[55] He believes that the texts that now constitute the canon of 'Third World' literature and which are used to serve as a counter-canon are, as a category, like any canon, a fabrication. He is critical of the neglect of authors who do not write in English, which causes 'the vast majority of literary texts' from Africa and Asia to be 'unavailable in the metropolises' (p. 97). Those (English-language) texts that are admitted are subject to 'the protocols that metropolitan criticism has developed for reading what it calls "minority literatures"'.[56] In Ahmad's not uncontroversial view, then, the metropolitan universities control by selection the syllabus of the new canon and by method how it is read.

Stereotypes

Stereotypes are often talked of as the product of unavoidable psychological processes. On the face of it this is undoubtedly true. But it must surely be the case that, within the inevitable constitution of the self against a stereotyped Other, the particular form that stereotype takes will differ at different periods and in different places. Homi Bhabha has suggested that 'It is the force of ambivalence that gives the colonial stereotype its currency' and that it is this ambivalence which 'ensures its repeatability in changing historical and discursive conjunctures'.[57] For Bhabha:

> To recognize the stereotype as an ambivalent mode of knowledge and power demands a theoretical and political response that challenges deterministic or functionalist modes of conceiving of the relationship between discourse and politics, *and questions dogmatic and moralistic positions on the meaning of oppression and discrimination.*[58]

This is a troubling passage for those of us who might actually want to be moralistic, if not dogmatic, about oppression and discrimination; perhaps it was words like Bhabha's that Ahmad had in mind when he complained of those poststructuralisms that proclaim the *'impossibility* of stable subject positions' and the *'death* of politics as such'.[59] Bhabha goes on:

> My reading of colonial discourse suggests that the point of inter-
> vention should shift from the *identification* of images as positive
> or negative, to an understanding of the *processes of subjectification*
> made possible (and plausible) through stereotypical discourse.[60]

But there is little reason for these points of intervention (in Bhabha's
phrase) to be separated at all. Analysis of racial stereotypes does
demand more than a simple labelling of good and bad, but since
the nature of subjectification depends on negative and positive views
of others, to refrain from identifying them as such is an abdication
of one's duty as a critic.

Bhabha writes of the 'processes of subjectification'. But these
must be seen in their historical and material contexts. Ambivalence
towards colonial stereotypes arises not from some unchanging psychic split but in response to cultural conditions. To argue otherwise
is not only to deny the truth that we are first and foremost social
creatures but to postulate a mysterious kind of psychic national
homogeneity in the country where stereotypes are circulated.

It is possible to keep hold of the psychological while viewing it
within the material world and historicising it. Rightly observing
that 'Social representation is a process and to this process there
is no end',[61] Jan Nederveen Pieterse emphasises that social representations 'arise out of a multiplicity of historical contexts and
configurations, and therefore cannot be reduced to a few simple
schemas'.[62] This suggests that stereotypes will tell us more about
the people who produce and circulate them than about those who
are stereotyped. Indeed, Nederveen Pieterse soon afterwards makes
this suggestion explicit, explaining that a 'recurring refrain' in his
book is the 'principle that the image-formation of outsiders is
determined primarily by the dynamics of one's own circle'.[63] These
images are likely to alter as cultural conditions 'at home' change.[64]

Before moving on it is necessary to note that not all critics
take such a negative view of stereotypes. Ritchie Robertson, for
instance, has defended them as essential ways of understanding
life. In Robertson's opinion:

> Stereotypes are not falsehoods, but simplified models which are
> necessary if we are to cope with the multiplicity of experience. The
> error lies not in using stereotypes, but in supposing that stereotypes
> are fully adequate representations . . . it is possible, though difficult,
> to use stereotypes in a critical and tentative manner, as frames within

which the reality of the Other can be perceived and described with precision. By such methods another culture can be accurately understood and represented; but this can only be done from an observer's specific historical standpoint, and within the conventions of representation that the observer employs.[65]

It is a pity that Robertson's zeal should lead him to overstate his case, for some stereotypes obviously are falsehoods, both on a general level (manufacturing an erroneous image of a group based on a misapprehension – wilful or otherwise – of their characteristics) and on an individual level (wrongly attributing to an individual the characteristics of a group to which it is mistakenly thought that individual belongs, or ascribing to an individual member of a group misconceived traits of that group). Stereotypes can be false; and serious, often murderous, consequences can result from their use.

An understanding of stereotyping is vital. As Nederveen Pieterse among other commentators has observed, the features applied to other races are 'also attributed to entirely different categories defined according to social status, gender, age, nationality, and so forth'. Given these similarities, 'we must conclude that it is not racial phenotype, colour, or ethnicity that is the decisive factor, but the *relationship* which exists between the labelling and the labelled group'.[66] This line is a way of returning discussions of images to analyses of power. Studies of representations need not and certainly should not obscure power relationships.

Writing and race

The collection begins with Michael K. Green's essay on 'Philosophers among the savages'. Green shows how philosophers share some of the prejudices of their time and culture. Contemporary ideas of race will inform their positions on fundamental concepts, such as the savage, whose designation and function Green traces from classical to modern times. Green clearly explains how this idea is used to denote something other that, by opposition, also identifies the self. The association of the savage with wildness, the outside, chaos and formlessness, allows the delineation of the philosopher and his culture (it usually is *his*) as civilised, organised, interior, domestic. The fascination with the savage is in part because it circumscribes acceptable behaviour and establishes normative rules by their negation. The formation of these rules can play an important part in fostering a sense of community or national identity, whose sense of values is reached by consensus within the group and by conflict with those (the savages) outside the group.

Like Green, Gesa Mackenthun goes back to the classics for the roots of discourses of race and monstrosity. Mackenthun gives a rich reading of *The Tempest* in the context of changes in the ideas of monstrosity and female sexuality and power. Her essay offers a case-study of how received images are adapted ideologically to new historical conditions. The early narratives of America that she considers alongside *The Tempest* draw on the already existing fund of imagined monsters. In Shakespeare's play, claims Mackenthun, one discovers the condensing of two discourses of monstrosity: that of the medieval monstrous races and that of witchcraft. The discussion of witchcraft signals Mackenthun's important focus on gender as she proceeds to make good the general critical neglect of Sycorax, Caliban's mother. Mackenthun suggests that *The Tempest* 'contributes to a post-Elizabethan regendering of rulership in dramatically exorcising the fear of an unmarried female sovereign'. Gender and state formations are connected, and the discourses of territorial possession and of witchcraft combine, in the gendered representations of the New World as monstrous.

Mackenthun's analysis, which draws on Bakhtin's theories of the grotesque (further evidence that our understanding of monsters is subject to historical change), concludes with the idea, following Foucault, that alternative knowledges and histories to the accepted (patriarchal, colonial) order of things are excluded. If they cannot be spoken of they are represented as monstrous. (Neither Caliban nor Sycorax, who are spoken of in derogatory terms of race and gender, are firmly visualised.) And thus 'the early modern discourse of possession has itself become monstrous and grotesque'.

David Murray's essay is also concerned with race in North America. Acknowledging the difficulties with terminology which continue to this day, Murray complicates recent discussions of hybridity by considering the cultural situation in which *three* main racial categories are constructed: black (African-American), red (Native American), and white (European immigrants). Here binary models are not applicable, not even with the in-between state of hybridity. Murray shows how, since the times of early contact, Native Americans have been depicted as both the villainous and the noble savage, while the African-American has generally been viewed more negatively. The values attached to these groups, and white men's practice (both physical and textual) of concealing their miscegenation with Native American and African-American women, contribute to the complexities of the interrelationship between them. Murray illustrates how identities are affected by all this when he considers a number of autobiographies, themselves often hybrid texts because of the part played by whites in editing and publishing them. In particular, through a fascinating comparison of Long Lance's autobiography with the actual biographical details of its subject's life (the twists and turns of which I will not disclose here), Murray reveals how even self-identity is not what it might seem.

Drawing on a distinction that others have already made between race and ethnicity, Murray notes that ethnicity may involve choice – it may be created – as opposed to the view of authenticity on which definitions of race depend. In Murray's words, 'You can choose to embrace ethnicity, which is defined in terms of group, whereas race is quite different.' Murray extends this observation to remark that

> ethnicity can be creative, an act of imagining and reimagining the past, a creative use of memory. Ethnicity therefore need not be reliant on authenticity except as an important rhetorical weapon.

Ethnic and racial memory is the subject of Liam Kennedy's contribution. Kennedy takes as his starting point the observation that there has been a new plurality and politicising of memory in the United States in the aftermath of the loss, in the mid-1960s, of the postwar ideological consensus. In this 'volatile cultural pluralism', memory has been used to shape ethnic identities. A crucial point of Kennedy's essay is that these memories are not just actual ones, but are constructions, with the aim of creating or negotiating an identity. They are not, however, necessarily counter-hegemonic since they may 'prescriptively memorialise the past and essentialise the cultural identities' they inscribe.

Kennedy chooses the city as his 'site of memory' and preserves a working distinction between the ethnic and racial by discussing the novels and non-fiction 'urban biography' of Irish-American

William Kennedy as examples of ethnic perspectives and Toni Morrison's *Jazz* as an instance of racial views. Both authors' works are set in New York: William Kennedy's in Albany and *Jazz* in Harlem.

William Kennedy's writings show his belief that Irish-Americans reinvent the past as a step towards self-definition but he is also engaged, writes Liam Kennedy, in the act of questioning Irish-Americans' 'deeply mythologised story of immigrant success and ethnic passage'. The Albany books reveal ethnic history and identity to be always shifting, according to interpretations of the past, a process in which the novelist is himself engaged.

If the urban experiences and outlooks of Irish-Americans and African-Americans differ, there are some shared concerns. The Harlem of *Jazz* is 'more expressively imagined than it is historically documented' in Morrison's investigation of what urban freedom means for her characters. Their 'interior lives', out of the view of the narrator but on which author and readers may reflect, involve the workings of memory and desire. While the narrator portrays the city as a place of desire and forgetfulness, the author suggests that it is also one of love and memory. As an African-American, Morrison wants to keep hold of the 'useful past' while keeping alive future possibilities.

In both authors, Kennedy concludes, the tension felt by characters as a result of their efforts to find their own position in the past, at the same time as they are themselves positioned by those narratives, is expressed in memory, and this exemplifies the problems and necessity of establishing a usable past for their ethnic and racial groups.

Reimagining the past is also a major theme of Guadaloupean novelist Maryse Condé, the subject of Sam Haigh's essay. Haigh discusses Condé as a woman author who is writing within the male-dominated literary tradition of the French Antilles, and who questions the position of women in – and outside – race liberation movements. Declarations of black opposition to racism, and manifestoes of racial identity, it is pointed out, have often been based on a male agenda which may do little to lift the burdens faced by black women.

Haigh concentrates on Condé's *I, Tituba, Black Witch of Salem*. The title character will be known to many from Arthur Miller's *The Crucible*, in which she is Parris's 'Negro slave' from Barbados, who is accused of having a compact with the Devil.[67] Condé's imaginative telling of Tituba's story writes the 'Black Witch' back into history from her own perspective. Haigh argues that it is Tituba's role as witch that 'allows her to resist and to undermine the various forms of colonial authority wielded over her'. It is 'via witchcraft' that Condé has Tituba 'enter her people's history as a specifically *female* figure of resistance'. We might contrast this with the writing out of Sycorax that Mackenthun has noted in *The Tempest*. Haigh aligns Tituba with other marginalised and disruptive women who have been repressed (the madwoman, the hysteric, the adulteress, the lesbian), but whose stories and story-telling are 'a powerful mediator of alternative histories of women'. Condé's blurring of fact and fiction is seen by Haigh as akin to the folktale, which marks the attempt by 'both communities and individuals to put themselves into a history of their own making, to "storytell" themselves into existence'. Thus Condé brings the oral and the written together, something which – 'the ability to be both print and oral literature'[68] – Toni Morrison regards as a major characteristic of black art.

Negritude, one of the black cultural movements whose male-dominance (or 'androcentric discourse') Haigh shows Condé to be subverting, is also mentioned in Simon Gikandi's essay, as is the Harlem that forms the setting of Toni Morrison's *Jazz* (whose treatment by Liam Kennedy I have mentioned above). But Gikandi, who, too, is concerned with the dynamics of gender and race, has a different focus: that of race and the modernist aesthetic. Intrigued that the significance of race and cultures is still largely overlooked in studies of modernism, Gikandi notes that it is primarily through the figure of the primitive that race enters modernism, as a critical counterpoint to the industrial and bourgeois culture that many artists reacted against. In the process of this turn to the primitive several aspects that were formerly derided – closeness to nature, lack of industry, lack of moral and physical restraint, primacy of feelings above the intellect – now became virtues. Gikandi makes the point, though, that even if this led to a more positive picture (and I use the word 'picture' advisedly since Gikandi also examines the presence of these themes in modernist paintings and the influence of paintings on writers), it none the less rested on a sub-jective view of the primitive as different. What modernism does, writes Gikandi, is to 'connect race and aesthetics at the most fundamental level'. Thus where, previously, aesthetic principles had excluded blacks from culture, 'modernism sought to make blackness an essential condition in the establishment of aesthetic principles'. Blackness comes to supply the vitality lacking in a stultifying urban and industrial society whose subjects are becoming alienated. Here anthropology and psychology combine to offer the primitive as a figure whose pre-industrial existence affords glimpses of what life before urban industrialism looked like and of what may still be hidden in the depths of the unconscious. Yet, despite this self-serving use by modernists of the primitive, there were ways 'in which modernism came to be read, especially by colonised black writers, as a mode of liberation of race itself'. Modernism, then, in spite of its exploitation of (an idea of) blackness, provides the impetus to black self-expression in cultural events such as the Harlem Renaissance of the 1920s. Where the two modernisms differ (though they have similarities) is in African-Americans' desire for the modern instead of critiquing it. The figurative or even actual return to Africa is, in Gikandi's view, not incompatible with this since it identifies a usable past that makes possible the 'New Negro' of the present.

The essays that follow Gikandi's, though they have their own agendas, may each be seen to explore a different theme of his essay. These may be listed as the vital (Youngs), the erotic (White), the anthropological (Turner), the exotic (Gair) and the political (King).

My own essay proceeds from the premise that the language of race is applied to groups within society as much as to those outside it. Racial imagery, in particular the figure of the savage, is employed in class and gender contexts. Whereas Gikandi shows how, in modernism, a more positive view of the primitive emerges to rejuvenate those who are deadened by Western European or North American culture, my attention is on the 1880s and 1890s, a time when feelings towards society (particularly among the middle class) were ambivalent. I argue that these feelings, conjoined with the profound uncertainty about the nature of humanity provoked by social Darwinism, found expression in the form of the white ape, a creature exhibiting a dangerous and bestial vitality. I look at the presence of this disturbing creature in several fictional texts of the period and argue that it embodies fears of the Other at the same time that it forces an admission that it may no longer be possible socially or psychologically to keep it confined to its own domain.

Gikandi suggests in passing that one of the uses the West made of the primitive was as the bearer of its erotic desires. Eroticism forms the subject of Chris White's essay on the extraordinary Sir Richard Francis Burton: traveller, explorer, linguist, quasi-anthropologist, and much else besides. White makes no effort to conceal Burton's racism or his participation in Orientalist discourses, but, through a close reading of the 'Terminal Essay' to his translation of *The Thousand Nights and a Night* (1885), argues that his ambivalent attitude towards pederasty has him criticising British and Judaean–Christian culture. If Haigh's essay posits gender as a complicating factor in racial discourse, then White's does the same for sexuality. Claiming that representations of Burton as racist and Orientalist do not tell the whole story, White maintains that 'what can be found in Burton's work, especially in his translations of erotic classics, are a plethora of satirical textual games in which he mocks western attitudes to sexuality, and elevates eastern mores and practices as superior, more ethical, more honest'. If to this be raised the objection that Burton is engaged in a kind of ethnographic allegory, White has a ready response: that in his many translations Burton is 'allowing eastern cultures to speak for themselves in their artistic products' and is demonstrating 'the complexity of the cultural formations from which those texts emerged'. White's reassessment of Burton concludes that it is neither useful nor wholly accurate to classify him as straightforwardly Orientalist or racist or sexually liberationist. Rather, in his invention of the Sotadic Zone, outside the Judaean–Christian world, and where pederasty is, according to Burton, popular and widely practised, he creates for his readers 'a space in literature, language and history in which to look for other definitions and treatments of homosexuality'. It is perhaps indicative of the time at which Burton wrote, just at the early dawning of the modernism described by Gikandi, that, in White's view, he gives his readers nowhere stable to place themselves in terms of race, gender, or sexuality. Physically and figuratively, neither home nor abroad is sufficient.

The relationship of home and abroad in anthropology is one of Lynnette Turner's concerns. Turner examines ways in which anthropological data were acquired. In particular, she considers the

role of the questionnaire (used extensively by 'armchair anthropologists' remote from the field) and the development of participant
observation. Turner concentrates on the work of Alfred Howitt and
Lorimer Fison on Aboriginal Australians. The writings of Howitt
and Fison reflect changes that were occurring in late nineteenth-
century anthropological inquiry, but also 'determined in significant
ways' its agenda. Turner contends that the already existing male
bias in anthropology was compounded by participant observation, which was usually carried out by men but also, as with
Howitt and Fison, was reinforced by the attention given to male
rituals, which themselves offered a male view of society. Turner's
essay emphasises the gender bias in anthropology, showing how
the method of research can further marginalise women, both as
informants and researchers. Her study of methodology underlines
the complexity of the politics and sexual politics of ethnography,
complicating the simple model of observer and observed. Turner's
conclusion that Howitt's use of the questionnaire gives more of
a voice to Aboriginal women (however filtered) than does his
later fieldwork offers a challenge to those who assume a line of
progression and who ask no questions of the 'brotherhood' of
anthropologists.

The exotic is the focus of Christopher Gair's piece on Jack
London's South Sea writings of 1907–11. Gair builds on the thesis
that self-definition is achieved through or against another and
examines how the effects of the closing of the Western frontier in
the United States affected perceptions of the South Pacific. Gair
maintains that these were (and are) firmly grounded in material
conditions. Thus the widely held view that the white race was
losing its vigour and could best rediscover it by turning to the
primitive in the South Pacific had much to do with the loss of
ground for the pioneer. The extension or shifting of the frontier
was made to betoken racial and imperial energy (and this, notes
Gair, at a time when the city, which had its own frontiers, was the
scene of much conflict).

Gair sees in the range of London's accounts of the region 'a
multiplicity of forms of *Otherness*, all highly illuminating in the
context of American hopes and fears in the early twentieth century'. One of those forms of Otherness is as a potential sanctuary
from the forces of modernity; this, too, is gendered as the natural
is associated with the recovery of a masculinity threatened by a

'feminising modernity'. But Gair identifies too the crisis that ensues when, in the face of European and North American imperialism, the Other disappears: there vanishes the site on which the Frontiersman (and it usually is the Frontiers*man*) can prove his identity. In some ways this crisis is resolved by the application to race of theories of natural selection, and in other ways by the turn to the conventions of the adventure story, 'a form that cannot permit the negative thinking which insists upon the end of the exotic', for if the self is defined against the exotic, then the destruction of the exotic must involve the destruction of the self.

The need constantly to examine – and where necessary oppose – racial constructions is terrifyingly obvious from the Nazis' slaughter of the Jews. This volume closes with Richard H. King's essay on the different attempts by Theodor Adorno and Hannah Arendt, both German-Jewish intellectuals, to understand what caused the Holocaust. Both examine the crisis of western modernity embodied in it, but each has a different approach. King's careful delineation of Adorno's aim to develop a theory of prejudiced thinking in general, and of Arendt's aim to produce a theory of totalitarianism, has him drawing together concerns about race that have informed all the preceding essays, whatever their particular foci. This is how King summarises 'two essential questions' Arendt and Adorno 'asked and tried to answer':

> did modern anti-Semitism represent something new or was it only superficially different from earlier forms of anti-Semitism? And second, were Jews picked out for discrimination because of certain fixed, determinate characteristics or were they tabulæ rasæ, as it were, upon which were inscribed the dominant society's rejected, negative qualities at certain historical junctures?

Primo Levi, that quietly eloquent survivor of Auschwitz, professed himself unable to understand Nazi hatred, but felt that 'If understanding is impossible, knowing is imperative, because what happened could happen again'.[69] For Levi, writing was 'first and foremost . . . an interior liberation'. He and other inmates felt an urgent need 'to tell our story to the "rest", to make "the rest" participate in it'.[70] Most of us are 'the rest'. To us he issues the warning that 'In every part of the world, wherever you begin by denying the fundamental liberties of mankind, and equality among people, you move toward the concentration camp system'.[71] Race is one of the factors used to deny those fundamental liberties.

Notes

1. The practice of placing race in inverted commas to signify its questionable status will not be followed in this volume. The contributors' questioning of racial concepts will be clear enough from the essays themselves. As far as the geographical coverage of *Writing and Race* is concerned, care has been taken to avoid overlaps with other volumes in the series. *Writing and Africa* has already been published and other proposed titles include *Writing and India*.

2. See, for example, besides the works that I do mention, Patrick Williams and Laura Chrisman, eds, *Colonial Discourse and Postcolonial Theory: a reader* (London: Harvester Wheatsheaf, 1993), and Peter Childs and Patrick Williams, *An Introduction to Post-Colonial Theory* (London: Harvester and Prentice Hall, 1996).

3. Much of the following discussion about recent problems and debates in anthropology applies also to anthropological film. See, for example, Jay Ruby, 'Ethnography as Trompe l'Oeil: Film and Anthropology', in Jay Ruby, ed., *A Crack in the Mirror: Reflexive Perspectives in Anthropology* (Philadelphia: University of Pennsylvania Press, 1982), pp. 121–31; and, from the same volume, Eric Michaels, 'How to Look at Us Looking at the Yanomami Looking at Us', pp. 133–46; Jean Rouch (trans. Steve Feld and Shari Robertson), 'On the Vicissitudes of the Self: The Possessed Dancer, the Magician, the Sorcerer, the Filmmaker, and the Ethnographer', *Studies in the Anthropology of Visual Communication* 5, 1 (1978), 2–8; Peter Loizos, *Innovation in Ethnographic Film: From Innocence to Self-Consciousness 1955–1985* (Manchester: Manchester University Press, 1993); and Leslie Devereux and Roger Hillman, eds, *Fields of Vision: Essays in Film Studies, Visual Anthropology, and Photography* (Berkeley: University of California Press, 1995).

4. George E. Marcus and Michael J. Fischer, *Anthropology as Cultural Critique: An Experimental Moment in the Human Sciences* (Chicago: University of Chicago Press, 1986), p. 8. The authors' assertion that 'This trend may have much to do with the unfavorable shift in the relative position of American power and influence in the world' (p. 9) will be met with incredulity by some. As Peter Hulme cautioned in the same year, 'it is important to keep in mind both that the conquest of America, begun in 1492, is still being pursued to completion in Central America and Brazil, and that the United States has inherited

the imperial mantles and tactics of England and Spain in the Caribbean and Central America'. Peter Hulme, *Colonial Encounters: Europe and the native Caribbean, 1492–1797* (London: Methuen, 1986), p. 6.

5. Jacques J. Maquet, 'Objectivity in Anthropology', *Current Anthropology 5*, 1 (February 1964), 50.
6. Edward W. Said, *Orientalism* (Harmondsworth: Penguin Books, 1978), p. 21.
7. Anthony Fothergill, 'Of Conrad, Cannibals, and Kin', in Mick Gidley, ed., *Representing Others: White Views of Indigenous Peoples* (Exeter: The University of Exeter Press, 1992), pp. 38–9.
8. The quotation is taken from Francis L.K. Hsu, 'Rethinking the Concept "Primitive"', *Current Anthropology 5*, 3 (June 1964), 169. Hsu is summarising pp. 1–18 of Tylor's book. Tylor (1832–1917) was given a readership at Oxford in 1884, the first university post in anthropology in Britain. This information is to be found in, among other places, Henrika Kuklick, *The Savage Within: The Social History of British Anthropology, 1885–1914* (Cambridge: Cambridge University Press, 1991), p. 6.
9. Johannes Fabian, *Time and the Other: How Anthropology Makes its Object* (New York: Columbia University Press, 1983), p. 15. Further page references will be given in parentheses.
10. James Clifford, 'On Ethnographic Allegory', in James Clifford and George E. Marcus, *Writing Culture: The Poetics and Politics of Ethnography* (Berkeley: University of California Press, 1986), pp. 98–121. Further page references will be given in parentheses.
11. See also Renato Rosaldo, 'Imperialist Nostalgia', *Representations 26* (Spring 1989), 107–22.
12. Kuklick, *The Savage Within*, p. 243.
13. Raymond Williams, *The Country and the City* [1973] (London: The Hogarth Press, 1985).
14. Kuklick, *The Savage Within*, p. 244. Kuklick goes on to stress that there was by no means a consensus about what constituted the virtues of rural society.
15. Claude Lévi-Strauss, *Tristes Tropiques* [1955], trans. John and Doreen Weightman (Harmondsworth: Penguin Books, 1976), p. 48.
16. Ibid., p. 51. For further comments on how Time features in and may resolve this dilemma see also pp. 51–2. Lévi-Strauss's book should itself be read as a volume which in its style and structure, as much as its content, explores some of the debates in ethnography that are outlined in the present introduction.
17. Edward W. Said, *Covering Islam: How the Media and the Experts Determine How We See the Rest of the World* (London: Routledge and Kegan Paul, 1985), p. 142.

18. James Clifford, 'On Ethnographic Authority', *Representations* 1, 2 (Spring 1983), 119.
19. See James Clifford, 'Introduction: Partial Truths', in Clifford and Marcus, eds, *Writing Culture*, p. 6.
20. Clifford, 'Introduction: Partial Truths', p. 7.
21. Ibid., p. 6.
22. Dennis Tedlock, 'The Analogical Tradition and the Emergence of a Dialogical Anthropology', *Journal of Anthropological Research* 35, 4 (Winter 1979), 389.
23. Kevin Dwyer, 'On the Dialogic of Field Work', *Dialectical Anthropology* 2, 2 (May 1977), 146.
24. Steven Webster, 'Dialogue and Fiction in Ethnography', *Dialectical Anthropology* 7, 2 (1982), 112.
25. Daniel R. Gross, 'Dialectics in the Forest', *Reviews in Anthropology* 2 (February 1975), 64.
26. Ibid.
27. Ibid. For a defence of the personal approach see, for example, John J. Honigmann, 'The Personal Approach in Cultural Anthropological Research', *Current Anthropology* 17, 2 (June 1976), 243–61. However, in stressing the ethnographer's 'unique biographical background' (p. 244) and 'unique perspective' (p. 245), Honigmann seems curiously to free his colleagues from shared cultural characteristics and determinants.
28. Comment by Frances Henry on Dennison Nash and Ronald Wintrob, 'The Emergence of Self-Consciousness in Ethnography', *Current Anthropology* 13, 5 (December 1972), 537.
29. George E. Marcus and Dick Cushman, 'Ethnographies as Texts', *Annual Review of Anthropology* 11 (1982), 26.
30. Diane Lewis, 'Anthropology and Colonialism', *Current Anthropology* 14, 5 (December 1973), 588.
31. Edward W. Said, 'Representing the Colonized: Anthropology's Interlocutors', *Critical Inquiry* 15, 2 (Winter 1989), 214.
32. Said, 'Representing the Colonized', 215. See also pp. 215–20.
33. Clifford Geertz, *Works and Lives: The Anthropologist as Author* (Cambridge: Polity Press, 1988), pp. 71–2. For a critique of Geertz's arguments in this book, see my review of it in *Theory and Society* 19 (1990), 382–6.
34. Henrietta L. Moore, *Feminism and Anthropology* (Oxford: Polity Press, 1988), p. 4. See also the same author's *A Passion for Difference: Essays in Anthropology and Gender* (Oxford: Polity Press, 1994).
35. Moore, *Feminism and Anthropology*, p. 6.
36. Lynnette Turner, 'Feminism, Femininity and Ethnographic Authority', *Women: a cultural review* 2, 3 (1991), 239.

37. Frances E. Mascia-Lees et al., 'The Postmodernist Turn in Anthropology: Cautions from a Feminist Perspective', *Signs: Journal of Women in Culture and Society* 15, 1 (1989), 11. Quoted in Turner, 'Feminism and Ethnographic Authority', p. 240.
38. Turner, 'Feminism and Ethnographic Authority', p. 240.
39. Moore, *Feminism and Anthropology*, p. 7.
40. Ibid., p. 9.
41. Judith Stacey, 'Can There be a Feminist Ethnography?', *Women's Studies International Forum* 11, 1 (1988), 24.
42. Inderpal Grewal, *Home and Harem: Nation, Gender, Empire, and the Cultures of Travel* (London: Leicester University Press, 1996), p. 12.
43. Turner, 'Feminism and Ethnographic Authority', p. 243. The text Turner is drawing on here is Marilyn Strathern, *The Gender of the Gift: Problems With Women and Problems With Society in Melanesia* (Berkeley: University of California Press, 1988).
44. My discussion of these will be brief and indicative. See note 2 above.
45. Hulme, *Colonial Encounters*, p. 2.
46. Ibid., p. 15.
47. Barbara Christian, 'The Race for Theory', in Abdul JanMohamed and David Lloyd, eds, *Cultural Critique: The Nature and Context of Minority Discourse* 6 (Spring 1987), 54.
48. Neil Lazarus, 'National consciousness and the specificity of (post) colonial intellectualism', in Francis Barker, Peter Hulme, and Margaret Iversen, eds, *Colonial discourse/postcolonial theory* (Manchester: Manchester University Press, 1994), p. 197.
49. Aijaz Ahmad, *In Theory: Classes, Nations, Literatures* (London: Verso, 1994), p. 44. (Ahmad's book was first published in 1992.) Further page references will be given in parentheses.
50. For contrary views see the essays, critical of Ahmad, in *Public Culture* 6 (1993).
51. See, for example, Ahmad, *In Theory*, p. 41.
52. For more on this idea and for arguments in favour of the historical materialism behind it, see the excellent issue, 'In Defense of History: Marxism and the Postmodern Agenda', of *Monthly Review* 3, 47 (July/August 1995), which, among its contributions, includes an interview with Ahmad.
53. Ahmad, *In Theory*, p. 185. Ahmad calls *Orientalism* 'a deeply flawed book'. Ahmad, *In Theory*, pp. 160–1.
54. Ahmad, *In Theory*, p. 36. See also his fierce attack on poststructuralism for being repressive, bourgeois, individualist, and promoting 'non-attachment as the necessary condition of true understanding' (p. 56).
55. For other discussions see, for example, Benita Parry, 'Problems in current theories of colonial discourse', *The Oxford Literary Review* 9,

1–2 (1987), 27–58; Patrick Williams, 'Problems of post-colonialism', *Paragraph* 16, 1 (1993), 91–102; and Kenneth Parker, 'Very like a whale: Post-Colonialism between canonicities and ethnicities', *Social Identities* 1, 1 (1995), 155–74.

56. Aijaz Ahmad, 'The politics of literary postcoloniality', *Race & Class* 36, 3 (1995), 8.

57. Homi K. Bhabha, 'The other question: difference, discrimination and the discourse of colonialism', in Francis Barker, Peter Hulme, Margaret Iversen, Diana Loxley, eds, *Literature, Politics and Theory: Papers from the Essex Conference* (London: Methuen, 1986), p. 148.

58. Ibid., p. 149, my emphasis.

59. Ahmad, *In Theory*, p. 65.

60. Bhabha, 'The other question', p. 149, my emphases.

61. Jan Nederveen Pieterse, *White on Black: Images of Africa and Blacks in Western Popular Culture* (New Haven: Yale University Press, 1992), p. 15.

62. Ibid., p. 12.

63. Ibid., p. 29.

64. For two studies of representations of Africa that make a similar point, see Tim Youngs, *Travellers in Africa: British Travelogues 1850–1900* (Manchester: Manchester University Press, 1994), and Annie E. Coombes, *Reinventing Africa: Museums, Material Culture and Popular Imagination in Late Victorian and Edwardian England* (London: Yale University Press, 1994), p. 3.

65. Ritchie Robertson, 'Introduction' to Urs Bitterli, *Cultures in Conflict: Encounters Between European and Non-European Cultures, 1492–1800*, trans. Ritchie Robertson (Oxford: Polity Press, 1989), p. 7.

66. Nederveen Pieterse, *White on Black*, pp. 222–3.

67. Arthur Miller, *The Crucible* [1953] (London: Penguin, 1968), pp. 17 and 46.

68. Toni Morrison, 'Rootedness: The Ancestor as Foundation', in Mari Evans, ed., *Black Women Writers: Arguments and Interviews* (London: Pluto Press, 1985), p. 341.

69. Primo Levi, 'Afterword' to *If This Is a Man and The Truce*, trans. Stuart Woolf, Afterword trans. Ruth Feldman (London: Abacus, 1987), p. 396.

70. Levi, 'Author's Preface' to *If This Is a Man and The Truce*, p. 15.

71. Levi, 'Afterword' to *If This Is a Man and The Truce*, pp. 390–1.

2 *Philosophers among the savages*

Michael K. Green

Introduction

Philosophers, as human beings, are typically not free from the most deeply held assumptions of their time. Since philosophers exercise their activity within a cultural context, it is not surprising to find that they often share the prejudices of their time held by individuals of their own culture against those outside that culture. For example, one can find Hume saying:

> I am apt to suspect that negroes and in general all the other species of men (for there are four or five different kinds) to be naturally inferior to the whites.[1]

Or, we can find Marx saying:

> With the same right with which France has taken Flanders, Lorraine and Alsace, and, sooner or later, will take Belgium, with that same right Germany takes Silesia: with the right of civilization against barbarism, of progress against stability ... this right is worth more than all treaties, for it is the right of historical development.[2]

It is generally presumed that such remarks express views that are extraneous to the philosopher's philosophy. As such, they can be separated from his/her philosophy, which remains untainted by such views. Whether this is indeed the case can be debated.

The aim of this article is to examine how conceptions of the outsider play not this extrinsic role, but an intrinsic one in the development of philosophical positions. I will begin with some general reflections on the concept of the savage. I will then show

how this concept functions in the positions developed by several prominent philosophers. I will end with some reflections on why the concept of the savage plays such a central role in philosophical discourse.

The concept of the savage[3]

> For so the glutted earth
> Swarms even now with savage beasts, even now
> Is filled with anxious terrors, thru the woods
> And mighty mountains and the forest deep–
> Quarters 'tis ours in general to avoid.[4]

The term 'savage' is most likely derived from the Latin word 'silva', meaning woods or forest. It came into the English language via Old French, presumably as a result of the Norman Conquest. The connection with the forest is clear in this case. It probably arose in the context of an agricultural people for whom forests had to be cleared and replaced with cultivated lands. English has another word, 'wild', which is of Germanic origin and which also serves much of the same function as 'savage' does in the Romance languages.

Presumably, the concept originally referred to a place. As the above quote indicates, this is a place where humans do not belong. Wild and savage areas are thought of as inhospitable and dangerous regions. Thus, deserts, mountains, oceans, jungles, forests, and vast dry plains can all be savage or wild. These are typically harsh environments in which human beings can survive with only great difficulty. Typically, a distinction is made between the territory that a group inhabits and wild, uncultivated foreign lands.[5] Indeed, the house can serve as a symbol for the separation between these two worlds. As one writer explains the distinction between *domi* and *peregri*:

> These different but parallel terms conjure up the image of an ancient relationship: the uncultivated ground, the waste land, as opposed to the inhabited area ... This is where the extraneous world begins, and what is strange is necessarily hostile.[6]

The outside is the realm of strife, disorder, or, more generally, chaos.[7] On the other hand, the inside is the realm of order and law. Once these distinctions have been made the two different areas are (as Mircia Eliade shows) assimilated to two different models. He states:

> the world in which the presence and the work of man are felt ... have an extraterrestrial archetype, be it conceived as a plan, as a form ... all these wild, uncultivated regions and the like are assimilated to chaos: they still participate in the undifferentiated, formless modality of pre-creation.[8]

This formlessness is basic to the concept of the savage and provides the continuous thread of meaning that ties all of its different applications together.

As the quote introducing this section indicates, a savage place is full of savage beings, the consummate form of which is the savage beast. Savage areas contain dangerous and threatening animals, such as lions, boars, hounds, wolves, tigers, sharks, sea-hawks, bulls, baboons, leopards, jackals, and elephants, or savage monsters, such as a Chimera, Gorgon, Cyclops, Erinys, Sphinx, Centaur, Echeon, Devil, or any of the other vicious monsters that were supposed to inhabit the world and wait to prey upon human beings. Typically, savage animals are carnivorous and deadly. If not, then strong and violent. These savage beasts and monsters came out of the forest or other savage regions, preyed upon those who thought they were safe in their homelands, and then disappeared back into the forest to attack again at any time.

As savage places contrast with familiar ones, so savage beings contrast with the humanised and cultured beings who share the same culture. Savagery represents the zero point of humanised and cultured existence and functions to make evident what types of behaviour are not culturally appropriate for a given group. It is here that the concept of the savage performs a limiting function by marking off what is acceptable behaviour for an individual with a certain cultural identity from what is totally outside the realm of action for such individuals. Thus, humans who act like savage beasts fall outside the limits of what constitutes acceptable ways of acting and living for individuals with a given shared cultural identity.

Since savages fall outside the scope of humanised and cultured existence, they are typically thought to be more like beasts than human beings. As such, they are subject to savage fits of passion, such as fury, anger, temper, hatred, jealousy, fearlessness, and joy. They are subject to savage urges, such as wild desire and sensuality. They perform actions of savage brutality and cruelty. They experience a wild joy in shedding human blood. They gloat over the death and wounds of the enemy. They are ungrateful, have a forbidding heart, and know neither respect nor pity. The emotions, desires, and actions of such individuals are uncurbed, unfettered, and uncontrolled. We are back to the formlessness that is at the heart of the concept of a savage.

The savage as a limiting concept

The concept of a savage represents a chaos and formlessness that is the complete absence of human social existence. Thus, the concept of the savage serves to mark off the boundaries of what constitutes human actions and deficiencies and to distinguish it from what goes beyond the boundaries or limits of all human acceptability. The functioning of this concept can be seen in several major Western philosophers.

Greek conceptions of outsiders can be found throughout the Greek literary and philosophical tradition. A literary example can be found in *The Odyssey* in which Odysseus states:

> And we came to the land of the Cyclops, a fierce, uncivilized people who never lifted a hand to plant or plough but put their trust in Providence. All the crops they require spring up unsown and untilled, wheat and barley and the vines whose generous clusters give them wine when ripened for them by the timely rains. The Cyclops have no assemblies for the making of laws, nor any settled customs, but live in hollow caverns in the mountain heights, where each man is lawgiver to his children and his wives, and nobody cares a jot for his neighbors.[9]

Aeschylus in *Prometheus Unbound* provides a similar view of 'savages'. They are speechless and senseless individuals who live in a dream-like stupor as infants do. They burrow into hills like ants. They have no skills or arts, such as carpentry and brickmaking, and they have none of the benefits of culture, such as numbers, an alphabet, domesticated animals, medicines, or metals.[10] The Cyclops and other such savages are not members of any political community. The images of a person for the Greeks included such characteristics as being an agriculturalist, making laws in an assembly, and being a member of a particular Greek city-state. All non-Greeks were barbarians, and hence, outside the Greek social community. Indeed the word 'barbarous' came from the nonsensical sounds ('bar, bar') that the Greeks thought were made by the outsiders. These individuals weren't even considered fully human. They were natural slaves who could be legitimately subdued by violence. Thus, as related by Thucydides, whole cities could be destroyed by the Greeks and all their inhabitants slain because none of these non-Greeks was a person, i.e. member of the Greek social community.

Now let us turn to two Greek philosophers in whose thought the concept of the savage as the complete negation of human social community plays a role. When Plato in the *Republic* turns to showing that the life of a tyrant is worse than the life of a virtuous person even if the tyrant were able to subdue everyone and get everything that he/she wants, he makes use of a distinction between bestiality and proper humanised and cultured conduct. In book IX, Plato identifies the tyrant by distinguishing between 'the rational and gentle, and dominant' part and the 'beastly and savage' part of the soul. This latter part of an individual prompts him/her to incest, all sorts of bloody deeds, and 'in a word, falls short of no extreme of folly and shamelessness'.[11] We see that Plato explicitly recognises the concept as an ideal in which one finds a complete realisation of evil. Later, he draws upon this distinction to make an image of the tyrant so that his/her inner nature can be examined. He tells us to imagine an outer shell that looks like a human being, but which has three components inside it. One component is:

> a manifold and many-headed beast that has a ring of heads of tame and wild beasts that can change them and cause them to spring forth from itself all such growths.[12]

Here we see the formlessness of the savage playing a central role. Another is a lion, and the third is a human being. The unjust person, as an example of the perfectly unjust individual, is one who subordinates the human aspect of his/her existence to the bestial ones.

One finds a similar distinction in Aristotle. In his *Politics*, Aristotle states:

For man, when perfected is the best of animals, but, when separated from law and justice, he is the worst of all; since armed injustice is the more dangerous, and he is equipped at birth with arms, meant to be used by intelligence and virtue, which he may use for the worst ends. Wherefore, if he have not virtue, he is the most unholy and the most savage of animals, and the most full of lust and gluttony.[13]

Aristotle continues this discussion in the *Nicomachean Ethics* in his consideration of brutishness. We find that the:

brutish type is rarely found among men; it is found chiefly among barbarians, but some brutish qualities are also produced by disease or deformity; and we also call by this evil name those men who go beyond all ordinary standards by reason of vice.[14]

As examples of brutish states, he discusses various forms of cannibalism and the eating of raw meat. Brutishness, he says, is 'beyond the limits of vice'.[15] It is a type of wickedness that is 'not on the human level'.[16] It thus delimits the boundary of acceptable human conduct and serves as a negative ideal, i.e. one indicating the direction in which human beings are not supposed to move.

In the Middle Ages, the role of the formless figure of the savage was played by the Devil, who served as the same limiting concept and possessed the aspects of formlessness and bestiality that are intrinsic to the concept of the savage. Kant captures this approach of the Medieval thinkers:

There are two by-paths of vice: the path of baseness or brutality, and that of devilish malice. The first of these leads by way of violation of the duties we owe to our person to a level below that of the beasts; the second is the way of the man who makes it his business to turn his mind to evil, until no good inclination survives in his soul. While he retains a single good disposition, a single wish to be good, he remains human, but if he is wholly given over to wickedness, he becomes a devil.[17]

Further he states:

the conception of satanic evil is pure in its kind, being the conception of something wholly free of any germ of good, even of any will to good,[18] and

> If we personify the perfection of evil, we have the Idea of the devil.[19]

According to Kant, such wickedness 'oversteps the limits of human nature and becomes inhuman'.[20]

Hell, as described in Dante's *Inferno*, is a savage place full of savage beings. It is the fitting abode of Satan, as the epitome of evil. The lustful are blown about by violent winds,[21] gluttons are beaten by cold and filthy rain,[22] heretics are entombed in red-hot sepulchres,[23] those who injure others boil in blood,[24] sodomites endlessly cross fiery sands beneath a rain of fire,[25] panders and seducers are scourged by horned demons, flatterers are immersed in excrement,[26] barrators are plunged into boiling pitch,[27] fraudulent counsellors are clothed in flames,[28] traitors to their kin are immersed in ice and gnaw upon each others' heads,[29] and finally in the deepest pit of Hell Satan, frozen in ice, tears to bits with his teeth and claws those who betray their benefactors.[30] Dante's Hell is a savage place full of savage beings.

The savage and its functional equivalent also play a role in several of the philosophers of the modern age. When Hobbes gives an example of a people in his state of nature in which 'the life of man [is] solitary, poore, nasty, brutish, and short',[31] he gives the example of the native people of America:

> For the savage people in many places of America, except the government of small families, the concord whereof dependeth on naturall lust, have no government at all; and live at this day in that brutish manner, as I said before.[32]

Locke's *Second Treatise* can be seen as a justification for overcoming two types of savage – those of the New World who let productive land lie idle[33] and those of the Old World (the Norman Lords) who took what they desired by force and lived like parasites off the productive labour of others.[34] In both Hobbes and Locke, savagism is something to be overcome, and the concept of the savage functions to delimit the arena and types of legitimate competition and conflict from those that place an individual outside all human communities.

Among the Germans, the concept of a savage provides an important limiting function in Immanuel Kant's philosophy. According to him,

> man can only become man by education. He is merely what education makes of him;[35]

and

> all the natural developments of mankind must be developed little by little out of man himself through his own effort.[36]

As Kant goes on to argue, although the development of a person's abilities is something that he/she must do for him/herself, it is not something that he/she can do by him/herself. Thus, he states:

> Education is an art which can only become perfect through the practice of many generations. Each generation, provided with the knowledge of the foregoing one, is able more and more to bring about an education which shall develop man's natural gifts in their due proportion and in relation to their end, and thus advance the whole human race towards its destiny.[37]

As a finite being, an individual comes into the world undeveloped. Culture consists of discipline to counteract natural unruliness and instruction to impart information and to develop ability. Initially, others have to provide this discipline and instruction so that the individual can begin to actualise his/her human potential. According to Kant, culture progresses by slow degrees and represents humanity's attempt to make itself human and to rise above barbarism and the lawlessness of the savage. One generation transmits via its culture its accomplishments, experience, and knowledge. The next generation acts upon this repository of knowledge and experience. They add, subtract, and refine, and then transmit it to the next. Thus, slowly humans realise their humanity as culture provides scope and opportunity for the realisation of their peculiar abilities as agents, and they in turn modify and reproduce the culture that makes a human life possible. According to Kant, it is possible for a human being's animal impulses to turn him aside 'from humanity, his appointed end',[38] i.e. to overpower or swamp his human potentialities so that these lie dormant with him – asleep from neglect and non-use. Such people suffer from what Kant calls barbarism – 'the animal, so to speak, not having yet developed its human nature'.[39] This is a human being, uncultured and uncultivated. In *Conjectural Beginnings of Human History*, Kant undertakes to describe this transition from an 'uncultivated, merely animal condition to the state of humanity'.[40] From this perspective, then, the savage is perpetually caught in a state of non-development, incapable of progressing or developing into a humanised condition.

The savage as a critical concept

The concept of the savage as a limiting concept marks a level of wickedness that goes beyond the limits of human capabilities. However, the concept of the Noble Savage as a critical concept marks a level of virtue that goes beyond the limits of human capabilities. These two limits mark the upper and the lower boundaries of culturally acceptable behaviour. The Noble Savage can play a critical function relative to existing social and cultural institutions and processes. As with the limiting concept of the savage, this concept begins with a place – not a savage place that is completely inhospitable to human beings, but one that is completely hospitable to humans. It often begins in paradise in which human needs are readily met by a bounteous and providing nature. Projected into the past, it becomes a Golden Age in which individuals lived simple and virtuous lives and were uncorrupted by the power and greed of civilisation. Identified with a place, it becomes Sir Thomas More's utopia, which exists in no place but which contains individuals that far exceed contemporary individuals in virtue. Montaigne's 'On Cannibalism' and 'On Coaches', as well as the writings of Rousseau, make use of the critical function of the concept of the savage to evaluate and judge their own societies. Typically, Noble Savages have no writing, law, private property, exchange, violence, or fraud. They exhibit charity, compassion, and honesty and have an equality and freedom that is lacking to civilised persons. While supposedly existing outside society, Noble Savages normally exhibit the social virtues more fully than any individual within society does. Typical of this is Rousseau's claim that:

> nothing is so gentle as man in his primitive state when, placed by nature at equal distances from the stupidity of brutes and the fatal

enlightenment of civil man, and limited equally by instinct and reason to protecting himself from the harm that threatens him, he is restrained by natural pity from harming anyone himself, and nothing leads him to do so even after he receives harm.[41]

Philosophy and cultural identity

It remains for us to discuss why the concept of the savage plays such a recurring role in philosophy. This requires us to examine the nature of cultural identity and the relation between philosophy as an activity and cultural identity.

We must begin with an appreciation of the importance of culture and of the process by which a cultural identity is constituted. By providing a set of settled pathways upon which individuals can develop their own variations, a culture provides a shared framework of expectations that allows them to work together. A cultural identity gives the individuals a sense of a common past and of a shared destiny. It unifies and integrates the individuals, gives them a sense of belonging, and a sense of their own uniqueness as a people. Further, a culture provides the individuals within that culture with a way of life that is constitutive of what it is to be a human being. It provides a framework in terms of which individuals can work out for themselves their own identities with their own styles, which are variations upon and a creative synthesis of the cultural styles of life available in their cultures. It is in terms of these that an individual finds meaning in life.

Deculturation can lead to severe psychological disorientation, such as dissolution of the self, a sense of meaninglessness, aimlessness, and depression. This creates a painful situation which the individual may then attempt to escape by the use of alcohol or drugs, or by self-stupefaction through pleasures.

To understand the process by which cultural identity is constituted and the importance of philosophy in this process, we must begin by making a distinction between populations, peoples, and nations. A group of individuals either have no significant cultural commonalities (a population), or they have some such commonalities. If the latter, either these commonalities are not consciously recognised as such (a people), or they are (a nation).[42] Nations have conceptions of themselves and of how they differ from other nations. They have relatively settled cultural identities. Peoples develop conceptions of themselves and of how they differ from others as they develop a distinctive cultural identity by which they define themselves.[43]

Cultural identity on the minimal level arises when a group of individuals share the same or closely similar cultural styles. They have similar styles in technology as well as in economic, social, and political systems. They have similar religious, philosophical, artistic, and scientific styles or themes. The groups with cultural identity on this level can be seen to be developing variations on a similar theme. In the fullest sense, though, individuals have a cultural identity when they are self-consciously aware of these similarities in these areas, and they consciously work within the same traditions and with the same themes.

Social scientists have found that a cultural group that constitutes itself as a nation-state goes through a typical set of stages. The process by which a self-conscious cultural identity is created begins with a people who have a common culture. Through conflict with other decidedly different cultural groups, these people become aware of their cultural similarity. They receive consensual validation from their fellow group members and conflictual validation from the members of the other culture.[44] The concept of the savage typically has an important role to play in this process. The other is thought of as a bloodthirsty savage who exhibits all of the violence and destruction of a mad beast of prey. Once this self-consciousness has arisen, steps are taken to institute some form of political institutions by which the group can govern itself and thus constitute itself as a nation-state.[45] In this stage, if one group forms its identity by conquering another, then the concept of the Civilisable Savage might also play an important role in that culture. Also, the concept of a savage might function abstractly as a marker indicating the limits of acceptable social behaviour. Witness the facility with which the different warring factions in the former Yugoslavia are labelled savages and condemned by others for their savage atrocities against each other.

When a cultural identity is constituted, a normative order constituting a way of life is identified and self-consciously taken as constitutive of what type of person an individual who shares that cultural identity should be. The humanised and cultured relations among individuals are bound by a web of normative rules that define that cultural identity. People who share that identity are such and such type of people who do such and such things because this is what they do as such and such individuals. Savage areas and beings represent the concept of the complete absence of these humanised, cultural, and normative relations among people. In savage areas, brute force alone operates. This is why such regions are so harsh, and why it is difficult for humanised beings to survive in them. Similarly, savage beings relate to each other and to their environment only in terms of brute force. Thus, humanised beings who are forced into savage regions or have to confront savage beings typically lose their humanity and themselves become savage.

The notion of cultural identity, then, has both an external and an internal component so that the question of identity unfolds on two levels. On the external level of institutions and actions, individuals have the same cultural identity when they share certain values and traditions which constitute a certain way of life which is passed on from generation to generation. The fullest sense of identity, though, requires consciousness of identity. On the level of consciousness, individuals share an identity when they self-consciously recognise themselves as sharing the same culture. Thus, a culture identity arises through the exercise of powers of self-determination by a group which defines itself. Identity in the fullest sense is internally constituted by a group, and thus is an act of self-definition on the part of that group.[46] In the constitution and maintenance of cultural identity, the concept of a savage plays a central role in defining the zero state of culture, i.e. the condition of having no culture at all. Cultural identity is defined by contrast with a state of humanity in which this cultural identity is missing. This savage state provides the basis for distinguishing between the human realm of culture and the non-human realm of nature in the form of bestiality. The concept marks the limits of the culturally-constituted moral community and of the actions appropriate in this community.

Once constituted, cultural identities do not remain unchanging. Indeed, cultural identities are worked and re-worked on a continual basis. Most cultures that no longer serve the needs of the individuals in them, however, undergo revitalisation processes in which cultural identity is re-thought and re-worked. These can be quite bloody and devastating affairs in which the culture attempts to remake itself in a new image. During such times of rapid social change or among marginal individuals, i.e. individuals excluded from the social structure, societies can undergo these revitalisation processes. As a social structure breaks down and individuals can no longer maintain a sense of worth and dignity within that social system, an individual or group can formulate a new, utopian image of society. Often, these codes are formulated as a result of a prophetic or mystical experience. The individual undergoes what Wallace calls a 'mazeway resynthesis' in which after a period of extreme stress the person's whole complex of values and beliefs are swept aside and replaced by new ones.[47] The existing culture is thought of as corrupt and hence as needing to be destroyed and replaced by another. The new code is presented as offering salvation for the individual and society. It offers a way for individuals to recapture their self-respect and sense of self-worth. By means of hysterical conversion large masses of people can be converted to the movement. The heightened sense of mutual concern present in such movements provides a foretaste of the liberation to be achieved after the dismantling of the existing social relations. After the extermination of all evil, there would be a return to the lost anarcho-communistic order that existed at the beginning of time. There would be no human authorities, taxes, rents, or dues. Such movements tend to conceive of the community as a homogeneous, unstructured unity that transcends the differentiations and contradictions of the established social order.[48] They emphasise what they see as universal human values, such as peace, harmony, fertility of the mind and body, universal justice, and the equality and brotherhood of all. During such phases of cultural reconstruction, the concept of a savage can play a critical role as the values and institutions of the culture are judged and evaluated in an attempt to return to nature from the artificiality of pseudo-culture and ritualisation.

Cultures tend to make a distinction between the orderly, 'rational' inside and the chaotic, disorderly outside. In this process of self-definition, philosophy has a special role to play. It is a working out of a group's consciousness and conception of itself. It serves to identify the shared values and core conceptions of people, society, and nature that are constitutive of the culture. If so, then by examining a philosophy one can identify the elements in it that serve to buttress a specific cultural identity. Using this hypothesis, we can look back at history through the lens of cultural diversity and examine the relation between philosophy and culture.

The Greeks, who were nomadic herders, moved to what is now Greece through a series of migrations in small tribal bands. Their possession of the horse and superior weapons allowed them to displace the indigenous cultures of Greece, which were more agricultural and less nomadic. Confronted with these different cultures and with their own lack of identity as Greeks, they developed various philosophies as attempts to understand themselves and their relations to the 'barbarians'. Since this was a tribal society in which membership was by birth and blood only, everyone outside the group became barbarians and savages. Greek philosophy was for Greeks, because they were the only ones capable of reason and thus of philosophy. Plato expresses this as follows:

> Consider, then, if this goes to the mark. I affirm that the Hellenic race is friendly to itself and akin, and foreign and alien to the barbarian.

Rightly, he said:

> We shall then say that Greeks fight and wage war with barbarians, and barbarians with Greeks, and are enemies by nature, and that war is the fit name for this enmity and hatred. Greeks, however, we shall say, are still by nature friends of Greeks when they act in this way, but that Greece is sick in that case and divided by faction, and faction is the name we must give to that enmity.[49]

The barbarians were those against whom Greek philosophy was developed.

The Middle Ages was ushered in by the expansion of the Franks and Normans, who were able to develop a cultural identity and make full use of the technology that made the armed knight possible. When they set themselves up as rulers over the natives and ushered in feudalism, they established a hierarchically organised society with members of their own cultural group set over the farmers and labourers in a system of lateral cultural solidarity. The invaders, who were herdsmen, extended the shepherd–sheep metaphor to human relations.[50] The rulers were the shepherds, who, through their loyal and obedient sheepdogs (priests and warriors), kept the flock from straying and protected it from wolves. Within this framework, each had a different station – shepherds weren't sheep, nor were sheep shepherds. Each station had its own appropriate duties. The sheep were to provide clothing and food for the shepherd. The sheepdogs were to be obedient to their superiors, to refrain from preying on the sheep, and to chase away wolves. The shepherd was to look after the welfare of the flock so that it would prosper. Authority was exercised from the top down, and all were expected to be obedient to that authority. The Christian community was different from the ancient ones in that it was not based on birth and blood, but upon Baptism, which initiated an individual into the natural hierarchy of being and put each in his/her natural place.

By the High Middle Ages, the hierarchical conception of the universe underlying Greek civilisation was elaborated into a metaphysics by Aquinas.[51] God became not only the head shepherd tending his flock but also an all-powerful authorising father, who, by His authorisations, created the world. The whole system of kinship terms with which the hierarchical control of the children by the father was conceptualised was used to formulate Aquinas's great metaphysical system and the world became populated with Natural Law that circumscribed the authorised sphere of each thing. Each thing was given a vocation, i.e. an authorised sphere of influence and activity.

The higher's rule over the lower was not an arbitrary one, though, but was governed by laws. Now a law is an ordinance of reason, directed to the common good, made by one who is entrusted with the care of the community, and promulgated to his subjects.[52] Justice consists of giving each his due, and one should pay one's debts – natural and contractual. The subjects owe their superior respect, honour, obedience, fidelity, reverence, and service,[53] while the superior owes his inferiors influence and care.[54] The inferior should be well-subordinated to that by which it is regulated so that it can be led to the good.[55] Barbarism and savagery are to be overcome by putting each thing in its proper place and subordinating it to its natural superior. Within this framework, the Devil, as the one who overturns order and hierarchy, played a role as the zero condition of civilised existence as defined through Christian philosophy. The Devil was the antithesis of all that was Christian and as such represented the zero degree of human existence.

Viewed through the lens of cultural diversity, the sixteenth through eighteenth centuries were times of cultural revival among the many cultures that had been suppressed by the Norman–Frankish culture. The cultural solidarity of the Frankish and Norman lords, which provided the basis for a unified Christendom under feudalism, was shattered as various groups, such as the Anglo-Saxons, the Gauls, and various Germanic groups underwent revitalisation and reconstitution. Protestantism was more a sign of the cultural reawakening of groups whose cultures had been disrupted by the Frankish and Norman lords than the cause of it.

The north European cultural complex out of which the code of private property and individual rights developed was distinctively different from the Latin cultural complex of southern Europe.[56] The warrior ethos was very highly developed, and the group consisted of the armed warriors who came to the assembly (the Thing) armed to decide issues of concern to its members. The basic unity for long periods of time in these societies was the *comitatus*, a group of warriors who competed with one another and with other groups of warriors for primacy of place within the group or society.[57] The social order was based on conflict and alliance. The problem of overcoming savagery and barbarism for such a cultural complex came to be conceived of as the subjecting of this conflict and competition to rules. This required individuals to move from a state of nature in which there were no rules to govern this conflict to the state of civil society in which there was a code that protected the individual rights of the competitors and distinguished between legitimate and illegitimate forms of conflict and competition. Individual rights were like social fortresses or defences that were erected around the individual so as to keep him/her from suffering harm at the hands of others, who were always willing to inflict it. Thus, the natural state of physical violence and destruction typical of savagery and barbarism was to be exchanged for a humanised one of a civil society based on individual rights and political, social, and economic competition.

What has been hidden by the tendency to see history as a unilinear process culminating in a world system modelled upon European models is the extent to which history has been driven by cultural factors. From this perspective, the most important aspect of the late twentieth century is the decline of monolithic world views and the rise of cultural pluralism. Both capitalism and communism, which was typically a revitalistic reaction to Westernisation, became modified and adapted to various cultural contexts so as to give rise to distinctive systems of both. Neither the Anglo-Saxon version of capitalism nor the Russian version of communism has been able to create a unified world view or a single world culture by melting all other cultural differences down and re-casting them in its own image. Instead, at this time in history, the movement is towards the constitution and/or reassertion of suppressed or denied cultural identities. Indeed, it is quite possible that the whole debate between the capitalists and communists will be seen to have been a diversion which masked the real issue of maintaining cultural identity.

The importance of cultural identity as we move forward towards a new century can be gathered from a cursory survey of the various movements that have arisen in recent years. Within the United Kingdom, there are cultural stirrings in Scotland, Wales, Cornwall, the Isle of Man, Shetland and the Orkneys – not to mention Northern Ireland.[58] In France, there are such rumblings among the Bretons, Corsicans, Occitanians, and Alsatians.[59] Spain is facing similar challenges from movements among the Basque, Catalan, Galician, Andalusian, and Canaries.[60] Holland has cultural stirrings among the Frisians, and Belgium has the Flemish–Walloon linguistic problem.[61] Switzerland must contend with the Jurassiens,[62] and Italy with the emergence of the Lega Lombard, Lega Venetia, Sicilians, and Tyroleans.[63] India has three hundred and fifty groups of indigenous peoples, and many of these groups desire to be self-determining.[64] The relations between the Bakonjo and Baamba peoples in Uganda is typical of numerous such problems in Africa.[65] Chile has to contend with the Mapuches;[66] Brazil with over two hundred different peoples within its borders.[67] There are similar tensions throughout South and Central America.[68] Turkey, Iran, and Iraq must contend with the Kurds.[69] In Rumania and Bulgaria, there are conflicts with the Hungarian and Turkish minorities.[70] Czechoslovakia has split along cultural lines. There are also cultural splits between the Danish and the Inuits in Greenland.[71] The United States has over four hundred indigenous nations within its borders.[72] Stirrings of cultural renewal can be found among them as well as among the African-Americans and the Hispanics within its borders. The problem of the future is whether we are willing to strive for cultural understandings and base our policies upon these, or whether we will continue to treat someone who is different as if he/she were less than a human being.

Notes

1. David Hume, 1882, 'Of National Character', in *The Philosophical Works*, ed. T.H. Green and T.H. Grose (London), 252 n.

2. Karl Marx, 12 August 1848, *Die Neue Rheinische Zeitung*, in Bertram D. Wolfe, 1965, *Marxism: One Hundred Years in the Life of a Doctrine* (New York: Dial), p. 26.

3. Let me make a brief note about method. The new CD-ROM technology has quick and efficient word-search capabilities. In order to delimit the semantic space of the concept of savage, I used a CD-ROM search of *The Library of the Future*, 1st edn, 1991, Automated Archives Inc. & InfoWare Inc. This is a collection of 450 literary, philosophical and historical texts. A search was conducted on two words – 'savage' and 'barbarian'. The results of this search provide the basis for the next section. Also, see Bernard Sheehan, 1980, *Savagism and Civility: Indians and Englishmen in Colonial Virginia* (Cambridge: Cambridge University Press).

4. Lucretius, 1952, *On the Nature of Things*, trans. H.A.J. Munro (Chicago: Encyclopedia Britannica, Inc.), book V, lines 40 ff.

5. See Emile Benveniste, 1973, *Indo-European Language And Society*, trans. Elizabeth Palmer (Coral Gables, Florida: University of Miami Press), pp. 307–12.

6. Ibid., pp. 256–7.

7. Zygmunt Bauman, 1973, *Culture as Praxis* (London: Routledge and Kegan Paul), p. 137.

8. Mircea Eliade, 1959, *Cosmos and History* (New York: Harper and Row Publishers), p. 9.

9. Homer, 1946, *The Odyssey*, trans. E.V. Rieu (Harmondsworth, England: Penguin Books), book IX.

10. Aeschylus, 1965, *Prometheus Unbound*, trans. Robert W. Corrigan (New York: Dell Publishing Co., Inc.), p. 142.

11. Plato, 1969, *Republic*, trans. Paul Shorey, in *Collected Dialogues of Plato*, ed. Edith Hamilton and Huntington Cairns (Princeton: Princeton University Press), pp. 571 ff, pp. 798 ff.

12. Ibid., pp. 588 ff., pp. 816 ff. Also, see Plato, *Laws* VI, trans. A.E. Taylor, *The Collected Dialogues of Plato*, ibid., p. 766, p. 1344.

13. Aristotle, 1941, *Politics*, trans. Benjamin Jowett, in Richard McKeon, *The Basic Works of Aristotle* (New York: Random House), 1253a 31–7, p. 1129.

14. Aristotle, 1941, *Nicomachean Ethics*, trans. W.D. Ross, in Richard McKeon, ibid., 1145a 29–33, p. 481.

15. Ibid., 1148b 36, p. 1045.

16. Ibid., 1149a 16, p. 1045.

17. Immanuel Kant, 1930, *Lectures on Ethics*, trans. Louis Infield (Indianapolis: Hackett Publishing Co.), p. 246.
18. Ibid., p. 91.
19. Ibid., p. 241.
20. Ibid., p. 220.
21. Dante Alighieri, 1980, *Inferno*, trans. Allen Mandelbaum (Berkeley, Ca.: University of California Press), Canto V.
22. Ibid., Canto VI.
23. Ibid., Canto X.
24. Ibid., Canto XII.
25. Ibid., Canto XV.
26. Ibid., Canto XVIII.
27. Ibid., Canto XXI.
28. Ibid., Canto XXVII.
29. Ibid., Canto XXXII.
30. Ibid., Canto XXXIV.
31. Thomas Hobbes, 1985 [1651], *Leviathan* (London: Penguin Books), p. 186.
32. Ibid., p. 187.
33. Michael K. Green, 1995, 'Cultural Identities: Challenges for the Twenty-First Century', in Michael K. Green, ed., 1995, *Issues in Native American Cultural Identity* (New York: Peter Lang), pp. 1–38.
34. John Locke, 1689, *Second Treatise on Civil Government* (London), XVI, 177.
35. Immanuel Kant, 1960, *Education*, trans. Annette Churton (Ann Arbor: The University of Michigan Press), p. 6.
36. Ibid., p. 3.
37. Ibid., p. 11.
38. Ibid., p. 3.
39. Ibid., p. 4.
40. Immanuel Kant, 1963, *The Conjectural Beginnings of Human History*, trans. Emil Fackenheim in *On History*, ed. Lewis White Beck (Indianapolis: Bobbs-Merrill), pp. 60 ff.
41. Jean-Jacques Rousseau, 1964, *Discourse on the Origin and Foundation of Inequality Among Men*, trans. Roger D. and Judith R. Masters, in Roger D. Masters, ed., *The First and Second Discourses* (New York: St Martin's Press), p. 150.
42. Anthony D. Smith, 1987, *The Ethnic Origins of Nations* (New York: Basil Blackwell Inc.), and Marc A. Sills, 1993, 'Political Interaction Between States and Indigenous Nations: A Point of Departure', in Marc A. Sills and Glenn T. Morris, 1993, *Indigenous Peoples' Politics: An Introduction* (University of Colorado at Denver, Fourth World Center for the Study of Indigenous Law and Politics), pp. 5–22.

43. Sills and Morris, ibid., pp. 5–22.
44. Alvin W. Gouldner and Richard A. Peterson, 1962, *Notes on Technology and the Moral Order* (Indianapolis: Bobbs-Merrill Company, Inc.), pp. 44–7; Peter Loewenberg, 1992, 'The Psychodynamics of Nationalism', *History of European Ideas*, vol. 15, nos. 1–3, pp. 93–103.
45. Smith, 1987, *supra* note 42.
46. Marc A. Sills, 1993, 'Political Interaction Between States and Indigenous Nations: A Point of Departure', Sills and Morris, 1993, *supra* note 42, pp. 5–22.
47. Anthony F.C. Wallace, 1961, *Culture and Personality* (New York: Random House) and, 1966, *Religion: An Anthropological View* (New York: Random House).
48. Victor W. Turner, 1969, *The Ritual Process: Structure and Anti-Structure* (Chicago: Aldine Publishing Company), p. 92.
49. Plato, *supra* note 11, 470c.
50. Benveniste, 1973, *supra* note 5, p. 376.
51. Etienne Gilson, 1983, trans. L.K. Shook, C.S.B., *The Christian Philosophy of St Thomas Aquinas* (New York: Octagon Books).
52. Thomas Aquinas, 1970, *Summa Theologicae*, trans. Thomas Gilby, O.P. (New York: McGraw-Hill), vol. 28, Ia–IIae, q. 90, a. 1–4.
53. Aquinas, 1969, *Summa Theologicae*, trans. David Bourke (New York: McGraw-Hill), vol. 29, Ia–IIae, q. 100, a. 5.
54. Aquinas, 1967, *Summa Theologicae*, trans. Thomas Gilby, O.P. (New York, McGraw-Hill), vol. 5, Ia–IIae, q. 26, a. 9.
55. Aquinas, 1970, *Summa Theologicae*, *supra* note 52, Ia–IIae, q. 92, a. 1.
56. On the identification of distinct cultural patterns within Europe, see the work of Geert Hofstede, 1980, *Culture's Consequences: International Differences in Work-Related Values* (London, Sage).
57. See Tacitus, *Germania*, 1963, trans. Maurice Hutton in *Tacitus Dialogus, Agricola, Germania* (Cambridge, Massachusetts: Harvard University Press), XIII. Also, see Georges Dumézil, 1970, *The Destiny of the Warrior*, trans. Alf Hiltebeitel (Chicago: University of Chicago Press).
58. Michael Hechter, 1975, *Internal Colonialism. The Celtic Fringe in British National Development, 1536–1966* (Berkeley: University of California Press), and Anthony D.D. Smith, 1979, *Nationalism in the Twentieth Century* (New York: New York University), p. 153.
59. William Safran, 1992, 'Language, Ideology, and the State in French Nation-Building: The Recent Debate', *History of European Ideas*, vol. 15, nos. 4–6, pp. 795–800, and Smith, 1979, *supra* note 58, p. 153.
60. Linda Frey and Marsha Frey, ' "I Have Become A Stranger To My Brethren:" The Role of Religious Dissent in Early Modern European

Revolts', *History of European Ideas*, vol. 15, nos. 1–3, pp. 437–41, and Smith, 1979, *supra* note 58, p. 153.
61. Smith, 1987, *supra* note 42, p. 28, and Smith, 1979, *supra* note 58, p. 153.
62. Peter Loewenberg, 1992, 'The Psychodynamics of Nationalism', *History of European Ideas*, vol. 15, nos. 1–3, pp. 93–103, and Smith, 1979, *supra* note 58, p. 153.
63. Ronald S. Cunsolo, 1993, 'Italian Nationalism in Historical Perspective', *History of European Ideas*, vol. 16, nos. 4–6, pp. 759–66.
64. Joseph Schechla, 1993, 'The State as Juggernaut: The Politics of India's Tribal Nations', Sills and Morris, 1993, *supra* note 42, pp. 46–74.
65. Joshua Rubongoya, 1993, 'The Bakonjo-Baamba and Uganda: Colonial and Postcolonial Integration and Ethnocide', Sills and Morris, 1993, *supra* note 42, pp. 75–86.
66. Clausia González-Parra, 1993, 'Aukin Wallmapu Ngulam: The Mapuche Nation and Its Struggle to Survive', Sills and Morris, 1993, *supra* note 42, pp. 87–102.
67. Ana Valéria Nascimento Araújo Leitão, 'Economic Development and Indian Peoples: Three Cases of Colonising Indian Lands in the Amazonian Rainforest', Sills and Morris, 1993, *supra* note 42, pp. 163–76.
68. Michel de Certeau, 1986, 'Heterologies Discourse on the Other', trans. Brian Massumi (Minneapolis: University of Minnesota Press).
69. Amin M. Kazak, 1993, 'The Kurds and Kurdistan: The Struggle for Statehood', Sills and Morris, 1993, *supra* note 42, pp. 147–62.
70. Nicholas Xenos, 1992, 'The State, Rights, and the Homogeneous Nation', *History of European Ideas*, vol. 15, nos. 1–3, pp. 77–82.
71. Gudmundur Alfredsson, 1982, 'Greenland and the Law of Political Decolonization', *German Yearbook on International Law*, no. 25, pp. 290–307.
72. Ward Churchill, 1993, *Struggle for the Land* (Monroe, Maine: Common Courage Press).

3 A monstrous race for possession. Discourses of monstrosity in The Tempest and early British America[1]

Gesa Mackenthun

> Within its own limits, each discipline recognises true and false pro-
> positions; but it pushes back a whole teratology of knowledge beyond
> its margins . . . There are monsters on the prowl whose form changes
> with the history of knowledge.
>
> (Foucault)[2]

Much recent criticism of Shakespeare's *The Tempest* has concentrated on the play's negotiations of the topics of colonialism and
treachery, exemplified in the 'colonial' master–slave relationship
between Prospero and Caliban.[3] These readings have further
developed some of the arguments of earlier 'Third World' critics,
whose rewritings and revisions of *The Tempest* formed part of the
intellectual decolonisation movement.[4] A figure that has, with a
few exceptions, been consistently avoided by Shakespeare criticism
is Caliban's mother, the 'foul witch' Sycorax.[5] This lack of attention in a way reiterates the marginalisation of Sycorax by the play
itself: having died long before Prospero's arrival on the island, she
is absent from the dramatic action. As this essay will try to show,
however, the figures of both Caliban and Sycorax evoke a whole
cluster of images and ideological meanings which situate *The
Tempest* squarely between changing discourses of monstrosity and
male colonial authority. The notion of monstrosity in fact functions as a link between the dramatic deployment of Prospero's
colonial fantasy, the actual scene of English colonialism in early
seventeenth-century America, and changing ideas about female

sexuality and power. This, then, will not be an essay on *The Tempest* which merely searches for new sources or intertextual connections of the play. It will rather discuss the play as a manifestation of a cultural problematic – as a cultural artefact which is at times very much aware of its own myth-making function. The essay will not come up with any single conclusion but will suggest that *The Tempest* combines various, often contradictory, cultural discourses of authority and possession.

Discourses are established and perpetuated by way of signs. But contrary to semiotics, which examines the traffic of signs within the closed system of the (mostly literary) text, it is my contention that textual signs are ideologically loaded metaphors or *ideologemes*.[6] They not only refer to other texts but also to a changing field of action which, though largely determined by 'textualised' cultural practices and conventions, should never be reduced to this textual aspect. Conceived in terms of discourse, the ideological sign is, in Stuart Hall's terms, 'always multi-accentual, and Janus-faced – that is, it can be discursively rearticulated to construct new meanings, connect with different social practices, and position social subjects differently'. Hall continues:

> As different currents constantly struggle within the same ideological field, what must be studied is the way in which they contest, often around the same idea or concept. The question is, as Gramsci put it, 'how these currents are born, how they are diffused and why in the process of diffusion they fracture along certain lines and in certain directions'.[7]

Discursive or ideological processes, as Hall emphasises, are always related to political and historical forces by adapting received images to the requirements of new historical conditions.

An ideologeme that has travelled a considerable way since its inception during the rule of the Christian Roman emperor Constantine in the fourth century is the idea of the 'westward course of empire', or the 'translation of empire' – *translatio imperii*. As Frances Yates has shown, the notion that one nation is predestined to rule over the rest of the world was particularly widespread during the early modern period, when Elizabethan England contested Spain's claim to divinely ordained universal kingship.[8] In this case, then, the ideological translation of the claim to universal empire

from Spain's Charles V to England's Queen Elizabeth was brought
about by reversing the gender of the ruler: Yates has shown this
process in her analysis of contemporary iconography.

A potential site for the imagined world rule was of course
America, and *The Tempest* in fact bridges the gap between Mediterranean discourses of cultural difference and the discourses of
the colonial encounter in the Atlantic. Prospero's island becomes
the site of events and human encounters that are very reminiscent
of similar encounters in the New World.[9] Already by way of his
name, Caliban (an anagram of 'canibal') is linked to the 'man-
eaters' Columbus expected to find in the Caribbean. But the birthplace of Caliban's mother, Africa, also allows us to visualise him
as a black man. It is precisely this multiple ideological inscription
of the characters of Caliban and Sycorax that I now want to look
at in some detail.

Puppy-headed monsters

As Peter Hulme has shown, *The Tempest* and the figure of Caliban,
in particular, are deeply inscribed with the general concern of early
modern colonial discourse to redraw the ideological boundaries of
European geography and anthropology by way of a tactical adaptation of medieval and Mediterranean discourses of intercultural
encounters to the colonial encounter in the Atlantic world.[10] In the
writings of both antiquity and the Middle Ages, cultural difference
was clearly defined along a centre–margin axis. A typical medieval
map would have at its centre the *oikumene* – that is Jerusalem and
the Christian nations. Beyond these would be found the Jews and
Moslems, and even further beyond the barbaric tribes inhabiting
areas like Scythia and the land of Gog and Magog. At the very
edges of the world (predominantly in India) we would find the
monstrous races – creatures whose human status was uncertain
and who were marked by physical and behavioural abnormities.[11]
As John Friedman notes, these strange 'Plinian races', named after
the Roman historian Pliny who gives one of the most exhaustive
descriptions of them, are deployed in most popular medieval texts,
from the Alexander romances and the writings of John Mandeville
and Marco Polo all the way to illustrations of religious texts.
Their psychological function, Friedman proposes, may have been

to control imaginatively the fear of the unknown or little known parts of the earth.

Their minds filled with the texts of Mandeville and Marco Polo, early explorers of America inevitably bumped into native tales of monstrous races. One of the most frequent species mentioned are the *bellmyae*, whom Sir Walter Ralegh claims to have heard of in Guiana. The Indians tell him of

> a nation of people, whose heads appeare not above their shoulders; which though it may be thought a meere fable, yet for mine owne part I am resolved it is true, because every childe in the provinces of Arromaia and Canuri affirme the same: they are called Ewaipanoma: they are reported to have their eyes in their shoulders, and their mouthes in the middle of their breasts, and that a long traine of haire groweth backward betweene their shoulders.[12]

While Ralegh's attitude towards the veracity of these tales is ambivalent, Columbus has little doubt that the Caribbean islands – according to his wrong geography a group of islands adjacent to Cipangu (Japan) – were inhabited by anthropophagi, bellmyae, cyclops, amazons and especially a race called *cynocephali*. Showing a few jewels to some of the older inhabitants of Cuba on November 4, 1492, Columbus receives the information that

> in a place that they called Bohío there was a vast amount and that they wore it on neck and in ears and on arms and legs; and also pearls. Moreover, he understood that they said that there were big ships and much trade and that all of this was to the southeast. He understood also that, far from there, there were one-eyed men, and others, with snouts of dogs, who are men, and that as soon as one was taken they cut his throat and drank his blood and cut off his genitals.[13]

In spite of the communication problem, the information seems to get more precise a few days later when Columbus is again assured of the Indians' fear of a place called Bohío because it is inhabited by 'those of Caniba or Canima' – which Columbus then translates into 'canibal'. The peaceful Indians, Columbus claims, were even afraid to speak of these *caníbales* because they feared that they would eat them, 'and they say that they have but one eye and the face of a dog; and the Admiral thought they were lying and felt that those who captured them must have been under the rule of the Grand Khan'.[14] Given the morphological vicinity between 'canibal' and 'can/khan', in addition to Columbus's expectation to be close to the court of the Grand Khan, his conclusion sounds quite logical. Only after having looked for Cathay in vain does Columbus accept the tale of an island of man-eaters – without, of course, having paid a visit.[15]

The description of 'cannibals' as dog-headed made its way into English accounts as well. In his oral testimony to Richard Hakluyt and others, the sailor David Ingram claims that 'the *Canibals* . . . haue teeth like dogs teeth, and thereby you may know them'.[16] One of his listeners and chief propagandist of Elizabethan settlement, George Peckham, summarises the knowledge gained from Ingram thus:

> The Sauages generally for the most part, are at continuall warres with their next adioyning neighbours, and especially the Cannibals, being a cruel kinde of people, whose foode is mans flesh, and haue teeth like dogges, and do pursue them with rauenous mindes to eate their flesh, and deuoure them. And it is not to be doubted, but that the Christians may in this case iustly and lawfully ayde the Sauages against the Cannibals.[17]

The last sentence neatly demonstrates the way in which the production of knowledge about America interacts with the interests of colonial power: according to the contemporary law of nations, the Europeans could not justify their invasion of America on the sole basis that the indigenous inhabitants lacked a certain standard of civilisation. Necessary intervention into intertribal warfare, however, could pave the way to victory.[18]

We can conclude, then, that the discourse about America appropriated more than one race out of Europe's store of monstrous imaginations. The low-life characters Stephano and Trinculo obsessively call Caliban a 'monster' (with different variations such as 'man-monster', 'servant-monster', 'Monsieur Monster', and 'moon-calf'). By referring to Caliban as 'puppy-headed monster', they certainly evoke the popular lore of the anthropophagous but potentially servile *cynocephali*.[19] But although their discourse is residually informed by the tradition of monstrous races, it more overtly articulates a contemporary fascination with 'monstrous' births – people born with deformed limbs, conjoined twins and the like. The topic of monsters in general and monstrous births in particular occupied pride of place within the popular discourses in early modern France, Germany, and England. Monsters were displayed in pubs and fairs for small fees – a custom which Trinculo and Stephano consider for financial gain themselves when first perceiving Caliban (II.ii.28–34). With the emergence of scientific approaches to the explanation of natural wonders, religious inter-pretations of monstrous births as prodigies slowly receded before an increasing exploitation of the topic for purposes of entertain-ment – which is not to say that the theory of monsters as divine cues disappeared, as we shall see below.[20] This double interpreta-tion of monstrous births is also contained in the double etymology of the term 'monster', which is derived both from the Latin word *monstrare*, to show, and *monere*, to warn.[21]

In a recent essay, Patricia Parker has suggested a relationship between the Early Modern fascination with monsters and the desire to discover hidden truths – a desire that pervaded the cultural dis-courses of Europe at that time.[22] The new culture of the catalogue and the scientific gaze no longer allowed for the hidden existence of medieval monsters at the margins of the known world, nor for unanatomised monstrosities of the human body. Both 'territories' were now increasingly 'opened up': they became the object of tax-onomic ordering and rational investigation.

This contemporary fascination with monsters has left its im-print on the representation of Caliban. What is more, *The Tempest* imaginatively condenses two discourses of monstrosity, that of the medieval monstrous races and that of witchcraft. As Prospero claims, Caliban has been 'got by the devil himself/Upon thy wicked dam' (I.ii.321–2). He accordingly calls Caliban 'devil', 'demi-devil', 'hag-seed' and similar names. That Caliban is a monster-of-all-trades, so to speak, becomes apparent from the fact that Stephano and Trinculo also call him 'moon-calf', thus evoking Martin Luther's famous treatise in which the pope is described as a monster called 'moonkish-calf' (III.ii.20).[23]

What can be gathered from Dudley Wilson's recent book on early modern broadsheets dealing with monstrous births is that there was a sudden rush of these pamphlets shortly after Elizabeth's succession to the throne in 1558. From 1562 onward, numerous broadsheets appeared interpreting monstrous births as portents of impending chaos, either with reference to the general situation of unrest in Europe or with more specific reference to the rule in

England. While they overtly addressed the popular fear inspired by England's fall from Catholic Rome, on a more subliminal level these pamphlets may be seen as signs of insecurity about the 'monstrous guise' of England's reign – a reign which was, quite extraordinarily, that of an unmarried female ruler.[24]

The gendering of sovereignty

Much has been written about the symbolic cult of virginity that dominated the genteel discourse in Elizabethan England. What is more interesting in the context of our discussion of *The Tempest* and will eventually bring us back to a very specific symbolism of the monstrous, is the way in which the play contributes to a post-Elizabethan regendering of rulership in dramatically exorcising the fear of an unmarried female sovereign. Both Claribel and Miranda, had they not been married in time, would have succeeded their fathers as autonomous female rulers. Antonio's excessive sarcasm upon being told by Sebastian that Claribel would have succeeded Alonso had she not been married off to an African king can be seen as symptomatic of an anxiety of patriarchal power in England (II.i.240–55). The play stages, and imaginatively solves, a particular fear of 'virgin queens'. This impression is reinforced by the almost incomprehensible debate between Gonzalo and the other courtiers about the geographical location of Carthage and about Dido's marital status, which represents a conflict between two views of history: Gonzalo's orthodox, and geographically largely correct, identification of ancient Carthage with modern Tunis and his similarly orthodox identification of Dido as the widow of Sychaeus collides with the other aristocrats' geographical ignorance and their view of Dido, queen of Carthage, as the lover of Aeneas.[25] *Their* literary source is Virgil's *Aeneid*, in which Dido kills herself after Aeneas has forsaken her in order to conquer Italy. They therefore mock Gonzalo for speaking of 'widow Dido', a phrase which evokes the pre-Virgilian Greek myth of Dido who fled to Africa after the murder of her husband Sychaeus, cheated the local king Iarbas off the land on which she founded the fortress of Carthage, and finally preferred death to a marriage with Iarbas. Whereas this older myth can already be seen as an attempt to 'romanticise' the political issue of female land ownership (Dido does not commit suicide because she prefers death to patriarchal bondage but because of her excessive posthumous emotional bond to Sychaeus), the Virgilian version of the *Aeneid* adds another twist to the romanticisation of the plot by reducing Dido to the role of the disappointed and raving lover. Neither version (valiant widow or raving lover) made Dido available as a model for Elizabeth.[26] The myth of the cunning and autonomous female ruler could only be remembered by the 'ancient morsel' Gonzalo. The courtiers, by contrast, who follow Virgil, seem to entertain a post-Elizabethan view of female sovereignty: the queen is deserted because unlike her warrior spouse she cannot lead her country to new conquests. That the play is complicit with this view of female sovereignty becomes apparent from the fact that Ferdinand echoes Aeneas when he first perceives Miranda (I.ii.422–3).

The conflict between the two versions of Dido which *The Tempest* articulates can be seen to refer to a larger conflict of how best to remember the rule of Elizabeth – how best to integrate her reign into a masculine history of the English kings.

The play finally draws together the themes of dynastic succession and colonial (dis)possession in the famous scene which shows Ferdinand and Miranda playing chess. During their symbolic struggle for rulership, Miranda accuses Ferdinand of cheating but at the same time lovingly forgives him for all future tricks in the acquisition of real kingdoms:

> *Mir.* Sweet lord, you play me false.
> *Fer.*   No, my dearest love,
>   I would not for the world.
> *Mir.* Yes, for a score of kingdoms you should wrangle,
>   And I would call it fair play.
>
> (V.i.172–5)

Applied to the nationalist–colonialist configuration of England, this scene tells us that the female rival to domestic rule may well be deprived of her rights as long as this served the dispossession of other nations in the pursuit of universal kingdom. In this 'romantic' conjunction, both misogyny and imperialism find their common rationale.

Sir Walter Ralegh's naming of the New World as 'Virginia' (after the 'virgin' queen Elizabeth) is an integral part of the complex symbolic gendering of rulership which preoccupied Elizabethan high culture. This gendering of sovereignty consisted in identifying Elizabeth with the traditionally feminised realm while also equipping her with the traditionally masculine characteristics of the imperial ruler. The ambivalence of the ideological construct 'Elizabeth' is that it symbolised both the 'virgin' land (or *hortus conclusus*) and masculine control over it.[27] After the death of Elizabeth, the political gender symbolism remained androgynous: in his *Basilicon Doron*, James I views himself as the 'husband' of his feminised realm, but at the same time as 'a loving nourish father' providing the commonwealth with 'their own nourish-milk'.[28] The Puritan patriarchs in New England likewise referred to themselves as 'nursing Fathers', whereas in their gendered relationship to Christ they usually occupied the position of Christ's bride.[29] Like the previous ideological construct of the 'Virgin Queen', then, post-Elizabethan discourse produced an ambivalently gendered ruler. The effect of such 'hybridisation' of male authority was that women were excluded from any access to power and from unmediated contact with Christ.

The representation of the land as a 'virgin' female body (as in 'Virginia') is one of the most powerful cultural conventions carried over to America by early explorers seeking to articulate their desire for territorial possession. In text and image, America is frequently deployed as a virgin awaiting her male seducer.[30]

The thought that America might already be the property of someone else who was not willing to part with it may have caused sufficient anxiety to the colonial project, but the issue became even more critical where the owner was a woman. Among the early colonisers, Sir Walter Ralegh was the one most obsessed with the problem of female rulership. Recording a meeting with a native 'inheritix' and recounting the myth of the Amazons, Ralegh eagerly entreats Elizabeth to take up arms against them: 'if not, I will judge those men worthy to be kings thereof, that by her grace and leave will undertake the same'.[31] Ralegh's idealised dialogue with the Queen cannot conceal the male Elizabethan's conviction that a female ruler, like the Virgilian Dido, is incapable of the masculine acts of colonisation and conquest. Thus the *Discovery of Guiana* performs 'a gendered struggle for mastery and agency, authority and will' between a female ruler and her ambitious male courtier.[32] At the same time, it develops a gendered strategy of colonial dispossession, imaginatively playing out several women rulers against one another.[33] In Ralegh's gendered view of colonial action, as the most famous passage in his text implies, there is no room for warrior queens, nor for 'un-husbanded' lands and women:

> To conclude, Guiana is a countrey that hath yet her maydenhead, never sackt, turned, nor wrought, the face of the earth hath not bene torne, nor the vertue and salt of the soyle spent by manurance, the graves have not bene opened for golde, the mines not broken with sledges, nor their Images puld downe out of their temples. It hath never bene entered by any armie of strength, and never conquered or possessed by any christian Prince.[34]

The passage suggests that to leave a land thus without masculine attention was deemed just as unacceptable as to leave a woman in a state of 'maidenhood'. Ralegh's imagery performs a violent shift away from an earlier colonial gendering and reflects a growing metaphorical misogyny, in the face of native resistance, as well as the misogynist turn in Protestant discourse to be discussed in the next section.

In effacing the topic of English violence, the Virgilian romance of Captain John Smith and Pocahontas provided a pleasant mythical beginning to the history of English colonial rule in America. But as Peter Hulme has argued, the myth was only complete once that romance represented a state of utopian anteriority, once the 'treacherous' violence of the (male) Indians had undone the dream of intercultural harmony.[35] Thus Hakluyt's successor Samuel Purchas could comment on the 1622 massacre of Jamestown settlers:

> Temperance and Justice had before kissed each other, and seemed to blesse the cohabitations of English and Indians in Virginia. But when Virginia was violently ravished by her owne ruder Natives, yea her Virgin cheekes dyed with the bloud of three Colonies ... Temperance could not temper her selfe, yea the stupid Earth seemes distempered with such bloudy potions and cries that shee is ready to spue out her Inhabitants.[36]

The gendering of colonial action enters a new stage with this passage where Virginia, in one of Purchas's typically tortuous images, is turned from a ravished virgin into the mother of a monstrous birth. The work of 'breaking', 'tearing', and 'sacking' the virgin land, which Ralegh had promoted as the task of the English colonisers, is now performed by the Indians themselves – however with the opposite effect. Like Caliban's attempt to rape Miranda, with which Prospero retrospectively justifies his dispossession, the natives in Purchas's metaphor 'forfeit' their just title to the ravished land, which unites within itself the qualities of both virtuous Miranda awaiting her English Ferdinand and vicious Sycorax 'littering' her monstrous offspring before her coast.

In Purchas's contradictory metaphor, Virginia mutates from a temperate virgin to a distempered witch. Her native rapists betray an equally disturbing sexuality in Purchas's claim that they were 'more wild and unmanly then that unmanned wild Countrey, which they range rather then inhabite'.[37] In one of his many figurative tightrope acts, Purchas represents the Algonkians as both rapists and impotent suitors at once. Such paradoxes are brought about by the intersection of various strands of colonial discourse.[38]

Monstrous mothers

Samuel Purchas's extraordinary metaphor can be implicated into changing European discourses about female sexuality and monstrosity and, more generally, into a changing conceptualisation of the human body. The representation of Virginia as a monstrous mother draws on a very old metaphorical tradition. At the same time it represents an interesting adaptation of the discourse of witchcraft to the discourse of colonialism, thereby testifying to a contemporary concern with various forms of 'demonic possession'. As *The Tempest* can be seen to negotiate this discursive transition, it deserves some investigation.

According to Prospero, Sycorax is a witch who had been exiled from Algiers for her 'mischiefs manifold, and sorceries terrible' and dumped on the island where she 'littered' her son Caliban (I.ii.164–84). Besides the obvious similarities between Sycorax and Circe (who was likewise banned to an uninhabited Mediterranean island for her sorceries), Sycorax, being an African and female sovereign, also recalls the Greek myth of Dido.

As several scholars have noted, the play is careful to make us aware of how Prospero in fact fashions Sycorax's history in order to legitimate retrospectively his own dispossession of Caliban. As Sycorax had died before Prospero's arrival, he learns of her history through the unreliable Ariel, and the play invites us to doubt the authenticity of the tale.[39] The question of Caliban's human status becomes crucial here, and although Prospero endows him with the notorious epithets ('hag-seed', etc.), the play again tends to counter his assertions, for example by equipping Caliban with a remarkable poetic capacity when intoxicated ('The isle is full of noises', III.ii.133–41). Thus, by exposing the fraudulency of Prospero's Machiavellian strategy of rewriting the pre-history of the island in order to make it fit his present claim of sovereignty, the play keeps a critical (though frequently disregarded) distance between us and the Milanese magus. When Caliban reinforces his own claim of sovereignty ('This island's mine, by Sycorax my mother,/Which thou tak'st from me', I.ii.333–4), we are likewise invited to recognise the inappropriateness of Prospero's response: he accuses Caliban of lying and of having attempted to rape Miranda (I.ii.346) – charges which hardly form legitimate excuses for having dispossessed and enslaved Caliban in the first place.[40] 'Historically', Prospero could only have justified these actions on the grounds of Caliban's and Sycorax's bestiality – a bestiality of a very specific kind, as we have in part already seen.

While the figure of Sycorax is obviously modelled on such classical 'witches' as Circe and Medea,[41] she also distinguishes herself from these mythic ancestresses in being simultaneously implicated in the contemporary witchcraft discourse. By the later Middle Ages, the supernatural magic of the classical enchantresses had been translated into the new category of *malefica* (from the Latin *maleficium*: evil deed, crime). Contrary to classical notions of female sorcery, this early modern witchcraft discourse foregrounds the connection between the evil deeds of the 'witches' and their alleged sexual intercourse with the devil. The witch-trial handbook of Heinrich Kramer, *Malleus Maleficarum* (1487), contains the famous equation of witchcraft with female sexuality.[42] Like Caliban then, who, as Peter Hulme shows, is inscribed with both Mediterranean and Atlantic discourses of savagery, Sycorax is also doubly inscribed: Prospero's claim that Caliban is the product of her copulation with an *incubus* identifies Sycorax as a 'modern witch' even while her 'pagan' aspect, expressed in her Medea-like control of the elements, is preserved: as Prospero asserts, Sycorax could 'control the moon' and 'make flows and ebbs' (V.i.270). But through her 'monstrous birth', the figure of Sycorax becomes an even more complex site of intersecting discourses: according to Kramer, the

children to which the *malefica* would give birth after her intercourse with the devil would be human, as the *incubi* (so the theory
goes) could only implant the woman with other men's semen,
none of their own.[43] Still, in the *medical* discourse around 1600, the
assumed causes of congenital defects included – besides God's will,
an inappropriate amount of semen, and inappropriate behaviour
of the mother – the mother's possession by the devil.

Due to the growing secularisation of knowledge, the notion
that a monstrous birth was the result of its mother's copulation
with the devil was on the retreat. As in many other cases, Shakespeare here taps the residual discourse of witchcraft beliefs which
was incompatible with the emerging scientific view of the causes of
monstrous progeny.[44] The medical treatises of the seventeenth and
eighteenth centuries increasingly propagated the theory that monstrous births were the result of a 'monstrous' maternal imagination.[45]

By having 'littered' a 'puppy-headed' monster, Sycorax is not
only marked as a witch but also bears the traces of a monstrous
female. The mythical concept of the monstrous mother came in
handy for the early modern discourse of possession, as is suggested by Samuel Purchas's metaphor of Virginia spewing forth
her native offspring. Virginia's probably best-known classical pre-
decessor is Scylla, one of the monsters barring the sea passage in
the strait of Messina. While Charybdis grasps passing ships, sucks
them down and spews them up again, Scylla, who inhabits the
right-hand rock, is (according to Ovid's *Metamorphoses*) 'ringed
below her hell-black waist/With raging dogs'. Having once been
a fair virgin, Scylla was punished for rejecting the love of Glaucus,
who caused Circe to transform her into a hideous monster whose
lower half consists of 'gaping jaws . . . like Hell's vile hound'.[46] In
the *Odyssey*, Scylla is said to have 'twelve feet, all dangling in the
air, and six long necks, each ending in a grisly head with triple
rows of teeth, set thick and close, and darkly menacing death'.
From her hidden cave high up in the rock, her heads rush forth
and swallow the sailors of passing ships.[47] Guarding the passage
to the western Mediterranean, the two devouring female monsters
can be read as symbols of interdiction, of a vehement 'non plus
ultra'. Odysseus, of course, evades Scylla's terrible *vagina dentata*
(to which her triple rows of teeth amount) by sacrificing six of his
sailors. With his habit of cunningly outwitting fate, he has become
the literary model of John Smith and other colonisers. The fear of

the 'cannibalist' potential of the new continent, however, remained:
like Odysseus's sailors, the settlers of England's first colony in Virginia, Roanoke, had been 'swallowed' by the land, never to be
spewed out again.

In the remainder of this essay, I shall try to show that the representation of the New World as monstrous, suggested by the
frequency of medievalist monsters in early prints and texts about
America, is implicitly gendered. The topos of monstrous female,
like the monstrous races, can be traced back to medieval European
literature. One of the earliest examples of a monstrous female in
English literature is the Questing Beast of Malory's *Le Morte
d'Arthur*.[48] The Questing Beast, which is persecuted by King Pellinor
and later by Sir Palomides, has 'a head like a serpent's head, and
a body like a leopard, buttocks like a lion, and [is] footed like a
hart'.[49] From its belly issues the noise of thirty hounds. A contemporary female monster can be found in Spenser's *Faerie Queene*,
where the Red Crosse knight encounters Errour,

> the ugly monster plaine,
> Halfe like a serpent horribly displaide,
> But th'other halfe did womans shape retaine,
> Most lothsom, filthie, foule, and full of vile disdaine.

Errour's huge tail is 'pointed with mortall sting', and she breeds

> A thousand yong ones, which she dayly fed,
> Sucking upon her poisonous dugs, eachone
> Of sundry shapes, yet all ill favoréd.

As soon as they perceive the light of the Red Crosse knight intruding into the darkness of their forest, these creatures creep into
Errour's mouth.[50] In the ensuing fight, the knight wounds Errour:

> Therewith she spewd out of her filthy maw
> A floud of poyson horrible and blacke,
> Full of great lumpes of flesh and gobbets raw,
> Which stunk so vildly, that it forst him slacke
> His grasping hold, and from her turne him backe:
> Her vomit full of bookes and papers was,
> With loathly frogs and toades, which eyes did lacke,
> And creeping sought way in the weedy gras:
> Her filthy parbreake all the place defiléd has.

(I.i.20)

Whereas the image of the monster vomiting books is part of both anti-Catholic and anti-Protestant propaganda, the characterisation of Errour evokes above all a feeling of loathing towards the female body in general and its capacity for reproduction in particular. Before she dies, Errour spews forth small serpents, 'Deforméd monsters, fowle, and blacke as inke' (I.i.22). After Red Crosse has chopped off Errour's head, her 'scattred brood' sucks up their dying mother's blood. But after having 'devoure[d] their dam', their bellies swell and burst and their bowels gush forth. Errour's monstrous and cannibalistic progeny has destroyed itself (I.i.24–6).

Errour provided the model for Milton's depiction of Sin, who 'seemed woman to the waist, and fair,/But ended foul in many a scaly fold'.[51] Like Errour, Sin is

> a serpent armed
> With mortal sting. About her middle round
> A cry of hell-hounds never ceasing barked
> With wide Cerberean mouths full loud, and rung
> A hideous peal; yet, when they list, would creep,
> If aught disturbed their noise, into her womb,
> And kennel there, yet there still barked and howled,
> Within unseen.

Paradise Lost, first published in 1667, could fully exploit the discursive tradition of witchcraft lore. The link which Milton draws between the tradition of monstrous mothers and that of the witch's sabbath not only unites two powerful misogynous discourses but also sheds new light on Sycorax, who, like Sin, Scylla and the Questing Beast, is the mother of a 'puppy-headed' monster but who is more clearly linked with both classical and early modern witchcraft.

But the representation of Sin is also one of the clearest examples of the Protestant hatred of the grotesque body: having been born from Satan's head, Sin is successively raped by her father and by her son, Death. The latter impregnates her with '[t]hese yelling monsters that with ceaseless cry/Surround me, as thou saw'st, hourly conceived/and hourly born' (II. 795–7). After having been born, the monsters return to her womb, 'and howl and gnaw/My bowels, their repast; then bursting forth/Afresh, with conscious terrors vex me round,/That rest or intermission none I find' (II.799–803). Uniting within itself the opposite functions of conceiving and giving birth, of being born and dying, the grotesque body, as Mikhail

Bakhtin has shown, belongs to a 'carnivalesque' folk tradition which was systematically suppressed (or, as in these examples, semantically exorcised) in early modern Europe. As Susan Gubar notes, the 'eternal breeding, eating, spewing, feeding, and redevouring that characterize Errour, Sin, and [Swift's] Criticism link them to biological cycles considered destructive to intellectual and spiritual forms of life'.[52] Once symbolic of the eternal succession of death and rebirth that characterises the seasonal cycle, the grotesque body underwent a negative valuation in the neoplatonic discourse of the early modern period which promoted spiritual purity as an ideal. The 'leaky vessel' of the material body became, on the one hand, an object of scientific scrutiny and, on the other, a symbol of masculine anxiety. (I think the two developments can actually be seen as two manifestations of the same act of cultural repression, in which the 'rational' dissection of the female body functions to exorcise the fear of its 'leakiness' and impurity – which, symbolically, refers to the 'leakiness' of the body politic, its vulnerability to foreign invasion.[53])

The grotesque body, Bakhtin argues, subverted the dominant ideals of homogeneity and completeness. Grotesque images are ambivalent and contradictory, 'they are ugly, monstrous, hideous from the point of view of "classic" aesthetics, that is the aesthetics of the ready-made and the completed'.[54] Moreover, each of these monstrous mothers 'forms with her brood a self-enclosed system – cannibalistic and solipsistic'.[55] Bakhtin was reluctant to link the early modern antipathy towards the grotesque body with the emergence of Protestantism and the misogynous turn associated with it. But these three developments, I think, are very much part of the same problem. As Marie-Hélène Huet reminds us, in the discourse of Protestantism 'the idea of the monstrous mother becomes a blasphemous parody of the cult of the Virgin Mary'.[56] Protestant iconoclasm was above all directed at the feminine aspects of piety which came to be replaced by a transcendent, overtly masculine god. The Protestant discourse about monstrosity not only brought about a renewal of Aristotle's famous insight that the birth of a female is already the first, if necessary, departure from the norm;[57] it also revived the interpretation of monsters as prodigies – not, as in earlier ecclesiastical writers, as divine portents of future events, but rather as divine announcements of a 'monstrous' female imagination or the mother's idolatrous beliefs.[58] These theories, as Ben

Barker-Benfield has argued, derived from the fear that women might gain an unmediated knowledge of God – unmediated, that is, by their husbands or ministers.[59] What all of this shows, I think, is that the early modern female monster not only articulates a masculine aversion towards the physical processes of reproduction but also functions as a spectre of 'unmanned' and autonomous women.

I want to conclude with an extraordinary set of events that took place in New England in the years 1637–38. On September 21, 1638, the Puritan leaders of the Boston Colony assembled representatives of the surrounding Indian tribes at Hartford, Connecticut, to distribute among them the remnant of the Pequot tribe. As John Mason, a captain of the previous war against the Pequots and a leader of the massacre of their town Mystic, recalls, the Pequots were 'bound by Covenant, That none should inhabit their native Country, nor should any of them be called Pequots any more, but Moheags and Narragansetts forever'.[60] At issue was the Puritans' attempt to 'cut off the Remembrance of them from the Earth', as Mason writes in his account of the massacre in 1637, during which the whole village and all its inhabitants had been burned to the ground.[61] Recalling the incident much later in 1656, Mason displays the zeal of a witch-hunting inquisitor in praising the Almighty's 'Terror' against the Indians, who

> would fly from us and run into the very Flames, where many of them perished . . . God was above them, who laughed his Enemies and the Enemies of his People to Scorn, making them as a fiery Oven . . . Thus did the Lord judge among the Heathen, filling the Place with dead Bodies! . . . Thus was God seen in the Mount, Crushing his proud Enemies and the Enemies of his People . . . burning them up in the fire of his Wrath and dunging the Ground with their Flesh: It was the Lord's Doings, and it is marvellous in our Eyes![62]

The Pequot War had actually been deferred by a few months because the Boston magistrates had been preoccupied with a trial against the religious dissenter Anne Hutchinson. A lay preacher and pupil of John Cotton, Hutchinson had attracted a remarkable congregation of her own which the patriarchs apparently regarded as a threat to their authority. In addition, Hutchinson preached an easier road to salvation than the male professionals, insinuating that one's gender was irrelevant in the eyes of God. Such a doctrine of course threatened to upset the orthodox view that a woman could reach salvation only through her husband or minister. It was during her trial that Governor John Winthrop referred to the ministers as 'nursing Fathers', thereby invalidating any female attempt to intervene with the role of ministers. Obviously, Hutchinson was tried and later expelled for preaching as a woman rather than for preaching a slightly different covenant.

Shortly after her banishment in 1638, Cotton publicly announced Hutchinson's monstrous birth. The physician Thomas Weld describes the birth as '30. monstrous births or thereabouts, at once; some of them bigger, some lesser, some of one shape, some of another; few of any perfect shape, none at all of them (as farre as I could ever learne) of humane shape'.[63]

In a way, according to Puritan theory, Hutchinson even *had* to give birth to a monster, as is implied by Thomas Weld: 'for looke as she had vented mishapen opinions, so she must bring forth deformed monsters; and as about 30. Opinions in number, so many monsters.'[64] Shortly thereafter, another prominent Antinomian woman, Mary Dyer, likewise had a monstrous birth, and magistrates and ministers busied themselves in interpreting the events as manifestations either of divine will or of female mental corruption. Neither Hutchinson nor Dyer was attacked in writing for being a witch, though their midwife, Jane Hawkins, was later tried and banished, partly on charges of witchcraft.[65] But the implications of Winthrop's epithet for Anne Hutchinson as 'American Jesabel' are revealing indeed.[66] Winthrop later repeated the comparison but now added that he 'meant' the Jezebel of St John's Revelation, not the by far more famous Jezebel of the Second Book of Kings.[67] But by taking shelter behind a claim of authorial intention, Winthrop also reveals the *cultural* significance of his comparison: the Jezebel of 2 Kings is the model witch of the Old Testament, referred to as an archetype of modern witchcraft by Heinrich Kramer in his *Malleus Maleficarum*, by Ambroise Paré in his chapter on demons, and by Jean Bodin in his *Daemonologie*.[68]

Jezebel is the wife of King Ahab. She first seduces him to become a servant of Baal and then helps him acquire a new vineyard by masterminding the murder of its previous owner Naboth through the hands of contract killers.[69] After numerous announcements of God's revenge, Jezebel is killed for her 'witchcraft' by King Jehu (while Ahab, typically, is forgiven his devil worship and responsibility for the murder). After having thrown her from his castle, Jehu orders his men to bury her, but they find only her skull, feet, and the palms of her hands. This indicates the fulfilment of the prophecy that 'dogs [shall] eat the flesh of Jezebel: And the carcass of Jezebel shall be as dung upon the face of the field . . . so that they shall not say, This is Jezebel'. The killing of Jezebel is preceded (and perhaps triggered) by a truly fantastic event: lifting his face to look at Jezebel, who gazes out of a window, Jehu strangely sees 'two or three eunuchs' (2 Kings 9, 30–7).

In well-known fashion, the patriarchal myth makes the female 'witch' responsible for a transaction of property between men while the divine revenge at the same time consists of a kind of spring-time sacrifice in which the ground is fertilised with the mutilated woman's body. In providing the common but necessarily occluded ideological ground for both Winthrop's vilification of Anne Hutchinson and Mason's representation of the Mystic battlefield as a ground 'dunged' with the burned flesh of its inhabitants, this biblical story marks the functional intersection of the discourses of territorial possession and witchcraft in early modern England and New England. The archaic biblical narrative evoked by the Puritans – a narrative of the establishment of male power over the dead and mutilated body of a 'foul witch' – links such otherwise diverse texts as Ralegh's *Discoverie*, which imagines Guiana as a uterine treasure cave to be torn open and sacked, and the pamphlet 'Virginias Verger' by Samuel Purchas, whose symbolisation of Virginia unites the image of ravished innocence with a Miltonic evocation of female monstrosity.

Both the biblical patriarchs and the Puritans were concerned with erasing the 'Remembrance' of the people whose bodies are made to fertilise their fields: 'They shall not say, This is Jezebel'; 'nor should any of them be called Pequots any more'. But as so often, the obsessive desire to forget also generates, in the very act of forgetting, a lasting image of the anxiety which has produced it in the first place. Thus the illustration which accompanies John Underhill's account of the Pequot massacre articulates the gendered struggle for power and possession that was haunting the colonial project in British America from its earliest beginnings (Figure 1). In its choice of bird-perspective and symmetrical representation, the map of Mystic is also a *vagina dentata*, besieged by soldiers and fired from within.[70]

Figure 1   Attack on the Pequot village Mystic. John Underhill, *Newes From America* (1638)

Through producing the most troubling symbol of social chaos by following a 'scientific' logic of reason and order (the order of the huts is a European projection; the anatomic accuracy of the engraving's 'second meaning' reflects the emergence of a medical science of the gaze), the Mystic 'map' also points towards the violent rituals of domestication and exclusion practised by contemporary Puritan society in New England – a struggle for absolute control that is epitomised in the signifiers of the enemy's defensive power, the Indian town's palisades, which are at the same time symbols of the severest threat against the vitality of the male Puritan *body politic*. The image unconsciously reproduces the man-devouring Scylla, symbol of the prohibition to move beyond the known world and steal the fruit of foreign nations. Uniting within itself such diverse discursive traditions, the Mystic 'map' speaks of the anxiety that accompanies the European project of imperial expansion. It gives evidence of the fact that patriarchal power has always been secretly aware of the wishfulness embedded in *The Tempest*'s dénouement that the hypocritical game at home would legitimate the hypocritical policy abroad. Above all, however, it demonstrates that, as Gilles Deleuze and Félix Guattari have remarked, '[it] is not the slumber of reason that engenders monsters, but vigilant and insomniac rationality'.[71]

Monstrous writing

The imaginative product of conflicting discourses, Caliban cannot be visualised, he is 'fundamentally and essentially beyond the bounds of representation'. Like him, and less obviously because she does not have to be visualised, Sycorax is a 'discursive monster, a compromise formation bearing the imprint of the conflict that has produced [her]'.[72] That conflict arises from the need of a patriarchal and colonising culture to make sense of, and to legitimate, its history of violence by translating it into a history of knowledge. As Foucault forcefully reminded us, that knowledge, the accepted order of things, is always selective, always contingent upon structures of power. In defining an acceptable norm (the rational, spiritual, European, masculine), the discourse of knowledge excludes other possible knowledges and histories (the grotesque, non-European, female). That of which a discourse cannot speak can only be represented as something monstrous – that is, its representation remains double-voiced and metaphorically overdetermined.[73]

The previous analysis, then, bears out Homi Bhabha's statement that 'within the apparatus of colonial power, the discourses
of sexuality and race relate in a process of functional overdetermination' – although, obviously, the early modern discourse of cultural difference did not include 'race' as a 'scientific' category such
as can be found in the nineteenth century.[74] Thus, in translating
the unrepresentable into the monstrous, the early modern discourse
of possession has itself become monstrous and grotesque. *The
Tempest* seems to endorse such a view: in a gesture whose ambivalence is responsible for the play's lack of closure (it is not at all
clear to me that Caliban is left on the island, as most scholars
seem to conclude), Prospero says of Caliban, 'this thing of darkness I/Acknowledge mine' (V.i.275–6).[75] This can mean both an
acknowledgment of the 'monstrous' undercurrent of Prospero's
'enlightened' civilisation and a final act of enslavement. Caliban
certainly hears the latter ('I shall be pinch'd to death'). This consistent ambivalence of the play, its juggling between different
positions and its condensation of incompatible cultural meanings
turn *The Tempest* into an invaluable manifestation of the cultural
unconscious of its time.

On the basis that the monstrous, just as the grotesque, is ambivalent, potentially subversive and open-ended, *The Tempest* could
be called a monstrous text.[76] Still, its monstrosity and ambivalence
have gone unnoticed by generations of Shakespeare criticism on
the lookout for a unified meaning. As I hope to have shown in my
discussion of the figures of Caliban and Sycorax and the complex
ways in which they relate to changing contemporary discourses of
colonialism and male authority, Shakespeare's play re-presents the
ideological and semantic shifts of a culture in transition, a culture
that is marked by a conflict of meaning. Its 'monstrosity' is not
mere evidence of an 'overdetermined' condition of textuality as
such but indicates the specific ideological crisis of a 'culture of
reason' that could only legitimate its actions by slaying the monsters
gnawing at its bowels.

Notes

1. For their critical comments on an earlier version of this essay, I
   would like to thank Peter Hulme, Francis Barker and Johannes Fischer.
   Susanne Scholz deserves my lasting gratitude for her faithful advice
   on matters of gender in the early modern period.

2. Michel Foucault, 'The Order of Discourse', in Robert Young, *Untying the Text. A Post-Structuralist Reader* (London: Routledge, 1981), p. 60.

3. Among the works I have consulted are Francis Barker and Peter Hulme, 'Nymphs and reapers heavily vanish: the discursive contexts of *The Tempest*', in John Drakakis, ed., *Alternative Shakespeares* (London: Methuen, 1985), pp. 191–205; Curt Breight, '"Treason doth never prosper": *The Tempest* and the Discourse of Treason', *Shakespeare Quarterly* 41 (1990), 1–28; Paul Brown, ' "This thing of darkness I acknowledge mine": *The Tempest* and the discourse of colonialism', in Jonathan Dollimore and Alan Sinfield, eds., *Political Shakespeare. New essays in cultural materialism* (Ithaca: Cornell University Press, 1985), pp. 48–71; Eric Cheyfitz, *The Poetics of Imperialism. Translation and Colonization from* The Tempest *to Tarzan* (Oxford: Oxford University Press, 1991); Stephen Greenblatt, 'Martial Law in the Land of Cockaigne', in *Shakespearean Negotiations. The Circulation of Social Energy in Renaissance England* (Berkeley: University of California Press, 1988), pp. 129–98; Peter Hulme, *Colonial Encounters. Europe and the native Caribbean, 1492–1797* (London: Methuen, 1986); Stephen Orgel, 'Prospero's Wife', in M.W. Ferguson, M. Quilligan, and N.J. Vickers, eds, *Rewriting the Renaissance. The Discourses of Sexual Difference in Early Modern Europe* (Chicago: University of Chicago Press, 1986), pp. 50–64; Stephen Orgel, 'Shakespeare and the Cannibals', in Marjorie Garber, ed., *Cannibals, Witches, and Divorce. Estranging the Renaissance* (Baltimore: Johns Hopkins University Press, 1985), pp. 40–66.

4. See, for example, Octave Mannoni, *Prospero and Caliban; The Psychology of Colonization* (1950), Aimé Césaire, *Une Tempête: D'après 'La Tempête' de Shakespeare – Adaptation pour un théâtre nègre* (Paris: Seuil, 1969), George Lamming, *The Pleasures of Exile* (London, 1984), and Roberto Fernández Retamar, *Caliban: Apuntes sobre la cultura en nuestra América* (Mexico City, 1971). For more recent critical treatments of these texts, see Rob Nixon, 'Caribbean and African Appropriations of *The Tempest*', *Critical Inquiry* 13 (1987), 557–78, and Peter Hulme, 'Rewriting the Caribbean Past: Cultural History in the Colonial Context', in *Interpretation and Cultural History*, ed. Joan H. Pittock and Andrew Wear (London: Macmillan, 1991), pp. 175–97.

5. For an exception, see Ania Loomba, *Gender, Race, Renaissance Drama* (Manchester: Manchester University Press, 1989).

6. Fredric Jameson defines 'ideologeme' as 'a historically determinate conceptual or semic complex which can project itself variously in the form of a "value system" or "philosophical concept", or in the form of a protonarrative, a private or collective narrative fantasy'. *The*

Political Unconscious. Narrative as a Socially Symbolic Act (Ithaca: Cornell University Press, 1981), p. 115.

7. Stuart Hall, *The Hard Road to Renewal* (London: Verso, 1988), p. 9. The quotation is from Antonio Gramsci, *Selections From The Prison Notebooks* (New York: Hoare and Smith, 1971), p. 327.

8. Frances Yates, *Astraea. The Imperial Theme in the Sixteenth Century* (London: Ark, 1975).

9. Hulme, *Colonial Encounters*, chap. 3.

10. Ibid., pp. 108–9.

11. John Block Friedman, *The Monstrous Races in Medieval Art and Thought* (Cambridge: Harvard University Press, 1981), p. 46.

12. Sir Walter Ralegh, 'The discoverie of the large, rich, and beautifull Empire of Guiana' (1596), in Richard Hakluyt, *The Principal Navigations Voyages Traffiques and Discoveries of the English Nation*, 12 vols (Glasgow, Maclehose: 1904), vol. 10, p. 406.

13. Christopher Columbus, *The Diario of Christopher Columbus' First Voyage to America: 1492–1493*, ed. and trans. Oliver Dunn and James E. Kelley (Norman: Oklahoma University Press, 1989), p. 133.

14. Columbus, *Diario*, p. 177.

15. See Hulme, *Colonial Encounters*, chap. 1.

16. David Ingram, 'The Relation of Dauid Ingram of Barking', in Richard Hakluyt, *The Principal Navigations, Voiages and Discoveries of the English Nation* (London, 1589). Facsimile reprint, ed. D.B. Quinn and R.A. Skelton (Cambridge, 1965), vol. 2, p. 558.

17. George Peckham, 'A True Report of the late discoveries ... by Sir Humphrey Gilbert', in Hakluyt, *Principal Navigations*, vol. 2, p. 706.

18. On the early modern international law with regard to America, see Lewis Hanke, *The Spanish Struggle for Justice in the Conquest of America* (Boston, 1965); Anthony Pagden, *Spanish Imperialism and the Political Imagination. Studies in European and Spanish-American Social and Political Theory* (New Haven: Yale University Press, 1990), chap. 1; Etienne Grisel, 'The Beginnings of International Law and General Public Law Doctrine: Francisco de Vitoria's *De Indiis prior*', in *First Images of America. The Impact of the New World on the Old*, ed. Fredi Chiapelli (Berkeley, 1976), vol. 2, pp. 305–25; Hulme, *Colonial Encounters*, pp. 156–68. On the rhetoric of treachery and voluntary submission, see Hulme, *Colonial Encounters*, chap. 4, and Gesa Mackenthun, *Metaphors of Dispossession. American Beginnings and the Translation of Empire, 1492–1637* (Norman: Oklahoma University Press, 1996, forthcoming), chap. 2 and 4.

19. William Shakespeare, *The Tempest*, Arden edition, ed. Frank Kermode (London: Methuen, 1985), II.ii.154; III.ii. Hereafter quoted directly in the text.

20. K. Park and L.J. Daston, 'Unnatural Conceptions: The Study of Monsters in Sixteenth- and Seventeenth-Century France and England', *Past & Present* 92 (1981), 20–54.
21. Marie-Hélène Huet, *Monstrous Imagination* (Cambridge: Harvard University Press, 1993), p. 6.
22. Patricia Parker, 'Fantasies of "Race" and "Gender": Africa, *Othello*, and bringing to light', in Margo Hendricks and Patricia Parker, eds, *Women, 'Race', and Writing in the Early Modern Period* (London: Routledge, 1994), pp. 85–7.
23. Dudley Wilson, *Signs and Portents. Monstrous births from the Middle Ages to the Enlightenment* (London: Routledge, 1993), p. 37. In the late seventeenth century, the term 'moon-calf' also referred to a mole, a specific kind of monstrous birth. See Paul-Gabriel Boucé, 'Imagination, pregnant women, and monsters, in eighteenth-century England and France', in G.S. Rousseau and Roy Porter, eds, *Sexual underworlds of the Enlightenment* (Manchester: Manchester University Press, 1987), p. 90.
24. Wilson, *Signs and Portents*, chap. 2, p. 42.
25. See Hulme, *Colonial Encounters*, p. 111. The centrality of the Dido passage has been pointed out by Leslie Fiedler, *The Stranger in Shakespeare* (London: Paladin, 1974), Hulme, *Colonial Encounters*, and Orgel, 'Shakespeare and the Cannibals'.
26. While the romantic version of Dido and Aeneas functioned as an explanation of the enmity between Rome and Carthage at Virgil's own time, his historiographical juggling (Virgil collapsed 340 years to make the fall of Troy coincide with Aeneas's voyage to Carthage) also came in handy for Elizabethan historians, some of whom claimed Aeneas as the ancestor of the British kings (Hulme, *Colonial Encounters*, p. 111; Orgel, 'Shakespeare and the Cannibals', p. 62). During the reign of Elizabeth, by contrast, the romantic episode was difficult to deal with: in the Sieve Portrait of ca. 1580, Elizabeth appears 'flanked by miniature scenes from the story of Dido and Aeneas' and holding the sieve, symbol of her virginity, in her hand. This modern Dido, the iconography suggests, 'will resist the temptations of any modern Aeneas' (Orgel, 'Shakespeare and the Cannibals', pp. 62–3).
27. Peter Stallybrass, 'Patriarchal Territories: The Body Enclosed', in M.W. Ferguson, M. Quilligan and N.J. Vickers, eds, *Rewriting the Renaissance. The Discourses of Sexual Difference in Early Modern Europe* (Chicago: University of Chicago Press, 1986), p. 130.
28. Orgel, 'Shakespeare and the Cannibals', p. 59.
29. Ben Barker-Benfield, 'Anne Hutchinson and the Puritan Attitude Toward Women', *Feminist Studies* 1, 2 (1972), pp. 73–6; David Hall,

ed., *The Antinomian Controversy, 1636–1638. A Documentary History* (Middletown: Wesleyan University Press, 1968), p. 250.

30. See, for example, Hulme, 'Polytropic Man', and Louis Montrose, 'The Work of Gender in the Discourse of Discovery', *Representations* 33 (1991), 1–41. A famous example may be found in Richard Hakluyt's epistle to Ralegh, in Peter Martyr, *De Orbe Novo* (Paris, 1587). Translation in E.G.R. Taylor, *The Original Writings and Correspondence of the Two Richard Hakluyts*, 2 vols (London: Hakluyt Society, 1935), vol. 2, pp. 367–8.

31. Sir Walter Ralegh, 'The discoverie of the large, rich, and beautifull Empire of Guiana', in Richard Hakluyt, ed., *The Principal Navigations Voyages Traffiques and Discoveries of the English Nation* (1598–1600, repr. Glasgow, 1904), vol. 10, pp. 423, 431.

32. Montrose, 'The Work of Gender', p. 32.

33. See my forthcoming *Metaphors of Dispossession*, chap. 3.

34. Ralegh, 'Discoverie', p. 428.

35. Hulme, *Colonial Encounters*, p. 172.

36. Samuel Purchas, 'Virginias Verger', in *Purchas His Pilgrimes* (1625, repr. Glasgow, 1905–7), vol. 19, p. 229.

37. Purchas, 'Virginias Verger', p. 231.

38. The representation of the Algonkians as both violent nomads and effeminate (in their incapacity to perform the act of 'husbandry') has a long anthropological tradition in Europe. It resembles the description of the Scythians in writers such as Herodotus and Aristotle who portray them as marauding but impotent males. See R. Jones and P. Stallybrass, 'Dismantling Irena: The Sexualizing of Ireland in Early Modern England', in P. Parker, M. Russo et al., eds, *Nationalisms and Sexualities* (London: Routledge, 1992), pp. 162–3.

39. See Barker and Hulme, '"Nymphs and Reapers"', p. 199; Brown, '"This Thing of Darkness"', p. 59; Hulme, *Colonial Encounters*, pp. 123–4; Breight, '"Treason doth never prosper"', pp. 9–10.

40. See Hulme, *Colonial Encounters*, pp. 123–4.

41. See Frank Kermode, 'Introduction', Shakespeare, *The Tempest*, p. XL.

42. See Sigrid Brauner, 'Cannibals, Witches, and Shrews in the "Civilizing Process"', unpublished ms, Amherst (1992), pp. 2–3, 9.

43. Heinrich Kramer (Jakob Sprenger and Heinrich Institoris), *Der Hexenhammer (Malleus Maleficarum)* (München: DTV, 1982), p. 55.

44. My use of the categories 'emerging' and 'residual' is indebted to Raymond Williams's theory of cultural change. See his *Marxism and Literature* (Oxford: Oxford University Press, 1977), pp. 121–7.

45. Huet, *Monstrous Imagination*, p. 5. On monstrous mothers, see also Marilyn Francus, 'The Monstrous Mother: Reproductive Anxiety in

Swift and Pope', *English Literary History* 61 (1994), 829–51; Susan Gubar, 'The Female Monster in Augustan Satire', *Signs* 3, 2 (1977), 380–94; Boucé, 'Imagination, pregnant women'.

46. Ovid, *Metamorphoses*, trans. A.D. Melville (Oxford: Oxford University Press, 1986), pp. 317, 326–7 (books XIII and XIV).
47. Homer, *The Odyssey*, trans. E.V. Rieu (Harmondsworth: Penguin, 1946), p. 191 (book XII).
48. I owe this reference to Elaine Jordan.
49. Sir Thomas Malory, *Le Morte d'Arthur*, 2 vols (Harmondsworth: Penguin, 1977), vol. 2, pp. 46, 401.
50. Edmund Spenser, *The Faerie Queene*, in *Edmund Spenser's Poetry*, ed. Hugh Maclean (New York: Norton, 1968), I.i.14 and 15. Further references will be in brackets in the text.
51. John Milton, *Paradise Lost*, in *Poetical Works*, ed. Douglas Bush (London: Oxford University Press, 1974), II.650–1. Further references will be in brackets in the text.
52. Mikhail Bakhtin, *Rabelais and His World*, trans. Hélène Iswolsky (Bloomington: Indiana University Press, 1984), Introduction; Gubar, 'Female Monster', p. 390.
53. For a discussion of some of these issues from an anthropological perspective, see Mary Douglas, *Purity and Danger: An Analysis of the Concepts of Pollution and Taboo* (London, 1978). With regard to the symbol of the 'Virgin Queen', see Philippa Berry, *Of Chastity and Power. Elizabethan Literature and the Unmarried Queen* (London: Routledge, 1989). See also the forthcoming doctoral thesis of Susanne Scholz (Frankfurt/M., 1996). Again, the issues of race and gender may be seen to converge. The fear of 'pollution' may symbolically be seen in moral terms, but with the growth of nation states and racial definitions of cultural-national identity we can also observe a growing fear of a physical racial 'mongrelisation'. On the fear of racial hybridisation in the nationalist discourses of nineteenth-century Europe and United States, see Robert Young, *Colonial Desire. Hybridity in Theory, Culture and Race* (London: Routledge, 1995).
54. Bakhtin, *Rabelais*, p. 25.
55. Gubar, 'Female Monster', p. 391.
56. Huet, *Monstrous Imagination*, pp. 28–30.
57. Wilson, *Signs and Portents*, p. 19.
58. Huet, *Monstrous Imagination*, p. 30.
59. Barker-Benfield, 'Anne Hutchinson'.
60. John Mason, 'A Brief History of the Pequot War', in *Collections of the Massachusetts Historical Society*, 2nd ser., vol. 8 (1819), p. 146.
61. Mason, 'History of the Pequot War', p. 144.
62. Ibid., pp. 139, 140–1, 144.

63. Hall, *Antinomian Controversy*, p. 214.
64. Ibid.
65. A.J. Schutte, ' "Such Monstrous Births", A Neglected Aspect of the Antinomian Controversy', *Renaissance Quarterly* 38 (1985), 104, n. 58.
66. Hall, *Antinomian Controversy*, p. 310.
67. Barker-Benfield, 'Anne Hutchinson', p. 79.
68. Kramer, *Malleus Maleficarum*, p. 104; Paré, *Des Monstres et Prodiges*, p. 83 and (for Bodin) p. 179, n. 184.
69. *King James Bible*, 1 Kings 15–16. Further references will be given in brackets.
70. Ann Kibbey has called attention to this second layer of meaning in her discussion of the synchronicity of Antinomian Crisis and Pequot War but in my view misses the full ideological and psychological implications of this 'coincidence'. See Ann Kibbey, *The interpretation of material shapes in Puritanism. A study of rhetoric, prejudice, and violence* (Cambridge: Cambridge University Press, 1987), p. 110.
71. *Anti-Oedipus*, quoted in Fred Botting, *Making Monstrous.* Franken-stein*, criticism, theory* (Manchester: Manchester University Press, 1991), p. 161.
72. Hulme, *Colonial Encounters*, pp. 108–9.
73. See Foucault, 'Order of Discourse', p. 61. In the interpretation of dreams, Freud speaks of overdetermination when one latent thought is expressed by various manifest elements, i.e. when one unconscious problematic is translated into a series of different images (or vice versa). Sigmund Freud, *Die Traumdeutung* (Frankfurt: Fischer, 1961), p. 257. Metaphorically speaking, such images as the rape and monstrous birth of Virginia activate more than one 'vehicle' or semantic field in order to transport an idea (or tenor). They are overdetermined because they condense various, and at times conflicting, semantic layers within one image.
74. Homi Bhabha, 'Difference, Discrimination and the Discourse of Colonialism', in Francis Barker et al., eds, *The Politics of Theory* (Colchester, 1983), p. 202.
75. I agree with Leslie Fiedler that the island is given back to Ariel, not to Caliban. Fiedler, *Stranger in Shakespeare*, p. 172.
76. Fred Botting has made such a diagnosis for *Frankenstein* which in his description amounts to a fictional anticipation of Roland Barthes's theory of the open and indeterminate text. See his *Making Monstrous*, p. 5.

4 Racial identity and self-invention in North America: the Red and the Black

David Murray

The underlying themes of this essay are race, hybridity, and mimicry, ideas which are in constant circulation in contemporary discussions of colonial and postcolonial discourse and practice. I want, though, to concentrate on a couple of particular North American instances, in order to suggest some further dimensions of the discussion, particularly in relation to the limits and possibilities of the choice and invention of identity within and across racial and ethnic categories. My starting point is the existence of a triangle of racial identities in the Americas, from the beginnings of European contact, rather than the binary terms of White and Other, which tend to dominate much theoretical discussion.[1]

I begin with a scene described by the French visitor Alexis de Tocqueville in 1835, and turned by him into a sort of allegorical tableau. Journeying through the forests of Alabama he comes across the log cabin of a pioneer. While resting, he sees an Indian woman, probably Creek, come up to a nearby spring,

> Holding by the hand a little girl of five or six and who was of the white race, and who, I supposed, must be the pioneer's daughter. A negro woman followed her. There was a sort of barbarous luxury in the Indian woman's dress; metal rings hung from her nostrils and ears; there were little glass beads in the hair that fell freely over her shoulders ... the Negro was dressed in European clothes almost in shreds. All three came and sat down by the edge of the spring, and the young savage, taking the child in her arms, lavished upon her such caresses as mothers give; the Negro, too, sought, by a thousand

innocent wiles, to attract the little Creole's attention. The latter showed by her slightest movements a sense of superiority which contrasted strangely with her weakness and age, as if she received the attention of her companions with a sort of condescension. Crouched down in front of her mistress, anticipating her every desire, the negro woman seemed equally divided between almost maternal affection and servile fear, whereas even in the effusions of her tenderness, the savage woman looked free, proud, and almost fierce.[2]

At de Tocqueville's approach, annoyed by his curiosity, the Indian woman then 'plunged into the forest'. De Tocqueville finds something 'particularly touching' in the scene, namely that 'here a bond of affection united oppressors and oppressed, and nature bringing them close together made the immense gap formed by prejudices and laws yet more striking'.

The different characteristics and relations of the races, which de Tocqueville fills out in the surrounding chapters of his book, are clearly sketched in here. The White is superior and acts accordingly, the Black is subservient, longing to be accepted, while the Indian is independent and natural, and this supposed distinction remains important in the representation of the races well beyond de Tocqueville.[3] What is particularly interesting in this passage, though, is the idea of nature, which, bringing them together in a 'bond of affection', is contrasted with the gap created 'by prejudices and by laws'. This is a familiar trope, opposing an original and natural harmony to the divisions and deformations of society, and yet de Tocqueville presents the behaviour as so marked and distinct as to serve to reinforce the idea of racial differences or propensities, just as James Fenimore Cooper's frontiersman Natty Bumppo would try to distinguish between a common nature and the particular 'gifts' of each race.[4] In this scene, for all of de Tocqueville's concern with the effects of society, we seem to be seeing a sort of elemental relation, and this reflects a wider ambivalence about innate and acquired traits.

What is missing from this scene, though, is even more interesting. The women are acting in a maternal role, but if they are the symbolic mothers, where is the father? De Tocqueville tells us the girl is the child of the white pioneer and presumably of his white wife, but she is displaced in this scene and he is absent. The widespread reality of miscegenation of white men with Indian and black women on the frontier and elsewhere was of course often

obscured by the absence of the father. This absence was an actual
one, through the lack of acknowledgment or responsibility for
paternity, particularly with black slaves and their white owners,
but it can also be seen in ideological and cultural terms through
the silence so often surrounding the white male's role, in contrast to
the well-worn images of black rapists, and white women threatened
by Indians. Thus the actuality of miscegenation involving white men
and black and Indian women appears in an ideological reversal
which effaces the role of white men.

For modern readers, the description of the child as 'the little
Creole' may suggest something that is not intended by de Tocqueville
and yet it leads us into the heart of the passage. As he is using it,
the word means simply born in America, native, but the many
overlays of racial mixing with which the word has been enriched
or contaminated also leak into this passage. We might note, too,
the way de Tocqueville sets the 'bonds of affection', implying a
nature which brings together, in opposition to prejudice and law
which keep people apart. While he is referring ostensibly to the
maternal impulse here, his terms are precisely those which haunt
discussions of miscegenation: desire, natural or unnatural, and its
transgression of laws and divisions which also claim their basis in
the natural.

I would argue, then, that the way in which the clear terms of
difference in the tableau are broken down in their very description, allowing the ideas of miscegenation and hybridity to seep in
at a symbolic level, points to a larger instability whenever such
clear divisions are set up. Robert Young is only one of those who
have recently shown the ways that 'colonial desire' has permeated
the thinking of Whites,[5] and the way that, while seemingly invisible, issues of race are operative at an intellectual level in the
whole concept of culture. In the United States the actual products
of desire are also very evidently and actually present, as real people, as well as in ideas such as the melting pot, but the actual
terms in which the United States has conceptualised racial identity
has meant a complex and differentialised effacement of the fact of
mixing. While greater interest has now been paid to the role and
the ubiquity of the mixed-blood and the hybrid (most of the terms
available are at least potentially offensive when applied to actual
people, which is itself significant, of course), the complex relation

between red and black and white has been less explored. So I want to examine the differential relation of the races indicated here, and the crucially different attitudes on the parts of Whites to miscegenation with Blacks and Indians, with a view to complicating some of the current conceptualisations of hybridity and ethnicity.

From the earliest accounts of Indian–white encounters the Indian woman was depicted as a 'natural' partner for the European discoverer. Best known in American literature through the many versions of Pocahontas and John Smith, the archetype can be found from the earliest images of the New World, and appears, for instance, in Mexico in the person of the helper of Cortes, La Malinche.[6] Of course, alongside this was the racist aversion, the depiction of savagery, and Robert Tilton has recently shown the way the Pocahontas myth plays down the historical actuality of her marriage to John Rolfe and her bearing of a son by him, in order to emphasise the rescue of Smith, with its conveniently unfulfilled romantic possibilities. We can trace the ways that desire is articulated, only to be blocked, in James Fenimore Cooper and many other writers,[7] but even allowing for this, there is a strong accompanying positive image of Indians, and particularly a pervasive idea of them as romantic vestige or trace. The idea of Indian ancestry has even had a certain appeal, especially if linked with an Indian princess like Pocahontas, and if we compare this with the attitude to having black ancestry we see clearly the difference. Furthermore, except in the most virulently racist quarters, it has been accepted that someone with a small percentage of Indian blood and larger percentage of white could decide to 'be' White, which is different from the attitude towards Blacks. As Karen Blu puts it, according to this view 'Black blood pollutes White blood absolutely, so that in the logical extreme, one drop of Black blood makes an otherwise White man Black', whereas with Indians the idea of purity operates quite differently: 'It may take only one drop of Black blood to make a person a Negro, but it takes a lot of Indian blood to make a person a "real" Indian.'[8]

While having a certain proportion of Indian blood might or might not be an active ingredient in one's racial identity, then, for Blacks the situation is quite different. As Carl Degler pointed out, in a comparison of the United States with Brazil, though there are terms like mulatto and quadroon,

they have been no more than descriptive; they carry no social or
legal significance. There are only two qualities in the United States
legal pattern: white and black. A person is one or the other; there
is no intermediate position.[9]

He points out that in Brazil a mulatto, or any of the other categories
of mixed-blood, 'occupies a special place, intermediate between white
and black; he is neither black nor white. No such place is reserved
for the so-called mixed blood in the United States: a person is either
a black or a white.'[10]

Degler is clear that this does not preclude prejudice against
colour in Brazil or elsewhere,[11] but it does mean that there is a
recognised place, within which there can be social mobility, for
people of mixed race, and thus a way in which social class can
intermingle with race, which then does not act as a watertight
category. It is precisely the absence of this 'special place' in North
America or in the British Empire of the past that recent discussions of hybridity have addressed, in order to liberate its decon-
structive potentialities. As Robert Young, following Homi Bhabha,
puts it:

> hybridity begins to become the form of cultural difference itself, the
> jarrings of a differentiated culture whose 'hybrid counter-energies', in
> Said's phrase, challenge the centred, dominant cultural norms, with
> their unsettling perplexities generated out of their 'disjunctive, liminal
> space'. Hybridity here becomes a third term which can never in fact
> be third because, as a monstrous inversion, a miscreated perversion
> of its progenitors, it exhausts the differences between them.[12]

One of the main contentions of the present essay is that this idea
of the non-third has to take account not only of the differences
between Indian–white and black–white hybridity, but of the particular complexities when all three races may be involved, and I
will be concentrating on the way in which Indianness is asserted
in the context of changes in the prevailing racial and ethnic discourses of origins, purity and genealogy.

The complex and shifting relation between villainous and noble
savage in American culture is by now well documented in accounts
of the representation of Indians. The role of the mixed-blood or
half-breed has been less explored and where it has been it is carefully distinguished from the Black–White mixed-bloods, or mulattos.[13] Positive images of interracial mingling between Indians and

Whites, seen as the promise of a unified autochthonous American race, needed to be carefully distinguished from any suggestion of black blood. Only where the representation was very negative, and half-breeds seen as the degenerate product of an unnatural mingling, was little distinction made between red and black, since any mixing was seen as mongrelisation. Even at its most positive, though, treatment of the mixed-blood, far from transcending or escaping the terms of race, depended on the delineation of fixed racial traits in its characterisation, and the more prevalent negative images predominate, whether in Twain's sinister figure of Injun Joe in *Tom Sawyer* (1876) or in the many doomed relationships, where the narrative line cannot allow the prospering of an inter-racial relationship.

While a great deal of writing by Indians themselves has also subscribed to this privileging of pure origins, there has also been a clearer awareness of the role and range of mixed-blood experience. In one of the earliest texts produced by an Indian woman, *Cogewea: The Halfblood: A Depiction of the Great Montana Cattle Range* (1927), Mourning Dove is at pains to dismiss the negative images of half-breeds.[14] At one point Cogewea actually burns a book she reads that is offensive about half-breeds. Entering in two races (running races, but the ambiguity is presumably deliberate), the ladies' and the squaws', Cogewea wins both but is paid only as a squaw, and rejects her prize. The book swings, like Cogewea, between an assertion of Indian traditional ways and a political engagement with the present, and even its provenance is suitably hybrid, being, like many Indian texts, particularly autobiographies, a composite work.[15]

For both Blacks and Indians, autobiographies have had a crucial role in self-definition. In both cases the earlier texts have been subject to conditions of white co-authorship or editing, so that the final product may be said to be a mediated one. While there are important differences, one thing that is crucial to these early texts is the question of the racial identity, which with white mediation is insistently labelled rather than really explored, whereas in fully-authored later texts, there is the possibility, at least, of problem-atising the very terms of race. For both Blacks and Indians, the questions of authorising and identity depend both on origins and on self-assertion. For Frederick Douglass, the absence of the father (whom he states simply is a white man and not known to him) and the shadowy and silent but powerfully moving presence of the mother, who, we are told, travelled miles merely to spend some time with her child during the night, means that his sense of identity needs to be made, and fought for.[16] In contrast, Indian identity is associated with ancestral connections, and Indian autobiographies assert identity by invoking lineage and tribal connection with the land and the past.

I want to concentrate on one of the most curious productions, published in its final form in 1852 as *A Sketch of the Life of Okah Tubbee, (called) William Chubbee, Son of the Head Chief, Mosholeh Tubbee, of the Choctaw Nation of Indians, by Laah Ceil Manatoi Elaah Tubbee, His Wife*. The text includes general sketches of Indian life and character, and is buttressed by letters of support and authentication from various respectable citizens, ranging from people who had been successfully cured by Tubbee's Indian remedies to the Commissioner of Indian Affairs, apparently affirming Tubbee's Indian status. The bulk of the book, though, is a first-person account of Tubbee's life, introduced as 'a true narrative drawn up from his own lips' written by his wife. As Daniel F. Littlefield, the modern editor, points out, many of the elements of the book seem to be based on their stage-show, which was built upon Tubbee's virtuosity as a flute-player, but also included songs and stories with a strong Indian emphasis, and it is certainly possible to see a very deliberate exploitation of those romantic and exotic aspects of Indianness which would ensure both a status and a living. His wife's Christianised and genteel message is combined with his music to offer a compendium of marketable Indianness.[17]

What is of particular interest here, though, is the way that Indian identity is affirmed in the narrative in the face of conflicting identities, because the actual biographical facts, according to Littlefield, offer a fascinating counterpoint to the narrative. A white slave-owner, James McCary, at his death manumitted a slave woman and two of her three children. The third child, Warner McCary, was left to the slave woman and her two children, to remain their slave. Warner McCary tried hard to ignore or escape this bond, taking the name of William McCary or William Chubbee, or McChubby, and eventually Okah Tubbee, and performing as musician and Indian herbalist.

Okah Tubbee's narrative begins with a double movement which is to be typical of the text as a whole:

The first recollections of my childhood are scenes of sorrow; though I have an imperfect recollection of a kind father, who was a very large man with dark, red skin, and his head was adorned with feathers of a most beautiful plumage . . . I seem to have been happy then, and remember the green woods . . . This scene soon changed, for I had a new father, or a man who took me to a new home, which proves to have been Natchez, Mississippi. (p. 17)

He describes how he soon realises that this man was not his father and he 'began to understand that I could have but one father'. This man was a white slave-holder, with a slave woman who had two older children. Though she was cruel to him and made him serve the other children, 'they obliged me to call her mother'. Throughout the text he refers to her as 'my unnatural mother' or 'the woman' or 'the coloured woman'. The shadowy existence of another, earlier existence is reflected in a strange uncertainty about tenses and sequence. The first recollections 'are scenes of sorrow'. But then we have the imperfect recollection of the kind father, which was prior to this, and 'I seem to have been happy then', where the present tense 'seem' emphasises the haziness of the present recollection rather than the past itself.

This dream-like effect appears at key moments throughout the book, with a whole series of parental or authority figures appearing as enigmatic irruptions into his life. Various white men hint at his ancestry (and one of these may in fact have been his father, according to Littlefield), and a black woman talks of looking after him before his present 'mother' but the effect is of a confused nightmare. He describes how, at one of his lowest points, while imprisoned for an attack after a racial taunt, 'a white man', not named in the book, visits him and tells him that he is a slave, the property of his black mother, and that his father, 'probably a white man', has not bought him out of slavery. He pleads to be told the truth, but the man 'turned coldly from me, while I stretched on the floor in despair, assuring him my blood was free, and pure. I crawled round where I could look him in the face . . .' (p. 28).

This demand for recognition, to be looked at, is present in black writing from the slave narratives onwards, but here it is also linked very basically to blood and descent, and to a denial of Tubbee's blackness. One of the most distinctive features of this particular account is the way that the basic family relationships are so confused and threatening. Rather than, for instance, the black mother being a positive, and the absent white father being the enigma, the black woman here represents the brutality of slavery itself. After Tubbee has tried to make a new identity for himself by ignoring his slave status, serving an apprenticeship and behaving as a free person of colour (a marginal possibility in Natchez at the time, according to Littlefield) his mother – 'the coloured woman' – recaptures him, and in a scene of maximum humiliation she ties him to the bed, flogs him, and tells him, 'Sir, I have taken this plan to show you, you have a master'. She demands that he buy his freedom from her, and in language that resonates with the ironies of the situation, insists 'nothing but your word that you will buy yourself will do; I will take your word for what a slave man is worth; and now promise me quickly, and be like an Indian in keeping your word' (p. 46).

The play of identities in this passage is fascinating. Tubbee must give his word to buy himself, thereby accepting his status as a black slave, but be 'like' an Indian in keeping it, and the constant reference to Indian identity as more fundamental and true recurs throughout the book. The idea of a wild nature dormant within him is alluded to obliquely within the opening pages, when, forced to wear filthy rags rather than the good clothes of the woman's other children, he 'often left them off in consequence'. In order to wash them he has to go 'in a naked state' and when reproached replies 'where did you ever see or hear of a child being born with clothes on?' (p. 18). (We may be reminded here of de Tocqueville's scene, where the black woman's ragged cast-off clothes are part of her difference from the Indian.) He is stirred by his 'mother's' references to Indians, in spite of her denials ('begone! outlandish savage, you never had any father' (p. 23)), and his description of his first encounter with Indians is atavistic enough to leave us in no doubt of his inclinations. They seem surprised at him and approach him. 'I was wild with delight, I thought I was their child, that they were seeking for me; I started and held out my hands, tears gushed from my eyes, I addressed them in a language to me unknown before.' It turns out, of course, that 'I had asked in Choctaw for my father, saying he had gone and left me and I was with bad people' (p. 31). His identification with them is resented by Whites, who insist on his black slave status, though the Indians insist that 'white man lie, he no good, him no slave no, bad white man steal him, his skin is red'.

This is the first of a series of recognition scenes, culminating in a set-piece scene at the Indian camp where an aged Choctaw remembers being told by Moshulatubbee of the loss of his son. Okah Tubbee is identified as this son by a scar on his leg, and the remembered speech of the loving father is given at some length. After the early death of the mother Moshulatubbee fulfils the role of both mother and father, so that here we have Tubbee's ideal and ultimate parent:

> I carried him in my arms by day and slept with him there at night. The tender mother's ready eye would have been less vigilant than mine. Would to heaven that I had suffered him to emerge into manhood while yet borne in a father's arms. (p. 69)

The particular circumstances of his life, in which race has corrupted and perverted family bonds, are transcended in his creation of a loving Indian father, but while his case may be particularly bizarre, he is performing his invention of identity within and between the prevailing conventions and stereotypes, and thereby throwing them into relief. The language of stylised nobility in which the Indians speak here invokes the peculiar cluster of values associated with the Indian as Noble Savage, which on a larger cultural level is an appeal to a nature prior to society or history, an origin beyond the complexities and duplicities of history and actual lineage. In this way Tubbee's own stratagem reveals a larger cultural and ideological contradiction in the idea of the Indian.

So far I have been focusing on Okah Tubbee to explore the relation of identity to lineage, actual or imagined, but an equally important element, and one also connected with hybridity, is that of mimicry. Tubbee's success as a performer was as a clearly labelled Indian, and even his musical virtuosity, which presumably could easily have typecast him as a Negro performer, is deliberately linked to his Indianness. In an amazing and almost comic passage, which seems to have much of the hokum of the medicine-show about it (he was also known as Dr O.K.), Tubbee describes a dream in which he gets the idea to develop new instruments. He is an ancient shepherd with scattered flocks, and a voice tells him to 'take the saucepan out of your pocket, and blow through the handle thereof, and there will come forth sweet strains of music'. Interpreting the flocks as the scattered Indian tribes he wants to unite, Tubbee makes and uses the new instrument, the 'saucepanana', and then has the idea of the musical tomahawk. 'I thought, if the tomahawk, the Indian's most deadly weapon, could be made into an instrument of music, it would be coming nearer to the Indian's heart' (p. 86).

In his act as a whole, the impersonation and play-acting involved, as well as the music, call to mind a crucial later development in the recycling and commercialisation of racial images: the minstrel shows. Originally performed entirely by Whites imitating Blacks, minstrel shows were only later taken over more by Blacks, who then, though, in order to ensure popularity, had to imitate the original white caricature of them. As a form, however, they offered the possibility of a certain degree of carnivalisation of racial roles. In 'Noble Savage', a minstrel show of the 1870s described by Robert C. Toll, a white Eastern writer who has an idealised view of Indians insists that the suitor for his daughter's hand bring him a real Indian. Rather than go West to find one, the suitor hires a black man to impersonate the Indian. When the bogus Indian appears before the writer, who is used to writing about the Noble Savage, the writer runs away in panic, screaming for someone to 'Shoot the savage'. The black imitator then gets carried away with the role and goes round scalping everyone, presumably to general amusement.[18] The overall point being made is that Easterners have a sentimental view of the 'real' savage Indian, but what interests me here is the level of mimicry involved, with Whites playing Blacks playing Indians, and it is this idea of mimicry which I want to add to the theme of hybridity, in order to accommodate the variability and instability involved in the representations of otherness.

If one aspect of the project of Western civilisation was to make the inferior others, by education and example, as much like the Whites as possible, another aspect was to maintain precisely that difference which justified white authority. As Homi Bhabha puts it,

> The 'part' (which must be the colonialist foreign body) must be representative of the 'whole' (conquered country), but the right of representation is based on its radical difference.[19]

Consequently, Bhabha has pointed to those places where the contradictions and ambivalences of mimicry are revealed. The real threat is not so much in the clear imitation, where the white mask conceals a black presence beneath, but in a more fundamental 'discursive process by which the excess or slippage produced by the ambivalence of mimicry (almost the same but not quite) does not merely "rupture" the discourse but becomes transformed into an uncertainty which fixes the colonial subject as a "partial" presence'.[20]

As the early minstrel shows indicate, the fascination with these uncertain borders means that Whites often feel drawn in very different ways to imitate what they have distinguished themselves from, and not always just to show their superiority to it. Michael Taussig has brilliantly discussed examples from the Americas where the mimicry has gone both ways, in a process which he calls the 'colonial mirror of production',[21] and where it is 'far from easy to say who is the imitator and who is the imitated, which is copy and which is original'.[22] He shows how the complex interplay of role-playing and mimicry threatens the white need for a clear and recognisable other, expressed in American terms in the ideal of the pure Indian. The complex interplay of races and roles threatens this pure ideal, though, and

> this infernal American identity machine thus composes a mosaic of alterities around a mysterious core of hybridity, seething with instability, threatening the First World quest for a decent fix of straightforward Othering – were it not for the degree zero provided by the black man.[23]

I want now to try to clarify some of the implications of this connection between hybridity and mimicry through a concrete example, and turn to my second chosen autobiography, *Long Lance*. Published in 1928 and steadily republished, it is presented as the authentic account of an Indian childhood as lived before the impact of modern white culture. By the time of its publication Long Lance was already widely known as a journalist and Indian spokesman, and the actor Irvin Cobb, in his Foreword, refers to the quite different book Long Lance might have written if he had covered his later life. It would have documented his achievements in going from a full-blood childhood to success at Carlisle Indian school, followed by decorations for bravery as an officer in World War I. Within a couple of years of the book's publication he was also to become a star in silent films. *Variety* described him as 'an ideal picture Indian, because he is a full-blooded one ... an author of Indian lore, and now an actor in fact'.[24] The book addressed a demand for stirring tales of the West with a nostalgia for the 'vanishing American' as a figure of nobility and simplicity, and the packaging of the book is meant to stress its authenticity. Cobb claims that 'there is authentic history in these pages and verity and most of all a power to describe in English words the thoughts, the instincts, the events which originally were framed in a native language'.[25]

Much of the book is an account of exploits and customs of a traditional Indian tribe, and this may be partly accounted for by the origins of the book as a fictionalised account of Blackfeet life. According to Long Lance, though, 'they thought it was too good for a boy's book, and forthwith decided to run it as my autobiography' (Smith, p. 199). The publishers were clearly aiming at the long-standing and continuing market for authentic accounts of or by Indians indicated by the success, before Long Lance, of Charles Eastman and Geronimo, and after him by Black Elk and many others.[26] In the figure of Long Lance, then, we have the appeal of the authentic full-blood Indian, reflected in numerous pictures of him from the time, in full traditional dress, but also the appeal of an Indian who has learned to be like a sophisticated white man, and other pictures of him reveal a dapper, dignified individual. As an influential columnist remarked, 'were it not for his straight black hair, which is cut close to his head, and his skin, which is not red but more the color of ivory-toned parchment, he might be taken for a Wall Street broker' (Smith, p. 199).

It is precisely this ability to be 'taken for' one race or another, the aspect of mimicry, which I want now to pursue through Long Lance, beginning with a particular instance recounted by an English visitor to a smart hotel in Banff, Canada, in 1924, where Long Lance worked as a sort of public relations man. He describes having a wide-ranging and cosmopolitan conversation with a charming stranger, who then challenges him. 'You are looking hard at me. Can you tell to what nationality I belong?' After a suitable pause, seeing the Englishman's bafflement, he announces, 'I am a full-blooded Blood Indian. I am Chief Buffalo Child Long Lance of the Blood tribe.' Walker's response is interesting: 'Had the heavens opened, I could not have had a greater surprise' (Smith, p. 121).

The point of the story, for Walker, lies partly in his expectations, and Long Lance is relying on this, as he does in many of his dealings with Whites. It is a pleasant surprise for Walker, because it reflected great credit on a full-blood to be able to mimic a white man so well. It is important to stress that this is allowed within the particular terms of similarity and difference operating for Indians in the period, and was in fact the governing principle of the Carlisle Indian school, founded in the previous century precisely for the purpose of civilising and Christianising the traditional Indian out of existence. Long Lance learned the lesson very well, and his address at graduation shows this:

> we do not wish to be designated as Cherokees, Sioux or Pawnees, but we wish to be known as Carlisle Indians, belonging to that great universal tribe of North American Indians, speaking the same language and having the same chief – the Great White Father at Washington. (Smith, p. 25)

So we can suggest that to be a Carlisle Indian was to be both Indian and not Indian, a success as a white man which was doubly admirable because 'really' an Indian, and this is what Long Lance in his whole career played on, and even exploited. If this were the whole story it could be seen as a positive one, revealing his ability to invent himself anew in ways which affirmed the assimilative policies of the time. But in 1932 Long Lance shot himself. All sorts of contradictions in his life were coming to a head, the main one brutally indicated by the report of a Pinkerton detective commissioned by one of his white Hollywood patrons:

> Subject's father full-blooded negro. Joe S. Long . . . Winston-Salem, North Carolina. Mother half Indian. Two brothers, one sister respected negroes. One brother negro detective. . . . Subject's name Sylvester Long. (Smith, p. 230)

Sylvester Long had been brought up as a Negro. Joining a circus for the summer and working with Indians he seems to have realised he could be taken as Indian if he identified himself as such, and began picking up odd words of Indian languages. Because of this, and the fact that the family had always claimed Indian ancestry, he applied to Carlisle Indian school and persuaded local officials, including the white minister, to endorse his claim to be 50 per cent Indian on both sides (though Carlisle often settled for less). He shrugged off suspicions there that he was black, and learned Indian words and background from other Indian pupils, and there is a wonderful irony about his career at Carlisle. Ostensibly there to become less Indian and more civilised, actually Long Lance was acquiring the Indianness on which he was to trade for the rest of his life. But he could only trade on it indirectly, in that it provided the basis from which he was supposed to have developed, and for which he was admirable. So we have the paradox of him needing to be an Indian in order to be congratulated for being like a White, civilised, which of course he always had been. This points to the asymmetry between different ways of being 'like' a white man, and we can see this very clearly by returning to Mr Walker in the hotel at Banff, and imagining his reaction if Long Lance had revealed he was a Negro from Winston-Salem. In fact we have an actual instance. The writer Irvin Cobb, who wrote a fulsome introduction to the autobiography, when he heard that Long Lance had Negro blood, is reported to have said, 'To think that we had him here in the house. We're so ashamed! We entertained a nigger' (Smith, p. 196).

Long Lance's story is certainly instructive about the different sorts of racism, the different ideas of difference and sameness acceptable in the early years of this century, and we could leave it there as a curiosity, as what Donald B. Smith calls the true story of an impostor.

To leave him as impostor, though, which would mean seeing him 'really' as a Negro from Winston-Salem who pretended to be an Indian, would be in some crucial ways to avoid the challenge to our categories which Long Lance offers, and to ignore the part which pretending and role-playing plays in issues of race and ethnicity. To develop this it is worth looking at the status of what were probably Long Lance's forebears. Within North Carolina and surrounding areas are a number of particularly interesting groups. These are people who have always had a recognisable group identity, with family names which recur over very long periods (Chavers, for instance, for the Lumbee, and Goins for the Melungeons), but the exact nature of that identity in the eyes of their white neighbours has often been ambiguous. As with Okah Tubbee further south in Natchez, the catch-all category, free persons of colour, has included free Blacks, together with people with varying or indeterminate amounts of black, white and Indian ancestry.

There are two complicating issues here. One is that, as Jack Forbes has shown, from very early on, Indians not clearly on a reservation (so mostly in the East), or living recognisably as Indians (speaking an Indian language, for instance), often were classed as free persons of colour. This was particularly so if there was any evidence of mixed blood, and here we come to the second and crucial complication. In his ground-breaking book Forbes has demonstrated the extreme slipperiness of a whole category of terms like mulatto, and their use from as early as the seventeenth century to refer to Indian–white as well as Black–white mixtures.[27] Once there is a large legal category of free persons of colour, non-traditional Indian groups find it well-nigh impossible to distinguish themselves from Blacks, which, of course, given the racial ideology that has prevailed for several centuries, means anyone with even a small percentage of black ancestry.

Perhaps the most significant of these groups of quite troublesome and problematic people, now called the Lumbee, were clearly in evidence by the end of the eighteenth century, especially in Robeson County, and ideas of where they came from have ranged from displaced Cherokee to the original Croatan people who were a mix of the first white colonists and Indians.[28] Once these people were legally classed as free persons of colour in 1835, they were disenfranchised and effectively counted as mulattos, a term to whose complications Forbes devotes several chapters. They were eventually recognised as Croatan Indians in 1885, and it was then a matter of vigilantly protecting this hard-won status. Of course, to do this involved them in the whole racial ideology of their white neighbours, including racial screening committees for their schools to exclude blacks. This shabby episode reflects in microcosm, though, what Forbes has described as 'a 100 year struggle to resist the "coloured" category, a struggle fought with uneven success and one which served to poison African–American Indian relations as well as to split communities'.[29] As he says, because the term coloured equalled Black 'its acceptance by Indians would have amounted to a voluntary change in ethnic identity' (p. 258). (In 1956 Congress recognised them as the Lumbee Indians, and perhaps their most publicised moment was their rout of the Ku Klux Klan in 1958. More recently they were involved in a Black–Indian coalition in 1968.)[30]

The Lumbee present a fundamental challenge to many of our assumptions not only about Indians but about ethnicity itself. There is no original language, and very few of the organisational or boundary-marking elements which might be expected in a traditional Indian group. It has often been pointed out that ethnicity can be seen as being about choice, whereas race is not. You can choose to embrace ethnicity, which is defined in terms of group, whereas race is quite different; in fact Blacks were in some ways negatively characterised as not having all of the elements which constituted ethnicity, like community and a sense of valued identity and origins. Another way to put this is to say that ethnicity can be creative, an act of imagining and reimagining the past, a creative use of memory. Ethnicity therefore need not be reliant on authenticity except as an important rhetorical weapon. So, present-day Indian writers may choose whether to invoke an Indian heritage. Louise Erdrich, as her name suggests, has German as well as Chippewa ancestry, and has written, in *The Beet Queen*, about German immigrants. Many contributors to collections of Native American writing choose to identify themselves as of mixed origins, and the implication is that the Indian element is in this context the operative one, but the prevailing racial climate is still such that for a writer who was part Black and part Indian to invent or present him- or herself as Indian would be a very different thing, resented by fellow-Blacks if not also by Indians or Whites, as overstepping some invisible line.

For as Okah Tubbee's and Long Lance's stories remind us, the ability to choose to be ethnic has been dependent on obscuring the non-choice of race. Unfortunately, as has often been pointed out, the resurgence of urban white ethnicity has all too often had an anti-Black orientation. I suppose only when being 'Black' is entirely a matter of individual choice and not a matter of assignment by others will Werner Sollors's 'invention of ethnicity' have worked its way through.[31] I want to argue, finally, for the importance of the larger challenges offered by figures such as Okah Tubbee and Long Lance. It is not just that there are such oddities, but that they reveal the fault-lines of a great deal of our theorising about hybridity and about race and ethnicity, as well as the terms in which Native Americans are studied.

In his powerful account of Lumbee communities and their attempts to negotiate racial and ethnic identities, Gerald Sider describes a scene he witnessed at one of the local courthouses, where a middle-aged black man (as his identity would seem to be) stood before 'three water fountains, with the signs over each that earlier had said WHITE, NEGRO, INDIAN, gone almost but not quite beyond recognition'.[32] In such an environment, with officials and other people of all sorts possibly watching, and with a knowledge of the dangers and intimidations connected with making the wrong choice, imagine the difficulty for this man in choosing where to drink.

> The man I saw stood momentarily in front of the water fountains and then walked away without drinking at all. It was not an intellectual game, seeking to situate one's public self in the uncertain connections between past, present, and future: not at those appalling stakes.

From de Tocqueville's trio at the spring, with which I began, to the baffled figure at the water fountains (perhaps a distant relative of Long Lance – who knows?), we have moved from an apparently clear and fixed racial relation to an area of ambiguity, of apparent choice, but one where the faded signs retain at least some of their meaning and their power to discriminate and to harm.

Notes

1. One of the themes of this essay, the inadequacy of the available categories and terminologies of race, is reflected in my own difficulties with terms. To maintain a certain symmetry in my formulations, which develop out of nineteenth-century ideas, I have retained the adjectives white, black and Indian, and the nouns White and Black, with the intention that the development of my argument will underline just how arbitrary and ideologically loaded all such terms are. Similarly, my retention of the terms mixed-blood and mixed-race is not intended to endorse the idea of fixed racial categories. The later sections of this essay will specifically address the ways in which race can be opposed to the invocation of ethnicity, with its possibilities of choice.
2. Alexis de Tocqueville, *Democracy in America* (1835), vol. 1, ed. P. Meyer and M. Levin (New York: Harper and Row, 1966), pp. 396–7.
3. See, from a huge field, George Frederickson, *The Black Image in the White Mind: The Debate on Afro-American Character and Destiny, 1817–1914* (New York and London: Harper, 1971), and Robert F. Berkhofer, Jr, *The White Man's Indian: Images of the American Indian from Columbus to the Present* (New York: Alfred A. Knopf,

1978). Comparative or combined studies of the representation of Blacks and Indians are less common, which is part of the rationale of this essay.

4. In *The Deerslayer*, Cooper's Leatherstocking uses the same tripartite division as de Tocqueville, and there is a similar concern to delineate what is 'nature'. 'God made us all, white, black and red; and, no doubt, had his wise intentions in coloring us differently. Still, he made us, in the main, much the same in feelin's; though I'll not deny that he gave each race its gifts. A white man's gifts are christianized, while a redskin's are more for the wilderness.' Elsewhere he distinguishes between nature as 'the creature itself', whereas 'gifts come of sarcumstances', but the underlying emphasis on the hierarchy of race seems to outweigh the possibilities of a more relativist view. See Roy Harvey Pearce, *Savagism and Civilisation: A Study of the Indian and the American Mind* (Baltimore: Johns Hopkins University Press, 1967), pp. 196–211 for a discussion of these passages.

5. Robert Young, *Colonial Desire: Hybridity in Theory, Culture and Race* (London and New York: Routledge, 1995).

6. See Annette Kolodny, *The Lay of the Land: Metaphor as Experience and History in American Life and Letters* (Chapel Hill: North Carolina University Press, 1975); Robert S. Tilton, *Pocahontas: The Evolution of a Narrative* (Cambridge and New York: Cambridge University Press, 1995); and Peter Hulme, *Colonial Encounters: Europe and the Native Caribbean, 1492–1797* (London and New York: Routledge, 1992).

7. See, for instance, Louise K. Barnett, *The Ignoble Savage: American Literary Racism, 1790–1890* (Westport, Conn. and London: Greenwood Press, 1975).

8. Karen I. Blu, *The Lumbee Problem: The Making of an American Indian People* (New York: Cambridge University Press, 1980), p. 25.

9. Carl N. Degler, *Neither White Nor Black: Slavery and Race Relations in Brazil and the United States* (New York: Macmillan, 1971), p. 102.

10. Degler, *Neither White Nor Black*, p. 107.

11. In Brazil, not only does the ideological acceptance and even celebration of mixed blood not preclude the continuation of the colonial racial hierarchy, but the terminology is still contentious. See Marvin Harris, Josildeth Gomes Consorte, Joseph Lang and Bryan Byrne, 'Who Are the Whites?: Imposed Census Categories and the Racial Demography of Brazil', *Social Forces*, 72, 2 (December 1993), 451–62. The authors point out the difficulties in translating Brazilian terms for race. The word cor (colour) appears on census forms rather than race, and morena (brown) is widely preferred to the official term parda. The article chooses the term 'race-colour'.

12. Robert Young, *Colonial Desire*, p. 23.
13. See, for instance, William J. Scheik, *The Half-Blood: A Cultural Symbol in Nineteenth-Century American Fiction* (Lexington: Kentucky University Press, 1979). For general accounts see Roy Harvey Pearce, *Savagism and Civilisation*, and Berkhofer, *White Man's Indian*. Louis Owens's recent study of contemporary Indian literature, *Other Destinies: Understanding the American Indian Novel* (Norman and London: Oklahoma University Press, 1992), concentrates on the idea of the mixed-blood to great effect. His prefatory epigraph from the Chippewa writer Gerald Vizenor reflects his approach: 'Mixedbloods loosen the seams in the shrouds of identities.' While Owens concentrates on white-Indian mixings, Sharon P. Holland, unusually, goes further, in ' "If You Know I Have a History, You Will Respect Me": A Perspective on Afro-Native American Literature', *Callaloo*, 17, 1 (1994), 334–50. It is perhaps significant that her essay appears in a journal usually devoted to African-American rather than Indian materials.
14. Mourning Dove, *Cogewea, the Half-Blood* (Lincoln: Nebraska University Press, 1981). Mary V. Dearborn places her in a useful context in *Pocahontas's Daughters: Gender and Ethnicity in American Culture* (New York and Oxford: Oxford University Press, 1986). For an account of the editorial complexities, see Alanna K. Brown, 'The Editorialised Mourning Dove' in Arnold Krupat, ed., *New Voices in Native American Literary Criticism* (Washington and London: Smithsonian Institution Press, 1993).
15. Recent scholarly attention to the peculiar status of Indian autobiographies as complex bicultural products is best represented by Arnold Krupat's work, particularly *For Those Who Come After: A Study of Native American Autobiography* (Berkeley: California University Press, 1985) and David H. Brumble, *American Indian Autobiography* (Berkeley: California University Press, 1988).
16. Frederick Douglass, *Narrative of the Life of Frederick Douglass, an American Slave, Written by Himself* [1845] (New York: Signet, 1968). The importance not only of Douglass's work but of the slave narrative in general, as an extensive body of early black writing which raises crucial questions of mediation and autonomy of expression, has been recognised in much recent criticism. See Charles T. Davis and Henry Louis Gates, Jr, eds, *The Slave's Narrative* (Oxford: Oxford University Press, 1985); Valerie Smith, *Self-discovery and Authority in Afro-American Narrative* (Cambridge: Harvard University Press, 1987); and Robert B. Stepto, Jr, *From Behind The Veil: A Study of Afro-American Narrative* (Urbana: Illinois University Press, 1989).
17. Daniel F. Littlefield, Jr, ed., *A Sketch of the Life of Okah Tubbee, (called) William Chubbee, Son of the Head Chief, Mosholeh Tubbee, of*

the Choctaw Nation of Indians, by Laah Ceil Manatoi Elaah Tubbee, His Wife [1852] (Lincoln and London: Nebraska University Press, 1988). Further references will be given parenthetically in the text.

In Long Lance there is no ambivalence, and scarcely any parental role either. References are generally to 'our mothers', or 'our fathers', reflecting its generalised origins.

27. Jack D. Forbes, *Black Africans and Native Americans: Color, Race and Caste in the Evolution of Red-Black Peoples* (Oxford and New York: Basil Blackwell, 1988).

28. The reference here is to Ralegh's lost colony, of which the only trace found was the word Croatan carved on a tree. This would certainly be a pedigree classy enough to rival the heirs of Pocahontas.

29. Forbes, *Black Africans and Native Americans*, p. 258.

30. The best acounts are to be found in Blu, *Lumbee Problem*, and Gerald M. Sider, *Lumbee Indian Histories: Race, Ethnicity and Indian Identity in the Southern United States* (Cambridge and New York: Cambridge University Press, 1993).

31. Werner Sollors, ed., *The Invention Of Ethnicity* (New York: Oxford University Press, 1989), and *Beyond Ethnicity: Consent and Descent in American Culture* (New York and Oxford: Oxford University Press, 1986). It is worth noting that census practices are very relevant and revealing here. The old system whereby one portion of Negro blood cancelled out all others in racial classification, which was the whole problem with the category free persons of colour, has had a stubborn persistence. Forbes points out that 1930s census-takers were told to count white–Indian mixed-bloods as Indians, except where the Indian percentage was very small, but Negro–Indian mixed-bloods 'shall be returned as a Negro unless the Indian blood predominates and the status as an Indian is accepted in the community'. The instruction for the 1940 census was changed from 'predominates' to 'very definitely predominates and he is universally accepted in the community as an Indian'. Even as late as 1980, when self-identification was the method, no mixed status was allowed, so that anyone checking Indian and Black would be counted as Black (Forbes, *Black Africans and Native Americans*, p. 203).

32. Sider, *Lumbee Indian Histories*, p. 10.

5 *Once upon a time in America: race, ethnicity and narrative remembrance*

Liam Kennedy

Memory has become a significant issue of representation in American literature in recent years, with many writers 'reclaiming' or 'retelling' the American past from distinctly ethnic and racial perspectives. This preoccupation with the past is not new, but it has never been so plural and politicised in the history of American literature. What is at issue, in the most general terms, in this writing is the formation and inscription of cultural identities in the act of narrative remembrance. Writers have sought to interrogate and revitalise the histories of their ethnic and racial groups and show how cultural identities in the present are shaped by narratives of the past. In this essay I shall examine some of the historical and ideological contexts of this literary turn to memory and analyse selected texts which share a specific focus on the American city as a key site of memory for ethnic and racial groups.

The turn to memory in American literature reflects the historical development of a volatile cultural pluralism which has characterised the fragmentation of coherent political and cultural publics in the United States over the last thirty years. With the disintegration of the postwar ideological consensus in the mid-1960s, as Frederick Buell observes,

> cultural pluralism emerged as a powerful public issue and force. On the one hand, this represented an extension of the ideologically sacred concept of the United States as a nation of immigrants, a nation of nations; on the other hand, it ruptured these traditions, as analyses of American racism and the failure of the melting pot were supplemented by advocacy of oppositional and revolutionary

forms of cultural nationalism. In race relations, in ethnic affairs, and in management of internal borders generally, the boundaries of American identity were being transgressed and shattered.[1]

Although the 'boundaries of American identity' were never securely fixed in an unchanging national ideology, they were deeply encoded in the concept of the American Creed as civil religion and in its master narrative of exceptionalist ethnogenesis.[2] This narrative did not simply dissolve in the 1960s but it lost its power to describe a collective, national experience and evoke a shared historical consciousness. Since this period Euro-American traditions have struggled to authorise the meanings of American identity. New patterns of cultural existence, global migration, and ethnic and racial boundary-marking have accentuated these decentring tendencies, fragmenting and dislocating the 'common culture' of reference and reconfiguring the meanings of whiteness as an ethnic identity.

The importance of memory in this decentring cannot be under-estimated, though it takes diverse forms and has no singular political impetus. There is a good deal of contemporary critical interest in memory as an affective agency of self-definition and resource of critical perspectives on dominant forms of historical consciousness.[3] However, memory should not be too casually privileged as a counter-hegemonic force, for it is always socially constructed; it both transforms and is transformed by history. Moreover, when memory is a motivated or strategic act – of cultural maintenance or community-building, for example – it threatens to prescriptively memorialise the past and essentialise the cultural identities it inscribes. As totalising historical consciousness gives way to a multiplicity of micro-histories and vernacular memories, American writers have had to question notions of cultural origin, agency and continuity even as they take account of the role memory can play in constituting meaningful cultural and historical bearings. The writers' self-conscious efforts to 'recover' the past, a willed remembering set against diverse forces of historical amnesia, creates what Pierre Nora terms *lieux de mémoire*, 'sites of memory'. As Nora explains, *lieux de mémoire* exist

> where memory crystallizes and secretes itself at a particular historical moment, a turning point where consciousness of a break with the past is bound up with the sense that memory has been torn – but

torn in such a way as to pose the problem of the embodiment of
memory in certain sites where a sense of historical continuity exists.[4]

Lieux de mémoire are products of the dynamic interaction of
history and memory, unstable signs of the past which are invested
with cultural significance in the present. They may be places, or
people, or objects, or events; they may be real or imagined.

American city spaces constitute key *lieux de mémoire* in the narratives of many writers. In this essay I shall examine how selected
narratives reconstruct the urban past and address 'the problem of
the embodiment of memory' Nora refers to. Much of my textual
analysis will focus on the work of two writers, William Kennedy
and Toni Morrison, who offer distinctively ethnic (Irish-American)
and racial (African-American) perspectives on relationships between
memory and urban space.

I

For white ethnic writers the American city has multiple and shifting significations which reflect their diverse responses to historical
patterns of immigrant settlement, economic progress and sociocultural assimilation. Ethnic attitudes towards and representations
of the city are not consistent, but differ between and within distinct
communities and across generations. Yet key themes and motifs do
recur in literary texts, particularly in relation to the spatial boundaries of self-identity in urban contexts. In, for example, Jewish-
American representations of New York throughout much of the early
twentieth century the city is depicted from localised and vernacular perspectives; it is a conglomeration of 'urban villages', of ethnic
cities within the metropolitan mass which have their own distinct
communities, customs, religions and languages. There is an intense
identification with the everyday culture of family and street life
and the urban iconography becomes a mirror of self-development.
It is common for texts to feature an admixture of responses to the
city, portraying ambivalent states of mind, particularly striking in
the work of second- and third-generation writers who are historically distant from the culture of the immigrants. Jewish-American
writers such as Saul Bellow, E.L. Doctorow, Grace Paley, and Sandra
Schor produce psychological studies of the hyphenated state of being

Jewish-American, of the sensation of being in a liminal position between worlds, both drawn to and repelled by the culture and traditions of the ancestors and yet struggling to define their meanings in contemporary contexts.[5] For these writers ethnicity is very much a discourse of foundations or origins, and memory and imagination are heavily relied upon to generate a continuous process of ethnic interpretation.

The writer whose work I have selected to comment on more closely here is the Irish-American author William Kennedy. I do this in part because his work is intensely concerned with ethnic memory and city life, but also because Irish-American literature is all too rarely recognised as a discrete entity in literary studies.[6] Irish-American writers have a distinctive imaginative investment in the American city. The first Irish immigrants who fled the famine in the mid-nineteenth century and those who followed through the early years of the twentieth century settled in American cities, in part because of their harrowing experiences of rural life in Ireland. Throughout the twentieth century urban experiences have significantly defined Irish-American politics and culture and have been central to literary representations of the ethnic group. From Finley Peter Dunne's satirical sketches of Irish life in Boston at the turn of the century, through James T. Farrell's extensive narratives of the ghetto Irish of Chicago in the 1930s and 1940s, to Mary Gordon's stories of Irish-American suburbanites in New York today, a history of the Irish-American urban experience has been documented and imagined.[7] Of the Irish-American novelists at work today it is William Kennedy who has made the most extensive efforts to interrogate critically the meanings of Irish-Americanness as a lived experience and as a historical legacy.

Kennedy has written a cycle of historical novels that constitute a richly imaginative and shrewdly revisionist history of Irish-American urban experiences.[8] He has situated all his narratives in Albany, New York, documenting and expanding genealogies from novel to novel, constructing an intimate fictional and historical tableau of ethnic life in the city. The novels closely tie historical memory to place and foreground the roles of reminiscence and anecdote, of what Kennedy terms 'memory and hearsay', in the retelling of the ethnic past.[9] With this focus on vernacular memories, in particular, Kennedy illuminates the everyday encodings of ethnic identity and distinctiveness and explores the cultural myths of the ethnic group. Believing that Albany's past is 'always-shifting' he seeks to show how Irish-Americans use (select and interpret) history and reinvent the past in the process of self-definition.[10] In doing this he questions his own group's deeply mythologised story of immigrant success and ethnic passage, and shows considerable empathy for those who do not fit neatly into this story.

Irish-American reinvention of an ethnic identity and an idealised past is a central feature of *Ironweed* (1983). The narrative opens, fittingly enough, in an Albany graveyard where Francis Phelan has taken a few days' work digging graves. Francis has returned to the city after twenty-two years 'on the bum', a life of seemingly self-induced 'exile' sustained by the guilt he feels about the deaths of a scab he felled during a strike and of his thirteen-day-old son Gerald, whom he accidentally dropped and killed. In the graveyard and in his movements through the streets of the city he begins to confront the ghosts of his past and re-examine the memories he has carried with him for many years. His movements are contained within a tightly structured and highly symbolic time frame. It is Halloween, 1938, and the narrative opens on All Souls Day and closes on All Saints Day, underlining the themes of sin and redemption and the idea of communication between the living and the dead that further particularise the author's ethnic perspective. Francis's personal dilemma is not consumed by abstractions, though, for Kennedy works to historicise it by showing how it is bound up with the Irish-American community's interpretation of its past. Francis re-enters Albany as a ghostly figure voided of a historical self by the mythological status he has been accorded by the community and has long accepted. For Irish-Americans he is a heroic figure for his action in killing the strike-breaker, an action written into a popular play which depicts him as a 'Divine Warrior' furthering the cause of immigrant struggle. The popular narrative conforms to the 'up from below' symbolism so important to white ethnic views of the past which build upon immigrant heroism.[11] In this context Francis's return to Albany takes on a potent symbolism, for he returns as a bum, a historical reality at odds with his mythical identity. He is at once a living signifier of the harsh socio-economic realities of the Depression and a ghost of the ethnic past, the harsh realities of which have been sentimentalised or 'forgotten'.

Francis's ghost-like existence also symbolises the sense of social exclusion he experiences in being designated a 'bum'. Early in the narrative, while digging graves in the Albany cemetery, he comments to his co-digger, 'I never knew a bum yet had a gravestone'.[12] The recognition of social invisibility takes on a particular ethnic signi- ficance in the context of the author's comments on the cemetery and the memories it stirs in his protagonist. When Francis muses that 'being dead here [the cemetery] would situate a man in place and time. It would give a man neighbours . . .' (p. 13), he responds to striking encodings of Irish-American history in this landscape of the dead. Scanning the cemetery he notices that the dead 'settled down in neighbourhoods', from the rich and powerful Irish-Americans 'vaulted in great tombs built like heavenly safe deposit boxes', to 'the flowing masses, row upon row of them under simple headstones and simpler crosses' (p. 12). The cemet- ery not only encodes class differentiation (a form of social differ- entiation which is largely obscured by imperatives of ethnic struggle), but also offers an intriguing figure of the passage from immigrant to ethnic. While the names on the oldest headstones at the foot of the cemetery hill have weathered away,

> the progeny of those growing nameless at the foot of the hill were ensured a more durable memory. Their new, and heavier, marble stones higher up on the slope had been cut doubly deep so their names would remain visible for an eternity, at least. (p. 13)

Francis is implicitly identified with the 'nameless' at the bottom of the hill, the virtually erased immigrant identity that has been dis- placed and incorporated by that of the ethnic. Denied the security of location 'in place and time' this Divine Warrior/bum haunts the Irish-American present, straddling and blurring the realms of his- tory and myth.

In *Ironweed* the Irish-American past is always under construc- tion, its reinvention important to the patterning of social relations in the present. This reinvention is neither a stable nor an easily controlled process, suggesting that ethnicity is no simple matter of group assimilation or socialisation. Because ethnicity is a dynamic process of identity formation, its reinvention requires repeated revelations and repressions that are experienced both privately and publicly. An important function of memory in *Ironweed* is to express an ethnic anxiety about the past which characterises the protagonist's struggle clearly to define and locate his identity.

Possession by the past is shown to be harmful, promoting a self-lacerating sense of guilt in Francis:

> In the deepest part of himself that could draw an unutterable conclusion . . . [Francis] told himself: My guilt is all that I have left. If I lose it, I have stood for nothing, done nothing, been nothing. (p. 216)

His return to Albany initiates a flood of memories and before long he is 'conjuring memories against his will' (p. 96). His task is to *re*interpret their meanings for him in the present, and Kennedy explicitly notes the therapeutic promise: if Francis 'can remember this stuff out in the open' he can 'finally start to forget about it' (p. 19). Throughout the narrative the process of remembering 'out in the open' is activated by the ghosts who challenge him to re-assess the causes and consequences of his violent past. This self-analysis disrupts Francis's deep psychological investment in the narrative of heroic exile. He begins to consider that the strike was 'simply the insanity of the Irish, poor against poor, a race, a class divided against itself', and that the strike-breaker he killed was an itinerant like himself, seeking 'to survive hostility in . . . strange cities' (p. 207).

Needing 'to believe in simple solutions', Francis finds that he is more and more confused by 'his own repetitive and fallible memory' (p. 223). However, if repetition signifies an ethnic anxiety, it also allows Francis to begin to come to terms with his violent past and with his vacated roles of husband and father. When he visits his family towards the end of the novel nothing is clearly resolved, though initial resentments and emotional conflicts slowly give way to a family dialogue about the past and present. The novel climaxes not in the family home but in yet another symbolic environment, an encampment of bums and hobos which constitutes an alternative 'city of essential transiency' (p. 208), and also a 'primal scene' (p. 209) in which Francis re-enacts his personal traumas. The first re-enactment is imaginative, as he tells others for the first time the story of how he accidentally killed his son. The second is physically violent as he kills one of a group of American Legion raiders who attack the encampment. The dramatic interactions of private and public actions and of ethnic and class politics are played out again. For Francis, this ritualistic return of the past leads to no ready release from his sense of guilt. The novel closes on an ambiguous note, a hallucinatory fantasy of Francis's return to his family. The meaning of this fantasy is not clear. Is Francis now about to 're-enter history' (p. 169), and locate himself 'in place and time'? The author refuses to tell us, and in the irresolution of this ending boldly re-emphasises the tensions between history, memory and desire in the construction of an ethnic identity.

In *O, Albany!* (1983), his non-fiction 'urban biography' of the city, Kennedy proposes that Albany is 'a magical place where the past becomes visible'.[13] In *Ironweed* this magical element is the activity of memory as it responds to charged associations with the past in everyday urban scenes and events of the present. The Albany streets in particular appear surfeited with echoes of past lives:

> Francis saw the street that lay before him: Pearl Street, the central vessel of this city, city once his, city lost. The commerce along with its walls jarred him; so much new, stores gone out of business he never even heard of. Some things remained: Whitney's, Myer's, the Old First Church, which rose over Clinton Square, the Pruyn Library. As he walked, the cobblestones turned to granite, houses became stores, life aged, died, renewed itself . . . (pp. 63–4)

There are echoes here and elsewhere in the novel of a modernist nostalgia, a melancholic romancing of the past, but Kennedy is not simply motivated by a sense of the loss of the ethnic past. In representing city spaces as *lieux de mémoire* and source of material and imaginary traces of the past in the present he asks readers to recognise the 'always-shifting' nature of ethnic history and identity as these depend upon interpretations of that past. Kennedy concentrates on both the internal mechanisms of ethnic identity formation and its historical conditions, aware that he is himself playing a part in the reinvention of the Irish-American past.

II

If the story of ethnic passage as a core myth of national identity is troubling for many white ethnic writers it is almost entirely alien to most African-American writers. The progressive urban narrative of immigrant arrival, ghetto communalisation and suburban assimilation has relatively little historical or imaginary relevance to the lives of African-Americans. The black urban experience in the twentieth century is one founded on *migration* and (the growth of a suburbanised black middle class notwithstanding) continues to be significantly defined as a 'ghetto' experience. Since the Great Migration of the early twentieth century when many thousands of Southern blacks moved northwards to cities such as Detroit, Chicago, Philadelphia and New York, urban experiences have crucially transformed African-American cultural identity and made the city a key site of collective memory within the broader diasporic consciousness. African-American writers have recorded, interrogated and contributed to this transformation. There is no singular, unified representation of this transformation in black literature. A utopian/dystopian dialectic operates within and across black city texts, dramatising the urban maps of possibility and prohibition for African-American subjects. The city is a space of refuge, recommunalisation and individual agency; but it is also a space of terror, segregation and environmental determinism. James Baldwin, in *Go Tell It On the Mountain* (1953), combines archetypal images of heaven and hell as his black protagonist John Grimes surveys the skyline of New York while standing on a hill in Central Park:

> there arose in him an exultation and a sense of power ... he would live in this shining city which his ancestors had seen with longing from far away ... And still, on the summit of that hill he paused. He remembered the people he had seen in that city, whose eyes held no love for him ... Then he remembered his father and his mother, and all the arms stretched out to hold him back, to save him from this city where, they said, his soul would find perdition ... It was the roar of the damned that filled Broadway.[14]

Ironically symbolising New York as the 'shining city' of Puritan vision, Baldwin underlines his protagonist's sense of exclusion from this crucible of American democracy. For African-American writers of recent years representations of the city continue to portray such doubleness or ambivalence, though within a more self-consciously historical framework as writers such as Gloria Naylor, Jerome Wideman, Toni Morrison, and Walter Mosley seek to rewrite the urban black past within the context of increasing economic and social immiseration for urban blacks in the United States.[15]

Of all the city spaces that symbolise the 'modern' African-American experience it is Harlem which has been most powerfully and prodigiously mythologised. The movement of blacks into

Harlem from 1915 onward represented not only a significant demographic shift but the emergence of a 'race capital' in the United
States. As Harlem began to take this emergent form in the 1920s
black writers were quick to interpret and advance the symbolic impetus. In *The New Negro* (1925) Alain Locke famously presented
his vision of a new black identity:

> Here in Manhattan is not merely the largest Negro community in
> the world, but the first concentration in history of so many diverse
> elements of Negro life. It has attracted the African, the West Indian,
> the Negro American; it has brought together the Negro of the city
> and the man from the town and village . . . Proscription and preju-
> dice have thrown these dissimilar elements into a common area of
> contact and interaction. Within this area, race sympathy and unity
> have determined a further fusing of sentiment and experience . . .
> In Harlem, Negro life is seizing upon its first chances for group
> expression and self-determination. It is – or promises to be – a race
> capital.[16]

Locke's vision was widely taken up in the period and has been
seen as a central statement of the Harlem Renaissance, though his
views were disputed then and later by writers who perceived his
to be an elitist discourse of Americanist renewal which ignored the
realities of black working-class life in the city and of continuing
racist discriminations. Locke's utopian vision is mediated through
more ambivalent black representations of Harlem in the work of
Langston Hughes and Nella Larsen in the 1920s, and of Ann Petry,
Ralph Ellison, and James Baldwin in the mid-century.[17] In his essay
'Harlem is Nowhere' (1948) Ralph Ellison emphasised the extreme
psychological and cultural impact of the transition from rural to
urban, from pre-modern to modern, symbolised in the black
peopling of Harlem. He argues that this transition epitomised the
African-American's sense of instability as 'a "displaced person" of
American democracy'. For Ellison, the 'nowhere' of Harlem is the
symbolic 'scene of the folk-Negro's death agony' and of 'his tran-
scendence'.[18] Writing forty-five years after Ellison, Toni Morrison
picks up these themes of psychological instability and cultural
transition in her novel *Jazz* ([1992] 1993), a historical romance of
Harlem lives in the 1920s.

In *Jazz* Toni Morrison presents a Harlem that is more expressively imagined than it is historically documented. It is a Harlem
of the mind, a symbolic locus of black memory and a primal scene

of African-American modernity. Morrison writes with an intimate knowledge of the mythological and fictional signifiers which convey 'Harlem' in the black imagination. Her aim is not to uncover the 'real', historical Harlem, but to tease out the meanings of the cultural transition Ellison refers to above. In doing this, she reworks her own abiding interest in the dialectics of remembering and forgetting in African-American culture. Though Morrison is certainly not the first black writer to view memory as a key site of racial consciousness, few have more deliberately and consistently sought to 'fret the pieces and fragments of memory' in black life. For Morrison the reconstruction of the past is a form of narrative 'archaeology': narrative remembrance, she observes, is 'a journey to a site to see what remains have been left behind and to reconstruct the world that these remains imply'. In this process she blends memory and imagination to enter into the 'interior lives' of black Americans: 'I'm looking to find and expose the truth about the interior life of people who didn't write it'.[19] The truth of her characters' interior lives is not only the social facts of their daily experiences but also their unconscious or semi-conscious desires, anxieties and yearnings. It is in this psychological territory that Morrison digs deep into individual and collective memories.

The relationship of the city to African-American memory is not a new concern for Morrison. In earlier novels and in several essays she has expressed an ambivalent attitude to the patterns of displacement and adjustment in urban spaces. Her second novel *Sula* (1973) begins: 'In that place, where they tore the nightshade and blackberry patches from their roots to make room for the Medallion City Golf Course, there was once a neighbourhood . . . It is called the suburbs now, but when black people lived there it was called the Bottom'.[20] The novel tells of the formation and the collapse of the black neighbourhood under the pressures of white suburbanisation and commodity capitalism, and indirectly chastises the 'young ones [who] kept talking about the community, but they left the hills to the poor, the old, the stubborn – and the rich white folks'.[21] In the novel the loss of 'a place' has a damaging impact on black culture and the sense of imminent or real loss of African-American experiences of localised community is one that underlies much of Morrison's writing. In her essay 'City Limits, Village Values: Concepts of Neighborhood in Black Fiction' (1983), she argues that 'the affection' black writers display for the city is usually limited to 'the village within it: the neighborhoods and the population of those neighborhoods'. In Morrison's view the key figure of this village community is that of 'the ancestor' who 'values racial connection, racial memory over individual commitment'. It is this memorial parent who provides the possibility of recommunalisation in the city based on 'village values'.[22] In *Jazz* this theme of urban amnesia is picked up again as Morrison makes more explicit her concern that the American city 'seduces' black people into forgetting the experiences of pre-urban black life in the United States. Even as she makes this explicit, though, she also subtly revises her earlier views to provide a complex meditation on the meanings of 'freedom' for African-Americans in the urban village of Harlem in the 1920s.

The unidentified first-person narrator of *Jazz* is self-confidently speculative about the lives narrated in the novel: 'Risky, I'd say, trying to figure out anybody's state of mind. But worth the trouble if you're like me – curious, inventive and well-informed'.[23] The narrator is all of these things but also only a partial witness to the life stories narrated and is notably seduced by the dynamism and aesthetics of city life. At the beginning of the novel the narrator speaks as a somewhat ironic proselytiser of the new:

> I'm crazy about this City.
> . . . A city like this one makes me dream tall and feel in on things. Hep . . . I'm strong. Alone, yes, but top-notch and indestructible – like the City in 1926 when all the wars are over and there will never be another one. The people down there in the shadow are happy about that. At last, at last, everything's ahead. The smart ones say so and people listening to them and reading what they write down agree: Here comes the new. Look out. There goes the sad stuff. The bad stuff. The things-nobody-could-help stuff. The way everybody was then and there. Forget that. History is over, you all, and everything's ahead at last. (p. 7)

This vision of the city is characterised by its aesthetic distance, echoing the (predominantly white) modernist perspectives on New York as a future-oriented city. It also echoes the bullish vision of Alain Locke (perhaps one of the 'smart ones' referred to above), an ideological championing of the black metropolis which will uplift the race. For the narrator, the city is a space of possibility and pleasure in which black people see and experience each other in new ways, such as 'how men accommodate themselves to tall buildings and wee porches, what a woman looks like moving in a crowd, or how shocking her profile is against the backdrop of the East River' (p. 34). The city 'pump[s] desire' into human relations, displacing love and inducing forgetfulness; it deceives people into feeling 'more like themselves, more like the people they always believed they were' (pp. 34–5). Black people are involved in exercises of individual and collective narcissism. Enduring economic deprivations on arrival in Harlem they none the less 'stayed to look at their number, hear themselves in an audience, feel themselves moving down the street among hundreds of others who moved the way they did' (pp. 32–3).

The narrator's exuberant representation of the city as 'back and frame' (p. 9) for the characters' lives is a richly expressive feature of the novel. But it also signals what the narrator finally admits is an error of vision and interpretation: 'It was loving the City that distracted me and gave me ideas. Made me think I could speak its loud voice and make that sound sound human. I missed the people altogether ... I believed I saw everything important [the main characters] did, and based on what I saw I could imagine what I didn't: how exotic they were, how driven. Like dangerous children' (pp. 220–1). The narrator errs in predicting the desires and actions of the main characters, having imagined them as 'exotic', 'driven' beings who are ignorant of the workings of history and prisoners of their passions and traumas. The narrator's self-censure and late admissions of unreliability are not intended to dissolve the lives narrated into arbitrary fictions or to diminish the reader's interest in them. On the contrary, the reflexivity of the novel draws attention to those elements of the characters' 'interior lives' that exceed the point of view of the narrator. What is absent, what is not seen or said, has a powerful narrative presence, motivating memory and desire in these interior lives. What the narrator 'misses' (and the reader is invited to reflect upon) is the significance of the workings of memory and desire – of loss, displacement, abandonment, and mourning – on the lives of the characters.

The plot of *Jazz* is narrated on the first page:

Sth, I know that woman. She used to live with a flock of birds on Lenox Avenue. Know her husband, too. He fell for an eighteen-year-old girl with one of those deepdown, spooky loves that made him so sad and happy he shot her just to keep the feeling going. When the woman, her name is Violet, went to the funeral to see the girl and to cut her dead face they threw her to the floor and out of the church. (p. 3)

The economy of this opening is deliberate and striking. In a few lines we are introduced to the garrulous narrator, to the three main characters – Joe Trace (the murderer), Violet (his wife), and Dorcas (the murdered girl) – and to key themes of obsessive love, betrayal and death. This plot and the attendant themes are the stuff of popular romance, though it is clear that Morrison views them as a representative subject of urban blues or jazz music. The plot, she has observed, is intended as 'the melody' of the text which the narrative departs from and circles around.[24] The bare plot of *Jazz* is itself a narrative improvisation based upon a photograph in James Van der Zee's *Harlem Book of the Dead* of an eighteen-year-old girl lying in her coffin.[25] Morrison constructs her digressive narrative around this image, positing the death of Dorcas as an allegory of desire in the estranged lives of Joe and Violet.

Clues as to how to interpret this allegory are scattered throughout the text, and as we follow the 'crooked line of mourning' (p. 17), which follows on Dorcas's death, we are led back in time to the Southern past. Joe, Violet and Dorcas are all orphaned migrants, haunted by the loss of parents and in particular the loss of mothers. Joe was rejected by his mother at birth and takes his enigmatic surname at an early age when he is told his parents had disappeared without trace. Violet's mother committed suicide, jumping down a well in rural Virginia. Dorcas's mother is burned alive in her house in East St Louis during the riots of 1917, only five days after her father's murder. The novel moves unevenly back in time to give us the stories of Joe's and Violet's childhoods and of their meeting in Palestine, Virginia, and even further back, the story of Joe's mother, Wild, and of Golden Gray, a white man (with a black father) whom Violet's grandmother raised. The stories are 'pieces and fragments of memory' which resist coherent narrative development, yet collectively constitute a distinctive genealogical legacy of loss and dispossession which shapes the memories and desires of the characters in the present.

As the disjointed narrative slowly begins to fill in details of Joe's and Violet's past lives we learn that they have emotionally grown away from each other, retreating into numbing consideration of their own lives. The death of Dorcas heightens their estrangement but also propels them into newly self-conscious investigations of prefiguring traumas. Violet becomes obsessed with Dorcas, and obtains a photograph of the dead girl which she places on the mantelpiece of their apartment. As 'a dead girl's face [becomes] a necessary thing for their nights', Joe and Violet in turn rise from bed to gaze at 'what seems like the only living presence in the house' (pp. 11–12). Joe sees a 'calm, generous' face absent of accusation or judgment. Violet sees a 'greedy, haughty' face that only 'sees its own self' (p. 12). The photograph becomes a focus for their diverse desires, reconfiguring other losses and absences in their memories. For Joe, Dorcas doubles for the mother he has lost and is haunted by. He discovered at the age of eighteen that his mother was a wild woman who lived in the woods and he searched for her on several occasions, at once ashamed and fascinated by the 'traces of her sloven unhousebroken self all over the county' (p. 178). For Violet, Dorcas's deathly presence in her life has distinctive if confused meanings. Even before the girl's death 'cracks' had begun to develop in Violet's consciousness, 'dark fissures in the globe light of the day' (p. 22), and as she 'stumbles onto these cracks' (p. 23) she becomes dissociated from the everyday course of her urban life. A major cause of this stumbling is her memory of her mother's death and her (too late) desire for a child. She is immured in 'mother-hunger' (p. 112) and as she gives herself to the memory of Dorcas it is clear that the dead girl becomes a substitute for the child she and Joe never had. Violet finds that 'not only is she losing Joe to a dead girl, but she wonders if she isn't falling in love with her too'. She further wonders: 'Who lay there asleep in that coffin? Who posed there awake in the photograph? . . . Was she the woman who took the man, or the daughter who fled her womb?' (p. 109)

As memories and desires are constructed around Dorcas we find that the identities of the main characters are complexly split between the past and present, between the rural South and the urban North. A damaging psychological pattern of dispossessions fashions the 'crooked line of mourning' that binds Joe and Violet despite their estrangement. Violet comes to wonder if the originating moment of love between Joe and herself was a form of displacement in which each stood in for the other's figure of desire: 'Which means from the very beginning I was a substitute and so was he' (p. 97). The allegory of desire which is Dorcas's death repeats this patterning of substitutions and the narrator is confident that Joe and Violet will compulsively repeat their traumas. When Felice, a young friend of Dorcas's, enters the lives of Joe and Violet to produce a 'scandalising threesome' (p. 6), the narrator views their relationship as a 'mirror image' of that involving Dorcas and predicts that 'one would kill the other' (p. 220). But the narrator is wrong and the patterns of the past are broken as Joe and Violet settle into a relationship of loving fulfilment at the end of the novel. The narrator ruefully expresses surprise:

> I was sure one would kill the other. I waited for it so I could describe it. I was so sure it would happen. That the past was an abused record with no choice but to repeat itself at the crack and no power on earth could lift the arm that held the needle. (p. 220)

How is it that the characters have stalled or defeated the metonymic drive of unfulfilled desires? The narrator does not tell us, indeed claims ignorance and suggests that there is something 'missing' or 'rogue' in the telling of the life stories (p. 228).

While Morrison refuses simply to explain Joe and Violet's loving resolution, she does work to suggest that it occurs as a result of their preparedness to confront the past so that they can find release from it. This confrontation and release, as much as the determining forces of history and desire, illuminates what I take to be Morrison's key concern in *Jazz*, to investigate the meanings of urban 'freedom' for African-Americans. The narrator represents the city as a space of desire and forgetfulness, while Morrison works to suggest that it is not only this but also a space of love and memory. The latter possibilities have to be struggled for against the seductive powers of the former and it is this struggle which defines the agency of her characters and their connection not only to the rural South but to the past of slavery. In interview Morrison states that she was

> fascinated by the thought of what the city must have meant to . . . second- and third-generation ex-slaves, to rural people living there

in their own number ... How did people love one another? What did they think was free?[26]

The significance of these questions about love and freedom is put into historical context by Morrison's observation in *Beloved* that 'not to need permission for desire – well now, *that* was freedom'.[27] In *Jazz* the city is the space of such freedom only imagined by the slaves and ex-slaves in the earlier novel who are forced to 'love small' or not at all. Dorcas (the symbolic descendant of Beloved) embodies an overwhelming desire that was not available to the ex-slaves and their children. For Morrison, there are profound questions of human agency bound up in her black characters' 'ownership' of their own bodies and emotions. The narrator of *Jazz* seems aware of this, believing it made urban blacks 'dangerous children' unable to understand or responsibly act upon their new urban freedoms. Joe and Violet confound this view, however, registering responsibility for their actions, signifying their ability to change on their own terms, and transmuting desire into love.

In *Playing in the Dark: Whiteness and the Literary Imagination* (1992) Morrison critically examines the American romance genre of the nineteenth century to argue that it most compellingly tells of 'the terror of human freedom – the thing [Americans] coveted most of all'.[28] In *Jazz*, her own historical romance, the 'terror of human freedom' is less a metaphysical force than a historical legacy of slavery. The discourse of 'freedom' in the novel is present in many registers, cutting across private and public realms of black lives and conjoining past and present. In the private lives of the characters it is most commonly reiterated in their references to 'choice' in deciding how to lead their lives and whom to love. Such choices can be delusory, representing the franchised 'freedom' on offer in an urban consumer culture. Morrison portrays such delusions in *Jazz* but also looks to deeper emotional meanings of human agency in the need of her characters to live an 'unslaved life'. The common dilemma for her characters is one that she has acutely posed for herself as an African-American writer: the need 'to find some way to hold on to the useful past without blocking off the possibilities of the future'.[29] She knows this is a delicate critical act of balancing the demands of remembering against those of forgetting. She also posits it as a cultural necessity for her African-American contemporaries.

III

In representing urban spaces as key *lieux de mémoire* Kennedy and Morrison recognise the fundamental instability of memory in the formation and maintenance of cultural identities. By foregrounding this instability they warn against memorialisation of the past while seeking to identify residual elements of alternative histories in acts of narrative remembrance. Both writers are aware that the American city acts as a totalising gauge of social and political progress, and both write with an eye on contemporary urban conditions of Irish-American and African-American experience. While their characters seek to negotiate their own positions within the narratives of the past they are also positioned by these narratives, and the resulting psychological tension finds expression in memory. In underscoring this tension both authors foreground the difficulties of establishing, as well as the need to establish, a usable past for their ethnic and racial groups in the present.

Notes

1. Frederick Buell, *National Culture and the New Global System* (Baltimore: Johns Hopkins University Press, 1994), p. 144.
2. See Buell, *National Culture and the New Global System*, pp. 145–6. On ideologies of American exceptionalism, see Byron E. Shafer, ed., *Is America Different?* (Oxford: Clarendon Press, 1991), and Kenneth Thompson, 'Identity and Belief', in *The United States in the Twentieth Century: Culture*, ed. Jeremy Mitchell and Richard Maidment (Milton Keynes: Open University, 1994), pp. 13–38. On the concept of civil religion (post-1960s), see Robert Bellah, R. Madsen, W.M. Sullivan, A. Swindler, and S.M. Tipton, *Habits of the Heart: Individualism and Commitment in American Life* (Berkeley: University of California Press, 1985).
3. There is a growing body of critical work on memory in the fields of American cultural history and literary studies. See, for example, George Lipsitz, *Time Passages: Collective Memory and American Popular Culture* (Minneapolis: University of Minnesota Press, 1990); John Bodnar, *Remaking America: Public Memory, Commemoration, and Patriotism in the Twentieth Century* (New Jersey: Princeton University Press, 1992); David Thelen, ed., *Memory and American History* (Bloomington: Indiana University Press, 1994); Geneviève Fabre and Robert O'Meally, eds, *History and Memory in African-American Culture* (New York and Oxford: Oxford University Press, 1994); Amritjit

Singh, Joseph T. Skerrett, Jr, and Robert E. Hogan, eds, *Memory and Cultural Politics: New Approaches to American Ethnic Literatures* (Boston: Northeastern University Press, 1996).

4. Pierre Nora, 'Between Memory and History: *Les Lieux de Mémoire*', *Representations*, 26 (Spring 1989), 7.

5. See, for example, Saul Bellow, *The Adventures of Augie March* (1953), E.L. Doctorow, *The Book of Daniel* (1971), Grace Paley, *Enormous Changes at the Last Minute* (1974), and Sandra Schor, *The Great Letter E* (1990).

6. The most comprehensive critical study of Irish-American literature to date is Charles Fanning, *The Irish Voice in America: Irish-American Fiction from the 1760s to the 1980s* (Lexington: University of Kentucky Press, 1990).

7. See, for example, Finley Peter Dunne, *Mr. Dooley in Peace and in War* (1898); James T. Farrell, *Young Lonigan* (1932); and Mary Gordon, *The Other Side* (1989).

8. William Kennedy's Albany novels include: *Legs* (1975), *Billy Phelan's Greatest Game* (1978), *Ironweed* (1983), *Quinn's Book* (1988), and *Very Old Bones* (1992).

9. William Kennedy, *O, Albany!* (New York: Penguin, 1983), p. 371. I have examined the role of memory in Kennedy's writings in more detail in 'Memory and Hearsay: Ethnic History and Identity in *Billy Phelan's Greatest Game* and *Ironweed*', *MELUS*, 18, 1 (Spring 1993), 71–82.

10. Kennedy refers to the 'always-shifting' past of Albany in *O, Albany!*, p. 7.

11. For a critical analysis of this symbolism, see Colin Greer, 'The Ethnic Question', in *The Sixties Without Apology*, ed. Sohnya Sayres, Anders Stephanson and Fredric Jameson (Minneapolis: University of Minnesota Press, 1984), pp. 119–20.

12. William Kennedy, *Ironweed* (Harmondsworth: Penguin, 1986), p. 12. All further references to this novel will be given parenthetically in the text.

13. Kennedy, *O, Albany!*, p. 7.

14. James Baldwin, *Go Tell It On The Mountain* (New York: Dell, 1985), pp. 33–4.

15. See, for example, Gloria Naylor, *The Women of Brewster Place* (1990); Jerome Wideman, *Philadelphia Fire* (1991); Toni Morrison, *Jazz* ([1992] 1993); and Walter Mosley, *Devil in a Blue Dress* (1989).

16. Alain Locke, 'Introduction', in *The New Negro: An Interpretation*, ed. A. Locke [1925] (New York: Athenaeum, 1968), p. 5.

17. See, for example, Nella Larsen, *Quicksand* (1928); Ann Petry, *The Street* (1946); and Ralph Ellison, *Invisible Man* (1952).

18. Ralph Ellison, 'Harlem is Nowhere', in *Shadow and Act* (New York: Vintage, 1972), pp. 294–302.

19. Toni Morrison, 'The Site of Memory', in *Out there: Marginalization and Contemporary Cultures*, eds Russell Ferguson, Martha Gever, Trinh T. Minh-ha, and Cornel West (Cambridge, M.A.: MIT Press, 1990), pp. 302–3.

20. Toni Morrison, *Sula* (London: Triad Panther, 1982), p. 11.

21. Ibid., p. 148.

22. Toni Morrison, 'City Limits, Village Values: Concepts of Neighborhood in Black Fiction', in *Literature and the American Urban Experience*, ed. Michael C. Jaye and Ann Chalmers Watts (Manchester: Manchester University Press, 1981), pp. 35–43.

23. Toni Morrison, *Jazz* (London: Picador, [1992] 1993), p. 137. All further references are given parenthetically in the text.

24. 'Interview: Toni Morrison with Elissa Schappell', *The Paris Review*, 35, 128 (Fall 1993), 118.

25. See Deborah A. McDowell, 'Harlem Nocturne', *The Women's Review of Books*, 9, 9 (June 1992), pp. 1, 3–5.

26. 'Interview', p. 120.

27. Toni Morrison, *Beloved* (London: Picador, 1988), p. 162.

28. Toni Morrison, *Playing in the Dark: Whiteness and the Literary Imagination* (Cambridge, MA: Harvard University Press, 1992), p. 57.

29. Toni Morrison, 'Rediscovering Black History', *New York Times Magazine* (11 August 1974), p. 15.

6 Appropriating a tradition: history and identity in the work of Maryse Condé

Sam Haigh

The still nascent literary tradition of the 'French Antilles'[1] is one that has always been overwhelmingly male-dominated. From the eighteenth- and nineteenth-century works of French settlers and explorers, to those of Antillean-born white Creoles;[2] from the first manifestations of racially aware black and mulatto forms of writing in the early twentieth century,[3] to well-known writers such as Aimé Césaire and Frantz Fanon; from novelists, playwrights and theorists like Joseph Zobel, Vincent Placoly and Edouard Glissant, to writers such as Jean Bernabé, Patrick Chamoiseau and Raphaël Confiant (recently celebrated for their manifesto *In Praise of Creoleness*),[4] it is a tradition which stretches, like a paternal line of descent, from colonisation to the present day. Of course, examples of Antillean women writers may certainly be found: the Creole, Drasta Houel, published a collection of poetry entitled *Vie Légères* (*Easy Lives*) in 1916;[5] while Suzanne Lacascade's *Claire-Solange, âme africaine* (*Claire-Solange, African Soul*) of 1924 was as radical as that of her more famous contemporaries Léon-Gontran Damas and René Maran; and Mayotte Capécia's novels *Je suis Martiniquaise* (*I am Martinican*), 1948, and *La Négresse blanche* (*The White Negress*), 1950, have become (in)famous examples of the Antillean anxiety of assimilation. It is not until the last two decades, however, that women have begun seriously to 'erupt' into the 'virile inheritance'[6] of writing from the Antilles.

Perhaps the most prolific of contemporary women writers – indeed of Antillean writers in general – is the Guadeloupean Maryse Condé. Her work, from the early plays *Dieu nous l'a donné* (*God*

Gave it to Us[7] and *Mort d'Oluwémi d'Ajumako* (*The Death of Oluwémi d'Ajumako*)[8] to the most recent novels *La Colonie du nouveau monde* (*The New World Colony*)[9] and *La Migration des coeurs* (*The Migration of Hearts*),[10] may in many ways be seen as emblematic of recent Antillean women's writing, for, like many of these writers,[11] she quite explicitly situates her work in relation to that of the male writers of the Antillean tradition. Indeed, as I shall suggest here, she may be seen to have worked, throughout her career, to interrogate, to disrupt and to attempt to appropriate their androcentric discourses of Antillean liberation.

Amongst these discourses of liberation, it is perhaps that of negritude which remains the most well-known and the most crucial, for it is with the birth of this political, literary and theoretical 'movement' in the Paris of the 1930s and 1940s that the black Antillean literary tradition as such is usually seen to have begun. Certainly, it marks the point at which entire groups of Antillean (and African) students, writers and intellectuals, rather than isolated individuals like Maran or Damas, began to rebel against the French colonial ideology of assimilation. It was with the essays and poetry of negritude that the quest for 'authentic', Antillean identity – however problematic it may subsequently seem to have been – began to be articulated. This was a quest which took the negritude writer, African or Antillean, on a literary (and often literal) journey to Africa, on a return to the 'native land' in search of his (or more rarely her) black self – of all that which had suffered systematic censorship and erasure during centuries of French colonialism. For the Antillean, such a return was also the necessary prerequisite of a second, and vital, return: to the Antilles. Here, newly confident of his non-European, yet noble, origins, he could finally undergo a process of 'rebirth', as a black Antillean proud of his 'negritude', or blackness.

The preoccupations of negritude have continued, in varying forms, to remain central to Antillean writing, and it is thus perhaps unsurprising that in her first attempts at the dominant Antillean genre, the novel, Condé should choose to engage with this 'founding discourse'. In fact, she had engaged with negritude before, attacking it virulently in two essays of the 1970s;[12] and both *Heremakonon*[13] (1976) and *A Season in Rihata*[14] (1981) in many ways consolidate these attacks. In both novels, Condé portrays the African nations in which her two Guadeloupean heroines find themselves not as the romantic, precolonial idylls familiar from Césaire's *Notebook of a Return to the Native Land*,[15] or from the work of Léopold Sédar Senghor, but as the corrupt, brutal dictatorships of Frantz Fanon's *The Wretched of the Earth*.[16] When set against contemporary reality, negritude's poetic evocations of Africa are shown by Condé to be fundamentally flawed.

Condé's interrogation of negritude does not stop with a Fanonian critique. Rather, she explores it from a point of view never contemplated by Fanon himself, and suggests that as a discourse of liberation negritude is flawed in terms also of what may be called its 'gendering'. Indeed, it is clear in the work both of African and Antillean poets that the quest for identity of negritude poetry is almost exclusively a male quest, the quest of Africa's exiled *sons* for a native land constantly figured as maternal: as 'Mother Africa'. More than this, the return to this 'motherland' is one which is typically effected through an imagined relationship with a variously exoticised and eroticised black woman. It is this woman–mother–lover who, celebrated and idealised, comes to represent all of the values and traditions of the African culture that the negritude hero wishes to rediscover. In negritude poetry, as A.J. Arnold points out, woman functions primarily as 'mediatrix between alienated self and fullness of being';[17] as the negritude hero's means of access to his identity as 'authentic' black of African origin.

This is true also when the specifically Antillean hero of negritude embarks upon his second return, from Africa to the Antilles. Here, woman functions both as the foundation of the black Antillean's new identity and as the foundation of a new nation of black Antilleans. What is clear is that this positioning of the black woman–mother as the 'ground' upon which black, male selfhood and the new nation are built, deprives her of any active role, of a place *in* that nation, and of an identity, herself, as a woman.

It is with such a reading of negritude in mind that Condé's first two novels, and in particular *Heremakonon*, may best be understood. Here – and, less explicitly, in *A Season in Rihata* – Condé explores what happens when the gendered terms of the negritude quest are reversed. That is, when a woman such as Véronica Mercier, an educated, assimilated Guadeloupean living in Paris, embarks on a journey to '*Father* Africa' in search of her identity as a black Antillean woman via a highly exoticised and eroticised relationship with 'a nigger with ancestors' (*Heremakonon*, p. 24),

Ibrahima Sory, a government minister descended from African kings. This quest, however, fails and Véronica, like *A Season in Rihata*'s Marie-Hélène, remains unable to make the vital, second 'return' to the real native land of Guadeloupe, and is left instead with a constant sense of exile and non-belonging. What Condé suggests is that the roles and terms of the negritude quest for identity may be so gendered and so fixed that as a discourse of liberation it is unable to function when those roles are reversed, leaving women such as Véronica with no means of imagining their identity as Antillean.

Condé's preoccupation with finding ways in which to figure the accession of women to a sense of Antillean identity continues to haunt her work, as does her engagement with the familiar preoccupations of Antillean theory and fiction generally. One such preoccupation – and one which, as Condé herself explains, necessarily accompanies the negritude quest for a *place* of origin – is the quest for an *explanation* of the origins of the Antillean people. Since slaves were typically separated from members of the same tribe upon arrival in the Caribbean, disparate tribal beliefs slowly disappeared, and this left Antilleans of African descent, as Condé points out, with no myth of origin.[18] As Edouard Glissant explains, myths of origin are of vital collective importance, for it is via such myths that:

> A community, without realizing it, unconsciously, but because it needs it to survive, to exist, at a time when the existence of one community is assured only at the expense of that of other communities, gives itself a reason for being in the land where it is, a land which then becomes its territory.[19]

Thus origin myths serve to 'legitimate' both the existence of a given people and its claim to the land in which it finds itself. As Glissant goes on to explain, such a function requires that the myth not only provides an explanation of the creation of the world but, most crucially, that it traces a clear line of descent back to an 'original ancestor'. Within the Western tradition – and, as Glissant reminds us, 'that is the one that prevails here'[20] – the biblical model predominates: the original ancestor must be a *father*-ancestor, for only a paternal line of descent is able to guarantee the legitimacy of an entire people.

It is thus perhaps unsurprising that within the Antillean literary tradition the recurring theme of the quest for motherland is accompanied by the equally recurring theme of the quest for the father-ancestor. This is especially evident in Condé's recent *Les Derniers rois mages* (*The Last of the Magi*),[21] in which the obsession of a Guadeloupean family with its putative African ancestor – a king of Dahomey exiled to Martinique during World War II – is explored. What is significant is that this literary search for a father-ancestor takes Condé to a figure who already exists in the Antillean imagination: the exiled king of *Les Derniers rois mages* closely resembles the figure of Béhanzin, 'king of Dahomey, who opposed the French penetration into Africa. [He was] exiled in Martinique'.[22] Such a resemblance is significant because Condé is by no means alone in evoking Béhanzin or figures like him. Glissant himself, in his novel *La Case du commandeur* (*The Commander's House*),[23] makes mention of the semi-legendary king, while Simone Schwarz-Bart, in her first novel, takes a folktale which exists in various parts of Africa and which has existed in the Antilles since slavery, and retells the story of another legendary figure, Ti Jean.[24] Similarly, both Daniel Maximin and Michèle Lacrosil evoke in their novels the figure of Louis Delgrès, the semi-legendary, semi-historical hero of Guadeloupe's 1802 rebellion against the reinstitution of slavery.[25]

The evocation of such figures, for Glissant, is vital because while oral stories of heroic figures by no means constitute origin myths themselves, they may be transformed, if they are written down, into the 'founding texts' of the Antillean people, providing them with a sense of 'belonging', and giving rise to something else which the Antilles have always lacked: their own history.

Of course, the Antilles, like the rest of the 'New World', are not literally 'historyless'. Rather, they possess no form of history as the West has defined it, and which Glissant himself defines as 'History . . . written with a capital H': linear, all-encompassing, *written* history, 'a totality that excludes other histories that do not fit into that of the West'.[26] Thus for Glissant, Antillean history can be reduced to a chronology of events which come from 'elsewhere', from France, and towards the beginning of *Caribbean Discourse* he sets out just such a chronology of Martinican history: from its 'discovery' in 1502, to departmentalisation in 1946 and the doctrine of economic assimilation in 1975. He then writes: 'once this

chronological table has been set up and completed, the whole history of Martinique remains to be unraveled'.[27] That which 'remains
to be unraveled', that which has been excluded, is what Glissant
terms '*h*istory', what Eloïse Brière calls 'the unofficial history . . .
[of] the oral tradition',[28] and it has been excluded precisely because it has not been written down, because it has not followed
the Western model of historical development: from oral story, to
origin myth, to written, official history. It is for this reason that
the vital movement from unofficial 'history' to 'History' must be
effected in the Antilles, in order that an alternative history may
finally be provided to counter Western history's erasure of the
Antilles. That is, in order that Antilleans, on the West's own terms,
may mark themselves off as a people and as a culture which is
distinct from the West.

Of course, such an undertaking is highly problematic, for it
betrays an investment in precisely the model of history which has
hitherto subsumed and erased the Antilles. As Glissant himself
points out, this is a model of history which, given the fundamental
'métissage' ('hybridity') of Antillean history and of the Antillean
people, may be seen to be both unsuitable and inadequate within
the Caribbean context.[29] It must be remembered that while the
vast majority of Antilleans are of African descent, large numbers of Guadeloupeans and Martinicans are descended from the
indentured labourers brought to the islands from India after the
abolition of slavery. Still other Antilleans are of European descent
or, more recently, of Chinese, Libyan and Syrian ancestry. Even if
one accepts the notion of 'progression' from oral to written (and
this is a point to which I shall return), to attempt to establish a
myth of origins based on the tracing of a line of descent back to
a single father-ancestor, and then to derive from that myth an all-
encompassing 'History' of the Antilles, would quite evidently entail the re-erasure of the disparate histor*ies* of the islands and of
their peoples.

The Antillean obsession with history, together with the Glissant-
ian search for alternative models of history-making, is explored in
several of Condé's novels – most notably perhaps in her African
trilogy *Ségou* and in her 1989 novel about Guadeloupe, *Traversée
de la mangrove* (*Crossing the Mangrove*).[30] In this latter novel, the
desire to rewrite history is coupled with a desire also to insert
women in history, as is the case in many of Condé's novels, though

perhaps most obviously in her *I, Tituba, Black Witch of Salem.*[31] Enormously successful in English translation, this is a novel which, as its title suggests, attempts to rehabilitate the story of a black woman into the dominant History of the Salem witch trials from which she had hitherto been erased. However, this is but part of the novel's project, for before following Tituba's journey to North America, and after describing her survival of the trials themselves, Tituba's narrative describes her experience of slavery in Barbados and, importantly, her part in movements of resistance against it. Indeed, it is this strong emphasis on resistance, along with the North American theme of *Tituba*, which is picked up also in its mode of writing. This time, Condé's search for a way in which to explore questions of Antillean history and identity quite evidently goes much further than the Antillean tradition itself – to the slave narrative, a mode of writing which, though popular in North America throughout the nineteenth century, never gained currency in the French-colonised Antilles.

Usually narrated by an escaped ex-slave to a Northern abolitionist who then wrote the story down, slave narratives are personalised accounts of the experience of slavery, and tell of the slave's journey to physical and spiritual freedom. For many, slave narrative represents the marginal tradition *par excellence* of counter-history: that is, the archetypal attempt both to seek to define one's own identity as hitherto marginalised subject, and to record, for the first time, the ignored and erased history of an entire people. Of course, this was not the principal motivation of the narratives' abolitionist ghostwriters and patrons. For them, these first-hand accounts provided an ideal means of exposing the system of slavery and thereby furthering the abolitionist cause. Indeed, it was in order to ensure that this function remained primary that both the form and content of the narratives were governed by a strict series of formulae and conventions.[32]

From its title and frontispiece – which bear both the narrator's name and her image – *Tituba* makes use of precisely these formulae and conventions. Prologues and epilogues, written by the narrator's abolitionist sponsor and patron, were an important part of the narratives: in *Tituba*, Condé provides a short explanatory note, prior to the text, which details her relationship with Tituba, as well as an 'Historical Note' in support of Tituba's narrative after it. Similarly in line with convention, there is a poetic epigraph, by seventeenth-century Puritan poet John Harrington, followed by the customary opening lines of the narrative itself, outlining the place, though not date, of the narrator's birth. As the text then proceeds, a text which is ostensibly narrated by an illiterate ex-slave to a sympathetic ghostwriter, conventional episodes are similarly described: hangings, escapes, incidents of violence, of bravery and of resistance.

Tituba is not, however, simply a latter-day replication of the nineteenth-century slave narrative. Rather, it is an attempt to expand and to disrupt the very tradition which it evokes, both because counter-history is by no means simply a secondary concern, and because slave narrative, like negritude, can be seen to be one more androcentric discourse of liberation, one more articulation of the quest for *male* identity. Once again, this is a quest in which women typically play a merely functional role, in which they are figured primarily in relation to men: as the mother of the heroic narrator, for example, or as the victim of a violence which serves only to accentuate the male narrator's own sense of powerlessness and emasculation.[33] Like the women figured within the poetry of negritude, those present in male-authored, nineteenth-century slave narratives were rarely represented as subjects in their own right: the realities of the female experience of slavery were thus subjected to a form of censorship that those of men were not.[34] Indeed, even those relatively few narratives to be written or narrated by ex-slaves who were women – like Harriet Jacobs's *Incidents in the Life of a Slave Girl*[35] – were censored in a very specific way. Jacobs, for example, was obliged to write under a pseudonym, and to present her story as a domestic or sentimental novel, as a search not for identity, but for the respectability of marriage and motherhood. Incidents of violence and of rape, not surprisingly, become 'polite stories of impolite "seductions"', and sexual desire is written out.[36]

It is clear from the beginning that Tituba's narrative works to resist this sort of self-censorship, for the opening scene itself at once recalls *and* reworks the convention it evokes, and tells of the all too common, but most usually unacknowledged, conditions of the narrator's birth: 'Abena, my mother, was raped by an English sailor on the deck of *Christ the King* one day in the year 16** while the ship was sailing for Barbados. I was born from this act of aggression. From this act of hatred and contempt' (p. 3). Here,

Tituba's mother, far from being erased as 'silent ground' of the narrator's coming into being, is, and continues to be, written into the text. What is more, throughout Tituba's life both in Salem and in Barbados, the reality of the female experience of slavery generally – sexual desire as well as rape and violence – is constantly evoked.

During the witch trials in Salem, Tituba is imprisoned, and once they are over she is sold to a Jewish trader, Benjamin Cohen d'Azevedo. When he finally dies, and frees her, she boards a ship bound for Barbados and is able, at last, to make her way home. It is upon her return to Barbados that we begin to see the reality not only of the female experience of slavery but also, more specifically, of female *resistance* to slavery. Indeed, it is at this point that Tituba herself discovers how the very possibilities of resistance are largely determined by gender, as she attempts to become involved with the revolutionary activities of a maroon community. When Tituba is first taken to their encampment in the hills, she is made rapidly aware that the community is highly patriarchal, as she is confronted by 'the Maroons . . . with their wives and children': the maroons are, by definition, men – and women, it seems, are not maroons (p. 144). Nevertheless, Tituba is anxious to act rather than be acted upon, and she continues to ask the maroon leader, and her lover, Christopher, to allow her to fight against the whites with him. His reply, unsurprisingly, is simply to tell her: 'a woman's duty, Tituba, is not to fight or make war, but to make love!' (p. 151).

Tituba's reaction is to leave the maroons, to return to the cabin that she had built for herself in the years before she left Barbados for North America, and to continue her role as healer to slaves on nearby plantations. It is when she meets and cures Iphigène, a slave who has been whipped and left for dead, that Tituba once more becomes interested in fighting directly against slavery, and the final scenes of Condé's text then follow the events of an attempted slave rebellion, in which Tituba plays a central role. Though Tituba, together with Iphigène and the others who rebelled, is hanged for her part in the uprising, her story does not end there. After Tituba's death Condé's text continues with an epilogue, and we learn that although Christopher had assured her that he alone would be immortalised – 'in song' – for his heroic deeds, it is she who has been remembered in the popular history of her island. As she herself exclaims, 'there *is* a song about Tituba!

I hear it from one end of the island to the other' (p. 175). She has become, it transpires, a heroine of the oral history of her people, 'a legend amongst the slaves' (p. 160) to stand beside those of other maroon heroes. What is more, she has become the legendary figure in Barbados that she never was in Salem. Significantly, she has done so by assuming the role that she had always refused to assume in Salem: as the colonial authorities make clear, it is *as a witch* that Tituba is finally hanged for her part in the rebellion, thereby meeting precisely the fate that she had escaped in Salem.

It is thus that archetypal counter-cultural role of 'witch' that links both parts of her story, and that enables her throughout to resist and to undermine the various forms of colonial authority wielded over her. It is her role as healer which enables her to help plan the slave rebellion undetected, for example, just as it enables her in Salem to resist the combined forces of slavery and Church. However, her role as 'witch' allows her also to resist and to undermine another form of authority: the patriarchal authority not only of the maroon community, but also of the religious community of Salem, and of the Parris household itself. Her 'magical' tales, for example, provide Samuel Parris's daughter Betsey and niece Abigail with an outlet for the energies and desires repressed by the religious education provided by the Reverend, while her knowledge of herbal remedies and of the female body succeeds in curing her mistress's long-term and indefinable illness – a 'dis-ease', it would seem, in patriarchy, brought on by the fear and revulsion inspired in her by her husband, and by the desires which she is forced to repress.

It is this specific counter-cultural form that her 'witchcraft' takes that points to the primary radicalness of Tituba's adoption of the role of witch, for it is thus via witchcraft that Tituba enters her people's history as a specifically *female* figure of resistance. Witchcraft, of course, as both Catherine Clément and Xavière Gauthier point out, is a disruptive role which has traditionally been assigned to and associated with women, and which has been seen as a 'feminine' force of rebellion, a threat to the prevailing order.[37] As Gauthier explains: 'if the figure of the witch appears wicked, it is because she poses a real danger to phallocratic society'.[38] It is a force of disruption, too, which has been handed down from generation to generation of women: just as, in *Tituba*, it is made clear that Tituba's powers have been inherited from her mothers – from

Abena, her biological mother, and from Man Yaya, who took care of her after her mother's death.

It was Man Yaya who taught Tituba 'herbs', 'the sea', 'sacrifices' and 'the upper spheres of knowledge': how to contact the 'invisibles', 'the dead [who] only die if they die in our hearts' (pp. 9–10). This latter power proves to be the most enabling for Tituba, for it means that, throughout her life, she is able to remain in contact with both Abena and Man Yaya, and to be assisted by them in times of need, long after their deaths. Furthermore, this chain of maternal support is continued also after her own death, for as she continues her work as healer to slaves and maroons, and incites numerous slave rebellions throughout the island, she saves the lives of a mother, Délices, and her newly-born daughter, Samantha, whom Tituba then chooses as her own descendant, and to whom she teaches everything that she herself had been taught by Man Yaya.

It is through her relationship with Samantha that Tituba ensures that her story is never finished, that it continues by way of a chain of female descent; a chain, what is more, of excluded, marginalised and disruptive women which goes far beyond that of Tituba's own immediate maternal family. As Clément points out, the disruptive power of the witch is only one form that women's rebellion may take: hers is a power which has been handed down to contemporary disruptive figures like the 'madwoman' or hysteric, the adulteress or the lesbian, all of whom may be seen to have inherited 'the repressed past . . . [the] reminiscence[s]' of those resisting and marginalised women like the witch who have come before her.[39] All of these women belong to what Clément calls the 'imaginary zone', in which all that is feared and thus rejected or marginalised by 'culture' is contained – 'myths . . . fantasies . . . fragments of evidence, these tail-ends of history'.[40] They belong to what Tituba herself refers to as 'the hidden side of things' (p. 156).

In other words, these women form part of an 'alternative' history, a history which has been absent from History and which, like 'the song about Tituba', has been 'taken from what is lost within us of oral tradition'.[41] This is a history arranged in the form of stories, and storytelling, as Clément and Gauthier point out, is a narrative form which in many cultures has been associated with women; with women who have hitherto had 'no cultural function in the transmission of knowledge'.[42] The 'conteuse', the 'tale-telling woman', is herself part of the chain of disruptive and marginal women to which the witch or the madwoman belongs. Indeed, the witch herself is a storyteller: her powers are handed down, from generation to generation, in stories and myths and in legends like 'the song about Tituba'.[43] Stories and storytelling may therefore be seen as a powerful mediator of alternative histories of women, as another way in which women link themselves together in order to resist the dominant order.

This is certainly the case throughout *Tituba*, which becomes, as does Toni Morrison's *Beloved* for Linda Anderson, 'a series of stories that characters tell themselves and each other about their lives'.[44] It is through story that women of different classes and different backgrounds link themselves in order to resist patriarchal and colonial power. For example, in order to form a friendship with her first mistress, Jennifer, a child-bride forced into marriage with the abusive Darnell Davis, Abena 'would tell her the stories that her mother had told her in the village of Akwapim, where she was born' (pp. 3–4). Equally, years later, Tituba's own relationship with Elizabeth Parris is in part sustained by the Caribbean tales which she tells to her mistress and her daughter, 'tales . . . of Anancy the Spider, people who had made a pact with the devil, zombies, *soukougnans*, and the hag who rides along on her three-legged horse' (p. 42).[45]

Perhaps the most important relationship between women, however, and certainly between black and white women, is that between Tituba and Hester, a white woman imprisoned for adultery at the same time as is Tituba for witchcraft. Hester (who in both name and biography would seem to resemble Hester Prynne from Nathaniel Hawthorne's *The Scarlet Letter* [1850]) has, like Tituba, rebelled against the strictures of a patriarchal culture. As she tells Tituba, who refers to the dominant, white society of New England as that to which Hester belongs: 'it's not my society. Aren't I an outcast like yourself? Locked up between these walls?' (p. 96). Despite the huge differences of education, class and aspirations, the two women find common ground through the stories that they tell each other about their lives. It is via storytelling, too, that Hester helps Tituba prepare for her trial, by first acquainting her with the Western conception of witchcraft with which she has remained unfamiliar throughout, and by then encouraging her to use her skills as a storyteller to her own advantage. Together, they invent stories which can be used by Tituba to denounce those who denounced her, and thus escape hanging. What is more, in an ultimate gesture of solidarity, Hester later hangs herself, both imposing upon herself the punishment usually reserved for women like Tituba, and connecting herself irrevocably with them.

After her death Hester then joins Abena and Man Yaya, becoming part of the chain of sustaining women who visit Tituba at various stages throughout her life. She had told Tituba, when they first met, of how she had always dreamt of writing a novel, and had lamented her exclusion from the realm of the written word, commenting: 'alas! Women don't write books! Only men bore us with their prose' (p. 101). Tituba, however, whose illiteracy excludes her all the more thoroughly from that realm, is content to accept that she does not belong to 'the civilisation of the Book',[46] and that instead, as we have seen, 'my people will keep my memory in their hearts and have no need for the written word. It's in their heads. In their hearts and in their heads' (p. 176). Now, through her deliberate attempts at allying herself with women such as Tituba and her mothers, Hester has succeeded in entering those same occluded histories to which they belong. That is, she has become one more 'heroine' of those forgotten, 'alternative histories' which, though they have never 'counted' because they have never been written down, have been handed from generation to generation of 'tale-telling women' like Tituba and herself.

Of course, Tituba does, eventually, become part also of 'the civilisation of the book' as, via Condé's text, her story enters the realm of written history, both dominant and marginal. Significantly, however, it is via the twin, and enabling, 'maternal traditions' of witchcraft and storytelling themselves that this takes place. As Condé explains in a brief statement before the text of *Tituba*: 'Tituba and I lived for a year on the closest of terms. During our endless conversations she told me things she had confided to nobody else.' It is by 'appearing' to Condé as her mothers have always appeared to her that Tituba tells her story to Condé and that Condé, too, then becomes a part of the matrilinear chain of resisting women whose history she and Tituba are engaged in recalling and recording. What is more, story is a vital element not only of Tituba's life and survival, and of her entrance into the realm of written history, but also of the very form which that written history takes. It is a form which, once more, simultaneously evokes and disrupts the tradition of history-writing – slave narrative – within which it positions itself.

Whether it is viewed as an attempt simply to gain support for the abolitionist cause or, on the narrator's part, as an attempt to attest to the existence of his or her people's past by bringing it into the realm of written history, slave narrative necessarily remains a part of the Western model of history outlined earlier. This is a model which, as James Olney points out, is based upon a separation between 'oral' and 'written', between 'fiction' and 'fact'.[47] That is, it is a model based, as Glissant pointed out, on the notion of 'progression' from oral story, to origin myth, to written history. If the slave narrative was to be taken seriously either as a plea for abolition or as the counter-history of an oppressed people, it was necessary for the narrator to demonstrate, via his or her adherence to the formulae and conventions of the genre, his or her successful progression from the 'primitive' realm of oral storytelling to the realm of 'true' history.

As Olney explains, it was demanded of the ex-slave that he give 'a true picture of slavery as it really [was]', and to do so he must claim that 'he is not emplotting, he is not fictionalising, and he is not performing any act of *poesis* (= shaping, making)'. For the narrator's memory to be 'creative' is for it to be 'faulty', for ' "creative" would be understood by sceptical readers as a synonym for "lying" '.[48] Fictionalising, storytelling, are therefore associated with 'untruth', in order that History alone may represent itself as true and authoritative.

It is via an incident which takes place between Tituba and Hester, as they make up stories and recount their own stories to each other, that Condé's rather different investment in the 'fictional' and the 'factual', in 'story' and 'history', is signalled. Hester asks Tituba, referring to the daughter with whom she is still pregnant: 'You know what she wants? She wants you to tell her a story. A story about your country' (p. 98). Tituba replies as would a traditional Antillean storyteller: 'Crick, crack! Is the court asleep?' and Hester replies: 'No, the court isn't asleep!' With that, Tituba proceeds: 'Long long time ago, when the devil was still in short pants, showing his knobbly knees covered with scars, there lived in the village of Wagabaha . . . a young girl who had neither father nor mother . . .' (p. 99). However, as Tituba's tale continues, Hester realises that it is more than an ordinary story, invented by Tituba to amuse and entertain her. Though Hester has recounted her own past to Tituba, and though Tituba has told her of her immediate past in Salem, Hester knows little of Tituba's life in Barbados. Here, Hester suspects, Tituba is recounting her own story, beginning with her birth, in fictionalised form. When Hester asks her for confirmation of these suspicions, Tituba refuses either to confirm or to deny them, and it is in so doing that she draws attention to the way in which her story is told also by Condé herself. As *Tituba* develops, it becomes apparent that it is precisely part-history, part-story: that it has sprung from a memory which is both 'creative' and 'emplotted'.

Tituba is a text which refuses to remove vestiges of the oral tradition, or to choose between fact and fiction. Rather than emphasising, as does the writer of slave narrative, her attempts to remain faithful to Tituba's story, Condé instead readily admits that her text is at least part invention, that it is a 'fictionalised' history. She foregrounds this throughout and, appropriately, it is at the points in her text when her role as 'ghostwriter' apparently replays most closely the conventions of slave narrative that her fictionalising becomes most evident. Such is the case during Tituba's trial, when Condé inserts what we are informed is part of Tituba's actual statement, taken from archives. The insertion of legal documentation is familiar from slave narrative, where it was used to authenticate the story further. In Condé's text, however, it serves instead to draw attention to those parts of Tituba's story which are 'inauthentic', for the archival material is clearly marked off from the rest of the text.

In her 'Historical Note', Condé makes this point much more clearly. It is, in fact, a 'Non-Historical Note', for she discusses how, at the point of Tituba's liberation from prison, all historical record of her disappears: 'To whom [was she sold]? Such is the intentional or unintentional racism of the historians that we shall never know' (p. 183). Condé assures us, however, of 'a vague tradition', presumably oral '[which] says that Tituba was sold to a slave dealer who took her back to Barbados', and goes on to state: 'I myself have given her an ending of my own choosing' (p. 183). We therefore learn that at least the second half of Tituba's story, which deals with her status as maroon heroine, is not based in 'fact'. Tituba is located, it would seem – as Linda Anderson feels is so often the case with 'the missing woman in History' – in 'the cracks, the slippage, between fact and fiction'.[49]

Condé's decision to blur the relationship between history and fiction is, however, radical in still another, important way, for storytelling – and especially in the Antilles – is a tradition which is not simply associated with women.[50] More generally, it is associated with, or *as*, the Antillean tradition itself. As we saw earlier, the oral tradition – 'tales, proverbs, "titim", nursery rhymes, songs ...'[51] – has always been an important aspect of Antillean culture and of the collective Antillean imagination. However, as we also saw, it has been an aspect consistently decoded as mere diversion or, as also for the African-American slave narrators, as a precursor to written history. What Condé reminds us, however, is that folktales are precisely a form of personal and communal history-making, the attempts of both communities and individuals to put themselves into a history of their own making, to 'storytell' themselves into existence.

For the writers of *In Praise of Creoleness*, the devaluation of the oral tradition represents one of the most significant dimensions of Antillean alienation. Not only because folktales vitally represent a suppressed and devalued mode of history-making, but also because the oral tradition is emblematic both of Antillean history and of Antillean identity. As they point out, the oral tradition is extremely diverse, containing within it remnants of the multiple cultures which make up 'Antillean culture'. The coexistence, for example, of elements from Carib mythology, from African tales, from European and Indian oral and written traditions attests to the complexity of Antillean culture, of the Antillean past, and of the Antillean people.[52] At the same time, the coexistence within the oral tradition of elements from already-existing oral *and* written traditions attests once more to the inadequacy of the Western model of 'progression' – from oral to written, from story to history – and points instead to the founding complexity of the Antillean situation in general.

As Bernabé, Chamoiseau and Confiant explain, this complexity is more than simply 'métissage', or hybridity. Rather, it is what they term 'creoleness': not a 'synthesis, not just ... a crossing or any other unicity' but, 'because of its constituent mosaic ... it is ... a kaleidoscopic totality' whose elements remain shifting and diverse.[53] It is this 'creoleness' which, for Bernabé, Chamoiseau and Confiant, must urgently be claimed; which must be reinvented rather than rediscovered. It is this 'creoleness' alone which forms the basis of Antillean identity, of 'Caribbeanness'; and it is thus this 'creoleness' alone which will provide a viable alternative to the Antillean obsession with single origins: historical, cultural and personal.[54] What is more, once the complex, Creole character of 'Caribbeanness' has been accepted, it will become possible for the Antillean people to move towards a wider sense of 'creoleness', towards a sense of solidarity with other peoples of the 'diaspora' community. These 'new solidarities', in turn, will expand the notion of 'creoleness' itself, and will enable the Antillean people to establish a sense of identity and of 'belonging' as both Antillean *and* as Creole, to position themselves as part of a wider community of transplanted populations: populations who, like African-Americans, the peoples of the rest of the Caribbean, or those of South America, share a similar history of colonisation and displacement.[55]

For the writers of *In Praise of Creoleness*, as for Glissant, cultural forms such as literature have a vital role in the reinvention and assertion of 'creoleness'. They point explicitly to the failure of negritude's characteristic obsession with single origins, for example (though they acknowledge its historical necessity),[56] and advocate instead the creation of a new, creole literature for the Antilles, 'a literature which will obey all the demands of modern writing while taking roots in the traditional configurations of our orality'.[57] It is within this context that Condé's project in *Tituba*, which was written three years prior to *In Praise of Creoleness*, may be seen to be radical indeed. The interaction of storytelling and history-writing, the *rapprochement* – or rather 'r*erapprochement*'[58] – of slave narrative and oral folktale in *Tituba*, make it part of the 'literary creoleness' which Bernabé, Chamoiseau and Confiant urge must be invented. At the same time, the very scope of Condé's text, which takes place between the Caribbean and North America, and in which positive links are forged also with other communities – with the Jewish Benjamin; with African-American women like Judah White, who sustains and supports Tituba in the absence of Man Yaya and Abena; with the Native Americans who work with John Indian; and even with white women such as Hester[59] – would appear to be looking forward precisely to the 'new solidarities' envisaged in *In Praise of Creoleness*.

Condé's *I, Tituba, Black Witch of Salem* may thus be seen to be a text which, in its search to redefine both Antillean history and Antillean identity, refuses to imagine either of them in the unitary and monologic terms which, until quite recently, have characterised the Antillean literary and theoretical tradition. Rather than see the Caribbean people as trapped by an impossible choice between two cultural identities – 'French' or 'African' – Condé's text, like that of Bernabé, Chamoiseau and Confiant, widens the terms of reference and moves towards a more open and more enabling notion of 'accepted creoleness'. At the same time, *Tituba* widens the terms of reference even further – beyond the still somewhat restricted form of creoleness imagined in the work of Bernabé, Chamoiseau and Confiant themselves. *In Praise of Creoleness*, as might be expected, is one more masculine discourse of liberation, one more narrative of resistance which fails either to take account of the Antillean women who precede it or to imagine a place for Antillean women in the Caribbean future which it envisions ahead.[60]

In *Tituba*, the form of creoleness which is beginning to be imagined by Condé – and which continues to be imagined in her most recent text *La Migration des coeurs* – is one which depends as much upon building solidarities of gender as it does upon building those of race or of culture. If Antillean discourses of liberation, literary or otherwise, have typically excluded women, contemporary women writers like Condé are now imagining discourses in which women are able to play much more active roles. At the same time, it is clear that writers such as Condé are themselves neither prepared to be excluded, like their foremothers, from the Antillean tradition, nor prepared simply to be 'included' within it. Rather, as I hope to have shown here, they are coming to occupy a position at the very forefront of contemporary efforts to expand and to redefine a burgeoning literary and theoretical tradition. That is, they are continuing to provide an important mode of intervention into, and disruption of, the basic tenets of that tradition; a constant commentary upon the difference that gender makes to what might otherwise be termed 'sexually indifferent' narratives of resistance.[61]

Notes

1. The term 'Antilles' will be used here to refer to the French 'overseas departments' of Martinique and Guadeloupe, situated in the Caribbean, although both neighbouring French Guiana, situated on the South American coast, and Haiti, independent from France since 1804,

are frequently also included in the term. Guadeloupe and Martinique were 'discovered' by Christopher Columbus in 1492 and 1502 respectively, and then colonised by the French in 1635. Up until this time, both islands were attacked continually by the Spanish until all resistance by the native Carib Indians was put down, and those who were not exterminated fled to neighbouring Dominica. From this point, the history of the Antilles is one of continued violence and colonial exploitation: from the replacement of French indentured labourers with the first slaves from Africa in 1680 to the introduction of the notorious 'Code Noir' (slave laws) in 1685; from slavery's first, and temporary, abolition in 1794 to its reinstatement in 1802; from slavery's definitive abolition in 1848 to the introduction of indentured labourers from India in 1853; and, finally, from the departmentalisation of the islands in 1946 to the present-day situation of mass unemployment and economic and social decline.

2. Père du Tertre's *Histoire générale des Antilles habitées par les Français* (*A General History of the French Caribbean*), published between 1667 and 1671, and père Labat's *Nouveaux voyages aux îles d'Amérique* (*New Voyages to the Islands of America*), published in 1722, provide the first examples of such writing. The white Guadeloupean Nicholas-Germain Léonard, who published three texts – *La Nouvelle Clémentine* (*The New Clementine*), 1744, *Idylles morales* (*Moral Love Affairs*), 1766, and *Lettre sur un voyage aux Antilles* (*Letter on a Voyage to the Antilles*), 1787 – became the first Antillean-born writer, though he, like the earlier French writers, spent most of his life in France and based his texts on observations he made as a visitor to the islands. Other texts by *béké*, or white Creole, writers followed: notably Louis Maynard de Queilhe's *Outre-Mer* (*Overseas*), 1835, and Poiré de Saint-Aurèle's *Les Veillées françaises* (*French Vigils*), 1826. See Richard Burton's entry on the West Indies in Peter France, ed., *The New Oxford Companion to Literature in French* (Oxford: Oxford University Press, 1995), pp. 851–4, as well as Patrick Chamoiseau and Raphaël Confiant, *Lettres créoles: Tracées antillaises et continentales de la littérature 1635–1975* (Paris: Hatier, 1991), pp. 21–9 and 207–14.

3. The mulatto population gained the right to full French citizenship in 1833, but they – and still less the black population – produced hardly any writing until the late nineteenth century. Both this and much early twentieth-century mulatto writing – poetry such as Victor Duquesnay's *Les Martiniquaises* (*Martinican Women*), 1903, and Oruno Lara's *Sous le ciel bleu de Guadeloupe* (*Beneath the Blue Skies of Guadeloupe*), 1912 – was, unsurprisingly, in a noticeably 'assimilated' style, a style derived from that of the white Creole writers, who

themselves emulated the work of their 'metropolitan' contemporaries. Although the 1885 novel *Atipa, roman guyanais* (*Atipa, A Guyanese Novel*) published in Creole under the pseudonym of Alfred Parépou by a Guyanese, and 'evidently non-white', writer offers, according to Richard Burton, 'a vivid and mordant picture of colonial society', René Maran's novel *Batouala* (1921), Oruno Lara's *Questions de couleur – noirs et blanches* (*A Question of Colour – Black Men and White Women*), 1923, and Léon-Gontran Damas's collection of poetry, *Pigments* (1937), are usually cited as the first examples of 'racially aware' writing by black or mulatto Antilleans (Burton, pp. 852–3).

4. Jean Bernabé, Patrick Chamoiseau and Raphael Confiant, *In Praise of Creoleness (bilingual edition)*, trans. M.B. Taleb-Khyar (Paris: Gallimard, 1993). First published as *Eloge de la créolité* (Paris: Gallimard, 1989).

5. In cases where no English edition of a French literary work exists, I shall supply my own, somewhat literal, translation of the French title in parentheses. Where an English edition does exist, I shall refer to that edition throughout.

6. A.J. Arnold, 'Poétique forcée et identité dans la littérature des Antilles francophones', in Maryse Condé, ed., *L'Héritage de Caliban* (Paris: Editions Jasor, 1992), pp. 19–28 (p. 21).

7. Maryse Condé, *Dieu nous l'a donné* (Paris: Pierre-Jean Oswald, 1972).

8. Maryse Condé, *Mort d'Oluwémi d'Ajumako* (Paris: Pierre-Jean Oswald, 1973).

9. Maryse Condé, *La Colonie du nouveau monde* (Paris: Robert Laffont, 1993).

10. Maryse Condé, *La Migration des coeurs* (Paris: Robert Laffont, 1995).

11. Although these other writers are numerous, perhaps the best-known are Michèle Lacrosil, *Sapotille ou le serein d'argile* (*Sapotille and the Clay Canary*), 1960; *Cajou* (*Cajou*), 1961; and *Demain Jab-Herma* (*Tomorrow, Jab-Herma*), 1967; Jacqueline Manicom, *Mon Examen de blanc* (*My Exam in Whiteness*), 1972; and *La Graine: journal d'une sage-femme* (*The Seed: Diary of a Midwife*), 1974; and Simone Schwarz-Bart, *Pluie et vent sur Télumée Miracle*, 1972 (*The Bridge of Beyond*, trans. Barbara Bray (London: Heinemann, 1982); *Ti Jean l'horizon* (*Ti Jean L'Horizon*), 1979; and *Mon beau capitaine* (*My Handsome Captain*), 1987.

12. See Maryse Condé, 'Pourquoi la négritude? Négritude ou révolution?', in Jeanne-Lydie Goré, ed., *Négritude Africaine, Négritude Caraïbe* (Université de Paris-Nord, Centre d'Etudes Francophones: Editions de la Francité, 1973), pp. 150–4, and 'Négritude césairienne, Négritude senghorienne', *Revue de la littérature comparée*, 3 (1974), 409–19.

13. Maryse Condé, *Heremakonon*, trans. Richard Philcox (Washington: Three Continents Press, 1982). First published as *Heremakonon* (Paris: Union générale d'éditions, 1976).
14. Maryse Condé, *A Season in Rihata*, trans. Richard Philcox (London: Heinemann, 1987). First published as *Une Saison à Rihata* (Paris: Robert Laffont, 1981).
15. Aimé Césaire, *Notebook of a Return to the Native Land*, trans. Clayton Eshelman and Annette Smith (Berkeley: University of California Press, 1983). First published as *Cahier d'un retour au pays natal* in the Paris magazine *Volontés* in 1939.
16. Frantz Fanon, *The Wretched of the Earth* (London: Penguin, 1990). First published as *Les Damnés de la terre* (Paris: Maspéro, 1961).
17. A. James Arnold, *Modernism and Negritude: The Poetry and Poetics of Aimé Césaire* (Cambridge, M.A.: Harvard University Press, 1981), pp. 153–4.
18. Maryse Condé, *La Civilisation du bossale: réflexions sur la littérature orale de la Guadeloupe et de la Martinique* (Paris: L'Harmattan, 1978), p. 7.
19. Edouard Glissant, 'Le chaos-monde, l'oral et l'écrit', in Ralph Ludwig, ed., *Ecrire la 'parole de nuit': La nouvelle littérature antillaise* (Paris: Gallimard, 1994), pp. 111–30 (p. 119). Translation mine.
20. Edouard Glissant, *Caribbean Discourse: Selected Essays*, trans. J. Michael Dash (Charlottesville: University Press of Virginia, 1989), p. 71. First published as *Le Discours antillais* (Paris: Seuil, 1981).
21. Maryse Condé, *Les Derniers rois mages* (Paris: Mercure de France, 1992).
22. Glissant, *Caribbean Discourse*, p. 262.
23. Edouard Glissant, *La Case du commandeur* (Paris: Seuil, 1981).
24. See Simone Schwarz-Bart, *Ti Jean l'horizon* (Paris: Seuil, 1979).
25. See Daniel Maximin, *Lone Sun*, trans. Clarisse Zimra (Charlottesville: University Press of Virginia, 1989). First published as *L'Isolé Soleil* (Paris: Seuil, 1981) and Michèle Lacrosil, *Demain Jab-Herma*, op. cit. Having been made an officer in the newly-established Antillean section of the French army when slavery was initially abolished in 1794, Delgrés became famous when in 1802 he and three hundred of his men jumped to their deaths from Fort Matouba, in a last and hopeless act of rebellion against Napoleon's attempts to reestablish slavery.
26. Glissant, *Caribbean Discourse*, p. 75.
27. Ibid., p. 13.
28. Eloïse Brière, 'L'inquiétude génélogique: tourment du Nouveau Monde', *Présence Francophone*, 36 (1990), 57–72 (58).
29. Of course, Glissant is by no means the only theorist to point out the exclusions inherent in dominant models of history. Numerous Western,

and particularly poststructuralist, theorists – with whose work that of Glissant has many affinities generally – have interrogated 'History' in similar terms, pointing out not only how 'Western' models of history are inappropriate in non-Western contexts, but also how their 'internal exclusions' render them equally inadequate within Western contexts themselves. See, for example, Derek Attridge, Geoff Bennington and Robert Young, eds., *Poststructuralism and the Question of History* (Cambridge: Cambridge University Press, 1987); Johannes Fabian, *Time and the Other: How Anthropology Makes Its Object* (New York: Columbia University Press, 1983); Tejaswini Niranjana, *Siting Translation: History, Poststructuralism and the Colonial Context* (Berkeley: University of California Press, 1992); Hayden White, *Metahistory: The Historical Imagination in Nineteenth Century Europe* (Baltimore: Johns Hopkins University Press, 1973); and Robert Young, *White Mythologies: Writing History and the West* (London: Routledge, 1990).

30. Maryse Condé, *The Children of Segu*, trans. Linda Coverdale (New York: Penguin, 1989) and *Segu*, trans. Barbara Bray (New York: Penguin, 1987). First published as: *Ségou: Les murailles de la terre* (1° tome, Paris: Robert Laffont, 1984) and *Ségou: La terre en miettes* (2° tome, Paris: Robert Laffont, 1985). Maryse Condé, *Traversée de la mangrove* (Paris: Mercure de France, 1989). All translations mine.

31. Maryse Condé, *I, Tituba, Black Witch of Salem*, trans. Richard Philcox (New York: Ballantine, 1992). First published as *Moi, Tituba, sorcière . . . noire de Salem* (Paris: Mercure de France, 1986). Page references will be given parenthetically in the text.

32. For a more detailed examination of the formulae and conventions of slave narrative, as well as of the reasons which lay behind the narratives' adherence to them, see James Olney, ' "I was born": Slave Narratives, Their Status as Autobiography and as Literature', in Charles T. Davis and Henry Louis Gates Jr, eds, *The Slave's Narrative* (New York: Oxford University Press, 1985), pp. 148–75.

33. This, as Molly Abel Travis points out, may be seen to be the function of Frederick's Aunt Esther in what is perhaps the best-known nineteenth-century African-American slave narrative, Frederick Douglass's *My Bondage and My Freedom, Part 1 – Life as a Slave, Part 2 – Life as a Freeman* (New York: Miller, Orton and Mulligan, 1855). Here, the whipping of Esther is primarily depicted not as an example of the violence inflicted upon Esther herself, but in order to fulfil the slave narrative convention that the narrator's first observed whipping should be described, and as an example of the emasculation felt by the male slave narrator (Molly Abel Travis, 'Speaking from

the Silence of the Slave Narrative: *Beloved* and African-American Women's History', *The Texas Review*, 13, 1992 (69–81), 73).

34. It must, of course, be acknowledged that all slave narratives, male or female, were subjected to an enormous amount of censorship, and most especially at the hands of the abolitionist ghostwriter or 'editor'. Unbeknown to the illiterate narrator, material was routinely reorganised and deselected, events were rearranged, 'repetitive' descriptions cut out, and the language of the ex-slave's narrative was modified, replaced, or 'translated' from African-American English into standard English, ostensibly for the sake of the approval of a 'wider audience' (see Miriam DeCosta-Willis, 'Self and Society in the Afro-Cuban Slave Narrative', *Latin American Literary Review*, 16, 1988 (6–15), 11).

35. Harriet Jacobs, *Incidents in the Life of a Slave Girl: Written by Herself* (Boston: Thayer and Eldridge, 1861).

36. Travis, 'Speaking from the Silence of the Slave Narrative', p. 73.

37. See, for example, Catherine Clément and Hélène Cixous, *The Newly Born Woman* (Manchester: Manchester University Press, 1986), first published as *La Jeune née* (Paris: Union Générale d'Editions, 1978), and Xavière Gauthier, 'Why Witches?', in Elaine Marks and Isabelle de Courtivron, eds, *New French Feminisms: An Anthology* (London: Harvester Wheatsheaf, 1981), pp. 199–203, first published in 1976 as 'Pourquoi sorcières?', an introduction to the first edition of a feminist journal entitled *Sorcières*.

38. Gauthier, 'Why Witches?', p. 103.

39. Clément and Cixous, *The Newly Born Woman*, p. 5.

40. Ibid., p. 6.

41. Ibid.

42. Ibid., p. 5.

43. See Trinh T. Minh-ha, *Woman, Native, Other: Writing Postcoloniality and Feminism* (Bloomington and Indianapolis: Indiana University Press 1989), p. 121. Man Sonson, too, the self-confessed storyteller of *Traversée de la mangrove*, is, herself, like Man Yaya in *Tituba*, a healer, or 'witch'.

44. Linda Anderson, 'The Re-Imagining of History in Contemporary Women's Fiction', in Linda Anderson, ed., *Plotting Change: Contemporary Women's Fiction* (Edward Arnold: London, 1990), pp. 129–44 (p. 138).

45. I do not wish to suggest here that solidarities between women of different classes and of different colours are in any way automatic or unproblematic. Tituba's relationship with Elizabeth, for example, does not survive her trial, and her relationship with her first mistress, Suzanna Endicott, is characterised not by understanding but by fear and loathing. Thus Tituba reveals how 'her eyes, the colour of sea water, made me lose my bearings. I was reduced to what she wanted

me to be: a gawk of a girl with skin of a repulsive colour' (*Tituba*, p. 26). Indeed, here Condé's work echoes that of her less famous precursor, Lacrosil, whose *Cajou* and *Sapotille ou le serein d'argile* chart abusive, rather than enabling, relationships between black and white women. Not only this, but they do so also in terms of the destructive power of the white gaze, terms which themselves recall Frantz Fanon's *Black Skin, White Masks* (trans. Charles Lam Markmann, London: Pluto, 1986; originally published as *Peau noire, masques blancs*, Paris: Seuil, 1952).

46. The translator of the English version of *Tituba* translates this phrase – in the French version 'la civilisation du Livre' – as 'the civilisation of the Bible'. When thus capitalised, 'Livre', meaning 'book', does indeed also mean 'Holy Book', or Bible. Given the context of my quotation of this phrase, I have thus chosen to modify the translation and to retain the ambiguity contained in the French 'Livre' by using the translation 'Book'.

47. James Olney, ed., *Studies in Autobiography* (Oxford: Oxford University Press, 1988), p. 150.

48. Ibid.

49. Anderson, 'The Re-Imagining of History', p. 129. This is also the position of Tituba in that other, well-known retelling of the Salem story, Arthur Miller's *The Crucible* (Oxford: Heinemann, 1953). Here, too, Tituba dreams of returning to Barbados, though, of course, the play never focuses on her particular story, and much less on what may have happened to her after the witch trials. Rather, Tituba remains throughout *The Crucible* a shadowy and somewhat stereotypical figure.

50. As Ina Césaire and Joëlle Laurent point out in the introduction to their collection *Contes de vie et de mort aux Antilles* (Paris: Nubia, 1976, p. 11), public storytellers are traditionally men while women tell stories, at night, to children. Women are thus marginalised participants in an already marginalised tradition.

51. Bernabé, Chamoiseau, Confiant, *In Praise of Creoleness*, p. 95.

52. Ibid., p. 96.

53. Ibid., p. 89.

54. Ibid., pp. 93–4.

55. Ibid., p. 94.

56. Ibid., p. 79.

57. Ibid., pp. 97–8.

58. It is important to note here that this is a 'rerapprochement', too, because despite the undeniable investment in history and truth on the part of the abolitionist sponsors of slave narrative, the ex-slave narrators did give frequent and very popular public *orations* of their work. What is more, the rhetoric of these orations, those elements

drawn precisely from the oral tradition, was often reproduced in the written text, and contributed greatly to the readers' appreciation of the narratives. Thus, once again, it is evident that the 'Western' notion of a split between history and fiction, of a 'progression' from the oral to the written, may be found to be especially inadequate in the context of marginal forms of 'history-making'.

59. Condé's very inclusion of Hester's story may be seen to be part of her text's literary 'creoleness', as well as to be part of her attempt to rewrite existing stories of marginalised and disruptive women.

60. The authors of *In Praise of Creoleness* not only dedicate their text to, and preface it with quotations from, writers such as Césaire, Glissant and Fanon, but within the text itself they position themselves quite explicitly as the last in a line of literary fathers and sons which extends from Césaire ('We are forever Césaire's sons', p. 80), through Fanon, to Glissant.

61. I borrow this term from Naomi Schor's 'Dreaming Dissymmetry: Barthes, Foucault and Sexual Difference', in Alice Jardine and Paul Smith, eds, *Men in Feminism* (New York: Methuen, 1987), pp. 98–110 (p. 100).

7 Race and the modernist aesthetic

Simon Gikandi

Race in modernism

I want to begin this examination of the relation between race and the modernist aesthetic by making two general statements: first, no student of literature and the arts can ignore the fact that the modernist movement in literature and the arts was one of the most important phenomena in the changing nature and function of culture in the twentieth century. Indeed, as every introduction to the most influential critical anthologies of modernism has been quick to point out, while there has never been a consensus on what modernism was – the term itself is surrounded by ideological disputes and generates what Monique Chefdor has called 'semantic confusion'[1] – there has never been much doubt about the centrality of the movement or even its uniqueness. As Malcolm Bradbury and James McFarlane observed in the 1991 preface to their influential book *Modernism: A Guide to European Literature 1890–1930*, the modernist movement is 'now generally seen as the dominant spirit in early-twentieth-century art and literature'; modernism in the arts 'transformed consciousness and artistic form just as the energies of modernity . . . transformed for ever the nature, the speed, the sensation of human life'.[2] The second point is that the global impact of modernism will remain incomplete so long as our desire to make the movement universal continues to ignore the central and constitutive role race played in the emergence of modernism both as a theory of art and culture and as a literary style. For the authority of modernism as the art form of the modern world, and indeed its identity as the first truly international literary and cultural movement, depended on its ability to deploy other cultures and experiences – those which seemed most removed from the European traditions the modernists were revolting against – as sources of alternative modes of representation and interpretation.

It was in the celebration of the mentality and body of what it considered to be its primitive other that modernism reinvented its aesthetic strategies as one way of freeing itself from what leading proponents of the movement considered to be the dogmatic authority of the nineteenth century. If so-called primitive peoples such as the Bororo of Brazil or the Fang of Gabon came to provide the mythologies and formats in which the modern European subject would come to be represented in such seminal works as T.S. Eliot's *The Waste Land* or Pablo Picasso's *Les Demoiselles d'Avignon*, then these primitives must begin to be read not as mere sources or influences in the establishment of a modernist aesthetic, but also as central objects in the project of modernism. In other words, it is no longer enough to read the Bororo as simple sources of Eliot's theories of myth and art as they were acquired through Frazer's anthropology; on the contrary, as David Richards has wonderfully observed, these 'noble savages' must be read as 'the very essence of modernism since it is their capacity to practise the relativity of the "mythical method", the poet's art, which will "make the modern world possible for art" '.[3] There is another way of putting this problem: if modernism was as much the art form of 'a rapidly modernising world' from which 'many traditional certainties had departed' and belief in 'the very solidity and visibility of reality itself has evaporated', as Bradbury has argued,[4] it is the product and ideology of an age in which the representation or recoding of the world can only be effected through the writing of what has come to be considered to be race, or the discourses that valorise this notion.

The surprising thing about many existing – and quite influential – studies of modernism is not so much how and why they ignore the visible presence of race, but that they fail to see how central it was in the construction of the modernist aesthetic and its ideologies. And the best place to examine this erasure is not so much in writing, where race tends to be more camouflaged, but in modern paintings, many of which had a great effect on the form and function of writing. The erasure of race in modernism, then, can be glimpsed most vividly in the critical history of those works of art which have come to function as the signature pieces of the culture of modernism – Manet's *Olympia* and Picasso's *Les Demoiselles d'Avignon*. The most prominent interpretations of these paintings have certainly commented both on their centrality in the emergence of the modernist style and on the influence of such non-traditional subjects as the prostitute or working-class woman; but when it comes to race, not even the most revisionist studies have much to say. T.J. Clark's influential interpretation of Manet's *Olympia* in *The Painting of Modern Life* relies on his radical claim that the modernity of this work lay in its proffering of 'a rich, exaggerated play with normal identities' in which ordinary experience was altered in the process of being represented.[5] More significantly, argues Clark, Manet's recoding of the experience of modernity depended on his audacious use of a prostitute (as both model and subject) to subvert bourgeois culture. The prostitute is thus indispensable to the emerging modern aesthetic, concludes Clark, because it simultaneously demands inclusion in the representation of modern life and threatens the ordering of this life:

> The category 'prostitute' is necessary, and thus must be allowed its representations. It must take its place in the various pictures of the social, the sexual, and the modern which bourgeois society puts in circulation. There is a sense in which it could even be said to anchor those representations: it is the limiting case of all three, and the point where they are mapped most neatly onto one another. It represents the danger or the price of modernity.[6]

The most radical claim in Clark's argument is that the prostitute, who exists marginally in the social sphere, has become the anchor around which the modern identity is represented.

But what of the black maid who stands in such powerful contrast to the prostitute? Clark does not have much to say on this subject. The truth is, even the best criticism of modernism has problems accounting for Manet's black maid. In his succinct attempt to account for the paradoxes of modernity, for example, Antoine Compagnon locates *Olympia* at 'a crucial moment in the modern tradition, a moment of crisis',[7] but while he is aware of the scandal aroused by the figure of the prostitute and its challenge to conventions of representation, he proceeds to locate its modernity elsewhere: '*Olympia* is the last of the great nudes in the history of painting; it is also a modern painting because of its subject and technique, and also because of the controversy it aroused: the black cat in the picture figures as a signature of modernity.'[8]

In a picture with the gleaming body of a white prostitute and her dark maid, Compagnon endows the black cat with the most dominant aesthetic value. In the process, he raises, but refuses to address, a question asked of Manet by Emile Zola in 1865: 'You needed dark patches and painted a black woman and a cat in a corner. What does all this mean?'[9] In his famous reading of Manet, Zola had suggested that not even the salon artist knew what the black woman and the black cat in his picture represented; nevertheless, both were inescapable figures in this painting.[10]

Now, as attention begins to focus on the palpable presence of blackness in paintings such as *Olympia*, students of art are beginning to see how race was both an overt concern of modernism and part of its larger scheme to reconfigure European strategies of representation. In the words of Albert Boime, 'decorative oppositions of black and white, or alternative passages of light and dark are translated into ideological statements about race, class, and gender'.[11] Like the courtesan whom she serves, the black maid is both inside and outside bourgeois culture: she demands representation in this culture because, through the expansion of global capitalism, she has become one of its inescapable figures; she disturbs our common view of this culture by both calling attention to the (perversely) privileged position of the white prostitute in the imperial system, and pointing to the irony of this situation in which whiteness is associated with nakedness. Manet juxtaposes inherited images of whiteness and blackness, but places them in unstable relationships. By doing so, he initiates one of the most important shifts in Western representations of others: race does not merely play a decorative function; on the contrary, it is one of the conditions of possibility of the modern aesthetic.

And if the most often asked question in studies of modernism is what is race doing in these cultural artifacts, the most obvious answer is that the modernist aesthetic could not have taken the shape it did without a sustained appeal to racial figures which came to play a decisive role in, first, the changing idea of the aesthetic and its connection to the representation and interpretation of the modern experience; second, in the transformation of the idea of culture in modern life; and, third, in some significant attempts to turn cultural differences into a powerful force in European self-representation. In the rest of this essay I will examine how modernism deployed race in these three areas.

Primitivism and modernism

Race enters modernism, first and foremost, in the form of the primitive.[12] Indeed, there is now enough documentation to show that almost every major modern writer, painter and theorist posited the exotic and the primitive as an alternative to the Western industrial culture many of them were revolting against. The primitive body, culture or mentality provided the modernist movement with its most powerful counterpoint:

> The interest in the Primitive as a critical instrument – as a counter-cultural battering ram – persisted in a different form when early twentieth-century vanguard artists engendered a shift of focus from Primitive life to Primitive art. Modernism is unique as compared to the artistic attitudes of past societies in its essentially critical posture, and its primitivism was to be consistent with this.[13]

The idea of the primitive as a counterpoint to bourgeois culture is persuasive in a kind of tautological way: the modernist artist's notion that there was something to be learned from cultures hitherto considered inferior could, in Rubin's words, 'be taken by bourgeois culture as an attack upon its values'.[14] But as David Richards has explained, the use of the primitive as a counterpoint to dominant notions of culture and representation also presupposed a positive function for the primitive – its capacity to reconfigure aesthetic codes and 'replenish the stock of cultural assets'.[15] But the manifest cultural difference of the primitive (and this is a point which needs to be stressed because it is easily lost in many studies of primitivism and modernism) was derived from certain dominant Western notions about race. True, writers such as T.S. Eliot or D.H. Lawrence were attracted to the Bororo or Aztecs because of what appeared to be these primitives' visible difference from modern civilisation, but it is also clear that the radicalness of this difference depended on Euro-American notions about race – the belief that the primitive constituted a different subject, with a different body, and a different system of cognition.[16]

But how did modern writers make the leap from race to the aesthetic?[17] This may seem to be a complex question because of what appears to be the philosophical separation between the two terms: the idea of the aesthetic lies at the very heart of modern

Western culture and criticism while the notion of race, especially in the post-Enlightenment, seems to be used with reference to people who were most removed from centres of European culture. But as Paul Gilroy has argued in 'Art of Darkness', even when the gap between the European self and the black other seemed to be most pronounced, as it was in the eighteenth century, it was difficult to talk about aesthetics outside the purview of race: 'the image of the black played an important role in debates over taste, judgment and the role of culturally specific experience in grounding aesthetic principles'.[18] One of modernism's most enduring achievements, however, was to connect race and aesthetics at the most fundamental level. While the idea of the aesthetics before modernism referred to art in order to exclude blacks from the realm of culture, modernism sought to make blackness an essential condition in the establishment of aesthetic principles.

Consider, for example, this powerful definition of the aesthetic in the eighteenth century, as provided by Terry Eagleton in *The Ideology of the Aesthetic*:

> Aesthetics is born as a discourse of the body. In its original formulation by the German philosopher Alexander Baumgarten, the term refers not in the first place to art, but, as the Greek *aisthesis* would suggest, to the whole region of human perception and sensation, in contrast to the more rarefied domain of conceptual thought. The distinction which the term 'aesthetic' initially enforces in the mid-eighteenth century is not one between 'art' and 'life', but between the material and the immaterial: between things and thoughts, sensations and ideas, that which is bound up with our creaturely life as opposed to that which conducts some shadowy existence in the recesses of the mind.[19]

Now, compare this definition of the aesthetic with Eliot's reflections on the Bororo mentality which he is going to try to incorporate into his poetics:

> In practical life, the Bororo never confuses himself with a parrot, nor is he so sophisticated as to think that black is white. But he is capable of a state of mind into which we cannot put ourselves, in which he *is* a parrot, while being at the same time a man. In other words, the mystical mentality, though at a lower level, plays a much greater part in the daily life of the savage than in that of the civilised man.[20]

Eliot is attracted to the Bororo mentality because of what he sees as its *aisthesis*. This mentality operates in a mystical area well beyond the domain of conceptual thought which, in post-Enlightenment Europe, defines modern culture; for this reason, the primitive's mystical mentality and its symbolistic modes of cognition provide the model for a modernist poetics. If Hegel sees the blacks' inability to make aesthetic judgments – their failure to objectify 'higher values' as 'artistic abstractions'[21] – as the mark of their state of cultural lack, Eliot and his contemporaries embrace the primitive as the fountain of a non-rational system of cognition. If Hegel sneers at the blacks' reduction of objects into fetishes rather than artistic objects, artists such as Picasso will draw on these same fetishes in their quest for alternative modes of perception.[22] Primitivism thus enters European theories of art in the form of a fetish.

But the modernist deployment of racialised figures is, nevertheless, marked by a double paradox: first, because it seeks regeneration in the most negative aspects of primitive culture – those that appear to be the most removed from Western cultural norms – what seems to be the modernist's identification with the black other is also a radical mode of dissociation. Secondly, modernism's quest for a new way of representing and perceiving modern industrial culture, a quest performed elsewhere, depends on a certain refusal to confer this elsewhere with its own instruments of interpretation or reflection. Let us examine these paradoxes in turn.

Let us begin by recalling how the most powerful modernist products – my examples here are Picasso's *Les Demoiselles d'Avignon* and Conrad's African texts – derive their narrative power from their representation of Africa as a space of death and darkness. In Conrad's 'Outpost of Progress', for example, the subjects' and narrator's mode of cognition depends on their ability to understand how the production of meaning no longer depends on the primacy of the subject over the object, or of the civilised over the primitive, but on a deliberate collapsing of such oppositions. Thus the trading post, originally intended to commemorate the ascendance of modernity in colonial Africa, has been reverted into a symbol of atavism and death. The European colonisers who used to claim ultimate authority over colonial spaces and subjects because of their unique subjectivity and mastery of nature are, in Conrad's short story, reduced to the same mechanical functions as the natives and goods they control:

> Society, not from any tenderness, but because of its strange needs, had taken care of those two men, forbidding them all independent thought, all initiative, all departure from routine; and forbidding it under pain of death. They could only live on condition of being machines.[23]

What is unique in this description is not Conrad's association of commerce and the death of the subject – this is, after all, one of the most dominant themes in modern texts – but the way in which the racialised image of Africa adds a radical dimension to this association. For it is the 'sensorial' meaning of Africa – its association with darkness and death – that makes it such a seductive instrument in the critique of the cognitive systems – the 'means/end opposition' inherited from the Enlightenment.[24] Africa does not merely nullify the authority of the European subject; it undermines the whole hermeneutical apparatus, leaving the Europeans in Africa victims of the worlds they came to master:

> They lived like blind men in a large room, aware only of what came into contact with them (and that only imperfectly), but unable to see the general aspect of things. The river, the forest, all the great land throbbing with life, were like a great emptiness. Even the brilliant sunshine disclosed nothing intelligible. Things appeared and disappeared before their eyes in an unconnected and aimless kind of way. The river seemed to come from nowhere and flow nowhither. It flowed through a void. Out of that void, at times, came canoes, and men with spears in their hands would suddenly crowd the yard of the station. They were naked, glossy black, ornamented with snowy shells and glistening brasswire, perfect of limb. (p. 218)

There are several paradoxes in this passage: because it is in the continent that the cognitive system of the European characters is shown to be incapacitated, Africa does provide both narrator and reader with important, albeit negative, knowledge. But Africa itself is an emptiness which discloses nothing – it is just the space in which the nihilism of modernity is exhibited. Have the Africans who move about in the yard derived any knowledge or meaning from their surroundings? Conrad's narrator forecloses the question of African cognition by reducing the blacks to mere bodies. Indeed, when he turns to questions of meaning and interpretation, perception and representation, Conrad's basic premise is that Africa and its bodies are simply the agents of the hermeneutical delirium that grips his characters in their moments of insight which are, significantly, also moments of death.

My basic premise here is that while Africa – and thus blackness – is an indispensable aspect of modernism, it does not demand, of the reader or writer, any kind of identification. Indeed, if we accept the basic philosophical premise that identity and identification depend on a positive notion of temporality (time leads to human progress and the growth of knowledge and understanding), we have to accord great significance to the modernist association of Africa with either an empty or regressive temporality. A sense of regressive time is, of course, a major mark of the modern aesthetic and its rejection of the progressive temporality of modern industrial culture. In Conrad's *Heart of Darkness*, to cite one of the most popular examples, the narrative is inaugurated and driven by regressive time: 'Going up the river was like traveling back in time to the earliest beginnings of the world, when vegetation rioted on the earth and the big trees were kings.'[25] We know that temporal regression drives Conrad's novel, but we have rarely considered how the power and authority of this regressiveness depends on his aesthetic appeal to the semantics of blackness. Indeed in a novel taking its readers back in time, there is a strange way in which moments of blackness become a substitute for the logic we usually associate with temporality in narrative. It used to be argued that the great transformations engendered by Conrad's novel – the changes it generates in conventions of novelistic language, temporality, and the status of the subject – could have been initiated in almost any geographical locality; and yet it is now clear that Africa plays such a specific role in the European imagination, that it is the ideal setting in which the central tenets of Western modes of cognition can be unsettled. For it is because Africa and blackness are populated with what Michael Taussig has called 'metamorphising images of evil and the underworld' that key signifiers can be shown to be 'strategically out of joint with what they signify'.[26] In other words, as Marlow discovers as he goes up the Congo, signs never seem to signify what we expect them to represent, and even key words such as civilisation and progress have been reduced to mere nonsense.[27]

And yet, it is this disjointedness between signs and signifiers that enables the author to comment on the modern condition. Thus in his struggle for a new language to express his revulsion for the female body and his terror of contamination and death, Picasso shifts, in *Les Demoiselles d'Avignon*, from the figure of the prostitute to that of the African mask; and in this masking of woman with blackness, he succeeds in provoking the 'thanatophobia' that becomes, in the words of his European viewers, a signature of his modernity:

> We sense the thanatophobia in the primordial horror evoked by the monstrously distorted heads of the two whores on the right of the picture, so opposite to those of the comparatively gracious Iberian courtesans in the center. One can hardly imagine the fear, the shock, and awe these heads must have imparted in 1907, given the vividness with which we still experience them. These 'African' faces express more ... than just the 'barbaric' character of pure sexuality ... their violence alludes to Woman as destroyer ... but they finally conjure something that transcends our sense of civilized experience, something ominous and monstrous such as Conrad's Kurtz discovered in the heart of darkness.[28]

But as we will see in the last section of this essay, this kind of reaction to the masks of darkness cannot be considered universal; it is indeed surprising that many students of modernism have assumed such universal responses to these texts.

Blackness and the psychology of modernism

An important aspect of the culture of modernism was its turn from epistemology to psychology. In so far as it was reacting against established forms of artistic and linguistic expression, modernism was also impelled to reject the modes of knowledge that sanctioned the literary canon it had inherited from the nineteenth century; and to revolt against tradition, it had to react against the rationalism inherited from the Enlightenment. For while the mind had become a driving force of European culture in its claim to rational reflection, modernism was part of a larger process which posited the mind as 'a realm of competing drives, incompatible systems, irreconcilable agencies or depositions, adjacent territories between which no reliable channels of communication could exist'.[29]

The new discipline of psychology attracted almost every major modern writer because it provided both what seemed to be a compelling diagnosis of the problems of modern industrial culture and a mode of cognition which, by privileging the unconscious and irrational aspects of experience, posited an alternative to the rationality of modernity. The diagnosis of the 'disease of modernity' was systematized by Freud in *Civilization and its Discontents* (1929) in which he considered the astonishing contention that 'what we call our civilization is largely responsible for our misery, and that we should be much happier if we gave it up and returned to primitive conditions'.[30] Freud considered this contention astonishing because 'in whatever way we may define the concept of civilization, it is a certain fact that all the things with which we seek to protect ourselves against the threats that emanate from the sources of suffering are part of that very civilization'.[31] If civilisation was the most logical justification for industrial culture, its most manifest failure was the ways in which its products – urban life, technological advancement, and the rationalisation of everyday life – had led to the alienation of the modern subject. Freud had, in fact, made an important connection between the crisis of modernity and its concomitant desire for primitive life in *Totem and Taboo* (1913), where he had argued that the primitive subject, often considered to be a figure of radical difference (the opposite of civilised culture), could function as a medium of understanding the irrational and the unconscious: the mental life of 'those whom we describe as savages or half-savages', Freud argued, has 'a peculiar interest for us if we are right in seeing it as a well-preserved picture of an early stage of our development'.[32] For the modernist writer, then, going back in time, travelling among the primitives, was a crucial aspect of understanding important aspects not only of what the moderns were before the corrupting influences of civilisation, but also what lay in the recesses of their psyche.

The implications of this turn to the primitive, however, went far beyond its psychological implications: it was at the very heart of the modernist quest for a new artistic language. As Michael North has noted in *The Dialect of Modernism*, the modernist movement was characterised by widespread 'racial cross-identification':

> Writers as far from Harlem as T.S. Eliot and Gertrude Stein reimagined themselves as black, spoke in a black voice, and used that voice to transform the literature of their time. In fact, three of the accepted landmarks of literary modernism in English depend on

racial ventriloquism of this kind: Conrad's *Nigger of the 'Narcissus'*, Stein's 'Melanctha', and Eliot's *The Waste Land*. If the racial status of these works is taken at all seriously, it seems that linguistic mimicry and racial masquerade were not just shallow fads but strategies without which modernism could not have arisen.[33]

Indeed, in works such as 'Melanctha' the racial masquerading and the imposition of a black mask over the white face allows the novelist to overcome several problems of linguistic self-representation. Stein had tried to write about her self and a failed love affair in *Q. E. D.*, a book that remained unpublished until her death; but finding it impossible to represent the self in the conventions and forms inherited from the nineteenth century, she rewrote the same story – her story – under the guise of the narrative of a young black woman. Thus it was through the mask of race that Stein could not only conceptualise her life in writing, but also make what she called 'the first definitive step away from the nineteenth century'.[34] Just as Picasso had to fashion a mask to capture her essence,[35] Stein had to fashion the language of dialect, the language of the black other, to represent her self *differently*. More significantly, the portrait of a black woman and her failed love affair could, through its representation in dialect, enable the author to fulfil one of the perhaps unspoken ambitions of modernism – its desire to capture reality in the language of surrealism, or even anti-realism.

Modernism and the liberation of race

From our discussion so far, it would appear that modernism was attracted to race as a way of dealing with the pathologies associated with industrial civilisation: it projected its worst fears and anxieties – and sometimes its erotic desires – on to the bodies of (black) others whom it also used as the conduit through which it could psychoanalyse its discontents and, at the same time, as a medium for developing a new language of self. In this view, then, race was part of the modern artist's entanglement with the culture of late capitalism – and especially the reification which was an inescapable part of this culture. And yet, as Jameson has argued, modernism 'can at one and the same time be read as a utopian compensation for everything reification brings with it' (p. 236). While Jameson reads this compensatory function in modernism as arising from the increasing abstraction of art in the modern period – art provides 'the place of quality in an increasingly quantified world' (p. 236) – there is also a sense in which modernism came to be read, especially by colonised black writers, as a mode of liberation of race itself. In other words, in spite of what appears to have been the sustained (mis)use of black subjects in modernism, the movement had a wide appeal to black writers in both Africa and the Americas: it was responsible for a major transformation in black writing in these regions, and it was to become the justification for various moments of cultural renaissance in places as diverse as Harlem in New York City and Haiti in the Caribbean.

Indeed, what are now considered to be the foundational texts of modern black writing – W.E.B. DuBois's *The Souls of Black Folk* and Aimé Césaire's *Cahier d'un retour au pays natal* (*Notebook of a Return to the Native Land*), to mention two of the most prominent texts in this tradition – were written either as part of the modernist reconfiguration of industrial culture (DuBois) or under the influence of its radical break-up of traditional linguistic forms (Césaire). Three questions arise from this claim of affinity between modernism and modern black writing: how could the project of black liberation (the motivating factor behind black writing in the early twentieth century) be reconciled to modernism's imprisonment of the black subject as its radical other; how did black writers deal with the tremendous baggage of racist thought inherent in the modernist return to the *volk* or primitivism; and what was the relation between this other modernism and what was to be canonised as high modernism – the modernism of Eliot, Pound, and Joyce?

If one were to pick up any manifesto of black modernism, let's say Alain Locke's *The New Negro*, one is struck by how often the desire or claim for a new black culture is linked to notions of collective freedom and individual emancipation. The cultural grammar of this important anthology is embodied in words such as enlightenment, self-expression, and self-determination; its driving philosophical claim is for a new black sense of being. Indeed, if the 'New Negro' was above everything else a cultural project, it was motivated by the desire, among its contributors, to free the black subject from what Locke called 'a mere external view' and to locate the inner essence of black being. Here is the key passage from Locke's introduction to the anthology:

> We turn therefore in the other direction to the elements of truest social portraiture, and discover in the artistic self-expression of the Negro to-day a new figure on the national canvas and a new force in the foreground of affairs. Whoever wishes to see the Negro in his essential traits, in the full perspective of his achievement and possibilities, must seek the enlightenment of that self-portraiture which the present developments of Negro culture are offering. In these pages, without ignoring either the fact that there are important interactions between the national and the race life, or that the attitude of America toward the Negro is as important a factor as the attitude of the Negro toward America, we have nevertheless concentrated upon self-expression and the forces and motives of self-determination. So far as he is culturally articulate, we shall let the Negro speak for himself.[36]

In this passage alone, one can see how advocates of cultural blackness existed both inside and outside the dominant notions of the modernist aesthetic. For one, the continuous insistence on the newness of the Negro echoed Baudelaire's definition of modernism as the art of the fleeting and the new. More importantly, like mainstream modernists, Locke would encapsulate black life in the metropolis in the form of a painting or portrait and then proceed to argue that the real essence of blackness was to be found in the way this painting was re-presented on the national canvas. But this appeal to such dominant modernist notions as newness and self-portraiture was also qualified in significant ways: because the black subject was to be foregrounded in the national canvas, he or she could not exist as a mere appendage to the modernist cultural project or an instrument of the other's quest for self-understanding; and since the black subject could not be reduced to a mere mask, he or she had to be recognised as an essential self whose identity depended on self-understanding and self-presentation, on his or her capacity for reflection. If self-reflection was what was missing when the black was deployed as a mask, as often seemed to be the case in Stein and Picasso, the 'New Negro' would acquire his or her identity through a capacity to speak for himself or herself. So while black modernism is explicitly linked to global modernity – 'Harlem has the same role to play for the New Negro as Dublin has had for the New Ireland or Prague for the New Czechoslovakia,' says Locke[37] – it was not to be imprisoned in the presentness of this modernity. On the contrary, Locke was to argue, black modernism would try to exceed the temporal moment of European modernism: 'Harlem, I grant you isn't typical – but it is significant, it is prophetic.'[38] The idea of prophecy is important here because it suggests identities that will be imagined and constituted in a utopian moment beyond the reification of modern American life.

The second question – that of how black modernism dealt with the racist baggage inherited from its European sources – is more complex. It is complex because there was a close relationship between the ideas which black writers found particularly appealing in the discourse of modernism and the racism that had imprisoned their societies and cultures over at least two centuries. Consider, for example, the movement of Caribbean and African writers which came to be known as Negritude: the poetics and politics of this movement were driven by ideas of race and *volk* culture which were, at the same time, popular in European racialist thinking, popularised in many cases by well-known racists such as the Count J.-A. de Gobineau. Why would the founders of Negritude, most notably the African poet Léopold Senghor, read and admire a writer such as Gobineau whose work sanctioned a philosophical tradition that was inimical to the essence and character of blackness? The most sensible answer to this question is provided by Senghor's compatriot, Aimé Césaire, in a 1967 interview: Senghor was grateful to Gobineau for having defined the province of art as essentially black, for having insisted, in Césaire's words, that 'If there are artists in Western civilization, it is because there are nonetheless a few drops of Negro blood in them.'[39] In an ironic twist of fate, then, the racialism of modernism was seen as legitimising blackness.

In these circumstances, it should not surprise us that the manifestos of 'black modernism' were driven by the same concerns as those of 'Anglo-American modernism'. In the *New Negro*, Locke seeks to register the transformation of black America not so much on the manifest cultural or social realm, but in the inner world of the mind; his search for the essence of blackness negates the materiality of black life as it ponders the meaning of the inner world of the mind, a world which, as we saw in the last section, has already been privileged by canonical modernism. If Locke seems contemptuous of material culture or rather the formulas in which black life has hitherto been represented, it is because he wants to focus on the 'new psychology' and 'new spirit' which denotes the modernity of the black experience: the younger generation of blacks, argues Locke, 'is vibrant with a new psychology; the new spirit is awake in the masses, and under the very eyes of the professional observers is transforming what has been a perennial problem into the progressive phases of contemporary Negro life'.[40] For long imprisoned in the rationalism of Western discourse, the true language of blackness can only emerge when the poet or artist develops mechanisms for probing the naturalness of black being. As another contributor to the *New Negro* observed, the most important element of black art is 'the psychological complexion of the Negro as he inherited it from his primitive ancestors and which he maintains to this day. The outstanding characteristics are his tremendous emotional endowment, his luxuriant and free imagination and a truly great power of individual expression.'[41] This, too, was the language of primitivism. The only difference was that while European artists had to appropriate forms of blackness from which they were separated by genealogy and tradition, the black artist was ostensibly connected to this art by his or her racial nature.

The black investment in the uses of primitivism inevitably leads us to the third question: what was the relation between black modernism and Anglo-American modernism? In one of the most influential books on this subject, Houston A. Baker, Jr, has argued that the concerns of Anglo-American modernism were irrelevant to the modernist project that emerged in centres of black culture such as Harlem.[42] Certainly, the ideologies of high modernism – the critique of civilisation and the privileging of the bourgeois subject – could seem to be at odds with the Harlem Renaissance's desire for the transformative power of civilisation and progress and its evocation of the collective character of the masses. But this radical difference conceals, I believe, an identity of means. In other words, 'black modernism' set out to deploy the aesthetic ideology of modernism to affirm and sustain what we may call the incomplete project of 'black modernity'. If Anglo-American modernism arose as a critique of modernity, black modernism seemed to be different in its desire for the modernising elements – and the civilisational authority – of western culture. It may have appeared to advocate a return to African sources with a renewed vigour and to invoke the name of the motherland as the foundation of blackness, but it also seemed to relate to, and value, this Africa in its pastness. If I may borrow a phrase from Jürgen Habermas, the new value placed on the transitory nature of black life in the modern metropolis, and the very celebration of the newness of the 'New Negro', 'discloses a longing for an undefiled, immaculate and stable present'.[43]

Black modernists such as W.E.B. DuBois now appear vulnerable to the charge that they invested in what Zamir has called 'the baggage of organicist primitivism of late-nineteenth-century American studies of folk culture',[44] but we should not forget that their evocation of a usable and classical black past was part of a difficult attempt to stabilise an intractable present. In this enterprise, both Anglo-American and Afro-American modernists sought, in the realm of the aesthetic, a resolution to the problems of everyday life. While these problems were, of course, different for each group, the philosophical and aesthetic strategies they demanded were surprisingly similar; by calling attention to these common means my goal is to promote a more comparative reading of these traditions against the wishes of some of their proponents – on both sides of the modernist divide – who would like to keep them separate and unequal.

Notes

1. Monique Chefdor, 'Modernism: Babel Revisited', *Modernism: Challenges and Perspectives*, ed. Monique Chefdor, Ricardo Quinones, and Albert Wachtel (Urbana: University of Illinois Press, 1986), p. 1.
2. Malcolm Bradbury and James McFarlane, *Modernism: A Guide to European Literature 1890–1930* (London: Penguin Books, 1991), p. 11.
3. David Richards, *Masks of Difference: Cultural Representations in Literature, Anthropology and Art* (Cambridge: Cambridge University Press, 1994), p. 211.
4. Bradbury, *Modernism*, p. 57.
5. T.J. Clark, *The Painting of Modern Life: Paris in the Art of Manet and His Followers* (New York: Alfred A. Knopf, 1985), p. 100.
6. Ibid., p. 103.

7. Antoine Compagnon, *The Five Paradoxes of Modernity*, trans. Franklin Philip (New York: Columbia University Press, 1994), p. xvii.
8. Ibid., p. 26.
9. Ibid., p. 27.
10. For a useful context for Zola's questions, see ibid. (pp. 27–8).
11. Boime, Albert, *The Art of Exclusion: Representing Blacks in the Nineteenth Century* (Washington, D.C.: Smithsonian Press, 1990), pp. 2–3.
12. Some of these questions are taken up in Marianna Torgovnick's *Gone Primitive: Savage Intellects, Modern Lives* (Chicago: University of Chicago Press, 1990).
13. William Rubin, 'Modernist Primitivism', *Primitivism in 20th Century Art*, vol. 1 (New York: The Museum of Modern Art, 1984), p. 7.
14. Ibid.
15. Richards, *Masks of Difference*, p. 189.
16. It is important to note that before it sought out the primitive, the aesthetic of modernism had already deployed women and the working class as radical figures of alterity. The most exemplary modernist here is, of course, D.H. Lawrence.
17. I am not suggesting that race and the aesthetic were not conjoined in earlier periods; see, for example, Sander Gilman, *On Blackness without Blacks* (Boston: G.K. Hall, 1982).
18. Paul Gilroy, 'Art of Darkness: Black Art and the Problem of Belonging to England', *Third Text* 10 (Spring 1990), 48. See also his *The Black Atlantic: Modernity and Double Consciousness* (Cambridge, Mass.: Harvard University Press, 1993).
19. Terry Eagleton, *The Ideology of the Aesthetic* (Oxford: Blackwell, 1990), p. 13.
20. T.S. Eliot, quoted in Richards, *Masks of Difference*, pp. 204–5.
21. Quoted in Gilroy, 'Art of Darkness', p. 47.
22. For a discussion of Hegel and the blacks, see Gilroy, 'Art of Darkness', p. 47, and *The Black Atlantic*, p. 41.
23. Joseph Conrad, 'The Outpost of Progress', *Eastern Skies and Western Seas: Two Complete Novels and Six Short Stories* (New York: Carroll and Graf, 1990), p. 217. Further references to this work will be made in parentheses in the text.
24. Fredric Jameson, *The Political Unconscious: Narrative as a Socially Symbolic Act* (Ithaca, N.Y.: Cornell University Press, 1981), p. 250. Further references will be given parenthetically.
25. Joseph Conrad, *Heart of Darkness*, ed. Robert Kimbrough, 3rd edn (New York: Norton, 1988), p. 35.
26. Michael Taussig, *Shamanism, Colonialism, and the Wild Man: A Study in Terror and Healing* (Chicago: The University of Chicago Press, 1987), p. 5.

27. I have developed this argument in *Maps of Englishness: Writing Identity in the Culture of Colonialism* (New York: Columbia University Press, in press). For slightly different examinations of Conrad and modern temporality, see Homi Bhabha, *The Location of Culture* (London and New York: Routledge, 1994), pp. 212–17; and Tim Youngs, *Travellers in Africa* (Manchester: Manchester University Press, 1994), pp. 202–5.

28. Rubin, 'Modernist Primitivism', p. 255. Since the *American Heritage Dictionary* defines thanatos both as the personification of death and as 'an alleged instinct to self-destruction', thanatophobia in this context refers to extreme revulsion against the figures that embody death (the African masks) but also suggests some self-destructive attraction to such figures.

29. Boime, *The Art of Exclusion*, p. 5.

30. Sigmund Freud, *Civilization and its Discontents*, 1929–30, *The Standard Edition of the Complete Psychological Works of Sigmund Freud*, trans. James Strachey and Anna Freud, vol. xxi (London: The Hogarth Press, 1961), p. 86.

31. Ibid., p. 80.

32. Sigmund Freud, *Totem and Taboo*, 1912–13, *The Standard Edition of the Complete Psychological Works of Sigmund Freud*, trans. James Strachey and Anna Freud, vol. xiii (London: The Hogarth Press, 1955), p. 1.

33. Michael North, *The Dialect of Modernism* (Oxford and New York: Oxford University Press, 1994), Preface.

34. Ibid., p. 61.

35. I am referring to Picasso's 'Portrait of Gertrude Stein' which superimposes a white mask on the subject's face.

36. Alain Locke, *The New Negro: An Interpretation* [1925] (New York: Arno Press, 1968), p. ix.

37. Ibid., p. 17.

38. Ibid., p. 7.

39. Quoted in A. James Arnold, *Modernism and Negritude: The Poetry and Poetics of Aimé Césaire* (Cambridge, Mass.: Harvard University Press, 1981), p. 41.

40. Locke, *The New Negro*, p. 3.

41. Ibid., p. 19.

42. Houston A. Baker, Jr, *Modernism and the Harlem Renaissance* (Chicago: University of Chicago Press, 1987), pp. 1–18.

43. Jürgen Habermas, 'Modernity – An Incomplete Project', *The Anti-Aesthetic: Essays on Postmodern Culture* (Port Townsend, Washington: Bay Press, 1983), p. 5.

44. Shamoon Zamir, *Dark Voices: W.E.B. DuBois and American Thought, 1888–1903* (Chicago: Chicago University Press, 1995), 174.

8 *White apes at the* fin de siècle

Tim Youngs

In a chapter headed 'The Races of Man', Charles Darwin set out in 1871 some of the arguments for and against the view that 'man' consisted of distinct species. Given the 'insuperable difficulties' in defining species, he decided that it would be more appropriate to use the term 'subspecies', and then wrote: 'But from long habit the term "race" will perhaps always be employed.'[1] A few pages later, Darwin, still exercised by the problem of definition, wondered whether 'primeval man', with 'arts of the rudest kind' and 'extremely imperfect' language, could be called 'man'. Darwin resolved that: 'In a series of forms graduating insensibly from some ape-like creature to man as he now exists, it would be impossible to fix on any definite point when the term "man" ought to be used.'[2] Darwin judged this 'a matter of very little importance'. He recorded his 'indifference' to 'whether the so-called races of man are thus designated, or are ranked as species or sub-species', though he inclined to the latter term as the 'most appropriate'. He trusted that the principles of evolution would soon be widely accepted and that with this acceptance the arguments between monogenists (who believed humanity was one species) and polygenists (who rejected evolution and maintained that humanity consisted of separate species) would soon die out.[3]

The idea that one could not identify the exact stage at which humanity may be distinguished from apedom discomposed those of Darwin's contemporaries who were anxious to demonstrate their remoteness from the simian and from the primitive. At issue here was something much more complicated than the demonstration of white racial superiority. As Darwin's problems with categorisation might suggest, the language of race was not fixed. As well as its application to groups of a different skin colour,[4] it was used to denote class and gender differences within 'civilised' societies. The ascription of inferior racial characteristics to various (white) groups within Britain was as important a means of self-definition and control of others at home as was the attribution of savagery to the domination of black Africans abroad.[5] If now we overlook distinctions that were made inside the so-called imperial centre, then we misperceive the latter as homogeneous, and to do *that* is to collude with the ideology of a common national interest against which groups were defined or within which they were subsumed.

The insistent, often desperate, conjunction of the languages of race, class and gender is greatest at precisely that time when the social order is felt to be under its most serious threat.[6] This essay will focus on the 1880s and 1890s, two decades in which 'there was ... a confluence of discourses ... about social and political disturbances, urban degeneration and racial decline, couched in social Darwinism'.[7] It is a particularly interesting feature of these years that the threats that members of the middle and upper classes felt were being made to the social order came increasingly to be registered against notions of the savage and the primitive. This is true not only of those texts that have an obvious external reference (travel, anthropology, imperialist writings, early science fiction, and so on), but also, and more intriguingly, of those that display a concern with internal danger.

The internal threat at this time can be seen to have three main aspects: the biological, psychological and social. These are, of course, interlinked, but in so far as distinctions may be drawn between them, the first, influenced by the popular understanding of Darwinism, combines a shuddering recognition of the origins and bestial nature of 'man' with alarm at the possibility of a degenerative adaptation down to one's (usually urban) environment; the second involves the actual or threatened return of repressed desires and instincts; and the third, which is embodied in the challenge posed to those characters who represent the values of civilised society, reflects their growing loss of power. The interrelation of these three aspects is evident in their shared imagery. In this essay I shall concentrate on the figure of the ape, which is common to all three concerns, and which is central to the idea of race. But I am interested in a particular kind of ape: the white ape, a creature that becomes highly visible at the *fin de siècle* and whose very designation is a strong indication of the coexistence of racial and social discourses. Before we can begin to describe it, though, we need to say something about its habitat.

The 1880s saw a 'deep-rooted' and 'comprehensive' social crisis.[8] According to Gareth Stedman Jones, this consisted of four main elements: a severe cyclical depression; the decline of some of the older central industries; a severe shortage of working-class housing in the inner industrial perimeter; and the emergence of socialism and collectivism.[9] The 1884 Reform Act had extended the franchise to around two million agricultural workers, giving the professional classes a 'deeply disturbing problem of social identity, as the boundaries between the lower bourgeoisie and their inferiors became increasingly blurred'.[10] The passing of the Act did not quell the unrest that had preceded it. In 1886 there were riots in Trafalgar Square, principally on 8 February when twenty thousand people, mostly unemployed dock and building workers, assembled. 'All forms of property were assailed, all signs of wealth and privilege were attacked',[11] and trouble continued for the next two days. In 1887 there were demonstrations of the unemployed, culminating in Bloody Sunday on 13 November.[12] The following year there was the match girls' strike and the year after that the great dock strike.[13] Between 1888 and 1892 trade-union membership doubled to over one and a half million.[14] Danger came from without, too. On 24 January 1885 Fenians exploded three bombs at Westminster Hall, the Houses of Parliament, and the Tower of London.[15] The Home Rule issue caused a realignment of the political parties in 1886, with a split in Gladstone's Liberal Party causing the defeat of his Home Rule Bill in June of that year.[16] The Irish, of course, were themselves caricatured as apes: 'The transformation of peasant Paddy into an ape-man or simianised Caliban was completed by the 1860s and 1870s.'[17]

Helen Lynd suggests that outbreaks of violence during the decade meant that 'the continued "docility" of labor was not to be counted on', and makes the fascinating point that 'While the depression lasted, rebellion could be crushed. Returning prosperity meant more power for labor.'[18] According to Jones, the dominant feeling of the 1880s among the propertied and intellectual classes was 'not guilt but fear'. The poor and unemployed of London 'were generally pictured as coarse, brutish, drunken, and immoral;

through years of neglect and complacency they had become an ominous threat to civilization'.[19] This would certainly seem to be the case in George Gissing's *The Nether World* (1889), whose narrator repeatedly expresses horror at Clem Peckover, against whom 'Civilization could bring no charge ... it and she had no common criterion'.[20] Peckover and her mother are 'two savages, whose characters so supplemented each other as to constitute an engine in tyranny' (p. 191).

Gissing's novel is saturated with racial imagery. Most of this is attached to Clem,[21] who is white. Clem 'would have liked dealing with some one with whom she could try savage issue in real tooth-and-claw conflict' (p. 8). She entertains a 'savage kind of admiration' for Bob Hewett (p. 36). Later, she is described thus:

> Reddened by the rays of the fire, her features had a splendid savagery which seemed strangely at discord with the paltry surroundings amid which she sat; her eyes just now were gleaming with a crafty and cruel speculation which would have become those of a barbarian in ambush. I wonder how it came about that her strain, after passing through the basest conditions of modern life, had thus reverted to a type of ancestral exuberance. (p. 120)

The reversion has come as Clem plots with her mother to marry Jane's father in the hope of gaining access to the money that they think he will have.

The association of wealth with savagery is made often in late nineteenth-century texts. On the face of it this may appear surprising, but it should become less so when it is viewed in the context of Darwinian doubts about the precise markers of humanity. For Gissing's narrator, Clem's savage regression is signalled in part by her self-abasing scheme to get money. Of course, it is only to be expected that novels that concern themselves, as Gissing's does, with the material conditions of the 'sordid struggle for existence' (p. 151) should delineate their characters in racial terms. Darwin's concept of the struggle for existence between and within species makes this unavoidable. (And in any case 'the working classes were often figured in *fin de siècle* texts as the lower "race"'.[22]) In viewing 'the army of industrialism as an army fighting with itself, rank against rank, man against man, that the survivors may have whereon to feed' (p. 274), it is but a short step to seeing the members of this army as the 'slaves of industrialism' (p. 104).

There may be nothing inherently racial about this reference to slaves but the connotation would have been clear. Besides, since Gissing's characters are moulded by their (economic) environment, they are slaves to it just as any species or (in the sense then current) race would have been. Furthermore, defenders of slavery in the American South had earlier compared their system favourably with industrial slavery in England.

The narrator of *The Nether World* thinks that 'To humanise the multitude' it is necessary to 'effect an entire change of economic conditions' (p. 109).[23] In Gissing's presentation of industrial capitalism 'not as a personality, but as an abstract, controlling principle', writes John Goode, the 'impersonality is historically very precise, because what emerges most clearly from the social history of the 1880s is an overwhelmingly dehumanised class relation'.[24] Gissing's grim belief in the force of that dehumanising environment is such that, as Stephen Gill remarks in his Introduction, 'What is so striking about *The Nether World* is how little is presented as a counter-force to this economic pressure' (p. xv).

In writing of the 'universal struggle for life', Darwin had used an economic metaphor: 'unless it be thoroughly ingrained in the mind, the whole economy of nature, with every fact on distribution, rarity, abundance, extinction, and variation, will be dimly seen or quite misunderstood'.[25] Since Darwin had described Natural Selection as 'a power incessantly ready for action ... and immeasurably superior to man's feeble efforts',[26] it is understandable that many novelists who saw the economic environment as the arena in which Natural Selection occurred should be pessimistic about the chances of resisting that power. And since Darwin also declared that 'natural selection acts by life and death – by the survival of the fittest, and by the destruction of the less well-fitted individuals',[27] much anxiety was expressed about who it was in society that seemed likely to survive and who it was that seemed destined for destruction.

In the social context I have outlined, the fear of destruction is felt mainly by the upper and middle classes. This might seem odd, given the ruinous health of those who lived in poverty and squalor, but the visible protests by those who suffered such conditions, combined with the financial precariousness felt by many members of the middle class, meant that there was a nervous perception of the inhabitants of the 'Nether World' as possessing greater strength.[28]

There is not, that I have noticed, any direct reference to apes in Gissing's novel. I have mentioned the book to illustrate how race, class and gender imagery came together at that time. However, in Robert Louis Stevenson's *The Strange Case of Dr. Jekyll and Mr. Hyde* (1886),[29] Hyde not only has a 'savage laugh' (p. 13), gives a screech 'as of mere animal terror' (p. 38), and has a hand 'lean, corded, knuckly, of a dusky pallor, and thickly shaded with a swart growth of hair' (p. 54); but he plays 'ape-like tricks' (p. 61), and seems to be 'a masked thing like a monkey' (p. 37). What is more, when he tramples to death Sir Danvers Carew, M.P., he exhibits 'ape-like fury' (p. 19). When we have a British gentleman metamorphosing into an ape-like creature and killing a Member of Parliament underfoot, something profoundly troublesome is happening.[30] To understand what this might be, the simian motif has, like everything, to be placed in its historical and social context.

Hyde drinks 'pleasure with bestial avidity' (p. 53). But Stevenson warns against so firm a denial of base enjoyments that they resurface in a deformed and damaging way. This is one lesson of Jekyll's statement that 'I concealed my pleasures; and ... when I reached years of reflection ... I stood already committed to a profound duplicity of life ... both sides of me were in dead earnest' (p. 48). This is not a simple morality tale about the duality of humankind. Jekyll, having been 'born ... to a large fortune ..., fond of the respect of the wise and good among my fellow-men, and thus, as might have been supposed, with every guarantee of an honourable and distinguished future' (p. 48), finds that it is exactly his social respectability and financial standing that have caused his crisis, for they cannot acknowledge his baser side. The conflict arises as the indicators of status become unsettled. This, as I have remarked elsewhere,[31] provokes the real horror of *Jekyll and Hyde*: that, in the event of Jekyll's death or disappearance for longer than three months (p. 9), Hyde stands to inherit Jekyll's 'quarter of a million sterling' (p. 20). The incongruity of this redirection of wealth is emblematised by the residence of Hyde in a 'dismal quarter of Soho', whose 'blackguardly surroundings' include

> a dingy street, a gin palace, a low French eating-house, a shop for the retail of penny numbers and two-penny salads, many ragged children huddled in the doorways, and many women of many different nationalities passing out, key in hand, to have a morning glass. (p. 20)

It is this horror of the inappropriate possession of wealth that so disturbs, and it is not surprising that the real fear of this shift in the base of power is masked, both in the tale and in subsequent adaptations of it, by the bestial. Indeed, at least two critics have argued that Jekyll's simian avatar connects with the audience for whom Stevenson is writing. Quoting from a letter of 1886 to Edmund Gosse in which Stevenson pronounces: 'Let us tell each other sad stories of the bestiality of the beast whom we feed',[32] Patrick Brantlinger and Richard Boyle contend that 'Hyde was thus both a chief cause of his creator's popular success and an ironic, albeit unconscious image of that popularity – the "ape-like", atavistic image of "the people" '.[33]

The social repression of pleasure, dramatised in *Jekyll and Hyde* by the transformation of the white gentleman into an ape-like figure, is also a theme of Oscar Wilde's *The Picture of Dorian Gray* (1891). Lord Henry Wotton tells Dorian:

> The mutilation of the savage has its tragic survival in the self-denial that mars our lives. We are punished for our refusals. Every impulse that we strive to strangle broods in the mind, and poisons us . . . The only way to get rid of a temptation is to yield to it. Resist it, and your soul grows sick with longing for the things it has forbidden to itself, with desire for what its monstrous laws have made monstrous and unlawful.[34]

Monstrosity recurs throughout Wilde's novel. Occasionally, its reference to race is direct, as when Dorian tells Henry of 'a hideous Jew' he has met outside an 'absurd little theatre' while he was searching through 'this grey, monstrous London of ours' for 'some adventure'. Dorian is amused by the Jew: with his 'amazing waistcoat', 'vile cigar', 'greasy ringlets . . . enormous diamond blazed in the centre of a soiled shirt', and 'gorgeous civility', he 'was such a monster' (p. 48). The commingling of danger and delight as Dorian pursues his quest for sin also brings together race and degradation; the repulsive Jew in keeping with the sordid environment.[35] Since cultural perceptions of the Jew conjoin race and money it is understandable (though none the less reprehensible) that this figure should emerge in a novel that exhibits the contemporary preoccupation with a disjunction between essential and financial or social worth.

As with *Jekyll and Hyde,* incompatibility between social status and natural inclination is figured by the animalistic pursuit of individual desires. Several times observing Basil's portrait of him on returning from 'one of those mysterious and prolonged absences that gave rise to such strange conjectures' (p. 128), Dorian grows ever more fascinated with the contrast between his own beauty and the corruption of his soul:

> He would examine with minute care, and sometimes with a monstrous and terrible delight, the hideous lines that seared the wrinkling forehead or crawled around the heavy sensual mouth, wondering sometimes which were the more horrible, the signs of sin or the signs of age. He would place his white hands beside the coarse bloated hands of the picture, and smile. He mocked the misshapen body and the failing limbs. (p. 128)

If this is supposed to be spiritual corruption then it has a peculiarly social basis. We are told by the narrator of how Dorian would sometimes reflect, while 'lying sleepless in his own delicately-scented chamber, or in the sordid room of the little ill-famed tavern near the Docks, which, under an assumed name, and in disguise, it was his habit to frequent', on 'the ruin he had brought upon his soul'. 'The more he knew, the more he desired to know' (p. 128). The interest lies in the location of the sin: it is the East End of London.

As in Stevenson's story, Wilde's tale turns to the figure of the simian to communicate the distaste that accompanies the pursuit of pleasure. When Dorian leaves Sybil Vane, who has 'spoiled the romance of [his] life' by letting the reality of her love for him overcome and spoil her acting (p. 87),

> where he went to he hardly knew. He remembered wandering through dimly-lit streets, past gaunt black-shadowed archways and evil-looking houses. Women with hoarse voices and harsh laughter had called after him. Drunkards had reeled by cursing, and chattering to themselves like *monstrous apes.* (p. 88, my emphasis)

The image is that of the urban jungle, of coarse humanity adapting down to a squalid environment. The threat to the well-to-do observer is physically real. Jim Vane, Sybil's sixteen-year-old brother, hates Dorian, 'through some curious race-instinct for which he could not account, and which for that reason was all the more dominant within him' (p. 66), for being a gentleman. The 'murderous hatred' he feels (p. 70) may be stirred by incestuous desire for his sister, but the class antagonism is dominant.

Class conflict is evident in Wells's *The Time Machine* (1895) in which the Morlocks, the future descendants of the proletariat, prey on the non-labouring Eloi. The Time Traveller describes the Morlocks he sees thus: running either 'on all-fours' or 'with its forearms held very low' (he cannot tell which), with 'strange large greyish-red eyes' and 'flaxen hair on its head and down its back', 'a Thing', 'like a human spider', a 'little monster', a 'Lemur',[36] 'human rats' (p. 69), and 'white', 'ape-like' creatures (pp. 43 and 44). It is perfectly appropriate that the Traveller should give the Morlocks such a range of bestial labels. His use of several terms fits his inability to decide between a social and a biological explanation for the Morlocks' existence.[37] He realises that 'Man had not remained one species, but had differentiated into two distinct animals' (p. 45); yet at the same time he speculates that

> the present merely temporary and social difference between the Capitalist and the Labourer was the key to the whole position ... There is a tendency to utilize underground space for the less orna-mental purposes of civilization; there is the Metropolitan Railway in London, for instance, there are new electric railways, there are subways, there are underground workrooms and restaurants, and they increase and multiply ... Even now, does not an East-End worker live in such artificial conditions as practically to be cut off from the natural surface of the earth? (p. 47)

Patently, the fact that the Morlocks reside underground, prey on the Eloi above ground, and are figured as 'this bleached, obscene, nocturnal Thing' (p. 45), admits a psychological interpretation too. Socially *and* psychologically, the repressed returns to threaten the civilised self. When the Traveller joins his guests for dinner back in the time from which he has journeyed, and prepares to tell his story, he is 'starving for a bit of meat' (p. 17), prefiguring the hints to the reader that the Morlocks are cannibals (e.g. p. 52). The suggestion is that 'man' and ape may not be so far apart.[38] This is largely why the Morlocks are *white* apes. There would other-wise be less alarm.

An ape man also figures largely in Wells's remarkable *The Island of Doctor Moreau* (1896). Although this ape is black-faced, his condition implicates so clearly, if allegorically, the white characters and readers of the novel that I feel quite justified in including him here.

The story is told mainly in the form of a manuscript written by Edward Prendick and discovered by his nephew, the framing narrator, Charles Edward Prendick. The manuscript tells how Edward, a 'private gentleman',[39] spent eleven months between February 1887 and January 1888 on an island after being shipwrecked. To his rescuer, Montgomery, who had studied biology at University College, London, Prendick reveals that he had himself 'taken to natural history as a relief from the dulness [sic] of my comfortable independence' (p. 7). We learn later that he had 'spent some years at the Royal College of Science, and had done some research in biology under Huxley' (pp. 27-8).[40] Like Dr Jekyll and Dorian Gray, Prendick is a comfortably well-off gentleman who feels that excitement is missing from his life. Like Jekyll and Dorian, he undergoes experiences that reconnect him with the primitive and the bestial.

Having heard Montgomery address Moreau, Prendick remembers that the latter was a physiologist caught in a scandal ten years before when he was exposed by a journalist as having conducted unwantonly cruel experiments. Moreau had been driven out of England. This, together with the description of the island as a kind of biological station (p. 28), introduces us to the question of the nature of humanity and animality and to its biological, theological and psychological implications.

Prendick's exchange with the black-faced 'simian creature' (p. 58) who had met him on the beach soon makes these themes apparent. The 'Ape Man' (p. 61) embodies the duality of the human and the animal that so troubled Wells's contemporaries. Prendick's 'ape-like companion' (p. 59) can speak, though the word Prendick first uses to denote this is 'chattering' (p. 58), with its connotations of a monkey's sounds. Admittedly, the creature's broken syntax, malformed hands, and – according to Prendick – idiocy mark him off from humanity, but the fact that he speaks at all, let alone his half-human appearance, makes the point of separation between the ape and the human as unclear as Darwin had suggested.

The problem of ascertaining this dividing line is compounded by the narrative uncertainty as to whether the Ape Man and his fellow Beast People are improved animals or degenerate humans (made so by Moreau). Prendick thinks the latter, stating of the

Beast People that 'I did not know yet how far they had forgotten the human heritage I ascribed them' (p. 59). But Moreau insists:

> The creatures ... were not men, had never been men. They were animals – humanized animals – triumphs of vivisection. (p. 77)

Moreau's declaration that 'These creatures you have seen are animals carven and wrought into new shapes ... to the study of the plasticity of living forms – my life has been devoted' (p. 78) is a thrilling testament to the impact both of Darwin's theories about the fluidity of form and of the concomitant challenge to ideas of fixity and wholeness. Darwin had written that 'if any one species does not become modified and improved in a corresponding degree with its competitors, it will be exterminated'.[41] The disclosure of, in Prendick's words, 'Monsters manufactured' (p. 78) draws attention to the potential mutability of humans and of their inseparability from beasts. Moreau confidently insists that 'the great difference between man and monkey is [only] in the larynx, ... in the incapacity to frame delicately different sound-symbols by which thought could be sustained' (p. 79). Although Prendick objects to this claim, the fact that Moreau has produced animals that talk supports his own case rather than that of his inquisitor.

The tenuous hold on humanity possessed by Moreau's Beast Folk is maintained only by the ritual saying of the Law. In this Prendick is persuaded by the Ape Man and other beasts to participate. The Law itself consists of injunctions to act in ways that would define its adherents as 'Men'. However, the directions are negative in their formulation:

> 'Not to go on all-Fours; *that* is the Law. Are we not Men?'
> 'Not to suck up Drink; *that* is the Law. Are we not Men?'
> 'Not to eat Flesh or Fish; *that* is the Law. Are we not Men?'
> 'Not to claw the Bark of trees; *that* is the Law. Are we not Men?'
> (p. 63)

And so on. Noticeably, each law prohibits the exhibition of bestial behaviour. It does not advocate conformity to a code that characterises civilised conduct because the Law recognises no such trait as identifiable in itself. Since, then, this part of the Law prohibits animal acts, it confirms their continuing hold, hinting at the constant threat of regression, rather than affirming human qualities in themselves.

An illustration of Moreau's project is provided by the relation of how he made his first man from a gorilla soon after landing on the island eleven years previously. He had spent a week moulding him, with the brain causing the most difficulty. The experiment's racial connotation is clear: 'I thought him a fair specimen of the negroid type when I had done him' (p. 83). The modified gorilla was taught the rudiments of English, the alphabet (at which he was very slow), and the basics of counting. The possibility of the gorilla's education might not have seemed so fantastic to Wells's readers as we might assume. Just a year after the publication of *The Island of Doctor Moreau*, for example, *The Strand Magazine* reported on the case of Joe, an 'arboreal anthropoid ape', who 'can, in fact, do almost anything that a human being can do except talk'.[42] Albeit mainly by imitation, Joe had learned how to sleep, bath, dress, eat, drink, work, and relax like a human. He even writes on command, though 'The result is a curious collection of Simian hieroglyphics which may be understood in the forests of Borneo, but not in ignorant America'.[43] Joe had been exhibited extensively throughout the United States, and had recently spent several months in Boston. The anonymous contributor of this article also reported that Professor William James of Harvard University had given a demonstration of Joe's intelligence to a select audience.

Whatever the potential accomplishments of the ape – and Moreau's improved gorilla begins his new existence 'with a clean sheet, mentally; [he] had no memories left in his mind of what he had been' (p. 83) – Wells's monkey reverts. Moreau finds him one day 'squatting up in a tree gibbering at two of the Kanakas who had been teasing him' (p. 84), and has to threaten and shame him.

Moreau, symbolic of God as creator, discovers that his contemplation of the beings that he at first thinks indisputably human, reveals ever more of their animal traits. Despite his determination that each experiment will manufacture a rational creature and will 'burn out all the animal', they revert. 'As soon as my hand is taken from them the beast begins to creep back, begins to assert itself again' (p. 86). The battle between the Beast People's instinct and their hypnotically induced requirement to obey the Law, which they often break, especially at night, may be taken as a reflection of the enduring struggle faced by humankind to fight off the animal urges from which we can never fully free ourselves.

In addition to the biological and theological readings of Wells's text, it is also possible to read the narrative as an allegory of colonialism in which the Beast People are the colonised. Prendick's adaptation to his surroundings – 'I say I became habituated to the Beast People, that a thousand things that had seemed unnatural and repulsive speedily became natural and ordinary to me' (p. 94) – sees him going native. However, by the time six more weeks have elapsed, Prendick has 'lost every feeling but dislike and abhorrence for these infamous experiments of Moreau's' and he is desperate to escape 'these horrible caricatures of my Maker's image' and to get back to the 'sweet and wholesome intercourse of men' (p. 109).

Prendick spends ten more months on the island 'as an intimate of these half-humanised brutes' (p. 138). He complains of this period that 'The Monkey Man' took himself to be his (Prendick's) equal because he has the same number of fingers and 'was for ever jabbering at me, jabbering the most arrant nonsense' (p. 140). The Monkey Man distinguishes 'little thinks', the 'sane everyday interests of life' (p. 140), from 'big thinks', which comprise larger speculations whose meanings may be lost on him but which he nevertheless enjoys memorising and reciting to others of the Beast People. The plain-thinking Prendick invents 'some very curious "big thinks" for his especial use' and thinks him 'the silliest creature I ever met; he had developed in the most wonderful way the distinctive silliness of man without losing one jot of the natural folly of a monkey' (p. 140).

After a while, however, the increase in loudness and decrease in comprehensibility of the Monkey Man's jabber as it grows 'more and more simian' (p. 140) is one of the signs by which the reversion of the Beast People is detected. The creatures' 'growing coarseness of articulation, a growing disinclination to talk' (p. 140) transmits their slide from human back to animal traits. 'Can you imagine language,' Prendick asks of us, 'once clear-cut and exact, softening and guttering, losing shape and import, becoming mere lumps of sound again?' (p. 140).

The alteration of states is as true of Prendick as it is of his bestial companions:

> I too must have undergone strange changes, [sic] My clothes hung
> about me as yellow rags, through whose rents glowed the tanned

skin. My hair grew long, and became matted together. I am told that even now my eyes have a strange brightness, a swift alertness of movement. (p. 142)

Once escaped from the island and returned to England, Prendick, for many years, 'could not persuade myself that the men and women I met were not also another, still passably human, Beast People . . . and that they would presently begin to revert, to show first this bestial mark and then that' (p. 149). The protagonist is left at the end with a dual vision as the perception gained from his experiences intrudes from time to time into the normality of everyday life around him which is thus rendered in some way alien to him and to us.[44] His discomfiture has led him to remove from London to 'near the broad free downland' (p. 150):

> When I lived in London the horror was wellnigh insupportable . . . I would go out into the streets to fight with my delusion, and prowling women would mew after me, furtive craving men glance jealously at me, weary pale workers go coughing by me, with tired eyes and eager paces like wounded deer dripping blood, old people, bent and dull, pass murmuring to themselves, and all unheeding a ragged tail of gibing children. (p. 150)

Even when he seeks relief in a chapel 'it seemed that the preacher gibbered Big Thinks even as the Ape Man had done' (p. 150). Prendick cuts a forlorn figure when he announces that his solace lies in solitude and the stars. In his contemplation of the heavens and his consolation that it must be there 'in the vast and eternal laws of matter, and not in the daily cares and sins and troubles of men, that whatever is more than animal within us must find its solace and its hope' (p. 151), the metaphysical and the misanthropic combine. In London Prendick had tried to avoid 'the blank expressionless faces of people in trains and omnibuses . . . [who] seemed no more my fellow-creatures than dead bodies would be' (p. 150). Prendick's diagnosis applies more to himself than to the denizens of the capital: 'And even it seemed that I, too, was not a reasonable creature, but only an animal tormented with some strange disorder in its brain, that sent it to wander alone, like a sheep stricken with the gid' (p. 150).

In the texts I have looked at so far, white apes (and the black-faced ape who is created by one white man and is the companion of another) have emerged to narrow the distance between the middle-class readership and those who have been branded as different by racial terminology. The fascination and fear evoked by these pallid primates reflects the growing conviction that socially and psychologically, as well as biologically, they could no longer be kept at bay.

For a better understanding of the movement I am describing here I want to turn to Freud's idea of the uncanny, which has to do with a feeling produced by unfamiliarity with one's environment, an unfamiliarity caused not by complete unacquaintance but by repression:

> an uncanny experience occurs either when infantile complexes which have been repressed are once more revived by some impression, or when primitive beliefs which have been surmounted seem once more to be confirmed ... When we consider that primitive beliefs are most intimately connected with infantile complexes, and are, in fact, based on them, we shall not be greatly astonished to find that the distinction is often a hazy one.[45]

Freud's identification of 'primitive' beliefs with 'infantile complexes' owes much to contemporary thought on race. By this time 'the idea that the mental processes of savage man were similar to those of civilized children had long been ... commonplace'.[46] Accordingly, Freud's explanation probably tells us more about these influences than they do about the uncanny itself. The beliefs that characterise the infant and the primitive and which define the uncanny would seem to be animism and the effacement of the distinction between the imagination (psychical reality) and material reality (p. 365). The point of the uncanny, writes Freud, is that through repetition and recurrence it forces our acquaintance with that which has been transformed by repression into anxiety so that what really is familiar seems strange and frightening (pp. 363–4).

In the texts I have discussed up to now the sense that the self is in some way incomplete is communicated by doubling. (The Nether World assumes an upper one; the Morlocks live below ground, feeding off the Eloi above ground; Jekyll transforms into Hyde; the Ape Man is animal and human, one of the Beast People; Dorian has his portrait.) Whether the narrative presents the self as an individual (Jekyll, for example) or as a society (*The Time*

Machine), the duality makes manifest something that has not been acknowledged; something that has been repressed.

Freud saw the double as playing a large part in the uncanny. Summarising Otto Rank, he writes that 'the "double" was originally an insurance against the destruction of the ego' (p. 356); in other words, a defence against mortality. This urge Freud attributes to 'the primary narcissism which dominates the mind of the child and of primitive man' (p. 357) (again setting the infant and the non-European on a level well below that of the civilised adult).

Freud looks at what happens to the double after this primary stage. He advances two later functions of the double. The first is its place in the formation of the conscience, that special part of the ego 'which is able to stand over against the rest of the ego, which has the function of observing and criticizing the self and of exercising a censorship within the mind' (p. 357). Here the idea of the double is associated with self-observation and self-criticism. The second function involves 'all the unfulfilled but possible futures to which we still like to cling in phantasy, all the strivings of the ego which adverse external circumstances have crushed, and all our suppressed acts of volition which nourish in us the illusion of free will' (p. 358).

The relevance of the uncanny to the sighting and habitat of the white ape seems quite clear. The whiteness of the ape subjectifies the other, while the apishness of the white creatures objectifies the self. The animal's appearance forces an admission of the damage that may occur if it is ignored – or repressed. Its discovery (really a rediscovery) will result in either a self-destructive fascination or the suffering of retribution. On one level, an important one, these texts are issuing a warning of what might happen if cognition does not alter or expand. In social terms, the evolution of the double, which Freud sees as originating from a self-defensive impulse and whose early friendly aspect later inspires terror, encourages (in the narrator or reader, if not in the protagonist) the creation of a social observer or conscience and the recognition of the social other.

Quoting the views of Jentsch, Freud cites as an instance of the uncanny 'doubts as to whether an apparently animate being is really alive; or conversely, whether a lifeless object might not be in fact animate' (p. 347). Dorian Gray's portrait exemplifies this, of course, and Wilde's text is also suggestive of another of Jentsch's attributions of the uncanny: the feeling of intellectual uncertainty that is essential to it. Freud glosses the theory thus: 'The better orientated in his environment a person is, the less readily will he get the impression of something uncanny in regard to the objects and events in it' (p. 341). We can infer from this that the prominence given to the uncanny in so many popular texts of the *fin de siècle* communicates the sense of a lack of knowledge of one's surroundings. Indeed, this point is strengthened when we recall that Freud's original word for the uncanny (unheimlich) translates literally as unhomely (p. 399, Editor's note). Worries about the invasion or loss of one's home or about encounters with creatures that are without (in the senses of outside and lacking a home) are fundamental here. That the 'unhomely' should turn out to have once been familiar before being repressed underscores its appropriateness to the social situation of the 1880s and the 1890s. The feeling of unfamiliarity, arising from the perception of a social threat from a discontented pool of the unemployed or from confident, organised labour, and from upward and downward social mobility, is often suggested by the projection of doubleness (Jekyll and Hyde, the Eloi and the Morlocks) or by confusion between the animate and the lifeless (Dorian's portrait). Easily discernible in these projections is the measure of objectification that allows for self-criticism and the pursuit of desire that is otherwise suppressed. The white ape is common to both these processes.

Of course, the most famous white ape of them all did not appear until 1912 and was the creation of a North American. Tarzan is a different manner of creature altogether, and the positive, romantic representation of him would seem to close down all those troublesome questions that were posed by the white apes of the *fin de siècle*, of whom he is, as a child, a contemporary. (His parents sailed for Africa in 1888, and his mother would give birth to him shortly after arrival.[47]) Even the geography of the Tarzan story provides a bulwark against the worried introspection of the late nineteenth century. Tarzan, in Africa, is at a safe distance from the society whose assumptions his existence seems to throw into doubt. And when, at the end of *Tarzan of the Apes*, Tarzan does enter white civilisation (in this case the United States) his appearance is threatening only to a few undesirable individuals, not to the idea of human nature or to the social fabric. Indeed, it also appears to mark his introduction into the world of money and capital, which shouldn't surprise anyone with any knowledge of his creator's wholehearted grasping of it.[48]

The phrase 'white ape' occurs several times in *Tarzan of the Apes*, though it is first applied not to Tarzan but to his father, Lord Greystoke, while Chapter V, the chapter after which the term is first used, is titled 'The White Ape'. In this chapter Kala, the ape, has adopted baby Greystoke, who has now been named 'tarzan', meaning 'White-Skin' in the ape language. Tarzan, the white ape, is blessed with the 'divine power of reason' (p. 44); his 'healthy mind' is 'endowed by inheritance with more than ordinary reasoning powers' (p. 56). His superiority of intelligence over that of the apes, whose language has very few words (pp. 45–6), is evident. At ten years old he is able, through his discovery of children's books and a dictionary in his late parents' cabin, to begin to teach himself to read, a process that continues over the next seven years, by which time he has learnt that he is 'a M-A-N' and his companions 'A-P-E-S' (p. 55). The boy Tarzan symbolises the white ape as a rational creature. By the age of eighteen he can read and write English but not speak it (p. 71).

Tarzan is not the only creature identified as a white ape. Jane Porter is referred to as a 'hairless white ape' (p. 168) as she is abducted by the cruel and capricious chief ape Terkoz.[49] Terkoz is carrying Jane 'toward a fate worse than death' (p. 168), a fate from which it is Tarzan's role to rescue her. When Tarzan fights Terkoz, Jane, resting passively, if not almost in orgasm, against a phallic growth – 'her lithe, young form flattened against the trunk of a great tree, her hands tight pressed against her rising and falling bosom, and her eyes wide with mingled horror, fascination, fear, and admiration' – looks on at the 'primordial ape battle with the primeval man for possession of a woman' (p. 171). The battle is not just between ape Terkoz and man Tarzan, but between ape and man ways of behaving towards women. It is true that, faced with Jane's repulsion of him, Tarzan 'took his woman in his arms and carried her into the jungle' just as 'his first ancestor would have done' (p. 172), but his conduct is superior to the bestial: it combines natural animality with social instinct. His face is 'A perfect type of the strongly masculine, unmarred by dissipation, or brutal or degrading passions' (p. 178). It is a 'noble face' that proclaims 'chivalry', and of his new predicament Tarzan 'felt rather than reasoned that he must meet it as a man and not as an ape'

(p. 179). Tarzan differs from the white apes discussed earlier in this essay in that he can blend positively the natural and the animal with the social and the human. His creator, it seems, seeks to instil the essence of natural but noble masculinity into a culture that has seen it either debased or rarefied. Thus, to Jane, Tarzan is: 'a perfect creature! There could be naught of cruelty or baseness beneath that godlike exterior' (p. 180).

Tarzan's recognition of Jane's struggle against being taken by force gives him choice, and it is in the awareness of this that he is distinguished fundamentally from the non-human (and from those other white apes we have encountered who slip towards bestiality rather than step up from it). When Tarzan leads Jane to a bower he responds to her alarm by giving her his knife for the night and by lying outside. We are told that 'He had not in one swift transition become a polished gentleman from a savage ape-man, but at last the instincts of the former predominated, and over all was the desire to please the woman he loved, and to appear well in her eyes' (p. 185). This, with his gesture moments before of kissing the locket he has just given her and which she has kissed, is seen as the 'hall-mark of his aristocratic birth, the natural out-cropping of many generations of fine breeding, an hereditary instinct of graciousness which a lifetime of uncouth and savage training and environment could not eradicate' (p. 185). There is an inversion of the conventional white-ape motif here, then. Instead of the threat posed by a natural inheritance to the social, cultured being, heredity overcomes nature. A deep, almost desperate conservatism is at play, for the manoeuvre can work only by naturalising social distinctions. Burroughs's stress on aristocratic fine breeding and graciousness suggests to us that a working-class Tarzan might have behaved very differently.

Besides Burroughs's use of the creature, there is another danger in the figure of the white ape. In separating by projection the beastly from the human, writers and their readers deny that which is human in them. As the scientist Stephen Jay Gould has quite properly complained, by attributing to our 'apish ancestry' the aspects of ourselves we want to criticise – 'brutality, aggression, selfishness; in short, general nastiness',[50] and contrasting it with our better sides, which we think of as uniquely human, we perpetuate a dualism of body and mind – of which Freud himself is guilty. The trouble with this, as Gould rightly says, is that it tries to remove us from biology by blaming our unpleasantnesses on past animality and trumpeting our virtues as the result of our humanity. Reminding us that the altruism on which we proudly rest our claims to civilisation may in fact be compatible with the selfish urge to preservation because the individual's chances of genetic and biological survival may sometimes best be found through the survival of kin, Gould suggests that 'Basic human kindness may be as "animal" as human nastiness' (p. 266). We must refute any thesis that specific behaviour is genetically determined; for to say so is to blame the beast and not ourselves for creating it:

> Our genetic make-up permits a wide range of behaviors ... Upbringing, culture, class, status, and all the intangibles that we call 'free will,' determine how we restrict our behaviors from the wide spectrum – extreme altruism to extreme selfishness – that our genes permit. (p. 266)

To blame brutish behaviour on an inheritance which we cannot always suppress is to allow for the identification of certain people in our society (at different times, the working classes, immigrants, sexually active women) as more bestial than others. This labelling is used to denote criminality. Gould, summarising Cesare Lombroso's ideas from the 1870s of a biological basis to crime, writes:

> Biological theories of criminality were scarcely new, but Lombroso gave the argument a novel, evolutionary twist. Born criminals are not simply deranged or diseased; they are, literally, throwbacks to a previous evolutionary stage. The hereditary characteristics of our primitive and apish ancestors remain in our genetic repertoire. Some unfortunate men are born with an unusually large number of these ancestral characters. (p. 223)

But these claims of biological determinism are 'used by the leaders of class-stratified societies to assert that a current social order must prevail because it is in the law of nature' (p. 224). Since the strategies and figures of domination *within* a society are similar to those employed against another society, it is not surprising that a key creature should be the ape, which combines social with racial savagery.

Gould writes of biological determinism that it shows our 'continuing attempt to exonerate a society in which so many of us flourish by blaming the victim' (p. 224). What Gould asks of the biological determinists, we might well say of the creation of the white ape:

> Why do we wish to fob off responsibility for our violence and sexism upon our genes? The hall-mark of humanity is not only our mental capacity but also our mental flexibility. We have made our world and we can change it. (p. 228)

We have no need to make apes of others.

Notes

1. Charles Darwin, *The Descent of Man, and Selection in Relation to Sex* [1871], with an Introduction by John Tyler Bonner and Robert M. May (Princeton: Princeton University Press, 1981), Part I, pp. 227–8.
2. Ibid., p. 235.
3. Ibid.
4. 'Of all the differences between the races of man, the colour of the skin is the most conspicuous and one of the best marked.' Ibid., p. 241.
5. George Stocking has distinguished between the 'soft' rural primitivism 'of the preindustrial world, marginalized in England and still flourishing on the Celtic fringe' and urban primitivism, whose subjects dwelt in slums which were 'so far removed from the amenities and the morality of civilized life that many observers, including Friedrich Engels and Henry Mayhew, were impelled to use racial analogies to capture the sense of difference'. George W. Stocking, Jr, *Victorian Anthropology* (New York: The Free Press, 1987), p. 213. Thus even to write against urban conditions was often to circulate racial images. My attention in this essay is more on urban than rural primitivism.

   For more on the intellectual and social contexts of views of the primitive and the savage, see Douglas Lorimer, *Colour, Class and the Victorians: English Attitudes to the Negro in the Mid-Nineteenth Century* (Leicester: Leicester University Press, 1978), and Brian V. Street, *The Savage in Literature: Representations of 'primitive' society in English fiction 1858–1920* (London: Routledge and Kegan Paul, 1975).
6. Nederveen Pieterse makes a similar observation: 'Stereotypes are reconstructed and reasserted precisely when existing hierarchies are

being challenged.' Jan Nederveen Pieterse, *White on Black: Images of Africa and Blacks in Western Popular Culture* (New Haven: Yale University Press, 1992), p. 223.

7. William Greenslade, *Degeneration, Culture and the Novel 1880–1940* (Cambridge: Cambridge University Press, 1994), p. 108.

8. Gareth Stedman Jones, *Outcast London: A Study in the Relationship between Classes in Victorian Society* (Oxford: Clarendon Press, 1971), p. 281.

9. Ibid.

10. Wim Neetens, *Writing and Democracy: Literature, Politics and Culture in Transition* (London: Harvester Wheatsheaf, 1991), p. 37. Women were denied the vote until 1918.

11. Jones, *Outcast London*, p. 291.

12. Ibid., pp. 290–6.

13. A concise summary of these events (of which there are many accounts) may be found in Helen Merrell Lynd, *England in the Eighteen-Eighties: Toward a Social Basis for Freedom* (London: Frank Cass & Co., Ltd, 1968), chap. 7, 'Organized Labor'.

14. Ibid., p. 289.

15. Karl Beckson, *London in the 1890s: A Cultural History* (New York: W.W. Norton & Co., 1992), p. 18.

16. J.F.C. Harrison, *Late Victorian Britain 1875–1901* (London: Fontana, 1990), p. 217.

17. L. Perry Curtis, *Apes and Angels: The Irishman in Victorian Caricature* (Newton Abbot: David & Charles, 1971), p. 2.

18. Lynd, *The Eighteen-Eighties*, p. 286.

19. Jones, *Outcast London*, p. 285.

20. George Gissing, *The Nether World* (Oxford: Oxford University Press, 1992), p. 6. Further page references will be given in parentheses.

21. Most, but not all. Using the Crystal Palace as a setting, the narrator offers a powerful criticism of those games that are designed to prove 'muscularity' at the same time as they 'appeal to the patriotism of the throng'. The coconut shy, for example, has wooden models of the 'treacherous Afghan' and the 'base African', while at another stall, where one's strength is measured by how far a ball can be sent flying when a spring is hit, the place where one strikes the mallet is marked by 'the head of some other recent foeman'. It is to Gissing's credit that he condemns through his narrator the use of these images, but in complaining that 'nowhere could be found any amusement appealing to the mere mind, or calculated to effeminate by encouraging a love of beauty' (p. 107), he replaces racial with gender stereotypes. Indeed, the descriptions of Clem as 'savage' deploy racial ideas to signal her failure to live up to the ideal of the feminine. For more on

how 'Clem's atavism is a function of her deviation from conventional womanhood', see Greenslade, *Degeneration, Culture and the Novel*, p. 76.

22. Sally Ledger, 'In Darkest England: The Terror of Degeneration in *Fin de Siècle* Britain', *Literature & History*, 3rd series, 4/2 (Autumn 1995), p. 81.

23. His other solution is to 'bring to bear on the new order of things the constant influence of music' (p. 109).

24. John Goode, 'George Gissing's *The Nether World*', in David Howard, John Lucas, John Goode, eds, *Tradition and tolerance in nineteenth-century fiction. Critical essays on some English and American novels* (London: Routledge and Kegan Paul, 1966), p. 238.

25. Charles Darwin, *The Origin of Species by Means of Natural Selection*, last (6) edn [1872] (London: Watts & Co. [n.d.]), p. 47.

26. Ibid.

27. Ibid., p. 148.

28. See, for example, William Greenslade, who summarises the belief of '[Francis] Galton and others ... that the "fittest", in the sense of "healthiest" stock – the countrymen – were less able to adapt, and so were ill-equipped to survive the special exigencies of urban life'. Greenslade, *Degeneration*, p. 42.

Greenslade comments more generally that:

> Degeneration was at the root of what was, in part, an enabling strategy by which the conventional and respectable classes could justify and articulate their hostility to the deviant, the diseased and the subversive. (p. 2)

29. I shall be referring to the following edition: Robert Louis Stevenson, 'The Strange Case of Dr. Jekyll and Mr. Hyde', in *Dr. Jekyll and Mr Hyde, The Merry Men and Other Tales* (London: Dent, 1925). Page references will be given parenthetically.

30. I discuss this in more detail in Tim Youngs, 'Stevenson's Monkey-Business: *The Strange Case of Dr Jekyll and Mr Hyde*', in Peter Liebregts and Wim Tigges, eds, *Beauty and the Beast: Christina Rossetti, Walter Pater, R.L. Stevenson and their Contemporaries* (Amsterdam: Rodopi, 1996), pp. 157–70.

31. Ibid., p. 168.

32. Quoted in Patrick Brantlinger and Richard Boyle, 'The Education of Edward Hyde: Stevenson's "Gothic Gnome" and the Mass Readership of Late-Victorian England', in William Veeder and Gordon Hirsch, eds, *Dr Jekyll and Mr Hyde after One Hundred Years* (Chicago: Chicago University Press, 1988), p. 272.

33. Ibid., p. 278.

34. Oscar Wilde, *The Picture of Dorian Gray* (Oxford: Oxford University Press, 1981), p. 18. Further page references will be given parenthetically.

35. The narrator seems to share Dorian's anti-Semitism. Chapter VII opens thus:

> For some reason or other, the house was crowded that night, and the fat Jew manager who met them at the door was beaming from ear to ear with an oily, tremulous smile. He escorted them to their box with a sort of pompous humility, waving his fat jewelled hands, and talking at the top of his voice. Dorian Gray loathed him more than ever. (p. 80)

36. H.G. Wells, 'The Time Machine', in *Selected Short Stories* (Harmondsworth: Penguin, 1958), p. 45. Further references will be given in the text.

37. I discuss this aspect of the story in relation to the tale's narrative structure in Tim Youngs, 'Wells's Fifth Dimension: *The Time Machine* at the Fin de Siècle', in Tracey Hill and Alan Marshall, eds, *Decadence and Danger: Writing, History and the Fin de Siècle* (Bath: Sulis Press, forthcoming).

38. I use 'man' advisedly. Elaine Showalter has described quest romances such as *The Time Machine* as allegorised journeys into the male self. Elaine Showalter, 'The Apocalyptic Fables of H.G. Wells', in John Stokes, ed., *Fin de Siècle/Fin du Globe: Fears and Fantasies of the Late Nineteenth Century* (Basingstoke: Macmillan, 1992), p. 73.

39. H.G. Wells, *The Island of Doctor Moreau* [1896] (Harmondsworth: Penguin, 1946), 'Introduction' [n.p.]. Further page references will be given parenthetically. This is not one of the most satisfactory editions of the novel, but it is probably one of the most accessible to readers of the present volume. See Nancy Steffen-Fluhr, 'The Definitive *Moreau*', *Science-Fiction Studies* 20, 3 (1993), 433–9.

40. Wells himself studied under Huxley in 1884–85, which he later called 'the most educational year of my life'. H.G. Wells, *Experiment in Autobiography: Discoveries and Conclusions of a Very Ordinary Brain (Since 1866)* (New York: The Macmillan Company, 1934), p. 161.

41. Darwin, *Origin of Species*, p. 76.

42. Anonymous, 'An Educated Monkey', *The Strand Magazine* XIV (July–December 1897), 473.

43. Ibid., p. 474.

44. Wells also adopts this technique in *The War of the Worlds* (1898).

45. Sigmund Freud, 'The Uncanny' [1919], in *Art and Literature*, The Penguin Freud Library, vol. 14, ed. Albert Dickson (London: Penguin, 1990), p. 372. Further page references will be given parenthetically.

46. George W. Stocking, Jr, 'The Dark-Skinned Savage: The Image of Primitive Man in Evolutionary Anthropology', in *Race, Culture, and Evolution: Essays in the History of Anthropology* (Chicago: The University of Chicago Press, 1982), p. 126. See pp. 125–7 for more on the development of recapitulationist theories.

47. Edgar Rice Burroughs, *Tarzan of the Apes*, 5th edn (London: Methuen & Co., Ltd, 1919), p. 3. Further page references will be given parenthetically.

48. On Burroughs's view of writing as a commercial activity and on his financial ventures, see the very interesting information in Irwin Porges, *Edgar Rice Burroughs: The Man Who Created Tarzan*, 2 vols (New York: Ballantine Books, 1975).

49. Torgovnick has noticed interestingly that Terkoz leaves behind Esmeralda, Jane's African-American servant (who is made a figure of fun throughout by Burroughs), and that this is 'typical of the [Tarzan] novels, in which black women invariably incite lust in villainous hearts'. Torgovnick also makes the astute comment that in this scene the threat of miscegenation is 'disguised as a species difference'. In other words, for Terkoz to have abducted Esmeralda would not have been so thrilling because it would have been like mating with like. 'Burroughs believed blacks to be a midway stage of evolution from ape to white humans.' Marianna Torgovnick, *Gone Primitive: Savage Intellects, Modern Lives* (Chicago: The University of Chicago Press), p. 53.

50. Stephen Jay Gould, *Ever Since Darwin: Reflections in Natural History* (London: Penguin Books, 1991), p. 260. Further page references will be given parenthetically.

9 Hunting the pederast: Richard Burton's exotic erotology

Chris White

Orientalist Man who has travelled extensively.[1]

In 1886 Richard Burton (1821–90) sent an account of his public
career to his civil service employers as part of his request to retire on
a full pension at the age of sixty-five. He listed his nineteen years
in the Bombay Army, the nine years he spent on active service with
the Sind Survey, the twenty-nine languages he had learnt and the
exams he had passed in eight eastern languages, and the forty-
eight works he had published.[2] His active participation in the material practices of colonialism and the anthropological bent in the
visiting and interpreting of alien cultures of his published works
make him in effect the epitome of the 'Orientalist'. Burton can be
seen, in his life and works, to accept and validate 'the basic distinction between East and West as the starting point for elaborate
theories, epics, novels, social descriptions . . . concerning the Orient,
its people, customs, "mind", destiny, and so on', and in his involvement in a quest to find 'a different type of sexuality, perhaps
more libertine and less guilt-ridden', as reinforcing the racist stereotype of Oriental eroticism as excessive, debauched and immoral.[3]
Edward Said sees Burton:

> both as a rebel against authority (hence his identification with the
> East as a place of freedom from Victorian moral authority) and as
> a potential agent of authority in the East. (p. 195)

This version of Burton is echoed in the work of other contemporary commentators, who refer to his 'semi-voyeuristic erudition in

matters of pederasty',[4] view him as 'delineat[ing] the geography of a transgressive space ... in which androgyny, pederasty and perversion held sway',[5] or as 'fascinated by the sex-life of Orientals'.[6] The combination of prurience and power ascribed to Burton positions him wholly within the Orientalist discourse. The white man has the power not only to determine the political and religious systems of the Orient, but also to interpret any existing culture, while also being able to seek gratification from those social structures and sexual practices rejected as inferior, corrupt and licentious. But Said allows that Burton was knowledgeable about the 'systems of information, behaviour and belief' (p. 195) of the Orient and Islam, to the extent that he was able, disguised as an Indian Muslim doctor, to perform a pilgrimage to Mecca at a time when westerners were liable to be put to death for entering the holy city. The representation of Burton as a racist imperialist or as just another exponent of Orientalism, however, is not adequate or wholly valid. In this essay I aim to demonstrate that what can be found in Burton's work, especially in his translations of erotic classics, are a plethora of satirical textual games in which he mocks western attitudes to sexuality, and elevates eastern mores and practices as superior, more ethical, more honest. Thus, in addition to those elements of Burton's works that inevitably reflect the prevailing ideas of racism and imperialism, there is a substantial critique of both the racial stereotypes and of the right relationship between East and West, performed not through explicit political challenge and argument, but rather through a combination of allowing eastern cultures to speak for themselves in their artistic products, and an extensive system of demonstrating the complexity of the cultural formations from which those texts emerged.

At the heart of this essay is an absence, a text that existed once, but which never proceeded beyond the stage of being a manuscript. During the 1880s, while suffering from ill health, Sir Richard Burton translated and published a series of erotic classics. Following publication of his translations of the *Kama Sutra* in 1883,[7] and *Ananga-Ranga* in 1885,[8] came *The Perfumed Garden of Sheikh Nefzawi* in 1886,[9] an incomplete edition omitting the sections on pederasty and sodomy. Then, in the days before his death, in 1890, Burton completed his translation of the missing parts of *The Perfumed Garden*, designing it to be published as a supplement to the original 1886 edition. His wife Isabel burnt the manuscript, along

with an unknown quantity of other material, an act which has led
to her going down in history as one of the greatest bowdlerising
vandals of all time.[10] Isabel defended her action in the *Morning
Post*, claiming that her aim was to save her husband's soul. Having defended the purity of his character and work, Isabel Burton
declared:

> What a gentleman, a scholar, a man of the world may write when
> living, he would see very differently to what the poor soul would
> see standing naked before God, with its good or evil deeds alone to
> answer for.[11]

The man may have been pure, but his work by implication was evil.

The reasons for the partial nature of the 1886 edition are unknown, but seem to demonstrate a caution concerning obscenity
in Burton's work. While the *Kama Sutra* and *Ananga-Ranga* are
religio-ethical works which incorporate material on sex and sexuality into their discussions, *The Perfumed Garden* is primarily
what the *Kama Sutra* has always been represented as in the West,
a how-to-do-it manual with an emphasis on stimulating the desires of the reader. In view of this, the omission of the pederastic
passages represents a strategic decision by Burton: the world might
tolerate instructions on heterosexual intercourse, but in a culture
where sodomy was punishable by life imprisonment,[12] the risk
of publishing this particular information must have appeared too
great.

Burton's translations of these erotic texts both partake of an
Orientalist discourse and offer a critique of the western judgment
of eastern mores and morals. As late as 1898, Sir Hugh Clifford
wrote:

> The glamour which will always hang about the rags of the East
> while our world lasts ... viewed at the right time, and seen in this
> deceptive light, [means] all manner of things in themselves hopelessly
> evil and unlovely have the power to fascinate as far more attractive
> objects too often fail to do ... The atmosphere is apt to destroy a
> man's ability to scale things accurately; it deprives him of his sense
> of proportion.[13]

Clifford's reference to the glamour of the East deploys an Orientalist exoticism, which he sees as a deception that will blind the

colonialists to the truth of their role and their rightness. The East is corrosive of the West's masculinity and plainness. That metaphor of 'glamour' stands in for a surface that is misleading and implicitly rather flashy, overstated, not marked by sobriety and understatement. The East's culture is 'evil' and 'unlovely', where the functional and reproductive West is good and lovely. Burton's accounts of eastern erotic exoticism are more modulated – more corrupted in Clifford's terms – than this crude condemnation. In the 'Terminal Essay' to his translation of *The Thousand Nights and a Night*,[14] published in 1885, and in the footnotes to Scheherezad's tales, he produces a version of eastern eroticism which is fantastical and ironic, despite its racist overtones.

Burton's inclusion of sexualised anecdotes and sexual information in the footnotes to the tales frequently seems to be purely gratuitous, their relevance to the text of the tale being at best tangential. In the convoluted plot of 'Nur Al-Din Ali' is an episode in which, to prove the true identity of the son, the Wazir fabricates a trick of condemning the son to death by crucifixion for not putting sufficient pepper in the pomegranate preserve. The Wazir asks the son about his thoughts, to which the son replies, 'Of maggoty heads like thine;[1] for an thou had one ounce of sense thou hadst not treated me thus.' Burton's note one reads as follows:

> Here good blood, driven to bay, speaks out boldly. But, as a rule, the humblest and mildest Eastern when in despair turns round upon his oppressors like a wild cat. Some of the criminals whom Fath Ali Shah of Persia put to death by chopping down the fork, beginning at the scrotum, abused his mother till the knife reached their vitals and they could no longer speak.[15]

The relationship between the text and the note is opaque at best. Bestial barbarism emerges as an accepted social relationship in eastern cultures, on a continuum with insults. But, more significantly for Burton, this footnote evidences the straightforward, physically courageous masculinity represented by eastern men in his Orientalist erotology.

While lauding the eastern male, Burton cannot be regarded as anti-racist, since he establishes a hierarchy of non-white races. Burton's racism admits of differences between the Arab and the 'negro', the former emerging as far superior to the latter. The difference that is foregrounded is that of penis size. He pursues his animalistic metaphors in one of the very first notes to *The Nights*, where the history behind the relationship between King Shahryar and his last wife Shahrázád is recounted. The cause of the King's murderous revenge, in marrying and killing a succession of women, lies in two episodes of finding his first wife, and that of his brother, in compromising situations with black men. In Burton's translation these two men are respectively described as 'a black cook of loathsome aspect and foul with kitchen grease and grime' (*Tales*, p. 4), and a 'big slobbering blackamoor' (*Tales*, p. 6). (In the most recent full translation of *The Nights*, the equivalent lines read 'a black slave' and a 'gigantic negro'.[16]) Burton's commentary on his blatantly racist version of these passages extends and elaborates his disparagement of black men:

> Debauched women prefer negroes on account of the size of their parts. I measured one man in Somali-land who, when quiescent, numbered nearly six inches. This is a characteristic of the negro race and of African animals; *e.g.* the horse; whereas the pure Arab, man and beast, is below the average of Europe; one of the best proofs by the by, that the Egyptian is not an Asiatic, but a negro partially white-washed. (*Tales*, p. 6)

The construction of such a scheme of differentiation reveals Burton's participation in the prevailing race ideas of his time, and the appropriation and partial transformation of those ideas, to his own ends. The Arab must be, according to this logic, closer to the European than to the negro, since Arabic culture and peoples are admirable for their cultural sophistication and historical longevity; negroes are not, and here is physical proof, gathered first hand by the author, as evidence for the superiority of some non-white races over other non-white races.

Fundamental to Burton's representation of Oriental erotology is a valuing of some aspects of Arab culture, but this is joined with a defensiveness about the content of the texts, which leads to effective self-censorship by Burton. His translation of *The Nights* appeared under the imprint of the Kama Shastra Society, which claimed to have offices in Benares and London, while actually being based solely in Stoke Newington. The man responsible for the printing of the work was Leonard Smithers, publisher and importer of pornography, prosecuted for, amongst other crimes, importing and selling Emile Zola's scandalously sexual novel *La Terre*.[17] Thus the translation, while it is claimed as an honourable and respectable project, is implicated in the mechanisms of the production of pornography. Yet Burton insists, despite the material production of the text, on the scholarly nature of his enterprise.

Burton claimed this edition as the first full and unexpurgated European translation of *The Nights*,[18] and calmed his wife's fears of scandal by portraying it as a scholarly and educative text. Since my object of study here is Burton, and not the texts of *The Nights* themselves, I shall be focusing on Burton's 'Terminal Essay' to the tales, rather than on the tales themselves. Included in Burton's 'Terminal Essay' to *The Nights* is Section D, a fifty-page disquisition on 'Pederasty'. The form of the 'Essay' is a scholarly supplement to his translation of *The Nights*, but it is almost entirely tangential to it. The 'Essay' makes a number of brief references and has comparative footnotes to the tales, making connections between Burton's historical and anthropological studies and the incidence of pederasty in the tales. The most blatant example of irrelevance is displayed in the discussion of lesbianism (notable for appearing under the heading 'Pederasty', where almost universally, in other texts of this period, male and female homosexuality are viewed as completely different activities), which Burton spends several paragraphs on, concluding his last lengthy footnote on the subject by saying that 'as the feminine perversion is only glanced at in *The Nights* I need hardly enlarge upon the subject' (fn. 2, p. 160). But, despite this rather self-indulgent provision of information to the reader, there is often a degree of defensiveness apparent in Burton's account of the Orientalist erotic. At the end of Section, 'Pornography', Burton warns the reader, in this edition 'for private subscribers only', that:

> There is another element in *The Nights*, and that is one of absolute obscenity utterly repugnant to English readers, even the least prudish. It is chiefly connected with what our neighbours call *Le Vice contre nature* – as if anything can be called contrary to nature which includes all things.[19]

Yet this seems to overstate the case, since there are only four pederastic episodes in *The Nights*.[20] But Burton does insist upon the naturalness of this Vice, reinforcing the point in a footnote in which he relates an anecdote about a dying fisherman telling his confessor that 'to amuse myself with little boys was natural to me as for to man to eat and drink' (p. 177). This contradiction, referring to pederasty as repugnant and obscene, while relaying anecdotes about how it is seen as wholly natural in other cultures, is what characterises Burton's discourse on pederasty, and what makes it so difficult and elusive to define and describe. But in this paradox is the production of a set of meanings about Oriental erotology and homosexual identity which serves to undermine the linear directedness of both western Christian morality and liberation campaigners.

Burton presents his analysis as a personal investigation into historical and contemporary practice of pederasty without any explicit investment in arguing for improved toleration of homosexuals. He writes very much as an antiquarian, very much like the authors and texts he is quoting from. Both the writer and the reader of this text are constructed into a convention of 'literariness', which makes the text appear a serious, high-minded thing. The scholarly appearance of 'Pederasty' is enhanced by the use of Latin and Greek, not only in quotations but to express ideas about sexual practice and history. This has an effect that is simultaneously serious and obfuscating. It requires a certain level of education to decipher and understand all the allusions in this text, the kind of education given to middle-class and upper-class males.

Burton interplays 'learned' quotations and illustrative stories. The coining of terms and the use of classical etymologies are central to the structure and purpose of the text. Latin is particularly used for references to sex organs, especially the use or unnatural conditions of them. This is not simply a matter of Burton concealing what he is talking about because very often he gives both English and Latin descriptions. He mixes English, Latin and Greek to build up a catalogue of sexual practices and of coded ways of referring to pederasty. He supplements his reference to 'the over-development of the clitoris' with the phrase 'veretrum muliebre ... habens cristam' (p. 160), a woman's genitals which have a crest or a cock's comb. The English translation of a text which would originally have been in Latin marks that text as something distinctive. There are very few of these, the most substantial being 'All things from Jove descend/Jove was a male, Jove was a deathless bride;/For men call Air, of two-fold sex, the Jove' (p. 173). If Latin were a device for concealment of the erotic content from those not in possession of a particular knowledge, then this would appear in Latin. Instead, any danger of the reader not understanding the quotation is avoided by putting it into English. More significantly, by presenting this as an English text, Burton is positioning this in British culture, not archaic, dead-and-gone classical culture, an ironic gesture given the content of the quotation. Burton effectively prioritises sexual and gender ambiguity as the highest form of meaning-generation. Plain, simple binaries (masculine and feminine, heterosexual and homosexual) are devalued, and figures which synthesise antitheses are foregrounded.

The illustrations accompanying the quotations are carefully annotated from classical sources. Scholarship is used to produce a different version of the history of pederasty. In arguing with authors who have 'made Sappho a model of purity' (p. 160), Burton cites Ovid as saying 'Lesbia quid docuit Sappho nisi amare puellas?', meaning what did Sappho teach the Lesbian women if not the love of girls? The 'nomenclature of pathologic love' (p. 165) in Greek language, in the way in which Burton narrates it, constructs the outsider-status and abnormality of pederasts as the site of perverse pleasure. Values such as 'dishonest love', non-conformity, the 'unspeakable' type of men, and 'Sotadic disease' (p. 166) are counterposed with terms and practices such as 'love a posteriori' (p. 166) and 'buttockry, because most actives end within the nates, being too much excited for further intromission' (p. 167). The implied practice of positive pleasure ironises the judgment of dishonesty and non-conformity, and the outside, abnormal nature of pederasty is made the source of pleasure.

Perhaps more than the translation itself, the analytical material and commentaries that attended it threatened Burton's public reputation as diplomat, army man and explorer, even though his editions of Orientalist erotica were for a very select audience, privately published and destined for a highly educated minority. This did not prevent contemporaries from equating the man with the content of the work, as in the judgment of Wilfrid Scawen Blunt, who described Burton as someone with 'a cross in his blood, gipsy or other', who wore 'a costume which his muscular frame and immense chest made singularly and incongruously hideous, above it a countenance the most sinister I have ever seen, dark, cruel, treacherous, with eyes like a wild beast's'.[21] Nor did it prevent the translation of *The Nights* from being vilified for its perceived immorality, for instance in an article by Henry Reeve in the *Edinburgh Review*, which described the work as fit only 'for the sewers',[22] and in Stanley Lane-Poole's *Personal Narrative*, which accused Burton of having 'an attitude of attraction towards all that is most repulsive in life and literature'.[23] More damningly, and more dangerously, Burton is implicitly presented by Lane-Poole as writing of these repulsive things from a position of too great a personal knowledge, given that 'the anthropological notes ... evince an intimate acquaintance with Oriental depravity' (p. xx).

In the opening paragraphs of the 'Pederasty' section Burton makes opaque reference to the manner in which he undertook part of the investigations that inform his anthropology, under the auspices of the Empire. Burton states that 'being then the only British officer who could speak Sindi, I was asked to make enquiries and to report upon' (p. 158) the incidence of male prostitution by the conqueror of Sind, Sir Charles Napier. This is used to legitimate what follows, since the work is claimed as a product of observed fact which can therefore contain only the truth, not as a dangerously subjective (fictional) version. However, 'I undertook the task on the express condition that my report should not be forwarded to the Bombay Government, from whom supporters of the Conqueror's policy could expect scant favour, mercy or justice' (p. 158). The officials of the government are compared unfavourably with Napier, who acted upon Burton's report by ordering the four brothels to be closed down, both because of their suppression of his report and also because they dismissed him for performing his investigatory duties as too much of a participant. By his own account, he performed his investigation dressed as an Arab merchant and visited the brothels *incognito*. Burton's status as a participant in the object of his investigations is established as that of an honourable official of the British Empire, an impression mitigated by the obscure conclusion to his account of the origins of the project. He states that the death of Napier 'compels me pacere sepulto [to suffer in silence]. But this excess of outraged modesty was not allowed' (p. 158). This constructs Burton in the role of someone compelled to write his history of pederasty, and makes modesty (or silence) far from a virtue.

Burton pre-empted negative judgments on his work in the 'Terminal Essay' to *The Nights*, locating sexuality in the stories themselves, rather than in his treatment of them, and refusing any suggestion that their erotic is excessive or unnatural:

> The naïve indecencies of the text are rather *gaudisserie* than prurience ... Crude and indelicate with infantile plainness; even gross and at times 'nasty' in their terrible frankness, they cannot be accused of corrupting suggestiveness or subtle insinuation of vicious sentiment. Theirs is a coarseness of language, not of idea; they are indecent, not depraved; and the pure and perfect naturalness of their nudity seems almost to purify it, showing that the matter is rather of manners than of morals.[24]

This defence, whilst arguing for tolerance of difference, is conflated with colonialist attitudes. While defending the culture that produced *The Nights* from charges of immorality, he infantilises that culture. The innocence of the culture and the childlikeness of the people mean that they don't know any better, and so cannot be legitimately castigated for beliefs and practices that developed which more mature cultures, such as the one Burton is writing for, would find repugnant. The child-Oriental may play with its 'excrements of wit',[25] but such behaviour is natural curiosity, indicative of an uncivilised ignorance about social mores, not an act of evil corruption with a sexual component. The Oriental body is a model for the Oriental mind in Burton's rendering of the Orientalist idea, in that it lacks mature, Christian discrimination about orifices and bodily products.

In a lecture delivered in Brazil in 1866, 'The Visitation at El Medinah', an account of his journey to the burial-place of Mohammed, disguised as a Dervish, Burton goes so far as to equate the geography of the East with the innocent bodily life of the Oriental:

> There was no ennui upon the road: to the traveller there is an interest in the wilderness
>
> > Where love is liberty and Nature law
>
> unknown to Cape seas and Alpine glaciers and even the boundless prairie.[26]

The quotation in this sentence is not referenced in the printed version of the lecture, unusually for Burton with his penchant for excessive footnoting, and seems to have no logical connection to the physical places described around it. But the interesting wilderness of the 'Desert between Cairo and Suez' speaks, in its very appearance and the experience of crossing it, of an amoral libertarianism that is natural and loving, not unnatural and degenerate. The stories of *The Nights* are thus true to their culture, and while the implication is that that culture is inferior by definition, it does have its own structure and integrity, albeit an alien one to Burton's readership, which it is Burton's task to present to those ignorant of it.

Egyptians and Persians come in for a high degree of condemnation in Burton's text, in ways which seem to undermine the case he is making elsewhere for tolerance of cultural difference. The Persians not only invented obscene language and 'that horror of travellers' (*Tales*, p. 66), bakhshish, but 'have bequeathed to the outer world worse things than bad language, *e.g.* heresy and sodomy' (*Tales*, p. 66). There appears to be a subtle distinction in Burton's thinking between sodomy and pederasty. Sodomy is a decided negative, both as a legacy to the world from the Persians and as a practice resulting in the neglect of women and the flourishing of adultery in Kabul, 'the husbands being notable sodomites as the song has it: The worth of slit the Afghan knows; / The worth of hole the Kabul-man' (*Tales*, p. 299). But pederasty, the love and sexual use of boys, is treated in a very different manner in a footnote to 'Nur Al-Din Ali'. Burton points out that Mohammed may have been an Arab, but he was not a Persian, therefore not a born pederast, and 'he was too fond of women to be charged with the love of boys' (*Tales*, p. 211), yet quotes from the Koran evidence that has been interpreted by the Chevaliers de la Paille as 'a hint that the use of boys, like that of wine, here forbidden, will be permitted in Paradise' (*Tales,* p. 211).[27] The word 'love' is never mentioned in connection with sodomy, and Burton implicitly maintains pederasty as a higher order of desire through the absence of any condemnation of the belief about the activities of the after-life.

Burton rejects other theories of pederasty very speedily, as when he declares that the three types of sodomy identified by Mantegazza, which he lists as anatomical, luxurious (pederasty providing the greatest erotic pleasure), and psychical, represent an idea that is 'evidently superficial' (p. 161). He declares himself concerned to find the causes of homosexuality. The primary cause is 'a mixed physical temperament affected by the manifold subtle influences massed together in the world climate' (p. 161). In the 'Essay' Burton invents the Sotadic Zone in which, he says, the Vice of pederasty is 'popular and endemic' (p. 159): a geographical area covering all of the inhabited countries of the world which fall outside Judeo-Christian control. While outside the Sotadic Zone pederasty is only practised sporadically in a hostile society, inside the Sotadic Zone it is universally practised and accepted or tolerated. Burton's only explicit comment on the oppression of pederasts appears towards the end of the text when he describes incidences of violent oppression as 'isolated cases' within the Zone which 'effect nothing' in his theory of universal and institutionalised pederasty. He defines pederasty as being determined by 'geographical and climatic, not racial' (p. 159) factors. (This is not spelt out by Burton, but it is calculable since he gives the latitudes of its boundaries and names specific geographical and national features.) This asserted, he argues that 'the origin of pederasty is lost in the night of ages' and then proceeds to recount its 'historique' (p. 162). Distinguishing between 'feminisme' (p. 160) in men, and pederasty, and sidestepping any idea of inverted physiognomy by declaring this possibility 'a medical question whose discussion would here be out of place' (p. 163), he rejects any sense of the pederast being a breed apart. Instead pederasty is less an essential identity than a universal institution, and asserting that it has an 'historique' produces a sense of lived practices and real societies. It is this insistence on pederasty's 'historique' which allows him to sidestep Judeo-Christian ideology and discourse.

The choice of terms is indicative of Burton's argument in 'Pederasty'. 'Invert' and 'homosexual' do not appear at all in the text. 'Invert' is a medico-scientific term,[28] and 'homosexual' emerged from the earliest form of liberation movement in Europe.[29] 'Sodomy' and 'sodomite' are older terms that belong to a legal, religious and medical frame of reference. Science, religion and liberation discourses have little or no part to play in Burton's project. The term 'pederasty' has within it an ambiguity, a history which removes it from Christian frames of meaning, but which participates in the highest manifestation of European culture, classical Greece. Etymologically, the word implies sexual relations with boys, but is a term which is used either for homosexual paedophilia or for any act of sodomy between males, regardless of age. This allows Burton to be talking about different types of desire and objects of desire within one term, just as he is able to indicate several ideas and attitudes simultaneously through the textual and linguistic methods he employs. He does use the word Vice, frenchifying it with the addition of Le, capitalising both words and often putting them into inverted commas. So, what might appear to be participating in a discourse of sin and corruption, in fact is made highly ironic. Burton makes it another quotation, and another part of an ideological, Judeo-Christian position, and not a position of truth.

'Sotadic' as a term might appear to give a clear sense of Burton's attitude to pederasty, in its meaning of something characterised by coarseness and scurrility. But Burton does not characterise pederasty as coarse or scurrilous. The other meaning of 'Sotadic', a satire of coarseness and scurrility in the manner of Sotades, arguably indicates that in the text of 'Pederasty' Burton is performing an elaborate, satirical game in which he creates a scientific-sounding means of describing and defining pederasty while making those descriptions and definitions meaningless in themselves as restricted and determinate categories, maintaining them as a textual device to be read and reinterpreted by the reader.

Burton's whole account is imbued with the framework and discourses of both scholarship and colonialism. Colonialists and scholars are both in danger from their close contact with pederastic practices in 'primitive', immoral, non-Judeo-Christian cultures. It is precisely at the margins of scholarship and the Empire that the inevitable difficulties of scholar and colonialist arise. The police and the judicial system may retain control at the centre, London, but at the margins pederastic influence and practice will inevitably come into play. While Burton goes into some detail in discussing pederasty in Paris and its accompanying scandals, he deals much more briefly with Berlin, and his account of London runs thus: 'it would be invidious to detail the scandals which of late years have startled the public in London and Dublin: for these the curious will consult the police reports' (p. 188). In part this is obviously written in the knowledge that his readers will be perfectly aware of those scandals, and the reference to police reports places the treatment of pederasty in those cities fully within the scope of the law rather than any other institutional or social context. This brevity and the emphasis on criminal prosecution is wholly at odds with the other accounts of various cultures. The brevity marks what is outside Burton's text, the Judeo-Christian ideology and the experience of homosexuals living in Judeo-Christian cultures. When the text returns to the (real) centre of Burton's text, which is not central to its purpose – in other words, the Judeo-Christian is the real centre, but it is marginalised in the ostensible and explicit meaning of the text – a different sort of language is forced into the text. It ceases to pretend or to assume to practise scholarship. The language becomes more mundane, more prosaic, more vague, less specific. It does not rely upon classical references here, but on legal and experiential knowledge. The effect is to point very clearly to the conditions under which English and Irish homosexuals lived, both through the implicit demarcation of England and Ireland and through the construction of a utopia that lies elsewhere geographically but present historically. This is further implied by the absence of any British names from the list of famous pederasts through history, with the notable exception of Shakespeare. He does, however, give details of a three-volume British publication for readers to consult for other names. The work he recommends as the source of information on this subject is that by Pisanus Fraxi, the pseudonym of Henry Ashbee. This is a catalogue of all published pornographic texts on all subjects, from flagellation to lesbianism, that Ashbee could locate.[30] To declare that 'the indices will supply the names' (p. 191) does rather pull a punch. Embedded within the text there is a store of information to be gathered by the reader. As well as the books listing famous pederasts, he recommends pederastic books like Petronius's *Satyricon*, giving a plot summary and the type of sexual activity that appears in them. He gives details of how 'debauchees had signals like freemasons whereby they recognised one another' (p. 168) and describes some of them. He also gives addresses and dates of former homosexual meeting places and clubs in Europe, and indicates the popularity of Naples as a place for Englishmen to go and have pederastic sex.

Yet the sexual tourist emerges very badly from Burton's account by contrast with the simple honesty of the Oriental. All the places and acts described by Burton are discreet, secretive and rather seedy. Concepts of difference and otherness are used to position the West in relation to the East, effectively making the East normative rather than deviant, and to critique Judeo-Christian ideas about sex and morality. Burton contrasts, not only in detail but also in language, the treatment of pederasty inside and outside the Zone. His discussion of what is outside the Zone is framed by the discourse and ideology of the Judeo-Christian viewpoint. Outside the Zone, for Burton, urban life induces earlier puberty which in turn causes 'modesty to decay and pederasty to flourish' (p. 187). Burton is looking for the 'natural', in the sense of the organic, essential origins of homosexuality. Such origins are innocent, and are set against the corruption of urban life. Cities are the site of corruption; within the Zone, the cultures are 'uncivilised', and there sexuality is innocent and uncorrupted, belonging to a culture with a younger consciousness, even though historically the cultures within the Zone tend to be older than western urban cultures discussed. Anthropology, like sexology, is not a neutral science, but it can lay claims to the objectivity asserted by science. Burton shapes it to produce a structure of difference that plays not on nature/unnatural and sin/morality, but on youth and innocence/ age and degeneration, where homosexuality can reside on either side of the difference, and is not inevitably produced on the negative side of the equation.

Some of the footnotes to the stories themselves appear to be almost gratuitous, even gleeful, in decrying religion. Burton glosses a reference to the Holy City in 'The Tale of Nur Al-Din Ali and His Son' as follows:

> There are few cities which in our day have less claim to this title than Jerusalem; and curious to say, the 'Holy Land' shows Jews, Christians and Moslems all in their worst form . . . Nothing can be meaner than the Christians while the Moslems are famed for treachery. (*Tales*, fn. 1, p. 199)

This even-handed put-down of both Christianity and Islam is unusual. The majority of footnotes which refer to morality are dedicated to mocking western values and practices. The wedding-night scene in 'Nur Al-Din Ali' earns a note which reads, in its entirety, 'On such occasions Miss Modesty shuts her eyes and looks as if about to faint' (*Tales*, p. 220), a telling sketch of western femininity, while a reference to eastern techniques of urinating in 'The Tale of the Hunchback' allows Burton to ask the rhetorical question, 'Will it be believed that Canon Rawlinson was too modest to leave this passage in his translation?' (*Tales*, p. 259). Pederasty is strongly tied to masculinity in Burton's construction. There is a marked degree of misogyny implicit in Burton's valuing of eastern mores, where mincing, lisping effeminate westerners are contrasted to the straightforward, unfussy, gutsy masculine easterner, an impression enhanced by Burton's inclusion of sexualised anecdotes apparently for their own sake in which westerners emerge as weak and feminised, and easterners as robustly masculine. There is no linking of sexual behaviour with an essential or inherent gender identity. Heterosexuality seems only to result in ignorance and hypocrisy.

Burton demonstrates that historically the repression of homosexuals and homosexual acts was a result and an aim of Judeo-Christian influence. What emerges here is that religion cannot prevent pederasty, only condemn and punish it if it so wishes. Sometimes explicitly, sometimes implicitly, he describes cultures in which pederasty was integral to the organisation and understanding of sexuality and desire, and then shows the difference effected by the actions of missionaries, Jewish thinkers and Judeo-Christian lawmakers. Burton characterises religious systems other than Judaism and Christianity in language that places them at least on a level with those systems. He capitalises crucial words – 'the Holy Books of the Hellenes, Homer and Hesiod' (p. 162) – thereby making them in some sense equal to the capitalised Bible, and uses religious language, like 'sanctified' (p. 163), when speaking of the Olympian gods. In Spartan culture there is 'the Holy Regiment composed of mutual lovers' (p. 165), and Saladin, the arch-pagan, is described as 'great and glorious' (p. 188). Judeo-Christian judgments of other races are put into inverted commas, as in the 'unspeakable Turk' (p. 177), making such phrases quotations and not Burton's own judgments.

The critical, ironic nature of the text is exemplified in Burton's comments on the myth of Sodom and Gomorrah. He identifies 'the earliest written notices of the Vice in the mythical destruction of the Pentapolis' (p. 174), but, having declared other commentaries on the moral meaning of this myth as 'most unsatisfactory' (p. 175), manages a bathetic deflation of this powerful cultural story with the line that 'the myth may probably reduce itself to very small proportions, a few Fellah villages destroyed by a storm' (p. 175). He does not find any stories of sodomy in the place supposedly destroyed by such activities, and the act of monumental importance to Judeo-Christian discourse in the justification of the persecution and destruction of sodomites is relegated to the level of mere myth.

Burton discusses two versions of the Sodom and Gomorrah myth, the Muslim version and that of the Judeo-Christian belief system. The Judeo-Christian version is given from the perspective of Jewish theologians and Christian commentators. Burton's discussion of the Muslim account opens with:

> Moslems, even of saintly houses, are permitted openly to keep catamites, nor do their disciples think worse of their sanctity for such licence; in one case the English wife failed to banish from the home 'that horrid boy'. (p. 170)

Placed against this is the assertion that 'pederasty is forbidden by the Koran' (p. 171). This difference between theory and practice is complicated by the terms in which Burton describes the story of Lot. The angels appear as 'beautiful youths' who are a 'sore temptation' to the Sodomites in their 'erotic vagaries' (p. 171). The erotic is not the only vagueness here. Burton inserts terms like 'generally supposed', in reference to the angels; 'if they ever existed', in relation to the 'cities' (in inverted commas); and the 'circumstantial unfacts' of the whole story. But the presence of the myth in two separate versions in the Koran is ascribed to 'an instance of Allah's power [rather] than as a warning against pederasty, which Mohammed seems to have regarded with philosophic indifference' (p. 171). Burton goes on to tell how the penalty for sodomy is the same as that for adultery, and comments that the 'law is somewhat too clement and will not convict unless four credible witnesses swear to have seen it rem in re' (p. 171). And this has to be seen in the context of Burton's footnote to this discussion, which refuses Christian condemnation of Muslims, 'this magnificent country [Morocco] which the petty jealousies of Europe condemn . . . to mere barbarism' (fn. 25, p. 170). Muslim cultures appear as highly sophisticated and all-embracing of differences and practices that European Judeo-Christianity is too petty to understand. Any law requiring four witnesses to proceed with prosecution is not a law that will often be put into effect. The image of the pettiness of European law and religion is enhanced by the anecdote about the wife. The 'horrid boy' as an insult is personalised and trivialising. Burton's discussion of the Koran makes the religious aspects vague and the sexual and cultural aspects specific. The indeterminacy of the 'circumstantial unfacts' of the biblical myth is there to be contrasted with the details of the relationships between men and angels, and pederastic practices in Muslim cultures, making Christianity more akin to fiction and lies than Islam.

Islam is not produced as the saving grace for pederasts. In North Africa 'the debauchery of the men was equalled only by the depravity of the women. Neither Christianity nor Al-Islam could effect a change for the better' (p. 172), which implies that both religions would wish to see the North Africans' act cleaned up, but neither religion could do anything about it. Burton's account of the Jewish response to the Pentapolis myth opens with the declaration that 'the legend has been amply embroidered by the Rabbis who made the Sodomites do everything à l'envers' (p. 174), in other words, to do that which is directly antithetical to the logical response to an act or event. Burton emphasises the racism of the Rabbis, who 'declare the people to have been a race of sharpers', but, Burton says, 'the traveller cannot accept it' (p. 174). Experience of those cultures and countries gives the lie to the judgments of such religious critiques, and also to the judgments from those sources on the morals of the peoples of the Pentapolis.

> I must therefore look upon the history as a myth which may have served a double purpose. The first would be to deter the Jew from the Malthusian practices of his pagan predecessors, upon whom obloquy was thus cast ... But the main object of the ancient lawgiver ... Moses ... was doubtless to discountenance a perversion prejudicial to the increase of population. (pp. 174–5)

Fundamental religious doctrine is constructed by Burton as expediency, where sodomy is condemned merely on the basis of the fear of a reduced birthrate, and not because it is unnatural in some theological sense. The implications of the position of Judeo-Christianity as set out by Burton are that, first, pederasty must be extremely attractive to the majority of people if it poses this big a threat to population levels, and, second, the answer to Malthusian anxieties about population explosions is for large numbers of people to practise pederasty.

Christianity is presented in two other relationships to pederastic practice, outside the Pentapolis myth. One anecdote is included in

Burton's discussion of Arab sexual practices and their punishment for sex offenders. One of these punishments is 'to strip and throw them and expose them to the embraces of the grooms and negro slaves' (p. 179). Burton appears to relish the details of this degradation, which successfully combines abasement to both class and race inferiors. 'I once asked a Shirázi how penetration was possible if the patient resisted with all the force of the sphincter muscle: he smiled and said, "Ah, we Persians know a trick to get over that; we apply a sharpened tent-peg to the crupper-bone (os coccygis) and knock till he opens." A well-known missionary to the East . . . was subjected to this gross insult by one of the Persian Prince-governors, whom he had infuriated by his conversion-mania' (p. 179). So, Christian zeal leads to pederasty. An outsider intruding into and interfering with a non-Christian culture is treated to the cultural formations of the original society.

Burton goes on to present the hypocrisy of Christianity, with the 'remarkable exceptions' he produces that go against its opposition to 'pathologic love' (p. 179). He cites the example of the 'Dominican Order, which systematically decried Le Vice, but which had presented a request to the Cardinal di Santa Lucia that sodomy might be lawful during three months per annum' (p. 188). The request was approved. Burton's judgment on the cause of 'such scandals' is the existence of a celibate priesthood (p. 188). The conditions of Catholicism produce the practice of sodomy. Christianity becomes in part the cause of pederasty in these anecdotes, not the moral force opposing it and not the means of saving pederasts from damnation.

An underlying element in Burton's accounts of imperialism and religion is the implication of the outsider into sodomitical practices. It is evident in the story about the over-zealous missionary, and appears in all the anecdotes about relationships between coloniser and colonised. There is 'the high-dried and highly respectable Consul-General for the Netherlands, who was solemnly advised to make the experiment, active and passive, before offering his opinion on the subject' (p. 172), and the European immigrants to Brazil, where 'till late years pederasty . . . was looked upon as a mere peccadillo' and who followed 'the practice of the wild men who were naked but not . . . "clothed in innocence" ' (p. 187). Christianity or European culture incites pederasty, or is condemned for rejecting something it has not tried, or is so fragile in the face of a culture which practises pederasty that all it can do is emulate or adopt the behaviour. The overlap between dominant ideology and marginal culture is evident in these anecdotes. The pederast is not the wholly other, but implicates and can contain the normal and the moral in itself.

Burton apparently is not setting out to define the essential character of pederasts in his emphasis on geographical and climatic determinations of sexual practice. But this appearance is countered by a brief comment early in the text when, in contrasting behaviour and attitudes inside and outside the Zone, he argues that those who practise pederasty inside the Zone do so 'amid the opprobrium of their fellows who, as a rule, are physically incapable of performing the operation and look upon it with the liveliest disgust' (p. 159). This seems to imply that either physical revulsion leads to physical incapability or that it is the incapability that produces hostility to pederasty, that if they were capable they would be positive about it; but which it is Burton does not make clear. The condition of practising pederasty is the determinate influence in producing a pederastic identity, rather than some pathological interior identity which produces the practice. Pederasty is thereby not separated from the rest of (heterosexual) humanity, but offered as the potential identity for all.

The object that dominant ideology produces as the most transparently natural, the body, in Burton's text becomes the site of ideological and erotic discourse construction. The physical nature of the body is determined by the erotic practices of the individual and the culture, and it is possible to change the physical nature of the body if it is subsumed into Oriental practices. It is not simply clothing and social habits that are produced for pederastic practice, but the 'nature' of the body itself may be socially produced. Burton rejects the theory of specific physical characteristics in pederasts, and passes over medical discussions as not relevant to his purpose, and this has the effect of making the implied theory of social construction of desire and body central to the causes and the practices of sodomy. Where bodily attributes and activities are not a priori, but a socially constructed effect of specific cultures, the identity is not a separate or distinct entity which occupies the physical object and subjectively determines the physical world, but it is a product of the body which is the primary site of social effect and control.

Bodily attributes are used in Burton's history to indicate identity and status. Writing about Native Americans, he says 'the objects of "unnatural" affection have their beards carefully plucked as soon as the face-hair begins to grow, and their chins are tattooed like those of the women' (p. 183), this of boys who are chosen by the elders to be treated and brought up like girls, by their mothers. From Greek culture Burton cites the example of Nero, who 'took to wife Sporus who was first subjected to castration of a peculiar fashion; he was then named Sabina after the deceased spouse and claimed queenly honours' (p. 168). The shaping and reconstruction of the body from orthodox male to acquired feminine is done to construct the social possibility of a feminine social identity for someone who is not female.

The practice of castration and the existence of hermaphrodites and transvestites are characterised by Christians as effeminate and 'a disgrace [to] their masculine sex' (p. 173). But Burton produces biblical support for castration which is anti-heterosexual sex, since St Paul 'preached that a man should live with his wife as if he had none' (fn. 30, p. 173). Where the Greek and Native American practices support the construction of a specific cultural gender identity, the Christian practice is proscriptive, misogynist and anti-erotic. This, for Burton, is 'an explanation of Sotadic love in its second stage, when it became, like cannibalism, a matter of superstition' (p. 174). The sacrifice of masculinity, where masculinity is equated with heterosexual activity, is placed on a par both with cannibalism and with the origin and practice of pederasty. The most radical act of anti-sexuality by Christians is reconstructed by Burton into an act of pederasty, because the act of castration goes against heterosexuality, and whatever goes against reproductive heterosexuality is sodomitical, because it is not masculine. Burton seems also to be recommending cannibalism in this sentence, through constructing current condemnation of it as 'superstition'. This kind of throwaway line, which connects disparate elements in a 'commonsense' manner, is what produces the difficulties of interpreting and evaluating Burton's writing. The reference to cannibalism may be nothing more than mischief, as much a joke as the Cannibal Club he formed with Lord Houghton and Swinburne, complete with rules and aims,[31] a whimsical piece of iconoclasm, but in that disruptive connection of cannibalism and pederasty resides an exemplum of the indeterminacy of Burton's text. It might be wholly racist, or gratuitously racist with the central aim of raising the hackles of the dominant.

The social production of the body is the site of social construction of sexual behaviour. The constructedness of pederastic practice and attitudes and the social nature of desire is revealed through the differences in the meaning of pederasty. Burton's position is not the universalising one of medicine or morals: his text is anti-morality and anti-pathology, and, in its implicit attack on Judeo-Christianity, constructs a history and anthropology of pederasty that emphasises variety and the relationship between specific desires and specific cultural formations.

Any sense of this being a campaigning text is ostensibly disarmed by the insistent documentation of the natural practice of pederasty within the Zone. Burton, by concentrating on conditions inside the Zone, need not detail the conditions outside the Zone, since the differences will be perfectly clear to the pederastic reader. Through inventing the Sotadic Zone Burton effectively and critically rejects all the debates about the sinful or pathological nature of homosexuality, and gives the reader a space in literature, language and history in which to look for other definitions and treatments of homosexuality. His writing on pederasty is not straightforwardly classifiable as Orientalist, or liberationist, or dogmatically uplifting of the social usefulness of the invert as Ellis and Symonds tend to be. Religion and science are rejected in favour of a looser, more relativist, cultural analysis, giving no big answers, and allowing readers nowhere stable to position themselves, either in terms of race or gender and sexuality, in relation to his arguments, which range from the spurious to the polemic, and which decline to address issues of national and moral importance with any sustained seriousness.

Notes

With grateful thanks to Elaine Hobby.
1. Gustave Flaubert, *The Dictionary of Received Ideas* (Harmondsworth: Syrens, 1994), p. 48.
2. Frank McLynn, *Burton: Snow upon the Desert* (London: John Murray, 1990), p. 8. See also Jean Burton, *Sir Richard Burton's Wife* (London: George Harrap, 1942), and Frank McLynn, ed., *Of No Country: an Anthology of the Works of Sir Richard Burton* (London: Scribners, 1990).

3. Edward W. Said, *Orientalism* (London: Peregrine, 1987), pp. 2–3, 190. Further references will be given parenthetically.

4. Rudi C. Bleys, *The Geography of Perversion: Male-to-male Sexual Behaviour outside the West and the Ethnographic Imagination 1750–1918* (London: Cassell, 1996), p. 216.

5. Elaine Showalter, *Sexual Anarchy: Gender and Culture at the Fin de Siècle* (London: Bloomsbury, 1991), p. 81.

6. Robert Aldrich, *The Seduction of the Mediterranean: Writing, Art and the Homosexual Fantasy* (London: Routledge, 1993), p. 173.

7. Richard Burton, *The Kama Sutra of Vatsayana* (London and Benares: Kama Shastra Society, 1883).

8. Richard Burton, *The Ananga-Ranga of Kalyana Malla* (London and Benares: Kama Shastra Society, 1885).

9. Richard Burton, *The Perfumed Garden of Sheikh Nefzawi* (London and Benares: Kàma Shastra Society, 1886).

10. Those who indulged in Isabel-bashing include Ernest Dowson in his poem 'Against My Lady Burton' (in Derek Stanford, ed., *Three Poets of the Rhymer's Club: Ernest Dowson, Lionel Johnson, John Davidson* (Cheadle Hulme: Fyfield Press, 1974), pp. 84–5). Isabel Burton acted to fuel the fire of such criticism with her cleaned-up version of *The Nights* (private publication, 1886), following in the tradition of Thomas Bowdler and his sister, whose *Family Shakespeare* was published by Longmans from 1818 onwards. See Noel Perrin, *Dr. Bowdler's Legacy: A History of Expurgated Books in England and America* (Boston: David R. Godine, 1992).

11. Isabel Burton writing in the *Morning Post,* 19 June 1891, cited in Frank McLynn, *Burton: Snow upon the Desert,* pp. 363, 416.

12. The penalty for attempted buggery was ten years' penal servitude. The Labouchere Amendment to the Criminal Offences Act 1885 made the penalty for gross indecency up to two years with hard labour.

13. Ronald Hyam, *Empire and Sexuality: the British Experience* (Manchester: Manchester University Press, 1990), p. 18.

14. Richard Burton, 'Terminal Essay', *The Thousand Nights and a Night* (London and Benares: Kama Shastra Society, 1885), vol. x. Because the original publication resides in the locked cabinet of the Special Collection of the British Library, and is laborious to gain access to, page references to Section D, 'Pederasty', of the 'Terminal Essay' in the text are to Brian Reade, *Sexual Heretics: Male Homosexuality in English Literature from 1850–1900* (London: Routledge and Kegan Paul, 1970).

15. Richard Burton, *Tales from the Arabian Nights: Selected from The Book of the Thousand Nights and a Night,* ed. David Shumaker (Avenal, New Jersey: Gramercy Books, 1977), p. 246. References to

the footnotes and quotations from the stories are taken from this edition, henceforth referred to as *Tales* in the text.

16. Powys Mathers, trans., *The Book of the Thousand Nights and One Night* (London: Routledge, 1994), vol. 1, pp. 1, 2. In Edward Forster's translation, *The Arabian Nights in Four Volumes* (London: William Miller, 1815), the equivalent references read 'another man in her arms' and 'another black descended instantly from a tree' (vol. 1, pp. 3, 6), the second episode of adultery being followed by a translator's addition, declaring that 'decency forbids us to enter into a detail of their conduct, nor is it at all necessary' (p. 6). Translations seem only to reflect the sensibilities of the time in which they appeared and the audience they were intended for.

17. For more information on the career of Leonard Smithers, see Ronald Pearsall, *The Worm in the Bud: the World of Victorian Sexuality* (Harmondsworth: Penguin, 1983), pp. 476–9.

18. Earlier editions of *The Nights* included the highly selective and censored Edward Forster, *The Arabian Nights in Four Volumes* (London: William Miller, 1815), and the text which comes in for most criticism in Burton's footnotes, Edward Lane, *Arabian Nights* (London: Dent, 1836), described by Said as 'uninspired' (p. 164).

19. Burton, 'Terminal Essay', *The Thousand Nights and a Night* (1885), vol. x, p. 204.

20. The four pederastic episodes appear in *The Thousand Nights and a Night* (1885) at vol. ii, p. 234: vol. iii, pp. 302–4: vol. v, pp. 65, 156–62.

21. Wilfrid Scawen Blunt, *My Diaries: Being a Personal Narrative of Events 1888–1914* (London: Martin Secker, 1932), pp. 546, 543.

22. Henry Reeve, *Edinburgh Review*, no. 164, 1886, pp. 166–99, in McLynn, *Burton: Snow upon the Desert*, p. 341.

23. McLynn, *Burton*, p. 341.

24. Burton, *Nights* (1885), vol. x, p. 203.

25. Ibid.

26. Burton, 'The Visitation at El Medinah', *Sir Richard Burton's Travels in Arabia and Africa: Four Lectures from a Huntington Library Manuscript*, ed. John Hayman (San Marino: Huntington Library, 1990), p. 24. See also Colin McEvedy, *Atlas of African History* (Harmondsworth: Penguin, 1983).

27. Burton's note to explain the Chevaliers de Paille reads 'Called Chevaliers de Paille because the sign was a straw in the mouth à la Palmerston' (Reade, n. 66, p. 189), which explains little now, but which may be a reference to Palmerston's public image as an arrogant, aristocratic lover of horses.

28. The term 'invert' achieved a degree of common currency amongst those writing in defence of same-sex desire in Britain in the last thirty years of the nineteenth century, as a kind of synonym for the 'intermediate sex' of Krafft-Ebing. The principal British work, *Sexual Inversion*, by Havelock Ellis and John Addington Symonds (London: Wilson and Macmillan, 1897), uses the word 'invert' to describe an innate and unalterable sexual identity, where sexual desire is turned upon a member of the same sex.

29. The bastard term 'homosexual' (half Latin, half Greek) was invented by Benkert, whom Frederic Silverstolpe, in 'Benkert was not a Doctor: on the Non-Medical Origins of the Homosexual Category in the Nineteenth Century', *Homosexuality, which Homosexuality? International Scientific Conference on Gay and Lesbian Studies* (Amsterdam: Free University/Schorer Foundation, 1987), has shown to be one of the first campaigners for liberation, a Swedish homosexual, and not a Hungarian doctor, as he has generally been seen.

30. Pisanus Fraxi [Henry Ashbee], *Index Librorum Prohibitorum* (London, private publication, 1877), *Centuria Librorum Absconditorum* (London, private publication, 1879), *Catena Librorum Tacendorum* (London, private publication, 1885). See also Roy Porter and Lesley Hall, *The Facts of Life: the Creation of Sexual Knowledge in Britain 1650–1950* (London: Yale University Press, 1995).

31. James Pope-Hennessey, *Monckton Milnes: The Flight of Youth 1851–1885* (London: Constable, 1951).

10 Alfred W. Howitt and Lorimer Fison: 'Victorian' ethnography and the gendered 'primitive'

Lynnette Turner

A defining characteristic of the formation of British anthropology as an academic discipline in the 1870s[1] is the concerted attempt to upgrade the quality of the ethnographic information drawn upon by the metropolitan anthropological theorists. Where previously the 'ethnographic' materials found in books by travellers, explorers, missionaries, naturalists and colonial officials provided the basis for the theoretical arguments of the major Victorian anthropological writers, the end of the nineteenth century witnessed the development of a more specialised form of ethnographic writing, and one which emerged under the aegis of 'disciplinary' anthropology. Central to this new disciplinary writing was an emphasis on the desirability – and attainability – of objectivity. The production and massive circulation throughout the British colonies of *Notes and Queries on Anthropology* (1874), a guide designed 'to promote *accurate* anthropological observation ... enabling the traveller to collect information *without prejudice* arising from his individual bias',[2] had certainly assisted anthropology's push towards scientific rigour.[3] But the arrival of the ethnographic monograph – as a privileged anthropological resource – represented a serious claim both to factual accuracy and to a mode of analysis informed by disciplinary methods and requirements.

This essay is concerned with the formalisation of ethnography as a mode of acquiring and representing knowledge of other cultures. My aim here is to analyse the claims to specialist knowledge made by the new generation of fieldwork practitioners who emerged during the late nineteenth century and within a climate of energetic attempts to standardise ethnographic practice. By scrutinising the manner in which their claims to authoritative knowledge are both registered and encoded, my main purpose is to open up and explore the gender biases at work in the production of stable (scientifically governed) ethnographic knowledge. Such an assessment will contribute to an understanding both of the structuring and informing presence of gender within the history of the ethnographic tradition, and of the gendered terms through which representational authenticity and factual accuracy are claimed.

What follows is an examination of the work of two pioneering 'ethnographers', the explorer and government official Alfred Howitt (1830–1908) and the missionary Lorimer Fison (1832–1907), whose collaborative anthropological work in Australia is regarded by Adam Kuper as having 'effectively established the tradition of Australian ethnography'.[4] Their monograph *Kamilaroi and Kurnai: Group Marriage and Relationship by Elopement* (1880)[5] was described by J.G. Frazer as 'a document of primary importance in the archives of anthropology', an 'important work ... [which] unquestionably laid the foundations of a scientific knowledge of the Australian aborigines'.[6] Many of the changes occurring in anthropological attitudes to the study of other cultures can be detected in the writings of Howitt and Fison. However, these two figures can also be seen as agents of change, since they determined in significant ways the methodological agenda of late nineteenth-century ethnography.

Howitt and Fison were among the first anthropologists to formulate a specific mode of sustained field research based on 'participant observation', and both writers advanced an ethnographic method based not just on intimacy and empathy with the group being studied, but on being able to discover forms of 'traditional knowledge' generally unavailable to the *amateur* white observer or interlocutor. Indeed, in the Australian context, formal ethnography can be distinguished from other types of ethnographic knowledge precisely through guarantees such as that made by Howitt to offer 'authentic, detailed description[s] ... from the observation of an eye-witness accustomed to *scientific* modes of investigation'.[7] As the authors of *Notes and Queries* had argued in 1874, 'the imperfections of the anthropological record surpass those of other sciences',[8] and the insistent need to purge the anthropological archive of unscientific forms of ethnographic knowledge is clearly expressed in the support given to the work of a select band of 'approved' observers in the field: generally those, like Howitt and Fison, who were active members of scientific societies.[9]

The implications of such exercises in selectivity had their greatest impact on the status of both indigenous and European women's testimony as legitimate ethnographic material. Even if European women had secured a greater scientific standing in Australia than was the case of women within English anthropological circles, there still remained a recalcitrant methodological problem. 'Authentic, detailed descriptions' resulted from observation as a *participant*, and both Howitt and Fison advocated the 'impersonation' technique of infiltrating and participating in 'traditional' cultural practices. The acquisition of 'authentic' knowledge was achieved through active participation 'as an initiated person' and participation was proved through the disclosure of 'secret' knowledge. These 'secrets' were gradually unfolded (or so Howitt and Fison believed) during the ceremony of *male* initiation, and male rites and rituals of initiation became for these writers the occasion *par excellence* for the transmission of the most meaningful knowledge. Male initiation is a group-based activity. It 'typically involves many more participants than female initiation' and, historically, male initiation 'has been more visible to ethnographic attention'.[10] Indeed, among the Australian groups studied by Howitt and Fison, 'secrets' were gender-specific gifts, and much of their ethnography attempts to replicate indigenous forms of gendering knowledge. However, their concentration on male 'secret ceremonies' involves their discourse in a series of exclusions and hierarchies whereby the forms of knowledge available to ('native' and white) women are regarded, at best, as an appendage to male knowledge, and more generally as the devalued surplus of 'authentic' male traditions and knowledges. For this reason, the connection forged in their writings between the procurement of primitive secrets (as the central focus of field-based anthropology) and participant observation (as the principal research method) provides an important opportunity to analyse both the role of gender in the formalisation of ethnography as a system of knowledge and the devaluation of native women's cultural expression in the participant-observation mode.

Howitt, Fison and the fieldwork method

The names of Alfred W. Howitt and Lorimer Fison have generally appeared in accounts of the history of anthropology as the
archetypal 'men on the spot': the valued correspondents of the
metropolitan comparative anthropologists.[11] Both men acted as
correspondents in the 'field', firstly for the North American evolutionist Lewis Henry Morgan (author of the influential *Ancient
Society*, 1877), and later for British comparative anthropologists
including Edward Burnett Tylor and James Frazer. As Adam Kuper
explains:

> Fison had been recruited by Morgan to fill in his kinship question-
> naire while working as a missionary in Fiji. In 1871 he went to
> Australia, and advertised in the newspapers for help in the study of
> Australian kinship. A response came from Alfred William Howitt
> ... In the 1860s [Howitt] had begun to read the new literature on
> evolution, and he was ripe for Fison's invitation.[12]

Fison and Howitt's working partnership lasted until the end of
the century. Their anthropological research spans a crucial transitional stage in British anthropological history, a period when the
recently established theoretical hegemony of 'classical evolutionism'[13] within anthropology was slowly but steadily giving way to
a more particularistic approach to the analysis of other communities and cultures. Within this context of transition and change, the
writings of Fison and Howitt do not easily correspond with those
of the typical Victorian 'overseas correspondent' whose ethnographic
findings would be ultimately subordinated to the hypotheses and
publications of the geographically remote metropolitan theorists.
As George Stocking has noted, in the early years of institutionalised anthropology, the leading figures within the Anthropological
Institute 'envisioned a sharp division of labor between those abroad
who would supply the necessary observations – but who "are not
anthropologists" – and those at home who would use that data
"for the scientific study of anthropology" '.[14] Despite the hierarchy
of knowledge suggested in this directive, both Fison and Howitt
published extensively on the anthropology of indigenous Australian communities, with essays appearing in British, Australian and
North American specialist journals.

Stocking reserves the phrase 'ethnographic correspondents'[15] to describe Fison and Howitt, a description which neatly encapsulates the peculiarity of their anthropological activities. They both retained a strong commitment to the orthodox Victorian questionnaire method as the most efficient means of 'enlarging the field of reference',[16] and Howitt's development of this method is regarded by D.J. Mulvaney as a 'landmark in the history of Australian anthropology'.[17] They also maintained a firm interest in 'Victorian' anthropological obsessions such as 'primitive promiscuity',[18] and many of the questionnaires sent out by Howitt in the 1870s repeat the major interests of English 'abstract' anthropology. Such a commitment to the questionnaire technique meant that Fison and Howitt inevitably relied upon the information supplied by indiscriminate informants, particularly within areas where neither Fison nor Howitt had 'any personal experience of the territory concerned'.[19] As Mulvaney points out, these questionnaires were despatched to 'local police, other officials and missionaries whose educational attainments were usually slight, or whose concern was to wipe all memory of the past from the Aboriginal minds'.[20] Regardless of the possible prejudices held by these correspondents, Fison and Howitt maintained throughout their anthropological careers an interest in the observations of others for the purposes of both corroboration and collation. At the same time, however, they were certainly aware of the problems inherent in field-research methods and especially concerned with the production of 'authoritative' ethnographic material. Fison and Howitt are transitional figures. While they were addressing and answering the concerns and queries of the geographically remote 'armchair' anthropologists, acting as their assistants and subordinates, they also show in their own field research a marked interest in the whole issue of producing authoritative ethnographic knowledge.

Howitt was distributing circulars and questionnaires as late as 1900. But he also pioneered the recognisably 'modern' type of participant observation predicated on intimacy and empathic identification with the group being studied. According to Mulvaney, Howitt was the 'first [European] to promote' an Aboriginal Australian initiation ceremony and the first to 'actively participate as a presumed initiated elder'.[21] Howitt may also have been the first anthropologist to regard his status as an initiated member of the group not as an obstacle to the rigour and impartiality of 'scientific' method, but as a necessary credential in the production of accurate scientific knowledge. As he confidently advised Edward Tylor:

> As to 'native mendacity', no such thing could arise between a black fellow and – another initiated person. I have over and over been able to check the accuracy of statements made to me by blacks who knew that I was one of the initiated and I never found that anything but the exact truth had been told to me. It is inconceivable that a man would dare to lie on such a sacred subject [the 'actual secrets of the Initiation'] to an initiated member.[22]

However, despite both Fison's and Howitt's interest in the 'authority' of participatory (identificatory) knowledge, much of their anthropology is dependent on the familiar organising categories of Notes and Queries,[23] and carries a distinctly comparative-evolutionary aura. Indeed, the extended subtitle of Kamilaroi and Kurnai (Group Marriage by Elopement. Drawn chiefly from the usage of the Australian Aborigines. Also the Kurnai Tribe. Their Customs in Peace and War) is clearly suggestive of a piece of work which cannot happily settle into either a traditional diachronic-comparative approach (where the interest in 'elopement' forms part of a broader attempt to understand the evolution of marriage laws) or an emergent synchronic systemic mode (signified in the book's interest in the 'customs' of a particular community, the Kurnai). The most remarkable feature of Kamilaroi and Kurnai is thus its split focus: 'Fison contributed the theoretical and synthesising element in the book, while Howitt's ethnography of the Kurnai formed the descriptive core.'[24] In standard Victorian anthropological monographs, the descriptive passages culled from correspondents' reports would be submerged within an overarching, systematising narrative.

What is also strange about Kamilaroi and Kurnai is that Howitt's descriptive section is not contained within and by Fison's synthesising and summational account. And neither is Fison's account of the 'Origin and Development of the Turanian System of Kinship, as shown in the Class Divisions of Australian Aborigines'[25] dependent on the information supplied by Howitt. It is also rare to see an account such as Howitt's – 'The Kurnai: Their Customs in Peace and War' – appearing in such a free-standing and authoritative form. Because of the distinction between theoretical and descriptive approaches which divides Fison's and Howitt's sections, the very structure of the *Kamilaroi and Kurnai* volume seems to dramatise the methodological and epistemological tensions caught up in the transition from ethnology (whose historical concerns involve or demand cross-cultural comparisons) to ethnography (which forms a description of a specific community or culture).

Yet the main way in which these methodological and epistemological tensions are disguised in their writings is through consistent appeals to the stability of gender as a communicative channel across and between different cultures. As I will go on to argue, the authority of participant-observers is inextricably linked to their active involvement in 'secret ceremonies':[26] the *performance* of secret ceremonies functions as the locus of the 'truth' of primitive cultures and, as such, it simultaneously defines and concentrates the authority both of the other culture (as autochthonous) and of the participant-observer who is one of the few Europeans able to report these otherwise *hidden* truths to European audiences.[27] The particular secret ceremony which became the focus of interest for ethnographers in late nineteenth-century Australia is that of male initiation: what Howitt euphemistically called the 'making of young men'.[28]

The methodological conversion occurring at the end of the century is thus predicated on an interest in the specific 'tribal' customs through which distinct (and diverse) versions of primitive masculinity are formalised. In this reformulation of anthropological interest, attention moves away from the categorisation and characterisation of 'primitive society' more generally. Instead, the *male* primitive is granted systemic significance, and in the process becomes a much more stratified analytical category than before. No longer is the male primitive defined by way of a comparative morality whereby, as John McLennan suggests in *Primitive Marriage*, primitivity is synonymous with promiscuity[29] and primitive masculinity is thus defined within an (abstract) system of inter-marrying relations. Rather, the male primitive is described *in situ*, and defined and *redefined* at particular moments in his own social-sexual development: as an 'infant', as a 'novice', as an 'initiated man', as an 'elder', and also in terms of relational and status names. This does not mean that the female primitive disappears altogether in the ethnographic mode, but her anthropological status is maintained – if it continues at all – as merely an explanatory index of primitive sexual activity. The male primitive, conversely, is not only granted the status of a social being, but his sociality is also given a narrative form.

Conventional disciplinary accounts of the demise within anthropology of evolutionary categories and assumptions and of the movement from abstract to empirical methods of inquiry have generally failed to explore the informing role of gender and sexual difference within anthropology's formal and informal epistemologies. Certainly, the analysis of Fison's and Howitt's work raises a series of complex questions concerning the relations of gender and anthropology (and gender and science) in the last two decades of the nineteenth century, yet the important insights offered by their writings into the relationship of gender and ethnographic authority in the early years of disciplinary anthropology have been consistently overlooked.

As a presumed initiated elder, Alfred Howitt's anthropological research, undertaken largely among the Kurnai and 'in a field anthropology situation which effectively extended from 1872 to 1886',[30] forms a series of important documents in the development of a specialised fieldwork method. Lorimer Fison's interest, on the other hand, was in system-building, and he was far less interested than Howitt in the personal observation of specific 'primitive' practices. Fison consequently assumed the role of 'metropolitan intellectual' while Howitt remained the 'experienced bushranger' with 'outstanding local knowledge'.[31] Fison, however, made a firm claim to being the first significant correspondent of professional anthropological theorists, and Edward Tylor repeatedly remarked that 'No man knows a savage's mind better than Fison does'.[32] Between the output of Fison and Howitt emerges a clear sense of the epistemological issues at stake in the discipline's investment in accurate anthropological observation.

Lorimer Fison: evolutionary themes and intercultural knowledge

Lorimer Fison was a long-term advocate of the 'collate and compile' approach to gathering anthropological data. From the early 1870s Fison acted as an intellectual conduit whereby information on Australian totemism, marriage regulations, and kinship terminologies from a variety of sources was relayed to foreign anthropological theorists. Edward Tylor's first contact with Fison occurred in 1879,

at a time when Fison and Howitt were seeking support for the publication of articles sent to the Anthropological Institute.

In his first letter to Tylor, Fison describes the process by which
he and Howitt had gathered information on the 'intersexual relations' of Aboriginal Australians through information 'from our
correspondents who were brought into communication with us by
means of printed circulars'.[33] By 1880 – that is, a decade after his
original use of the questionnaire technique and when *Kamilaroi
and Kurnai* had been written – Fison was keen to stress to Tylor
that 'The more I learn of savage customs the more plainly do I see
the necessity of unlearning our own notions as a preliminary to
understanding the working of the native's mind'.[34] Clearly, Fison's
attitude to research technique is moving towards a more *empathic*
mode of inquiry, one which the crudeness of the question and
answer format could not insist upon. Fison's notion of 'personal
inquiry' is still largely based on interviews conducted through a
'thoroughly trustworthy & efficient interpreter',[35] but even better
was the evidence of

> a countryman of one's own who has been long enough among the
> natives, has had sufficient interest in the subject, & has neither
> looked at native things from an European standpoint, nor allowed
> preconceived notions as to idolatry, Satanic agency, & so forth to
> influence his view of native customs.[36]

What preoccupies Fison's discussions of fieldwork at this stage
is the indomitable problem of the accuracy of the European informant's testimony. Possibly because Fison's role as a missionary
meant that his closest and most accessible native community was
that immediately surrounding him, he does not appear to treat the
Aboriginal Australians based on mission stations as potentially
unreliable informants. Instead – and with little irony – Fison focuses
obsessively on the possible misinformation provided by (other) missionaries: 'Missionaries especially are sometimes apt to look upon
all heathen customs, which are innocent in themselves, because
they suppose them to have a meaning which the natives most
certainly do not attach to them.'[37]

Native informants, it would seem, would continue to behave
authentically – or at least retain unmediated 'traditional knowledge' – regardless of their present circumstances. Thus when Fison
argues that 'There are many things the natives won't tell to any

white man, but there are still more which he won't tell to his missionary',[38] the implication here is that all Christianised Aboriginal Australians would continue to be the repositories of traditional knowledge; their stubbornness merely results from an awareness of how such information would be interpreted. However, as Bain Attwood has pointed out, there were also many things that 'traditionally oriented men and women' would not tell to 'mission Aborigines'.[39] But such strategic (and potentially insurgent) interruptions in the supposedly unbreakable oral chain of tribal knowledge seem not to have been considered by Fison. As a missionary himself, it seems likely that Fison's own 'authority' is necessarily dependent on a firmly essentialist conviction that the 'truths' of primitivity can be yielded from *any* native source; it just required the right European person to unlock them.

Attwood's argument raises important questions about nativist *agency* in the context of early ethnography by acknowledging that certain Aboriginal Australians were in resolute control of the transmission of tribal knowledge. Whether or not this can be immediately attributable to an emergent Aboriginal Australian political consciousness,[40] such forms of resistance to the anthropological attempt to 'exaggerate . . . how traditional some Aborigines were',[41] form an important political context for analysis of the late nineteenth-century native informant. For Fison, however, the 'native' – as with the 'primitive' – was a homogeneous, ahistorical anthropological category, and his community of informants was unlikely to be riven by internal conflict and political differences. Time and again, Fison stresses that the problems of accuracy and authenticity lie principally in the trustworthiness of the European interlocutor, and following the publication of *Kamilaroi and Kurnai*, he was supplementing his remarks on the 'trustworthy correspondent' in a significant way. Writing to Tylor of a new informant based in Fiji, Fison comments:

> He is a good authority . . . He married a Fijian woman, & thereby took the position of *Kai tani* who is admitted to a connection with the tribe by marriage. For many years he lived as a Fijian among Fijians, & now that he has attained a respectable position as a Govt. official of some consideration, he finds his old ties somewhat inconvenient. I told him for his comfort that they were extremely convenient to me, inasmuch as without them he would not have been qualified to help me.[42]

The informant described here undoubtedly meets Fison's requirements of sympathetic or empathic knowledge. Yet what is most notable here is that Fison's use of the term 'authority' seems conditioned by a broader discourse of (colonial) authority. Although the informant's status as an 'insider' is a situation which 'qualifies' him as an appropriate informant, his 'respectable position as a Government official' also offsets the potential threat that assimilation into another culture poses to the objectivity and competence of his 'scientific' testimony. In this case, the 'trustworthiness' that Fison considered to be of vital importance in an informant is not located solely in the informant's proximity to native life, but is crucially bound up with some form of public or official confirmation of the reliability of his knowledge. Fison's good fortune is that such a hybrid informant simultaneously offers 'inside' and 'outside' knowledge, and both 'personal' and 'impersonal' modes of inquiry.

The close relationship of anthropological authority and colonial governmental authority presents a situation which inevitably disqualifies European women as authorising or authoritative informants. Once this strategy of disqualification is further combined with indigenous practices which gender 'traditional' knowledge, the implications for the place of native women and women's knowledge in late nineteenth-century anthropological discourse are significant. What appears in the anthropological archive as 'important knowledge' is patrilineal, and the figure of the 'traditionally oriented' Aboriginal Australian together with the concept of nativist agency has a firmly masculine basis.[43]

Fison's account of his 'Fijian' informant articulates a gendered ethnographic model of male activity and female passivity ('He is a good authority ... He married a Fijian woman'); a model not unusual in a late nineteenth-century context. But a key characteristic of this gendered division is the fact that the observer's entry or admission into tribal knowledge is achieved through his sexual relationship with a native woman. As Fison went on to propose, to be an authoritative observer, 'One wants to be an adopted member of a clan, & take unto himself a native wife, in order [to] get fully into the people's confidence.'[44] Such a sexualised definition of ethnographic authority in the colonial context is not an unusual statement of scientific veracity.[45] But in Fison's formulation, 'getting at what is in the mind of the natives' is firmly a male prerogative, being achieved through 'connection' with (entry through) a native woman. Not only, then, does the native woman remain fixed within a sexed and sexual categorisation, but Fison's discussion of a model of ethnographic practice based on trans-cultural identification is one in which the emergent necessity for insider knowledge *converges* with the classical evolutionist interest in primitive (female) sexuality.

'Adoption' in transition

Fison's evolving conviction that 'adopt[ion] into a clan' was a prerequisite for authoritative knowledge certainly indicates a much more self-conscious fieldwork mode, and one in which the non-specialist interlocutor is giving way to the authoritative (parti-cipant) observer. However, the emergence of ethnography in the modern sense of participant observation is generally regarded as the defining method of *modern* social anthropology, and thus coincides with the theoretical and methodological rejection of classical evolutionism. The tendency to argue for a neat 'paradigm shift' in anthropology is remarkably strong. Most histories of the twentieth-century 'break' from distinctively Victorian modes of anthropological inquiry tend to focus on the *theoretical* appara-tuses which conditioned the ethnographic move towards more localised, intensive and holistic accounts of pre-industrial commun-ities.[46] But the omission from these accounts of the transitional ethnography means that no analysis has been made of the status of the secret ceremony as the key analytical vehicle for the deter-mination of the sexual politics of ethnography at this time.

Once 'participant-observation' began to replace the question-naire method, the type of 'tribal' secrets disclosed of necessity changed. Certainly, in the Australian context, an ethnographic method which did not insist upon *participatory* knowledge allowed for dialogue between European male interlocutors and indigenous women. Thus, in *Kamilaroi and Kurnai* Howitt writes about mar-riage classes 'on the authority of "old Nanny"',[47] a mission-based native informant. But within the emergent participatory mode, direct involvement in the disclosure of secret knowledge is clearly a gender-specific activity, as Howitt notes in *The Native Tribes of South-East Australia*:

> During the morning an incident occurred which was very significant
> of the profound feeling of secrecy in regard to the central mysteries
> which is felt by the Kurnai. One of the Headmen came to me, and
> intimated that the old men, before proceeding further, desired to be
> satisfied that I had in very deed been fully initiated by the Brajerak
> blackfellows in the *Kuringal*. I caused them all to come to me in the
> recesses of a thick scrub, far from the possibility of a woman's
> presence, and I there exhibited to them the bull-roarer, which had
> been used at the 'Brajerak' initiations previously attended by me . . .
> I also fully satisfied them that I had witnessed all the ceremonies of
> the *Kuringal*.[48]

Howitt's comments regarding the gendering of indigenous knowledge indicate that the development of participant-observation is
commensurate with three key methodological imperatives. First,
Fison's ethnographic objective of getting 'fully into the people's
confidence'[49] demanded active involvement in the most secret ceremonies. This, in turn, depended on the ethnographer being able
to prove his 'insider' credentials. But given the strict taboos surrounding the involvement of Aboriginal Australian women in male
ceremonies, such a development leads to the inevitable suppression
within anthropological discourse of the native woman's voice, authority and history. Second, what Howitt describes as the 'central
mysteries' – as his own translation indeed suggests – begin to take
on a major defining or interpretative function. Howitt's interest
moves from the scattered and multifarious 'secrets' which evolutionists worked with, and begins to focus more and more on the
central mysteries. The move is towards an abstracted, concentrated
cultural form which 'speaks' the very essence of primitive life. Third,
the scientific investment in participant-observation of secret ceremonies as a more 'rigorous' or 'trustworthy' method of inquiry
leads to a firm rejection of the testimony of the mission-based
Aborigine. These three defining factors are heavily interlinked.

   Christian missionaries played an important role in European
attempts to reform the existing cultural order of the Aboriginal
Australians throughout the nineteenth century. Mission stations
were notorious in distorting and changing Aboriginal Australians'
'notions of space and time'[50] and Bain Attwood notes the attempts
by missionaries to 'structure Aborigines as *individuals* . . . The
missionaries sought to make each an integrated centre of consciousness, distinct from the natural world and other Aborigines.'[51]

A significant element of such attempts to sever the mission-based Aborigines from indigenous meaning systems was the missionaries' objection to movement on and off the missions, 'what many Australians would later deride as "blacks going walkabout" '.[52] The intention of most missionaries was to keep the Aboriginal Australians isolated from land which they regarded as their own, and to prevent them from leaving the missions to take part in ceremonies disruptive of Christian notions of order and morality. Significantly, the *questionnaire method* of anthropological inquiry was endorsed by both mission and government bodies. Conversely, the participant mode – which encouraged Aboriginal Australians to move off mission and government stations – posed a challenge to contemporary policies of native welfare.[53] The first technique, which allowed native informants – particularly women – to discuss their 'traditions' from within the confines of regulated encampments, relied upon personal memory:

> As my friend and correspondent, the Rev. J. Bulmer, of Lake Tyers mission, expressed doubts as to the accuracy of my informants' statements on this point [elopement], I not only re-examined them, but, in order to obtain a check, I went to the Ramahyuck mission, and there questioned four women who were most likely to be able to speak positively. They were of the Briakolung and Bratauolung clans. I questioned them as to the marriage customs of the Kurnai *before the white man came*.[54]

Under the auspices of the questionnaire method, native anecdotal evidence was admissible as anthropological data. But the methodological refinement occurring in the move towards participant-observation displaced both the testimony of mission Aborigines and the *historical* experience of Aboriginal Australians by focusing only on a *performable* and *observable* tradition reproduced[55] in a dehistoricised form. Furthermore, as Howitt's comments on Kurnai secrecy maintain, once the (male) ethnographer assumes a participatory role in Aboriginal Australian ceremonies he is bound – theoretically at least – to indigenous codes of behaviour which condition and regulate the disclosure of sacred knowledge.

These indigenous regulations meant, among other things, that white men could not participate in native women's ceremonies.[56] Despite the view endorsed by Howitt's close friend and colleague Walter Baldwin Spencer that the 'white man stands outside the laws which govern the native tribe',[57] this did not mean that he could contravene indigenous gender-specific laws attached to the ceremonies: 'If an Australian black ... had the slightest idea that either Gillen or myself were attempting to get information from the women they would tell us nothing.'[58] Furthermore, the testimony of native women informants based at the mission stations – women such as 'Bessy' and 'Nanny', who are featured in Howitt's section of *Kamilaroi and Kurnai* – disappears in the experiential ethnographic mode. Thus the politics of ethnography – more specifically, the sexual politics of *transitional* ethnography – are highly complex, and certainly not reducible to simple binary distinctions between observer and observed. The questionnaire method, which emerges from an evolutionary and thus abstract model of cultural analysis, had granted the native informant – though in mediated form – the 'authority' to narrate. The experiential method, on the other hand, marginalises the native 'source' and substitutes the European observer as the authoritative and knowing participant. In addition, because late nineteenth-century ethnography saw its purpose as getting to 'bed rock',[59] everyday social and domestic activities did not hold the same ethnographic value as a (frequently fantasised) *deeper* truth only accessible through the enactment of secret rituals.

Ethnographic authority: the international fraternity

The drive towards a more 'perfected'[60] fieldwork mode structured on adoption, impersonation and identification inevitably delimits the field of analysis to a closed circle of men speaking to men about exclusively male secrets. Significantly, at the point where Fison questions the opposition between theorist and fieldworker, his comments are marked by a masculinising register different from the one conditioning the previous sexualised model of participatory access. Fison's discussion of authority comes to be dominated, as does Howitt's, by the language of 'Masonic' camaraderie. Fison writes of Howitt:

> He is succeeding wonderfully in gathering fresh information. I am full of delight at his success, though, as I tell him, the next work must be his alone, for I can give no help as to the Australians. He is becoming known far & wide among them as a great Grand Warden & Grand Master of the mysteries, & wonderful things he is finding out.[61]

By the time that Fison had developed a professional interest in the field-based anthropological work being undertaken by Walter Baldwin Spencer in the late 1890s his attitude to anthropological inquiry is marked by a noticeable move away from abstract theorising. In encouraging Spencer's fieldwork Fison advises him that: 'I have come to care little about theories. If I had money & leisure, I should spend the rest of my days gathering facts.'[62] Though the legacy of the division between the activities of theorising and data-collecting still shadows Fison's comments, his resolute rejection of theory occurs repeatedly in his 1890s' correspondence. For Fison, the new brand of ethnographer is an 'invaluable' figure: a 'real worker, not a mere theorist ... It is most refreshing to get hold of a man who has "been there", & who has used his eyes.'[63]

Questionnaire or being there? Two moments in Howitt's anthropology

Alfred Howitt's brand of intimate participant-observation as an initiated person was conducted sporadically over a fifteen-year period, and his ethnographic writings fall into two distinctive moments. *Kamilaroi and Kurnai*, published in 1880, is clearly marked as emerging from an evolutionary paradigm. His monograph *The Native Tribes of South-East Australia* (1904) was based on fieldwork undertaken in the 1870s and 1880s and written under the guidance of Walter Baldwin Spencer, whose jointly-authored ethnographic monograph *The Native Tribes of Central Australia* (1899, with Francis Gillen) was received in England, Australia and North America as a ground-breaking study. Though Howitt's *Native Tribes* is clearly an uneven text, the push towards experiential knowledge and participant-observation is clearly registered. Coming between these two monographs is Howitt's 'On some Australian Ceremonies of Initiation' (1884), an essay which lays down the principle of participation 'as an initiated person'[64] as the most reliable course for an 'explanation of the meaning and intention of the ceremonies themselves':[65]

> My account will be drawn partly from that which I have witnessed and taken part in as an initiated person, and partly from conversation which I have held with blacks as to the ceremonies of their own tribes. On these statements I can rely, not only by being in a

position, from my own knowledge, to form an opinion as to their truthfulness, but also because between the initiated there is, as I have found, no reservation, but a feeling of confidence – I might even add almost of brotherhood.[66]

The candidness, openness, and 'truthfulness' affirmed in this notion of transcultural 'brotherhood' produces an exclusively masculine version of ethnographic authority. Howitt's statement may voice the ethnographic ambition of integration with the other, but it simultaneously signals the fact that such forms of participatory knowledge rely heavily upon commonality of gender, or, indeed, on the stable transmission of the meaning of the masculine body across and between different cultures. Indeed, the baldness of Howitt's allusion to notions of an international fraternity not only suggests the firmly patriarchal basis of such an international brotherhood but also incorporates the important secondary signification of freemasonry as instinctive sympathy or understanding.

In *Kamilaroi and Kurnai* Howitt's dependence on the organising categories of the anthropological questionnaire forces him to consider feminine aspects of primitive culture, but *only* through familiar categories of analysis such as 'infanticide', 'marriage customs', and 'marriage classes'. Though native women are not accorded equal social status with native men, nor are they transposed into the vacuous, antisocial margin of masculine cultural activity. Indeed, Howitt includes details of his discussions with native women on the Ramahyuck mission station, and uses their testimony as evidence which 'proves the rule' regarding elopement.[67] Howitt is able to argue that women, like men, are historical subjects, preservers of traditions:

> The authority which is inherent to age attaches not alone to the man, but also to the woman. In affairs of moment the women have a voice, and it is not without weight. They consulted with the men about the ceremonies of initiation. They kept alive the stringent marriage laws. They are also, with the men, repositories of the ancient customs, and strongly influence public opinion.[68]

In *Native Tribes*, however, Howitt's observation of women's social authority is given a different gloss:

> The authority of age also attached to certain women who had gained the confidence of their tribes-people. Such people were consulted by

the men, and had great weight and authority in the tribe. I knew
two of them, who being aged, represented the condition of the
Kurnai before Gippsland was settled. Together with the old men,
they were the depositaries of the tribal legends and customs, and
they kept alive the stringent marriage rules ... thus influencing
public opinion very strongly. Possibly the reason for this may have
been in part that in this tribe the women take part in the initiation
ceremonies up to a certain point.[69]

This revised version of women's authority changes the position
of indigenous women in ways which accord with the ongoing
transformation in the fieldwork process. In the first version women
are 'repositories' of ancient customs: not merely receptacles, but,
importantly, legitimate recipients of confidences or secrets. In the
later version women's 'authority' is both explained and delimited,
and women's authority is seen to accrue only in proportion to their
involvement in *male* ceremonies. In other words, Howitt acknowledges women's authority in the 1880 text, but by the turn of the
century, masculine activity (and masculine knowledge) enters the
text as the yardstick against which women's authority is measured.

'Being there' and being accepted: Howitt and the gendering of 'authentic' knowledge

Howitt's ethnographic studies emphasise a masculine primitive
social world and utilise masculine modes of participation and access
to 'traditional' knowledge. 'Ancestral beliefs', the 'central mysteries',
and 'tribal morality' are undoubtedly equivalent and exchange-
able terms in Howitt's discourse, and male initiation is assumed by
Howitt to represent the very core of the customs and practices by
which the Kurnai organise themselves as a social community. Such
an exclusive focus on the young men's initiation into 'traditional'
or 'authentic' knowledge has the effect of positioning all uninitiated
members, particularly women, as without access to social, ancestral
or, importantly, moral knowledge.

Howitt's account of the Kurnai – and particularly his concentration on the 'central mysteries' – is working towards a 'Modernist' appreciation of the Kurnai *Jerraeil* ceremonies as a totalising
sociocultural performance. In *Kamilaroi and Kurnai* the ceremony
of initiation described – the 'great ceremonial of *Jerraeil*'[70] – is an

extended male ceremony, a significant section of which the 'women
are not allowed to know anything about' (p. 197). Despite the fact
that the ceremony witnessed is a 'representation' (p. 194) (restaged
for Howitt's benefit), its function for Howitt is none the less
definitional, restoring the simple and unmediated truths of Kurnai
existence:

> The past seemed to revive in them. They were no longer the wretched
> remnant of a native tribe dressed in the cast-off garments of the
> white men, but *Kurnai* – the descendants of Yeerung – performing
> a ceremony handed down to them through their ancestors. (p. 194)

Although the 'representation' witnessed is interpreted by Howitt
as an unveiling of the Kurnais' authentic being, the ethnographic
model offered here is at once external and non-participatory. Within
the development of an ethnographic enterprise founded on a model
of transcultural identification, it is not insignificant that Howitt's
definitional gaze turns away from the pretences of the *restaged*
performance as a whole and on to something more succinctly and
peculiarly 'primitive': the 'turndun', a 'wooden instrument' made
by the men, the manufacture of which the 'women are not permitted
to know anything about' (p. 197). It is not the totality of the cultural performance that fascinates Howitt. Rather, the ceremonial
unveiling of the 'turndun' becomes *the* exemplary moment in the
Kurnais' dramatisation of their primitiveness:

> It is kept secret and hidden from light by the head chief, and is
> considered to possess some mysterious and supernatural power or
> influence . . . if seen by a woman, or shown by a man to a woman,
> the punishment to both is *death*. (p. 268)

The 'turndun', then, is precisely that object which acts as material
confirmation of his integration into 'primitive' ceremonial life and
knowledge, and in *Native Tribes* Howitt is quite candid about his
strategy of intercultural subterfuge:

> After a little I brought up the subject of the ceremonies, and he
> [Turlburn[71]] finally said, 'There is one thing you do not know.' . . .
> Looking all round, he then said, 'Come down here', going under
> the bridge and speaking in a low tone of voice. I went there and sat
> down, and he then, with much mystery and a watchful air, lest any
> one might come, told me of the *Turndun*, that is the Bull-roarer,
> and of the part it plays in their ceremonies. If I had not known this,

I should never have gained the influence I afterwards had, which
enabled me to cause the *Jerraeil* to be revived.[72]

So the status of the 'turndun' in Howitt's discourse is ambiguous.
It certainly functions as a material sign of transcultural identification, yet at the same time his knowledge of the turndun is the
main factor which compromises his myth of simple, unmediated,
assimilation and integration. Native informants in Australia were
frequently killed for passing on to Europeans details of tribal
secrets and, as D.J. Mulvaney has noted, Tulaba (Billy MacLeod)
– Howitt's later informant and co-ordinator of the restaged
ceremonies – demanded to know from whom Howitt had learned
of the turndun. Fortunately for Howitt, he was able to argue that
his 'brother' Turlburn (Long Harry) had died in 1881, three years
before the commencement of these ceremonies.[73] But Howitt generally fails to mention these material details in his ethnography, and
neglects to state that his research was dependent on the exchange
of food and tobacco for secret knowledge; a commodification of
knowledge which tellingly undermines the romance of fieldwork
among uncontaminated, ingenuous peoples. But though a complex
identification, Howitt restabilises the potentially problematic status
of the turndun by observing that it 'much resembles, in general
character, the wooden toy which I remember to have made as a
boy, called a "bull-roarer"'.[74] Although he is clearly positioning
the Kurnai as infant humanity, his appeal to a *shared knowledge*
and thus to a shared history works both to consolidate Howitt's
participant authority and to endorse the masculine terms of the
process of transcultural identification.

In this way the text attempts to smooth over the invasive presence
of the European witness, by inscribing the process of the acquisition
of knowledge as an exchange of knowledge among a fantasised
international and intercultural fraternity. The process of exchange
is predicated on a homosocial bond of togetherness[75] which further reinforces the textual and actual exclusion of women from
authentic knowledge.

Native women and the cultural performance

At the end of the nineteenth century, the defining feature of the
emergence of 'scientific' ethnography in Australia is the acquisition

of 'authentic' indigenous truths unavailable to the missionary or amateur anthropologist. In Howitt's discourse – as with other Australian ethnographers such as Walter Baldwin Spencer – these 'deep truths' consistently translate as 'primitive secrets' or sacred knowledge, and the procurement and possession of secret knowledge works to confirm the authority of the field-based anthropologist. But because this exchange of knowledge occurs within and around the controlled performance of male initiation, the indigenous participants' demand for proof of initiation (of being a 'full man'[76]) enforces a rigid gendering of the mechanics of transcultural identification. Ethnography's recognisably modern(ist) investment in the 'cultural performance' produces an ethnographic process and ethnographic discourse which is at once gender-specific and exclusory. Women's knowledge – supposedly devalued because it is a cultural form available to both the 'uninitiated' and the amateur anthropologist – inevitably slips into the margins of anthropological interest. Thus being an ethnographer in the disciplinary sense is an identity which cannot recognise or countenance feminine systems of indigenous knowledge.

Indigenous women are not wholly absent from Howitt's final monograph. Women are the central object of the 'Marriage Rules' chapter and the sexual activity of women is decisive in the determination of 'regular and irregular intersexual relations'.[77] But the categories of names and naming granted the native woman reflect only her sexual (not her social) status. Where indigenous women make an appearance in the text as a differentiated category of analysis they do so in little other than specifically sexual contexts. In *Native Tribes* the life of the male primitive is more finely calibrated. He is defined and – importantly – redefined at particular moments of his social-sexual development, and the variety of terms through which the Aboriginal Australian man is both written and understood is strikingly different from the terminology of reducibility and homogenisation that surrounds the native woman.

If we accept Howitt's claim that his 1884 essay is the first account to combine the observation of 'authentic' ceremonies with 'scientific modes of investigation', then the transformation of the role of indigenous women within an *ethnographic* mode of inquiry has far-reaching consequences. From the subject of social authority of 1880 to the figure of cultural vacuity and restricted meaning which emerges in 1884, the native woman is not only rendered obsolete within the mechanics of identification that condition empathic and participatory *scientific* knowledge, but the text converts the multifarious Aboriginal Australian woman into little other than a fixed, stereotyped, and potentially *inauthentic* appendage to her more meaningful masculine peer.

Intimacy, brotherliness, fellow-feeling, and masculine interaction are the central motifs of Howitt's ethnographic epistemology. The strictly homosocial register of these terms both replace and reject the much more sexualised model of intimacy and participatory access to knowledge (predicated on interracial sexual relations) which was formulated within the terms of the evolutionist interest in the links between promiscuity and primitivity. Yet both models emphasise the authority of the white male anthropologist. But between these two modes of knowing and writing about pre-industrial communities is the 'interview' format adopted by Howitt in *Kamilaroi and Kurnai*: an intermediate form of cross-cultural interaction which grants the native woman (no matter how minimally) both narrative competence[78] and cultural integrity. The emergence of the 'modern' mode of participant-observation, as traced through in Howitt's writings, seems to be constituted by a significant – indeed emphatic – cognitive failure. Howitt's ethnography refuses to recognise the native woman as a cultural practitioner; a form of rejection which inevitably dooms the de-authorised native woman to the shadowy silences of ethnographic subalternity.

Notes

1. 1871 is the year in which 'Anthropology' was recognised as a distinct department by the British Association for the Advancement of Science. In the same year the Anthropological Institute was founded.
2. British Association for the Advancement of Science, *Notes and Queries on Anthropology: For the Use of Travellers and Residents in Uncivilized Lands* (London: Edward Stanford, 1874), pp. iv–v.
3. I am using the term 'science' in the same, somewhat vague, sense used by the compilers of *Notes and Queries* which shows a strongly held belief in positivist epistemology, advancing the belief in the possibility of recording unmediated, unconstituted, directly observable 'facts'.
4. Adam Kuper, *The Invention of Primitive Society: Transformations of an Illusion* (London and New York: Routledge, 1991), p. 94.
5. Lorimer Fison and A.W. Howitt, *Kamilaroi and Kurnai: Group Marriage and Relationship, and Marriage by Elopement. Drawn Chiefly*

from the Usage of the Australian Aborigines. Also the Kurnai Tribe. Their Customs in Peace and War (Melbourne, Sydney, Adelaide and Brisbane: George Robertson, 1880).

6. J.G. Frazer, 'Howitt and Fison', *Folk-Lore*, vol. 20, no. 2 (1909), p. 151.

7. A.W. Howitt, *The Native Tribes of South-East Australia* (London and New York: Macmillan and Co. Ltd., 1904), p. 509.

8. BAAS, *Notes and Queries*, p. v.

9. Howitt and Fison were Honorary Fellows of the Royal Anthropological Institute of Great Britain and leading figures in the establishment of a department of Ethnology within the Australasian Association for the Advancement of Science.

10. Nancy C. Lutkehaus and Paul B. Roscoe, 'Preface', in Lutkehaus and Roscoe, eds, *Gender Rituals: Female Initiation in Melanesia* (New York and London: Routledge, 1995), p. xiv.

11. Adam Kuper describes Fison and Howitt as 'ethnographers' but notes the 'subservience of the Australian ethnographers to anthropological theorists' (see Kuper, *The Invention of Primitive Society*, p. 93). George Stocking describes Fison as the 'regular correspondent' of E.B. Tylor and J.G. Frazer (*Victorian Anthropology* [New York and Toronto, The Free Press: 1987], p. 79). It was James Frazer who most notably wished to preserve the distinction between 'descriptive' and 'comparative' anthropology, that is, between the less-specialised activity of data-collecting and the system-building and synthesis regarded by Frazer as anthropology proper. See Frazer's letter to Walter Baldwin Spencer, 13 July 1898, in R.R. Marett and T.K. Penniman, *Spencer's Scientific Correspondence with Sir J.G. Frazer and Others* (Oxford: Clarendon Press, 1932), p. 23.

12. Kuper, *The Invention of Primitive Society*, p. 93. See also James Frazer's version of their initial meeting in 'Howitt and Fison', *Folk-Lore*, pp. 150–1.

13. The phrase 'classical evolutionism' is used by Stocking in *Victorian Anthropology*. Stocking points out that 'there was a general sense in British anthropology in the early 1870s that the period of institutional and intellectual controversy and self-definition had passed, and that it was possible to turn toward a more normal form of scientific activity' (p. 258). The compromises achieved included agreement on the 'ultimate monogenetic origin' of humankind, and an 'accepted framework, one that would be remembered as having established the new science on a solid empirical, theoretical, and institutional footing' (p. 258). This 'accepted framework' was sociocultural evolutionism. Although this did not mean, as Stocking stresses, that the ethnographic material appearing in the *Journal of the Anthropological Institute* in

the 1870s and 1880s was directly informed by the theoretical issues of sociocultural evolutionism, the situation for first-generation Australian ethnographers was somewhat different. Fison and Howitt looked to the major evolutionists such as E.B. Tylor for theoretical guidance and their research is much more obedient to disciplinary demands than is the case of other contibutors to the *Journal*. To concur with Stocking's observations is not to argue for the transcendent status of anthropology as a body of thinking removed from wider cultural influences. My interest in the constraints, limitations, and boundaries imposed around 'the discipline' forms an attempt to understand the implications of such processes of standardisation.

14. Stocking, *Victorian Anthropology*, p. 259. Stocking is quoting from the 1874 edition of *Notes and Queries*.

15. Ibid.

16. D.J. Mulvaney, 'The Anthropologist as Tribal Elder', *Mankind*, vol. 7, no. 3 (1970), p. 206.

17. Ibid., p. 206.

18. See especially John McLennan, *Primitive Marriage: An Inquiry into the Origin of the Form of Capture in Marriage Ceremonies* (Edinburgh: Black & Co., 1865).

19. D.J. Mulvaney, 'The Australian Aborigines 1606–1929: Opinion and Fieldwork', in Susan Johnson and Stuart Macintyre, eds, *Through White Eyes* (Sydney, Wellington, London and Boston: Allen and Unwin, 1990) p. 38.

20. Ibid., p. 38.

21. Mulvaney, 'The Anthropologist as Tribal Elder', p. 205.

22. A.W. Howitt, letter to E.B. Tylor, 15 August 1899, Tylor Papers (Howitt 36), Archives, Pitt Rivers Museum, University of Oxford. I wish here to express my thanks to Elizabeth Edwards, Assistant Curator at the Pitt Rivers Museum, for permission to consult and reproduce this material.

23. The 1874 (1st) version of *Notes and Queries* is split into two sections: Part 1, 'Constitution of Man', and Part 2, 'Culture'. The 1892 edition is 'divided into two main divisions, namely, ANTHROPOGRAPHY and ETHNOGRAPHY. The former treats of man and the varieties of the human family from a purely animal point of view; while the latter deals with him as a social and intellectual being.' BAAS, *Notes and Queries on Anthropology*, p. 1.

24. Kuper, *The Invention of Primitive Society*, p. 97.

25. The full title of Fison's essay is 'Kamilaroi Marriage, Descent and Relationship: An Attempt to Trace the Origin and Development of the Turanian System of Kinship, as shown in the Class Divisions of the Australian Aborigines, with their Laws of Marriage and Descent'.

26. The ethnographic interest in 'secret societies' and 'sacred rituals', which dominates first-generation ethnography in Australia (reproduced also in Mary Kingsley's research on 'fetish' in West Africa), seems to reflect the intellectual dominance of E.B. Tylor and James Frazer over disciplinary ethnography. Both Tylor and Frazer were building up documentary evidence of 'primitive' religions, but the fact of 'participation' in the rituals themselves seems to have a significant place in the intellectual shift from a focus on 'belief' to that of 'ritual'.

27. The activity of penetrating the closed cultural circle as proof of the 'outsider's' successful strategy of impersonation is not restricted to ethnography. But it certainly functions as the hallmark of participant observation at this time.

28. Howitt, *The Native Tribes of South-East Australia*, p. 509.

29. McLennan, *Primitive Marriage*, p. 12.

30. Mulvaney, 'The Anthropologist as Tribal Elder', p. 205.

31. Kuper, *The Invention of Primitive Culture*, pp. 101 and 93.

32. Edward Burnett Tylor, 'Presidential Address', *Journal of the Anthropological Institute*, vol. 10 (1881), p. 92. See also Tylor's remarks in his review of *Kamilaroi and Kurnai* in the *Academy*, 9 April 1881, no. 466, pp. 264–6.

33. Lorimer Fison, letter to E.B. Tylor, 17 August 1879, Tylor Papers (Fison 2).

34. Fison, letter to E.B. Tylor, 16 January 1880, Tylor Papers (Fison 5).

35. Ibid.

36. Ibid.

37. Ibid. See also letters to Tylor dated 24 January 1881 ('Missionaries especially are at a disadvantage in inquiring into such matters' [Fison 7]); 26 September 1881 ('a missionary is, as a rule, the worst man of all men to go to for such information' [Fison 17]); 26 January 1883 ('a Presbyterian minister, during a discussion in the Melbourne Presbyterian Assembly a few months ago, [argued] that the heathen could not be saved because "they have not an atom of morality"' [Fison 27]); etc., Tylor Papers.

38. Fison, letter to E.B. Tylor, 26 September 1881, Tylor Papers (Fison 17).

39. Bain Attwood, *The Making of the Aborigines* (Sydney: Allen and Unwin, 1992), p. 79.

40. Gordon Briscoe locates the emergence of an Aboriginal Australian political consciousness around the 1880s ('Aboriginal Australian Identity: the historiography of relations between indigenous ethnic groups and other Australians, 1788–1988', *History Workshop Journal*, no. 36 (1993), p. 154).

41. Attwood, *The Making of the Aborigines*, p. 78.

42. Fison, letter to E.B. Tylor, 27 September 1881, Tylor Papers [Fison 18].
43. I do not wish to suggest that late nineteenth-century ethnography represents a privileged discourse on Aboriginal Australian knowledge. However, the anthropological omission or downgrading of indigenous women's knowledge forms a significant blow to an interest in gender as a category of Aboriginal historical analysis. The historical and analytical consequences of women's marginal anthropological status is also tellingly present in Nicholas Thomas's otherwise quite brilliant analysis of nativist agency in the Pacific region in the 1890s. Thomas's reading of the archive of colonial relations consistently focuses on the indigenous male as the figure of native resistance. In particular, his analysis of the photographic evidence of restaged/re-enacted performances of 'traditional' customs and rituals constantly grants the indigenous male exclusive rights to both 'agency and willed involvement' (p. 36). The attention Thomas gives to photographs of indigenous male customs and rituals effectively reproduces the significance attributed to the male ceremony in the 1890s as the paradigmatic primitive performance. See Thomas, *Colonialism's Culture* (Cambridge: Polity Press, 1994), pp. 33–65. For a fuller discussion of this bias in Thomas's book, see Lynnette Turner, 'Consuming colonialism', *Critique of Anthropology*, vol. 15, no. 2 (1995), pp. 203–12.
44. Lorimer Fison, letter to E.B. Tylor, 3 March 1882, Tylor Papers (Fison 21).
45. Mary Jacobus, Evelyn Fox Keller and Sally Shuttleworth argue that

> It is a truism that whereas nature, the body that scientific knowledge takes as its object, is traditionally constructed as feminine, the subject of science, i.e. the scientist, has usually been seen as masculine. The fantasies that attend such gendering of the production and reproduction of knowledge are at once sexualised and territorial.

See 'Introduction', in Jacobus et al., eds, *Body/Politics: Women and the Discourses of Science* (New York and London: Routledge, 1990), p. 6.
46. See especially Stocking, *Victorian Anthropology*, pp. 284–329, Adam Kuper, *Anthropologists and Anthropology: The British School 1922–72* (Harmondsworth: Penguin Books, 1975), 'Preface' and chap. 1, 'Malinowski', and George Stocking, 'From Chronology to Ethnology: James Cowles Prichard and British Anthropology 1800–1850', Introduction to James Cowles Prichard, *Researches into the Physical History of Man* (facs: from 1813 edn), ed. George W. Stocking (Chicago and London: University of Chicago Press, 1973).
47. Fison and Howitt, *Kamilaroi and Kurnai*, p. 230.

48. Howitt, *The Native Tribes of South-East Australia*, p. 627.
49. See note 44 above.
50. Attwood, *The Making of the Aborigines*, p. 7.
51. Ibid., p. 19.
52. Ibid., p. 66.
53. Few of the recent debates on anthropology as colonial discourse look at the material context and political ramifications of particular methodological changes. The modern method of participant-observation is generally regarded as politically damaging to indigenous peoples because of its tendency to reproduce them as hypostasised: as without history and a complex culture. Revivals such as those encouraged by Howitt were certainly exploitative of Aboriginal Australians whom in another capacity he was responsible for, but they were none the less regarded by governmental bodies such as the Victorian Board for the Protection of the Aborigines as counter-colonial, seditionary practices.
54. Fison and Howitt, *Kamilaroi and Kurnai*, p. 200 [original emphasis].
55. The *Jeraeil* that Howitt observed was indeed a 'reproduction': the initiated men presented an 'exact reproduction of the Jeraeil of their fathers', A.W. Howitt, 'The Jeraeil, or initiation ceremonies of the Kurnai Tribe', *Journal of the Anthropological Institute*, vol. 15 (1885), p. 303.
56. White women did not undertake 'approved' ethnographic work in Australia until well into the 1920s. Daisy Bates took up Walter Baldwin Spencer's suggestion that Australian anthropology needed 'an investigation of beliefs and customs from a woman's point of view ... *by a woman trained in anthropological methods*' [emphasis added]. Significantly, however, she was reluctant to embark on the enterprise of ethnographic writing without Spencer's assistance and urged Spencer to be her 'collaborator and collator in the enormous material I have collected'. See D.J. Mulvaney and J.H. Calaby, *'So Much That is New': Baldwin Spencer 1860–1929* (Melbourne: Melbourne University Press, 1985), p. 370. Bates's case raises important issues concerning women and the issue of authority in disciplinary anthropology.
57. Walter Baldwin Spencer and Francis Gillen, *The Native Tribes of Central Australia* (London and New York: Macmillan and Co., 1899), p. 102.
58. Walter Baldwin Spencer, letter to Henry Balfour, 20 September 1897, Spencer Papers (item 14), Archives, Pitt Rivers Museum, University of Oxford.
59. This is Lorimer Fison's phrase. As Francis Gillen recalls, 'I felt cocksure that I had learnt everything there was to know about the ceremonies but Mr Fison's question "Are you quite sure you have learnt everything? It is so difficult to know when one gets to bed rock

with these people" started me making further enquiries.' Gillen, letter to Walter Baldwin Spencer, 20 December 1895, Spencer Papers (Gillen 10).

60. Howitt frequently expresses frustration with the 'very imperfect' knowledge acquired through the questionnaire method. See *Kamilaroi and Kurnai*, pp. 225 and 230.

61. Lorimer Fison, letter to E.B. Tylor, 7 November 1881, Tylor Papers (Fison 19).

62. Fison, letter to Walter Baldwin Spencer, undated, c. late 1899, Spencer Papers (Fison 3).

63. Fison, letter to E.B. Tylor, 29 September 1893, Tylor Papers (Fison 42).

64. Howitt, 'On Some Australian Ceremonies of Initiation', *Journal of the Anthropological Institute*, vol. 13 (1884), p. 433.

65. Ibid., p. 432.

66. Ibid., p. 433. The pervasiveness of the discourse of 'brotherhood' is evident in the sarcastic remarks of the Ramahyuck mission superintendent, Rev. A.H. Hagenauer, to the Board for the Protection of the Aborigines: 'it seems as if Mr Howitt is becoming a Black brother himself'. Cited in Mulvaney, 'The Anthropologist as Tribal Elder', p. 214.

67. Howitt, 'The Kurnai' (*Kamilaroi and Kurnai*), p. 200.

68. Ibid., pp. 211–12.

69. Howitt, *Native Tribes*, pp. 316–17.

70. Howitt, 'The Kurnai' (*Kamilaroi and Kurnai*), p. 232. Further page references are included in the text.

71. Turlburn (also known as 'Long Harry', c. 1835–81) was one of Howitt's chief Aboriginal Australian informants. See Mulvaney, 'The Anthropologist as Tribal Elder', p. 209.

72. Howitt, *Native Tribes*, p. 510.

73. Mulvaney, 'The Anthropologist as Tribal Elder', pp. 208–9.

74. Fison and Howitt, *Kamilaroi and Kurnai*, p. 267.

75. For a detailed discussion of the term 'homosocial' and of the 'male homosocial spectrum', see Eve Kosofsky Sedgewick, *Between Men: English Literature and Male Homosocial Desire* (New York: Columbia University Press, 1985).

76. Howitt, *Native Tribes*, p. 320.

77. Ibid., p. 187.

78. See note 54 above. Howitt questioned women on aspects of Kurnai history 'before the white men came'.

11 *The disappearing Other: exoticism and destruction in Jack London's South Sea writings*

Christopher Gair

It was the island of Fitu-Iva – the last independent Polynesian strong-hold in the South Seas. Three factors conduced to Fitu-Iva's independence. The first and second were its isolation and the warlikeness of its population. But these would not have saved it in the end had it not been for the fact that Japan, France, Great Britain, Germany, and the United States discovered its desirableness simultaneously. It was like gamins scrambling for a penny. They got in one another's way. The war vessels of the five Powers cluttered Fitu-Iva's one small harbour. There were rumours of war and threats of war. Over its morning toast all the world read columns about Fitu-Iva. As a Yankee bluejacket epitomised it at the time, they all got their feet in the trough at once.

Jack London, 'The Feathers of the Sun'[1]

Society acquires new arts and loses old instincts. What a contrast between the well-clad, reading, writing, thinking American, with a watch, a pencil and a bill of exchange in his pocket, and the naked New Zealander, whose property is a club, a spear, a mat and an undivided twentieth of a shed to sleep under! But compare the health of the two men, and you shall see that the white man has lost his aboriginal strength.

Ralph Waldo Emerson, 'Self-Reliance'[2]

In the September 1896 issue of *Atlantic Monthly*, the historian of the American Frontier, Frederick Jackson Turner, asked: 'What is the West? What has it become?' Going on to suggest that the answers to these questions provided an understanding of 'the most significant features of the United States of to-day', Turner described the cultural rejuvenation he saw as historically emanating from the freedom of opportunity available in the 'wilderness'. Portraying an effete, Eurocentric culture ruling the Eastern Seaboard, Turner argued that the pioneering spirit and the prevalence of 'free lands' 'promoted equality among the Western settlers, and acted as a check on the aristocratic influences of the East', where accumulation of property by the few had become the norm. Thus, within a model articulating competing definitions of nationhood, the West was 'another name for opportunity', and the Frontiersman had prophetic visions of a 'golden' future.

After nearly three centuries of Westward expansion, however, Turner contended that the settlement of the mid-West and the Pacific coast, the huge influx of poor (non-Anglo-Saxon) European immigrants, rapid technological development, and the acquisition of capital by corporate organisations had '[brought] this movement to a check'. The result would be an inward turn 'into channels of agitation', exacerbated by the West's directness in its expressions of dissatisfaction with the industrial conditions confronting it.[3]

In one way, Turner was right. The 1880s and 1890s saw unprecedented levels of violence in repeated battles between the forces of labour and capital. One need only think of much of the literature of the time – William Dean Howells's *A Hazard of New Fortunes* (1889), for instance, or Stephen Crane's *Maggie* (1893) – to understand that, as David Halliburton has argued in his discussion of Crane, conflict was a *condition* of much urban existence.[4] A brief extract from Howells's novel neatly illustrates the interaction between capitalism, immigration, and the desire to control definitions of nationhood:

[Conrad] stood at the corner of an avenue, and in the middle of it, a little way off, was a street-car, and around the car a tumult of shouting, cursing, struggling men. The driver was lashing his horses forward, and a policeman was at their heads, with the conductor, pulling them; stones, clubs, brick-bats hailed upon the car, the horses, the men trying to move them. The mob closed upon them in a body, and then a patrol wagon whirled up from the other side, and a squad of policemen leaped out, and began to club the rioters . . .

[Conrad] saw at his side a tall old man with a long white beard. He was calling out at the policeman: 'Ah, yes! Glup the strikers – gif it to them! Why don't you co and glup the bresidents that insoalt your laws, and gick your Boart of Arpitration out-of-toors? Glup the strikers – they cot no friendts! They cot no money to pribe you, to dreat you!'

The officer whirled his club and the old man threw his left arm up to shield his head ... The policeman stood there; [Conrad] saw his face: it was not bad, not cruel; it was like the face of a statue, fixed, perdurable; a mere image of irresponsible and involuntary authority.[5]

Clearly, for an author appalled by the collective hysteria emanating from Chicago's Haymarket Square atrocity of 4 May 1886, as a result of which four well-known anarchists were (as Howells put it) 'civically murdered' in a highly public miscarriage of justice,[6] there has been a near-total breakdown of hegemonic American ideology. In place of individualism – here parodied as the right to scab, whatever the cost to others – Howells represents a power struggle between unthinking enforcers of corporate law and, equally threatening even to the socialist Howells, a 'mob' of violent, de-humanised rioters. Howells employs the voice of the immigrant to expose the real economic conditions beneath the veneer of freedom and opportunity integral to the myth of the American Self-Made Man. Instead of a land of open spaces – and even in 1885, Howells had permitted the bankrupt Silas Lapham the luxury of a return to the 'pre-capitalist' family values of the (in his case, Northern) frontier – A Hazard of New Fortunes anticipates Turner's own dystopian images of a nation denied its historical safety valve.

And yet, in another way, Turner was mistaken to equate the settlement of the 'empty' Western spaces with the end of American Frontier mythology. The outbreak of 'Klondicitis' after the return of the gold-laden steamships Excelsior and Portland in July 1897 witnessed the same combination of regeneration and profit in the rush to the Northlands as Turner had described in his account of the West. Similarly, the wars in Cuba and the Philippines,[7] and the annexation of Hawaii in 1898 indicated the continuing import-ance of the Frontier myth to American rhetoric, a point that can be extended into the twentieth century with well-known examples as diverse as Kennedy's political 'New Frontier', Star Trek's 'Final Frontier', and the perennially popular Western. The 'filling-in' of the United States did not necessitate the rewriting of the myths upon which it had been constructed, even if the rapid growth of the U.S. Navy in the closing years of the nineteenth century seemed to undermine those myths by helping to marginalise the role of the individual pioneer.[8] Indeed, defending United States imperialism in 1899, Theodore Roosevelt singled out the continuing importance of the moving Frontier as a key metaphor of American youth and vitality:

> In every instance the expansion has taken place because the race was a great race. It was a sign and proof of greatness in the expanding nation, and moreover bear in mind that it was of incalculable benefit to mankind ... When great nations fear to expand, shrink from expansion, it is because their greatness is coming to an end. Are we still in the prime of our lusty youth, still at the beginning of our glorious manhood, to sit down among the outworn people, to take our place with the weak and craven? A thousand times no![9]

For Roosevelt, it is self-evident that a racial hierarchy exists and that the colonised will benefit from the very occupation of their lands that confirms and sustains the 'greatness' of the coloniser. It should be plain that such expansion and the textual strategies employed to record it will finally be concerned with anxieties about America itself, and with the self-definition of the writer as 'White Anglo-Saxon Western American', even where such self-definition necessitates representations of other communities. As such, 'new' lands and peoples tend to be incorporated into *American* history, their own myths and histories erased or reduced to a homogeneous Otherness rather than being accorded their own significance.

Of course, the United States were not unique in harbouring imperialist impulses at the turn of the century. Although the European New Imperialism tends to be thought of principally as constructing Joseph Conrad's multi-coloured map of Africa,[10] Chris Bongie is right to point out that 'this unprecedented period of expansion marks the moment when nineteenth-century colonialism, and with it its immeasurable problematic of modernity, first asserts itself as a *global* phenomenon'. As a result of the growing recognition by the Euro-American powers that the world was finite, each Great Power sought (as British Foreign Secretary Lord Rosebery put it in 1893) to 'peg out' its own claims as quickly as possible.[11] In the South Pacific, such construction was enacted swiftly and comprehensively, with the islands shared out between France, Germany, the U.S.A., Great Britain, the Netherlands, Australia, and New

Zealand.[12] It was to this region that Jack London departed from Oakland, California, with his wife Charmian and a small crew, in his forty-five-foot sail-boat the *Snark*, in April 1907. The voyage, intended as a seven-year, round-the-world expedition, but aborted due to ill-health and pressing financial difficulties after two years in the South Seas, provides the material that is the focus of the remainder of this essay.

I

Best remembered now for his 'dog-stories', *The Call of the Wild* and *White Fang*, Jack London (1876–1916) was a prolific writer on a host of factual and fictional subjects. His novels alone range from the revolutionary socialism of *The Iron Heel* (1908), through tales of adventure in the Klondike and the South Seas, boxing, prison reform, literary professionalism, to near-Emersonian paeans to self-sufficiency and the regenerative powers of the American landscape. In addition, he was the author of almost two hundred short stories; of accounts of his experiences as a young hobo (*The Road*, 1907), as an 'undercover' researcher into conditions in the East End of London (*The People of the Abyss*, 1903), and as an adventurer in the South Seas (*The Cruise of the 'Snark'*, 1911); of numerous socialist essays; and of war and sports journalism. He was also a hugely popular writer, commanding $1,000 per story at his peak and selling vast quantities of his novels and collected tales. As a result, London was able to purchase and develop a large estate at Glen Ellen, north of San Francisco, and enjoy a lifestyle often uncomfortably at odds with his socialist principles.

London's contradictions are apparent in his treatment of the South Seas.[13] The essays collected in *The Cruise of the 'Snark'*, the stories published in book form as *South Sea Tales* (1911) and *A Son of the Sun* (1912), and the novel *Adventure* (1911) range from extraordinarily sensitive attempts to understand local cultures,[14] through deployments of the 'wilderness' as a proving ground for overcivilised whites, to out-and-out endorsements of Anglo-Saxon supremacy and Manifest Destiny. The land and its indigenous populations thus take on a multiplicity of forms of *Otherness*, all highly illuminating in the context of American hopes and fears in the early twentieth century.

Indeed, the account of 'The First Landfall', recording the arrival of the *Snark* at Hawaii, immediately highlights many of the tensions inherent in London's narratives:

> For twenty-seven days we had been on the deserted deep, and it was pretty hard to realize that there was so much life in the world. We were made dizzy by it. We could not take it all in at once. We were like awakened Rip Van Winkles, and it seemed to us that we were dreaming. On one side the azure sea lapped across the horizon into the azure sky; on the other hand the sea lifted itself into great breakers of emerald that fell in a snowy smother upon a white coral beach. Beyond the beach, green plantations of sugar-cane undulated gently upward to steeper slopes, which, in turn, became jagged volcanic crests, drenched with tropic showers and capped by stupendous masses of trade-wind clouds. At any rate, it was a most beautiful dream ...
>
> Abruptly the land itself, in a riot of olive-greens of a thousand hues, reached out its arms and folded the *Snark* in. There was no perilous passage through the reef, no emerald surf and azure sea – nothing but a warm soft land, a motionless lagoon, and tiny beaches on which swam dark-skinned tropic children. The sea had disappeared. The *Snark*'s anchor rumbled the chain through the hawsepipe, and we lay without movement on a 'lineless, level floor'. It was all so beautiful and strange that we could not accept it as real.[15]

Initially, the language employed here seems to work within an established literary form. The impression of dreaming upon arrival in a new world is a familiar generic trait of the travel writer or explorer, and, in this case, directly echoes the 'vision' experienced by Mark Twain when *he* first arrived at Hawaii.[16] The landscape and native inhabitants are placed within a picture-frame, and are appreciated for their beauty by an observer familiar with the conventions of romantic landscape painting and writing. What attracts the outsider is what Paul Sharrad calls the 'colorist backdrop [that] counters the conflict a Westerner may be seeking to escape', but the description only serves to underlie 'his psychology, history, and art'.[17]

This leisure-class representation is deceptive, however, and the passage finally subordinates such transcendent values, based on romantic escape, to those of capital and the (American) West. Despite the final disclaimer – 'we could not accept it as real' – London simultaneously 'reads' the natural world in a very different manner.

The aesthetic response is displaced by the canny eye of the Frontiersman, who fears a 'perilous passage through the reef', but is delighted by the sudden appearance of the 'motionless lagoon' and 'lineless level floor'. To London, the lagoon is not merely another detail in the beautiful landscape: instead, it is a natural harbour, a place that has enabled the colonisation and exploitation of the island's resources, already observed as part of the introductory description.[18] For any more recent reader of The Cruise of the 'Snark', the significance of London's observations is made clear when he confesses that although he named it 'Dream Harbour', 'on the chart this place was called Pearl Harbour' (p. 76).

Such tensions dominate the Hawaiian chapters of The Cruise of the 'Snark'. London's narrative constantly leaps between what Bongie calls 'imperialist exoticism [which] affirms the hegemony of modern civilisation over less developed, savage territories', and 'exoticising exoticism [which] privileges those very territories and their peoples, figuring them as a possible refuge from an overbearing modernity'.[19] The former appears not only in examples such as the one above, but also in unashamed invocations of Anglo-Saxon supremacy, such as large sections of Adventure, as well as short stories like 'Yah! Yah! Yah!' (in South Sea Tales) and the account of 'Cruising in the Solomons' in The Cruise of the 'Snark'. On the other hand, London echoes Emerson's nostalgic yearning for the 'pre-modern' vitality of the natives (and of the white settlers), by contrasting these 'clean men . . . with their unsmirched souls' with the 'panicky little merchants with rusty dollars for souls' (pp. 76–7) that he has left behind him in San Francisco.[20]

The accounts of the dangers of overcivilisation reach their zenith in Tahiti, a place already lost as a pre-modern paradise. In 'The Nature Man', London tells of Ernest Darling, an American Socialist, ex-teacher, and the epitome of countercultural vigour. The chapter commences with a description of London's first sight of Darling, on a 'wet and drizzly afternoon' in San Francisco, when the author is amazed by the 'glowing and radiant' contrast made by the sunburnt, unshaven 'prophet' (p. 175). The juxtaposition of 'society' and nature is continued via a brief allusion to Tahiti, 'one of the most beautiful spots in the world, inhabited by thieves and robbers and liars'. As a result of the 'blight cast upon Tahiti's wonderful beauty by the spidery human vermin that infest it' (pp. 177–8), London announces that he will write about the

Nature Man instead, though his account necessarily (given the destruction of the exotic) contains descriptions of the bureaucratic efforts to stifle Darling's lifestyle.

Darling himself is the model of all that London admires in the Frontiersman, and is the vehicle for an inventory of the degeneration of American society with the 'Easternisation' of North America. As a result of 'overstudy' and repeated attacks of pneumonia, he has been 'close to death', and 'too weak to speak'. American medicine – including that prescribed by his physician father – proves useless, and Darling becomes a 'mental wreck ... sick and tired of persons'. He decides, therefore, to take the classic American step into the wilderness to seek an antidote to overcivilisation.[21] In the 'brush', of course, Darling finds relief, 'feeling that the sunshine was an elixir of health'. He studies the robust, carefree animals, and concludes that they are 'splendidly vigorous' because 'they lived naturally, while he lived most unnaturally' (pp. 180–1). By the time London meets him in Tahiti, and despite the efforts of insanity commissions to certify him for his dissidence, he is almost entirely self-sufficient and has imitated the natural world to such an extent that his health – considered ruined by the experts – is 'perfect' (p. 184). As with Emerson's emphasis on the relative 'manhood' of the American and the New Zealander in 'Self-Reliance', the 'natural' is equated with the recovery of a masculinity perceived as being under threat from a 'feminising' modernity.[22]

London is attracted to the Nature Man because of the latter's rejection of the values of corporate modernity. And yet he is forced to recognise the increasingly problematic status of such a lifestyle. Darling is branded an 'undesirable' by the authorities, threatened with the asylum and with prison, is deported from Hawaii, and the road from his land to market is closed by the 'conservative element' (p. 188). As with the other representations of both imperial and exotic exoticism in London's South Sea writings, there exists a desire to believe that modernity is not yet a global phenomenon. In London's writings, however, produced during and in the immediate aftermath of rapid American and European geopolitical imperialism, such a configuration becomes increasingly desperate, with the disappearance of the Other necessarily denying the Westerner the proving ground for his own Frontier identity.

The crisis hinted at in 'The Nature Man' is made even more explicit in another chapter of *The Cruise of the 'Snark'*, by London's visit to Typee, a trip informed by (and frequently quoting) Herman Melville's novel of 1846. While Ernest Darling is still just about able to inhabit a space where he can imitate the 'natural' world, London's account of the fate of Melville's 'brawny warriors', 'Noble-looking chiefs', and 'lovely damsels',[23] is synecdochal of the destruction of the exotic in the latter part of the nineteenth century. Not only does the chapter record the plundering of native art, which is taken to Europe, 'the ultimate abiding-place for all good heathen idols' (p. 159),[24] it also charts the fate of the indigenous people. Despite London's attempts to describe the place as 'fairyland', and to map his own experiences on to those in *Typee*, he is forced to acknowledge that what he witnesses bears little or no resemblance to Melville's text. The 'truly terrestrial paradise' – that is, the myth conventionalised by Melville, Stevenson, Gauguin, and others – has become a place where 'asthma, phthisis, and tuberculosis flourish as luxuriantly as the vegetation'. Where Melville saw a 'garden', London sees a 'wilderness . . . jungle, nothing but jungle . . . The valley of Typee was the abode of death, and the dozen survivors of the tribe were gasping feebly the last painful breaths of the race' (pp. 164–7).[25]

The collapse of the Typeans reveals a further rupture in London's discourse. First, he attempts to explain the fate of the 'strongest and the most beautiful' inhabitants of the South Seas as what Stephen Greenblatt has called (in a somewhat inverted context) a 'moral phenomenon'.[26] According to this reading, London is '*almost* driven to the conclusion that the white race flourishes on impurity and corruption' (pp. 168–9, my italics). As a result of their spiritual and physical purity, the Typeans are doomed to perish within a corrupt global modernity. Such an interpretation conforms neatly with London's repeated antagonism towards American culture, and with his desire to offer nature as an alternative to overcivilisation, even if it also recognises the totalising thrust of that modernity.

And yet it will not quite suffice. London's own narrative voice is also incorporated within the system he tries to attack, and morality is supplanted by the 'rational' scientific discourse of 'natural selection':

> We of the white race are the survivors and the descendants of the thousands of generations of survivors in the war with the microorganisms . . . We who are alive are the immune, the fit – the ones

best constituted to live in the world of hostile micro-organisms . . .
And they, who had made a custom of eating their enemies, were
now eaten by enemies so microscopic as to be invisible, and against
whom no war of dart and javelin was possible. (pp. 169–70)

The racial and cultural superiority encoded within London's participation in territorial expansion (remember 'Dream Harbour')
and the removal of native 'idols' to Europe and America is here
reinforced by the impression that what London is witnessing is a
repeat of an earlier point in his own racial 'history'. The Typeans
are portrayed as being at a 'primitive' stage of evolution and, if
they are to survive – which seems improbable – must repeat the
'regeneration' (p. 170) practised by the whites on the Frontier.
What is minimised in *The Cruise of the 'Snark'* is the significance of
London's own inability to survive the sicknesses of the South Seas.[27]
The final chapter ('The Amateur M.D.') and the 'Backword' are a
long inventory of the afflictions suffered by London and his crew,
as a result of which the voyage was abandoned, and London spent
five weeks in hospital in Australia and 'five months miserably sick
in hotels' (p. 305). These illnesses, however, are *never* described
as racial, though the ability to recover may be. Rather, they are
results of the environment and London claims that he has 'completely recovered . . . Without the use of drugs, merely by living
in the wholesome California climate' (pp. 306–7). By contrasting
his own recuperation with the demise of the native peoples, London sets out to 'prove' the superiority of one race over all others.

II

Although London was forced to abandon his round-the-world
expedition as a result of an inability to survive in the South Seas,
there was no reason why his fictional protagonists should do the
same. Having examined *The Cruise of the 'Snark'*, I shall now
offer a brief reading of the textual transformation of the geopolitical landscape necessary for the production of popular fiction. I
shall commence by looking at the collection of stories featuring
David Grief (*A Son of the Sun*), before concluding with an analysis of *Adventure* that seeks to illustrate the inseparability of self
and Other, domestic and exotic, in the construction of (and crisis
facing) meaningful American subjectivity.

If 'Typee' provides an example of 'natural selection' at work in the destruction of non-white peoples, then the description of David Grief offers an extreme intra-racial example of the same phenomenon. Hugely successful as a capitalist, worth 'many millions', and with 'holdings and ventures ... everywhere in the great South Pacific' (p. 29), Grief is also the supreme physical specimen, immune to the sun, to sickness, and to the alcoholism that is the fate of most white men in London's Pacific writings. Indeed, London maps out Grief's exceptional nature and constitution in great detail, making clear that: 'Unlike other white men in the tropics, he was there because he liked it ... One he was in ten thousand in the matter of sun-resistance' (p. 31). And yet, having made Grief's financial success explicit – one prerequisite of the popular hero being that he should be successful in all areas – London then repeatedly down-plays the economics of his presence. Instead, Grief epitomises the Western individualist out to assert his 'manhood':

> His was the golden touch, but he played the game, not for the gold, but for the game's sake. It was a man's game, the rough contacts and fierce give and take of the adventurers of his own blood and of half the bloods of Europe and the rest of the world, and it was a good game; but over and beyond was his love of all the other things that go to make up a South Seas rover's life – the smell of the reef; the infinite exquisiteness of the shoals of living coral in the mirror-surfaced lagoons ... and even the howling savages of Melanesia, head-hunters and man-eaters, half-devil and all beast. (p. 33)

It should already be apparent that a tension lies at the centre of Grief's character. On the one hand, he is the adventurer and nature lover, constantly seeking to test himself against other men and the 'wilderness'. On the other, he is in the vanguard of the colonisation of that world, in charge of a huge business involving the transformation of the land ('rip[ping] out' plants and replacing them with 'commercial' crops), the recruitment of 'the head-hunting cannibals of Malaita to the plantations of New Georgia' (p. 30), and the buying up of smaller business ventures. His actions, therefore, are instrumental in the destruction of the lifestyle he loves, and it is no surprise that he acknowledges the rapid disappearance of the 'old South Seas Romance' (p. 49). He has little interest in the business side of his success save as a proving ground. Instead, he repeatedly seeks out 'adventure' beyond the imperial marketplace,

in what Bongie calls the 'last-gasp enclaves of difference that ...
have no place in the world of colonial reproduction'.[28]

But this kind of tension needs to be disguised within the generic
conventions of the adventure story, a form that cannot permit the
negative thinking which insists upon the end of the exotic. Grief's
function is to act as a moral regulator, imposing the 'strong arm
of the [Frontier] law' on a lawless environment, and it is no surprise that when we first hear of him, a small-time crook is warned
that 'only a straight man can buck a straight man like him, and
the man's never hit the Solomons that could do it' (p. 17). Thus,
although he can show a concern with and respect for native customs (and even has a blood brother called Mauriri with whom
he converses in Polynesian), the descriptions of the land and its
inhabitants largely serve as backdrops to the reconstruction of
white identity, a process repeatedly undertaken via the application
of the moral code to 'degenerates', under Grief's supervision.

The formulaic nature of such an education, which is at the
heart of almost all the stories, makes it unnecessary to witness
every instance of its practice in *A Son of the Sun*. London admitted that the David Grief stories were 'pot-boilers',[29] produced at
a time when he was in need of quick money. Nevertheless, this
conformity to type becomes valuable in itself as a way of gauging
popular nostalgia for a rapidly vanishing part of American life,
and as a measure of idealised representations of 'whiteness' in an
age of considerable anxiety about overcivilisation. Time after time,
alcoholic, cowardly, or crooked Euro-American males are taught
a lesson by Grief, before demonstrating their own internalisation
of the Western ethos through the admission that his often sadistic
treatment of them was for their own good. Thus, when Alfred
Deacon, a racist bully who has been compelling 'a half-caste Chinese
pearl-buyer' named Peter Gee (p. 181)[30] into playing cards against
his will, is defeated by Grief in a wager that sends Deacon (with
a hand-written set of 'rules' to repeat every morning[31]) to Karo-
Karo, 'a God-forsaken little hole' (p. 197), for two years as Grief's
employee, he responds in predictably stoical fashion:

> Carefully and slowly, with trembling fingers, Deacon counted the
> cards he had taken. There were twenty-five. He reached over to the
> corner of the table, took up the rules Grief had written, folded
> them, and put them in his pocket. Then he emptied his glass, and

stood up ... Deacon shook hands all round, after receiving a final
pledge of good luck on Karo-Karo. (p. 203)

In place of the brash and boorish behaviour that has characterised
his lack of control until this point, Deacon manifests the calm
under duress required of the *real* man. He accepts his punishment
graciously, and his announcement that he is not a 'quitter' (p. 201)
earns him the admiration of the other men present, who meet
Grief's rules impeccably throughout. Paradoxically, two years in
the 'wilderness' are expected to make a gentleman of him, a task
at which the 'civilised' world has clearly failed miserably.

III

Given my introductory comments on Turner's image of the Frontier and the fact that, as a professional writer, London shared the
historian's distinctively urban stance as an investigative 'specialist',
writing about the 'wilderness' as a means of making a career in
a chosen discipline, it is unsurprising that there are similarities
between their projects. Both seek to hang the 'romance' of the
West within a frame repeatedly stressing the 'scientific' basis for
their discourse, relying on Darwinian evolutionary assumptions
and on a 'rational' and 'detached' style of writing. In addition,
both accept, and thus help to authenticate, the 'Western' creed of
'dominant individualism', and as London's South Sea novel *Adventure* makes clear through the victory of its protagonist, Joan
Lackland, over corporate financiers, and through her Grief-like
transformation of the lacklustre Englishman Dave Sheldon and
his decaying plantation, both believed that even if the Western
Frontier had been closed, the characters it bred would be ready
to adapt their abilities to other landscapes as well as the demands
of market capitalism.

It is therefore no surprise that London should provide Lackland
with a family history rooted in the pioneering tradition. Her father
had once owned cattle ranches, but lost his fortune thanks to 'the
big money panic in Wall Street' – that is, the lack of nerve manifested by Eastern financiers.[32] Joan herself is a combination of
Frontier spirit and cultural sophistication familiar in much of London's work. Educated in the saddle and the seminary, her talents

range from shooting to cooking to shrewd business dealings and discussions of poetry. Unable to contemplate the prospect of marriage, she sees the only alternative in the 'romance' (p. 57) of adventure in uncharted territories.

But as her name suggests, Joan Lackland (named after London's daughter, but sharing her creator's initials and a near anagram of 'Jack London') inhabits the post-Turnerian world. When Sheldon tries to guess her origins, he starts with 'Chicago or Wyoming', proceeds west to Nevada and California, and finally, after much prompting, arrives at the Philippines. Joan then corrects him, and announces her birthplace as the recently annexed Hawaii (pp. 59–60). But, like the David Grief stories, *Adventure* recognises that the closing of the Frontier is by no means an exclusively American affair. Following her father's financial collapse, Joan accompanied him on a voyage through the South Seas. But 'everything was changed' from the lands of his youth, with the islands 'annexed or divided by one power or another, while big companies had stepped in and gobbled land, trading rights, fishing rights, everything' (p. 65). Everywhere they sail, they encounter French, German, or English bureaucracy, the near-extinction of the natives, and the pessimistic acknowledgment that global modernity precludes the possibility of the romance of the Other.

These themes are familiar from other London novels of the period. Indeed, if one concern can be said to run through his work from *Martin Eden* (1909) via *Burning Daylight* (1910), *A Son of the Sun*, *Adventure*, and *The Valley of the Moon* (1913), to *The Star Rover* (1915), it is the fear of containment and the struggle to locate a space in which individual identity can be asserted. In each case the story told is one of loss, and in particular the loss of the possibility of authentic experience in a world made increasingly homogeneous. *Martin Eden*'s trajectory is an exercise in alienation, and the novel ends with the protagonist's suicide during his planned journey to the South Seas, where he had aimed to establish a new and unified selfhood. The conclusion of *Burning Daylight* envisages a return to a pre-corporate world, in which family values and a harmonious relationship with the land prevail. Its scenes depicting the colonisation of the Klondike and the development of Oakland, however, present a closed Frontier and an abuse of natural resources, in which the protagonist leads the way. Though the novel ends on a positive and regenerative note, it can only do so by imagining an escape from the forces of history, and a retreat into a world that no longer exists. *The Valley of the Moon* is even more concerned with the loss of the Anglo-Saxon pioneering tradition. Faced with an amoral urban world, in which the self is defined by forces over which it has no control, and by hordes of non-Anglo-Saxon immigrants, Billy and *Saxon* Roberts recreate the journey made by their ancestors and re-invent themselves as *real* Anglo-Saxons, looking for a place to settle.

Each of these journeys is associated with the physical or cultural destruction of indigenous peoples. Martin Eden plans to live 'like a prince', and 'build a patriarchal grass house . . . and have it and the valley and the schooner filled with dark-skinned servitors'.[33] Both *Burning Daylight* and *The Valley of the Moon* repeatedly represent the Native American population as doomed to perish in the face of the Anglo-Saxon onslaught, and even *The Star Rover* is predominantly concerned with white expansionism in its series of mini-adventures. And yet, at the very moment when other cultures are seen to be disappearing in the face of industrialisation and global capitalism, the sense of alienation felt by London's protagonists in their own society means that they must look towards and identify with the very Otherness they are simultaneously helping to destroy. Denied 'authentic' experience in their own monoculture, Martin Eden, the Robertses, Joan Lackland and the others can only approach any kind of 'wholeness' through the paradoxical step of identifying with what they claim to be above – other races.[34]

Although, in *Adventure*, no space is available in America for Lackland's pioneer spirit, the Native American retains certain essential values cherished by the alienated white protagonist. In her life story, Joan recounts how she and her friends were 'like Indians . . . wild to run wild' (p. 61), and she plainly finds the seminary atmosphere stifling and *un*natural. Though Joan is trained in European and American 'culture', she chooses to define herself through her association with Tahitian sailors, with Native Americans,[35] and even with 'cannibals' (p. 63). Although she expounds London's familiar doctrine of white mastery (p. 92), and shares Sheldon's belief that the 'unfit must perish' and that the 'blacks will die off' (p. 98), she feels as much threatened by the emergence of global capitalism as by the 'unanimous, unstable mob-mind' (p. 123) of the native island population in an echo of Howells's anxieties, here substituting racial for class Otherness.[36]

It is this marginality – the sense, on the Frontier, of being between something too well known and standardised, and an entirely unknown 'bush' culture that cannot be described or contained by available discourse (pp. 154–5) – which generates such contradictory representations of native culture.[37] On the one hand, Gogoomy, the ringleader of an abortive revolt, is described as having a 'primitive aristocraticness' and being 'dandyish in the extreme' (pp. 246–7), suggesting the kind of individualised identity no longer possible in Western society, and offering an alternative to that society. Likewise, the contest of 'head-hunters against head-hunters' is seen as representing 'The ecstasy of living' (p. 268), again promising a wholeness denied by consumer capitalism. On the other, the life of the Solomon Islanders is so alien that London is sometimes unable to find words to capture it:

> It was the largest house in the village ... Into it they went, in the obscure light stumbling across the sleeping-logs of the village bachelors and knocking their heads against strings of weird votive-offerings, dried and shrivelled, that hung from the roof-beams. On either side were rude gods, some grotesquely carved, others no more than shapeless logs in rotten and indescribably filthy matting. (pp. 278–9)

The imprecise language employed here – 'shapeless', 'indescribably', etc. – breaks down into total silence when the smoked heads of some white prospectors are discovered. Joan stumbles out of the hut, 'deathly sick', a phrase that will reveal its full meaning only in the final pages of the novel.

J. Gerald Kennedy's analysis of Poe's *The Narrative of Arthur Gordon Pym of Nantucket* (1838) examines the novel's scenes of decay, and makes a persuasive parallel between decomposing bodily figures and Pym's own virtual loss of language. Kennedy argues that:

> The spectacle of corruption exposes the inability of speech or writing to signify the 'inconceivable' or to conventionalize and regulate the attendant disgust. This sense of decomposition as a defiance of language comes closest to the radical, theoretical implications of *Pym*. For Poe's recurrent staging of human decay leads even the obtuse narrator to admit the failure of language, to realize that the odor from the brig was 'a stench, such as the whole world had no name for'.[38]

The same is true of Joan's response in *Adventure*, since she too is unable to use language, intellect, or culture to normalise the reality of what she has seen. By resisting this kind of control, the sight and smell of native tribal customs demonstrate the fact that there *is* still a space beyond the monoculture, but it is not a space into which Joan is able to step. From this moment, she (together with London's novel) rapidly retreats into cultural homogeneity. The native village is burned as punishment for what it contained; in their duel, Sheldon and his rival for Joan's love, Tudor, are described as being 'like a couple of wild Indians' (p. 297), now stressing the ludicrous nature of the fight and, implicitly, the culture; and Joan plunges into the very act of marriage that is anathema to her sense of individualism. Where Martin Eden committed suicide as the only way to preserve a sense of self, the 'deathly sick' Joan metaphorically commits the same act, both in her participation in the destruction of the exotic, and in her hasty retreat from 'romance' and 'adventure' into marriage and the marketplace. For her, as for David Grief and even for the Jack London adventuring through the 'wilderness' of the South Seas, the destruction of the exotic is inseparable from the destruction of the self.

Notes

1. Jack London, *A Son of the Son* (Collected Stories) (Garden City, New York: Doubleday and Page, 1912; London: Mills and Boon, 1912), p. 204. Subsequent page references from this edition are referred to in parentheses in the text.
2. Ralph Waldo Emerson, *Selected Essays*, edited with an Introduction by Larzer Ziff (Harmondsworth: Penguin, 1982), pp. 199–200.
3. Frederick Jackson Turner: 'The Problem of the West', in *Atlantic Monthly*, LXXVIII, September 1896, pp. 289–97. Reprinted in Donald Pizer, ed., *American Thought and Writing: The 1890's* (New York: Houghton Mifflin, 1972), pp. 156–67, esp. pp. 156, 160–1, 165–6. Of course, Turner's account was a very partial reading of the American experience. As Alan Trachtenberg elaborates:

   > Seeking a 'connected and unified account' of the American past at a time of disunity ... Turner thus arrived at his conception of the American character as an emblem of national coherence ... [The account] fails to acknowledge cultural multiplicity ... It makes its claims on the basis of a decidedly partial experience

– of chiefly Anglo-Saxon settlers and farmers flowing from New England into the Midwest. Moreover, the thesis ignores or obscures the real policies of the West ... [and] is as much an invention of cultural belief as a genuine historical fact: an invention of an America 'connected and unified' in the imagination if nowhere else.

Nevertheless, as Trachtenberg makes clear, Turner's frontier thesis articulated widely shared anxieties, and, rather than being an isolated tract of revolutionary import, was a document firmly rooted in the emergent enunciative fields of evolutionary science and professionalised academic discourse. (See Trachtenberg, *The Incorporation of America: Culture and Society in the Gilded Age* (New York: Hill and Wang, 1982), pp. 16–17.)

4. David Halliburton, *The Color of the Sky: A Study of Stephen Crane* (Cambridge: Cambridge University Press, 1989), pp. 38–9.
5. William Dean Howells, *A Hazard of New Fortunes* (1889) (Oxford and New York: Oxford University Press, 1990), pp. 383–4.
6. In a letter to Hamlin Garland, quoted in Tony Tanner's *Introduction* to the O.U.P. edition of *A Hazard of New Fortunes*, p. x.
7. By the 1890s, American investment in the Cuban sugar and mining industries, increased trade, and the island's strategic importance made it the inevitable focus of American jingoism. A revolution broke out in Cuba in 1895, largely as a result of Spanish oppression, and the United States officially entered the war in April 1898. The Spanish surrendered on 16 July. Perhaps the most significant battle of the war took place, however, in the Philippines, with the destruction of the Spanish fleet on 30 April by Commodore Dewey's Asiatic Squadron. On 13 August, one day after the signing of the peace protocol, an American force took Manilla. See Samuel Eliot Morison, Henry Steele Commager, William E. Leuchtenburg, eds, *A Concise History of the American Republic* (2nd edn) (New York and Oxford: Oxford University Press, 1983), pp. 477–98. For more detailed readings of the racial aspects of the war (in terms of American attitudes to both the external and internal racial fronts), and of subsequent colonisation, see Vincente L. Rafael, 'White Love: Surveillance and Nationalist Resistance in the U.S. Colonisation of the Philippines', and Amy Kaplan, 'Black and Blue on San Juan Hill', both in Amy Kaplan and Donald E. Pease, eds, *Cultures of United States Imperialism* (Durham and London: Duke University Press, 1993), pp. 185–218 and pp. 219–36.
8. See Morison, p. 483. In 1880 the United States Navy was ranked twelfth by size in the world. By 1900, it was third, with 17 battleships and 6 armoured cruisers.

9. Quoted in Richard Hofstadter, *The American Political Tradition and the Men Who Made It* (1948) (New York: Vintage Books, 1974), pp. 274–5.

10. When Marlow visits 'the Company's' offices (in *Heart of Darkness*), he studies 'a large shining map [of Africa], marked with all the colours of a rainbow', representing the imperial claims of the European powers. Joseph Conrad, *Heart of Darkness* (1902) (London: Penguin, 1985), p. 36.

11. Chris Bongie, *Exotic Memories: Literature, Colonialism, and the Fin de Siècle* (Stanford: Stanford University Press, 1991), p. 18.

12. See D.K. Fieldhouse, *Economics and Empire 1830–1914* (London: Weidenfeld and Nicolson, pp. 437–56), for an account of the rapid colonisation of the region between 1880 and 1910.

13. For the purposes of this essay, I restrict myself to London's writing on this subject from 1907–11. The complex Jungian material found in his late short stories (London had abandoned the genre for four years from 1912) is beyond the scope of my present interest in the Euro-American New Imperialism and the popular fictional representations of it. For a reading of this aspect of London's late fiction, see Earle Labor and Jeanne Campbell Reesman, *Jack London* (rev. edn) (New York: Twayne, 1994), esp. chap. 5.

14. Although, again, there is insufficient space to include a detailed account of these attempts, it is important to note not only the content of such stories – myths and detailed histories of the times before colonisation, usually ignored by white chroniclers – but also their form. Tales like 'The Bones of Kahekili' and 'Shin Bones' (both collected in *On the Makaloa Mat*, 1919, and recently reprinted in Jack London, *Tales of the Pacific*, with an Introduction and Afterword by Andrew Sinclair (London: Penguin, 1989)) do more than analyse and record other cultures. Rather, they incorporate the native tradition of spoken storytelling within their structure, in a fusion of orality and literacy, traditional myth and literary professionalism.

15. Jack London, *The Cruise of the 'Snark'* (New York: Macmillan, 1911; reprinted London: Mills and Boon, 1911), pp. 75–6. Subsequent page references from this edition are referred to in parentheses in the text.

16. Mark Twain, *Roughing It*, edited with an Introduction by Hamlin Hill (Harmondsworth: Penguin, 1981, p. 452). This sense of wonder is extended through Twain's description of Honolulu, pp. 452–6, though, typically, Twain finally undermines it with an inventory of the horrors inflicted by Hawaii's insect life.

17. Paul Sharrad, 'Making Beginnings: Johnny Frisbie and Pacific Literature', in *New Literary History*, 25.1 (Winter 1994), pp. 121–36, esp. p. 122. Also see Howard Horwitz, *By the Law of Nature: Form and*

Value in Nineteenth Century America (New York and Oxford: Oxford University Press, 1991), especially his analysis of Thomas Cole's five paintings, *The Course of Empire*, pp. 38–56.

18. My argument is partly informed here by Leo Marx's excellent reading of the similarly contrasting 'meanings' of the landscape in Twain's *Life on the Mississippi*. See Leo Marx, *The Machine in the Garden: Technology and the Pastoral Ideal in America* (Oxford and New York: Oxford University Press, 1964), pp. 320–5. London's descriptions of Hawaiian agriculture here and throughout *The Cruise of the 'Snark'* imply that the high yields of a variety of crops are the result of imperial ingenuity. David E. Stannard's brilliant account of the contact between European and Hawaiian histories, however, records that in 1778 Captain Cook and his men were 'astonished by the sight of vast agricultural fields that often covered entire valleys, fields employing enormously sophisticated irrigation techniques that, said one early visitor, reached "an incredible degree of perfection" and, added another, "surpassed anything of the kind we had ever seen before" '. Given Edward W. Said's 'moral epistemology of imperialism', it is unsurprising that London's narrative should contain a 'blotting out of [such] knowledge'. See David E. Stannard, 'Recounting the Fables of Savagery: Native Infanticide and the Functions of Political Myth', *Journal of American Studies*, 25.3 (December 1991), pp. 381–418, esp. pp. 382, 388.

19. Bongie, *Exotic Memories*, p. 17.

20. Such fears about overcivilisation reached their peak at the turn of the century. London's adventure stories in which, time after time, educated, urban enervated young men are transformed into bemuscled supermen parallel Teddy Roosevelt's call for the strenuous life, a new passion for sport, and the revived interest in war. In almost every instance, these manifestations of strenuosity combined the cult of Anglo-Saxon supremacism with the fear of modern softness. The best study of the period from this perspective is T.J. Jackson Lears's *No Place of Grace: Antimodernism and the Transformation of American Culture* (1981) (Chicago and London: University of Chicago Press, 1994).

21. Of course, this is one of the defining tropes of American literature. Focusing solely on the nineteenth and twentieth centuries, Cooper's 'Leatherstocking' novels, *Walden*, *Moby-Dick*, *Go Down, Moses*, and *Why Are We In Vietnam?*, are only a handful of the canonical texts employing errands into the wilderness as opportunities to critique hegemonic American culture.

22. For a reading of the links between the adventure story and the recovery of lost masculinity, see my 'Gender and Genre: Nature, Naturalism, and Authority in *The Sea-Wolf*', in *Studies in American Fiction*, 22.2 (Autumn 1994), pp. 131–47.

23. Herman Melville, *Typee* (1846) (Harmondsworth: Penguin, 1938), pp. 75, 92.

24. London participates in such theft, noting that one such 'idol . . . grins beside me as I write' (p. 160).

25. Stannard's description of Hawaii paints a similar picture. In the century following the arrival of Captain Cook, there was a 'population collapse (primarily disease-induced, but with powerful secondary side-effects, such as infertility and subfecundity) of about 95 per cent . . . a demographic disaster proportionately much worse than the Black Death that nearly crushed fourteenth century Europe' (p. 390, p. 397). In the second half of *Typee*, of course, Melville both qualifies his initial representation of an earthly paradise and foreshadows the destruction of the exotic in his representation of imperial warships and in his analysis of imperialism. I concentrate on his initial responses here since they largely inform London's own account.

26. Stephen Greenblatt, *Shakespearean Negotiations: The Circulation of Social Energy in Renaissance England* (Oxford: Clarendon Press, 1988), pp. 35–6. In Greenblatt's account of Thomas Hariot's *A Brief and True Report of the New Found Land of Virginia* (1588), disease in the natives is both proof of and divine punishment for secret conspiracy against the English.

27. It would have been impossible for London to ignore his afflictions in his own account of the voyage, since the *Snark*'s many disasters were chronicled in detail in the American press. Labor and Reesman point out that this was 'the most highly publicised of all Jack London's many wanderings' (p. 83), taking place when his fame was at its peak and when his movements were subjected to close scrutiny.

28. Bongie, *Exotic Memories*, p. 19.

29. See James L. McClintock, *White Logic: Jack London's Short Stories* (Cedar Springs, Michigan: Wolf House Books, 1976), p. 121.

30. The story's defence of Gee does not mask the narrator's own racism. One of the characters says that Gee is 'whiter than most white men', a point confirmed by the narrator, who suggests that he 'was that rare creature, a good as well as clever Eurasian' (p. 182). Whiteness, then, represents more than mere skin tone: rather, it signifies particular patterns of behaviour.

31.

> 'I must always remember that one man is as good as another, save and except when he thinks he is better.
>
> 'No matter how drunk I am I must not fail to be a gentleman. A gentleman is a man who is gentle. Note: It would be better not to get drunk.
>
> 'When I play a man's game with men, I must play like a man.
>
> 'A good curse, rightly used and rarely, is an efficient thing. Too

many curses spoil the cursing. Note: A curse cannot change a card sequence nor cause the wind to blow.

'There is no licence for a man to be less than a man. Ten thousand pounds cannot produce such a licence.' (p. 200, italics London's).

These rules sum up not only Deacon's new mantra, but also the code by which Grief lives, and which he imposes on a series of converts to the 'ideal' of Anglo-Saxon masculinity.

32. Jack London, *Adventure* (New York: Macmillan, 1911; reprinted London: Mills and Boon, 1911), p. 63. Subsequent page references from this edition are referred to in parentheses in the text. One major difference between London and Turner is that Joan, like many of London's protagonists, is female. For Turner, as Margaret Walsh has pointed out, 'When the frontier is considered as a condition moulding American character then the traits which emerge out of the struggle with the wilderness ... are masculine in identity'. In addition to women like Joan, or Frona Welse of his first novel, *A Daughter of the Snows* (1902), who are in many ways as much 'real men' as David Grief, London also populates his frontiers with wives, prostitutes and entrepreneurs, the very women absent from Turner and subsequent male histories of the West. See Margaret Walsh, 'State of the Art: Women's Place on the American Frontier', *Journal of American Studies*, 29.2 (August 1995), pp. 241–55, esp. pp. 241–2.

33. Jack London, *Martin Eden*, in London, *Novels and Social Writings*, ed. Donald Pizer (New York and Cambridge: Library of America, 1982), p. 880.

34. See my ' "The Way Our People Came": Citizenship, Capitalism and Racial Difference in *The Valley of the Moon*', *Studies in the Novel*, 25.4 (Winter 1993), pp. 418–35, for a detailed discussion of this process in London's California novels. For Saxon and Billy Roberts, it is only in the Valley of the Moon, the translation of the American Indian name 'Sonoma', and a place so far uncolonised by 'foreigners' that the 'true' Americanness of the family unit can be established.

35. Identification with the Indian was, of course, by no means universal. Frontier discourse generally constructed an Indian bereft of the 'pioneer' virtues described by Turner and London. For example, Theodore Roosevelt, President at the time of London's voyage, had confessed in 1886 (claiming to take the Western view):

> I don't go so far as to think that the only good Indians are the dead Indians, but I believe nine out of every ten are, and I shouldn't like to inquire too closely into the case of the tenth. The most vicious cowboy has more moral principle than the average Indian.

See Hofstadter, p. 274. In *Burning Daylight*, and in many short stories, London is considerably more sympathetic to Native American traditions.

36. This echo is more than simple coincidence. In *The Social Construction of American Realism* (Chicago and London: University of Chicago Press, 1988), Amy Kaplan illustrates the ways in which 'Journalists, reformers and pulp novelists [at the turn of the century] depicted the city as a new frontier or foreign territory to settle and explore and regarded its inhabitants – usually immigrants – as natives to civilise and control' (p. 45). In both cases (the Frontier and the urban centre), it is 'mob-like' foreign forces that are constructed as threatening Other, though there are also clear differences, most notably the association of the former with an (unknowable) primitive and the latter with old world decadence.

37. The point, of course, is that these are *representations* rather than an insight into the reality of native tribal customs.

38. J. Gerald Kennedy, '*Pym* Pourri: Decomposing the Textual Body', in Richard Kopley, ed., *Poe's 'Pym': Critical Explorations* (Durham, N.C.: Duke University Press, 1992), pp. 167–74, esp. pp. 172–3.

12 Modernity and racism

Richard H. King

It would be wrong to claim that the Holocaust first called attention to the pervasive effects of anti-Semitism and racism in the West. But reflecting upon the Holocaust after the end of World War II, some were moved to wonder whether western culture, particularly in its 'modern' incarnation, was fatally flawed. Two of the most important efforts to deal with this issue came from Theodor Wiesengrund Adorno (1903–69) and Hannah Arendt (1906–75). Both were from secular, German-Jewish backgrounds; both were trained in, among other things, philosophy; and both developed their analyses of the Holocaust and the role played by racism and anti-Semitism after they emigrated, Adorno in 1938 and Arendt in 1941, to the United States.[1]

Beyond this, however, the two had little in common. Their approaches to and conclusions about the Holocaust, expressed in Adorno's (and Max Horkheimer's) *The Dialectic of Enlightenment*, published privately in 1944 and then by a Dutch publisher in 1947, and *The Authoritarian Personality* (1950), which Adorno co-authored with four American psychologists; and in Arendt's *The Origins of Totalitarianism* (1951),[2] reveal numerous disparities. I know of no reference to Arendt in Adorno's work; nor is there evidence that Arendt was influenced by Adorno, although Arendt's controversial *Eichmann in Jerusalem* (1963) could be considered Arendt's 'answer' to *The Authoritarian Personality*.[3] For several reasons, both personal and intellectual, Arendt kept her distance from Adorno, despite the fact that they shared several friends, including theologian Paul Tillich, poet and playwright Bertolt Brecht, and the cultural critic and thinker Walter Benjamin. Indeed after Benjamin committed suicide rather than risk detection by the Spanish border patrol as he was attempting to leave France for Spain and eventually the United States, it was Arendt who delivered the text of Benjamin's short but immensely influential 'Theses on the Philosophy of History' to Adorno when she arrived in America in 1941. What they had to say to each other on that occasion is not recorded.[4]

Though the personal relationship between Arendt and Adorno is a fascinating topic, what I want to explore here are the differences between their understanding and evaluation of the crisis of western modernity as embodied in the Holocaust. Indeed, what their different approaches and disparate conclusions reflect was the difficulty in those early postwar years of figuring out why or how 'it' had happened. Indeed, there still is no consensus, nor perhaps should there be, about the best way to approach the Holocaust (with an emphasis upon the theoretical–conceptual or upon the historical), the appropriate focus (genocide against the Jews or the emergence of totalitarianism), the causes of racism and anti-Semitism (ideological–cultural or economic–social) and what these phenomena suggest about the western tradition (fatally compromised or salvageable, though seriously damaged).

Background

The differences in their backgrounds were considerable. Adorno studied philosophy and wrote his doctoral dissertation on Husserl and his *Habilitation* thesis on Kierkegaard, two figures with whom Arendt also concerned herself, though never in print. But the two formative influences on Adorno's intellectual development were, first, the modern avant-garde music tradition developed by Arnold Schoenberg and Alban Berg (Adorno had hopes of becoming a composer, was himself a skilled pianist and went to Vienna in the 1920s to study with both composers); and, second, the tradition of 'western' Marxism, specifically the work of figures such as Georg Lukács and Ernst Bloch (and in the background the great non-Marxist Max Weber) which shifted the focus of Marxism from economic to cultural concerns. Underlying Adorno's thought generally was a quasi-religious assumption, as Jürgen Habermas has put it in a slightly different context, that 'Matter is in need of redemption', while Rolf Wiggershaus notes the way the 'theological category of a materially corrupted world was translated into the Marxist category of the commodity fetish'. Both claims help us to understand the redemptive orientation of Adorno's work, the attempt to discover in the most marginal event or in the most recondite piece of avant-garde music the promise of some better order of reality than this one.[5]

However, the 'fact' is that most forms of western Marxism stubbornly refused to take phenomena such as racial, ethnic or national consciousness seriously in theoretical terms or to pay them much attention in the inter-war years. And this is where Arendt's intellectual *Lebenslauf* differs significantly from Adorno's. For, as she later responded when accused by Gershom Scholem of being a typical left-wing German intellectual: 'If I can be said to "have come from anywhere", it is from the tradition of German philosophy.'[6] This is not to say that the tradition linking Kant and Hegel with Arendt's two mentors, Martin Heidegger and Karl Jaspers, was particularly sensitive to matters of race or anti-Semitism, but it did mean that when Hitler acceded to power in 1933, it was easier for Arendt, who had previously taken little interest in her Jewish background, to comprehend that her own identity as a Jew and the dangerous plight of Germany's Jews could scarcely be avoided. She realised that Nazi anti-Semitism was more than just a smokescreen generated by monopoly capitalists to divert attention from the sharpening class conflict in Germany. (Max Horkheimer could write as late as 1939 that 'The [Nazi] pogroms are aimed politically more at the spectators than the Jews'.[7]) After interrogation by the Gestapo in 1934, Arendt fled to Paris and there engaged in work with a Zionist children's group. Later she reflected upon her discovery, as it were, that she was Jewish. What she said about her reactions is perhaps the best way to grasp her basic position: 'If I am attacked as a Jew, I must defend myself as a Jew. Not as a German, not as a world-citizen, not as an upholder of the Rights of Man, or whatever.'[8] Indeed, this sensitivity to historical experience was one of the salient features of her personality and of her thought. It was necessary to begin with experience itself and try to 'think what we are doing' rather than imposing an all-encompassing ideology upon it.

There are other ways to contrast Adorno and Arendt. Where Marxism was the great source of Adorno's thought, it was Heidegger who defined what thought, and hence philosophy, was for Arendt. Yet Arendt also had to make a decisive break with the Heideggerian spell in a way that Adorno never felt compelled to break with his theoretical precursors, though by the end of his life, his thought showed only the most tenuous link with orthodox Marxism. While Heidegger made 'historicity' and 'temporality' central categories in his phenomenology of *Dasein*, Arendt actually engaged with history as event and action and her analysis of totalitarianism reflected that concrete involvement. The account she offered in *Origins* was basically historical rather than conceptual: 'an analysis in terms of history' of the elements which constituted her 'explanation' for the 'origins' of totalitarianism.[9] These elements were the economic (the imperialist expansion after the mid-nineteenth century), the social (the transformation of European institutions after World War I) and the political (the collapse of the nation-state).

Adorno, the quasi-Marxist, hardly ever referred to specific events in developing his idea of modernity. For him and Horkheimer, the dialectic of Enlightenment involved 'the disenchantment of the world; the dissolution of myths and the substitution of knowledge for fancy' in combination with the domination of nature: 'knowledge is power'.[10] Their thesis was that this process had created not only progress but barbarism. In Adorno's work there were often sweeping evocations of the dominant system or larger social forces but never anything approaching a detailed analysis of the economic, social or political realities to accompany his analysis of anti-Semitism or the authoritarian personality.

Overall, then, Adorno and Arendt might be placed in two fundamentally different traditions of radical analysis. The tradition of 'social utopianism', to which Adorno and the Frankfurt School clearly belong, emphasises the achievement of happiness or satisfaction, however defined, while the tradition of 'natural law thinking', to which Arendt might be assigned, stresses the centrality of dignity and respect. The former is a response to deprivation; the latter, a response to degradation.[11] With this in mind, it is easier to see why *Origins* would emphasise that, in the wake of the Holocaust, it was a minimal but necessary requirement that since 'only the loss of a polity expels him [the individual] from humanity', all people should have a political home where they enjoy the 'right to have rights'.[12]

Though a redemptive politics was inimical to Arendt, the utopian moment in her thought was later to emerge as the political space, where citizens talked and acted together in concert. It was this emphasis upon public speech that helps explain her objections to psychoanalysis, particularly of the applied sort that Adorno and his associates used in *The Authoritarian Personality*. She held psychoanalysis to be a 'modern form of indiscretion' which failed to take public speech – or action – seriously.[13] Nor would she have thought that focusing only on German (or American) national character was to the point, since anti-Semitism in particular and totalitarian conditions in general were European-wide rather than just a German phenomenon. Finally, what was most relevant for Arendt was action, not the state of mind accompanying that action. The rare moments of psychologising in her thought come in reference to the loneliness and isolation in mass society which make individuals susceptible to the appeal of a totalised view of the world, which can mobilise people for political purposes, and to which the 'masses' man give themselves selflessly. Generally, she identified as fatal for modern European, specifically German and Jewish, political and moral life the historical denigration of the public and political in favour of the private and personal. The results for both peoples had been disastrous.

With Adorno, it was quite different. Like most of the Frankfurt School, he had been concerned to bring Marx and Freud into some sort of fruitful conjunction, to merge their vocabularies so that the quest for happiness so central to the Frankfurt analysis might be given materialist and subjective expression. Though notoriously short on specifics about how a future community should look, much of Adorno's analysis, particularly in *The Authoritarian Personality*, implied the need for a kind of theoretical–therapeutic élite to apply the lessons of his work to social reality, all the while realising that the larger 'objective', i.e. systemic, features of the system would have to change – somehow. Overall, then, Arendt's analysis generally pointed towards action rather than to beliefs (conscious or unconscious), while Adorno's investigated the individual character structure, how it generated and sustained beliefs, such as anti-Semitism, and how that character structure, anchored in social reality, might be transformed.

Yet another way to contrast Adorno and Arendt is to examine the meaning that the term 'totalitarianism' had for each of them. Adorno and his Frankfurt School colleagues used the term quite readily in the 1930s, an indication, among other things, that the term itself was not just the private property of Cold War ideologists.

But it functioned as a synonym for 'fascism', and that in turn referred primarily to Nazi Germany, never to the Soviet Union. Indeed, the Frankfurt School identified those who pinned the term on both Nazi Germany and the Soviet Union as conservatives who had lost their nerve and had, in particular among the emigré community in New York, moved to the right politically. With Arendt, of course, it was a different story. Her *Origins* made the point precisely that both Nazi Germany and Stalin's Soviet Union defined the category 'totalitarian' and were in that respect alike, all differences in informing ideologies and historical circumstances aside.

The problem with Arendt's view was (and is) not the comparative linkage of the two regimes as such. Indeed, a strong argument for it can be made. It was rather that Arendt began her study just after the war with an exclusive focus on Nazi Germany and only in the third section ('Totalitarianism') really switched to the comparative focus. As her biographer notes, the term 'race-imperialism' is used most frequently in the first two-thirds of the book where Arendt develops her analysis of imperialism, racism and anti-Semitism in relation to the rise of National Socialism.[14] By the time she completed *Origins*, her view was that racism, including anti-Semitism, was not integral to totalitarianism; as Stalin's regime showed, the group picked out for elimination could be a class as well: '[p]ractically speaking, it will make little difference whether totalitarian movements . . . organize the masses in the name of race or class . . .'[15] All this aside, the very fact that Arendt linked Germany and the Soviet Union as totalitarian regimes was reason enough for Adorno and the Frankfurt School to ignore her work.

But if Arendt's totalitarian linkage of Nazi Germany and the Soviet Union offended the Frankfurt group's political sensibilities, Adorno (and his colleagues) could be criticised for assuming that anti-Semitism in particular and authoritarian thinking in general were roughly the same in Germany and the United States. Where the analysis of anti-Semitism in *The Dialectic of Enlightenment* was exclusively focused on the German case (except for an addendum to the 1947 edition), the data, provided by questionnaires, psychological tests and the interviews upon which *The Authoritarian Personality* was built, were gathered from Americans in the mid-1940s. This is not to deny either that anti-Semitism was strong in the United States or that there were 'objective' factors in the social and economic system which created the preconditions for the 'authoritarian personality'. It is to suggest, however, that Adorno knew little about the country and made no effort, once the project was underway in 1944, to get better acquainted with it.[16] Nor did he take into account the liberal-democratic political culture which had some meliorating effect on the harsher aspects of racism and of anti-Semitism in the United States, but which had been all but absent in the Germany of the inter-war years. Moreover, if anti-Semitism was in part a revolt against modernity, a dimension which Adorno and Horkheimer strangely downplayed in *The Dialectic of Enlightenment*, then the lack of an entrenched, feudal social structure or feudal cultural ideals in America meant that anti-Semitism, for instance, should have had a different aetiology than in Germany. In Adorno's defence, his purpose in *The Authoritarian Personality* was to develop a general account of prejudiced thinking and thus he could have argued that the similarities overrode the national differences. In adopting this approach, however, he and his colleagues lost the historical detail and specificity which would have allowed differences to emerge.

In sum, once Arendt and Adorno moved into the comparative aspects of their investigations of anti-Semitism and racism, they ran into difficulties. This was due in part to the ambitions of both of them to develop more than just an analysis of anti-Semitism. In Arendt's case, it was to develop a theory of totalitarianism and in Adorno's case, as mentioned, it was to develop a theory of prejudiced thinking in general. Thus the work of both thinkers was marked by a tension between the specific and the general, the concrete historical and the abstract conceptual.

Anti-Semitism: a theory or a history?

In retrospect, one of the most important contributions Adorno and Arendt made was to pose the initial kinds of questions which they felt would illuminate anti-Semitism. As I see it, they asked and tried to answer two essential questions: did modern anti-Semitism represent something new or was it only superficially different from earlier forms of anti-Semitism? And second, were Jews picked out for discrimination because of certain fixed, determinate characteristics or were they tabulae rasae, as it were, upon which were inscribed the dominant society's rejected, negative qualities at certain historical junctures?

In some respects, their answers did not differ widely. Generally Arendt's answers were more detailed and historical, while Adorno's were more general and conceptual. On the question of the 'modernity' of anti-Semitism, Adorno was ambiguous but, overall, inclined to stress the conditions of modernity, particular modern forms of thought, that had generated anti-Semitism as a widespread phenomenon. A certain ambiguity in his thought was created by a shift in emphasis between *The Dialectic of Enlightenment* and *The Authoritarian Personality*. In the former text, Adorno first emphasised the historical and economic conditions under which Jews had been made expendable. Their role as middlemen, facilitating consumption and production in their roles as bankers and merchants, had, with the development of capitalism towards monopoly conditions, been rendered otiose and the resentment of those who were dependent on them financially was stimulated and then channelled into anti-Semitic sentiments and politicised. Thus, Jews could then be made scapegoats for the economic and social insecurities of the modern world.

And yet in the second part of 'Elements of Anti-Semitism', the chapter of *The Dialectic of Enlightenment* which directly addressed the issue, Adorno and Horkheimer posited a deep structure to anti-Semitism which all but assumed a kind of inevitability about anti-Semitism. Their theory of cognitive functioning assumed that we deal with the world optimally by balancing 'projection' out onto the world with 'mimesis' or reflection of it. However, for normal functioning it is also necessary that a self-reflexive element be present, a kind of monitor upon projection to keep it in touch with reality. When that self-reflexive capacity in an individual or a group is disabled, then it becomes more likely that forbidden or resented traits are projected onto others.

But it was the Jews, specifically, that were the object of projection and, in Adorno and Horkheimer's account, this was more than accidental. First, they suggested that the religious conflict between Judaism and Christianity, a cause of enmity in itself in terms of conflicting religious ideologies, was driven by collective Oedipal impulses in which the (Christian) sons seek to do away with the (Jewish) fathers. As they wrote: 'The adherents of the religion of the Father are hated by those who support the religion of the Son – hated by those who know better.'[17] Second, and most interesting, they suggested that there was a deep Gentile ambivalence regarding

Jews, since the latter were unconsciously identified as one group which had not been completely subordinated to the imperatives of civilisation such as a settled existence and steady work. As Adorno stated in an early memo to Horkheimer on the topic of anti-Semitism: 'the abandonment of nomadism was apparently one of the most difficult sacrifices demanded in human history'.[18] Their (the Jews') relationship to nature was a mimetic one and hence closer to nature, as reflected in their inherited rituals, symbols, texts and traditions, than to the modern domination of nature. When confronted with this, Gentiles were both attracted and repulsed; and they could express both envy through imitation ('a mimesis of a mimesis'), while rejecting Jews as a threat to civilisation itself.[19] As Adorno and Horkheimer suggested, the Nazi obsession with ritual, symbol and ceremony and their attraction to the 'natural' and the 'pagan', combined with the mass production and containment of these forces in Nürnberg-type rallies or the Olympic Games, was an attempt both to evoke and to contain the natural: 'Fascism is also totalitarian in that it seeks to make the rebellion of suppressed nature against domination directly useful to domination.'[20]

Overall, then, the picture was mixed. On the one hand Adorno and Horkheimer paid some attention to the contemporary conditions leading to the economic expendability of the Jews. Yet the core of their analysis suggested something much more deep-seated about anti-Semitism and that Jews were not just accidentally chosen to scapegoat since they were identified with certain relatively fixed traits and relationships to the dominant society. Yet why the Germans rather than the Poles or French had politicised what was a kind of fundamental anthropological impulse was neither asked nor answered.

In *The Authoritarian Personality* the emphasis perforce had shifted. Conceived as part of a large project funded by the American Jewish Committee and under the general direction of Horkheimer, there was little place in the volume for psychoanalytic-anthropological speculation and thus the emphasis fell much more on the present and relatively accessible manifestations of prejudiced behaviour. Also, the project was devoted to investigating the 'subjective', i.e. psychological, factors rather than 'objective' economic and social or cultural factors producing prejudice. That said, Adorno's general assumption in his section of *The Authoritarian Personality* was that authoritarian individuals could only be understood against the horizon of a capitalist social system which alienated individuals from their own purposes and desires. Anti-Semitism was best understood as a way of dealing with 'alienation' from, and incomprehension of, larger 'supra-individual laws' and 'social processes' through stereotyping and personalisation.[21]

But what flowed from, and re-enforced, this emphasis upon the subjective was Adorno's focus upon the 'functional' dimension of authoritarian thinking, that is, the psychological gain experienced by the prejudiced person. On the one hand, this meant he made no attempt to see conscious or even unconscious economic interests as underlying prejudice. Rather, the basic analysis, one informed by psychoanalytic ego psychology, was that the authoritarian personality, ostensibly strong and hard, had a fragile ego and was barely able to contain feelings of hostility directed against those in authority or to tolerate weaknesses in itself or in others. This ambivalence in the character structure of the authoritarian personality tended towards a 'sadomasochistic resolution'.[22] At the same time, he or she usually identified with conservatives as upholders of tradition against radicalism. This was what Adorno in one formulation named 'pseudo-conservatism'; and one of the most interesting parts of his contribution to *The Authoritarian Personality* was his construction of a typology of authoritarian personalities, including the 'manipulative' type which he exemplified with Heinrich Himmler and, later, with Adolph Eichmann.[23]

On the other hand, this emphasis upon the psychological and functional made it easy to ignore features of the 'objective' world that dictated authoritarian behaviour. As Edward Shils commented at the time and Zygmunt Bauman has more recently emphasised, the importance of institutional roles and settings was significantly underplayed in Adorno's analysis and this led Bauman to insist, following Stanley Milgram (and implicitly Arendt on Eichmann), that it was less the aggression built into the character structure of the individual than it was the 'obedience to authority' built into the institutions that was the key to how 'it' could have happened.[24]

What this meant was that the characteristics of the object of prejudice, in this case of the Jews, were relatively less important than what was projected onto them. Jews could be and were characterised in diametrically opposed ways (e.g. as revolutionaries or as monopoly capitalists). Thus it wasn't their qualities, but their existence as such that made them likely objects of prejudice and worse. In this respect Adorno's analysis, as he acknowledged, resembled Jean-Paul Sartre's in its emphasis upon the way the anti-Semite 'creates' the Jew, in this view a kind of category without inherent or fixed characteristics rather than a member of a tradition with determinate characteristics. From this point of view, prejudice, including racism and anti-Semitism, is basically grounded in 'heterophobia', fundamental suspicion of the other.[25] Thus a complex conclusion was arrived at in reference to the two questions raised earlier. On the one hand, in *The Authoritarian Personality*, Adorno emphasised the peculiarly modern dimensions of authoritarian thinking. Yet in doing so, he lost the specificity of analysis and the collective depth dimension so central to *The Dialectic of Enlightenment*. Finally, one cannot help but feel that the whole post-war analysis of anti-Semitism, developed by Sartre and Adorno – and to a degree, Arendt – according to which Jews were mobile, floating signifiers who could be attached to a wide variety of meanings or images and who had a stable identity only in their otherness, could have been produced only by thoroughly assimilated Jews, who themselves lacked much sense of a specifically Jewish identity. Overall, Adorno's theory of authoritarianism, convincing and powerful as it was in certain respects, left history far behind.

Arendt's approach was quite different from Adorno's, though why she approached her subject historically is something of a puzzle. Her frame of reference was Europe between the French Revolution and the early 1930s, with an emphasis upon the imperialist expansion of Europe in the mid- to late nineteenth century; the decline of the post-Revolution nation-state based on equality of citizens' rights; and the collapse of the basic institutions of Europe in the wake of World War I and the emergence of a mass society. Indeed, so insistent was Arendt upon stressing the 'objective' elements which 'crystallised' (one of her favourite metaphors) into the preconditions for totalitarianism that she refused causal primacy to the development of racism and anti-Semitism as ideologies. Rather, these phenomena were generated by and woven into the fabric of these larger economic, political and social developments and then worked their influence back on them. Nor did Arendt think that what had happened in Germany and the Soviet Union was inevitable. In fact, in the 'Conclusion' to the first edition of *Origins*, she suggested that all the tendencies and trends that she had analysed had been but 'shadowy forebodings of Hitler's and Stalin's gigantic principled opportunism . . .'[26] All she could and wanted to do was to identify the 'elements' which had come together at that specific point in history to produce modern totalitarianism.

But where was anti-Semitism and race in all this? First of all, Arendt insisted that modern anti-Semitism was a peculiarly modern phenomenon rather than an extension of long-standing Christian hostility to Jews and Judaism. On Arendt's account, the intellectual history of these phenomena saw a fundamental shift in the nineteenth century from what she called 'race-thinking', a relatively familiar concept implying a family rather than a hierarchy of races, to 'racism' as a coherent, all-purpose ideology. Running parallel to and interacting with this development was, she claimed, a shift in the nature of the nation-state. Where the achievement of the French Revolution had been to emphasise the 'state' as a constitutional order of citizens enjoying equal rights, the trend over the course of the nineteenth century was to emphasise the 'nation', which implied the supremacy of the 'people' (*Volk*), encouraged a hostility to the existing order of nation-states, and led to the politicising of ethnic differences in Europe. Finally, she saw parallel shifts in Gentile–Jewish relations as the century unfolded. Where once the emphasis had fallen upon 'Judaism', a relatively objective entity of tradition, beliefs and institutions, by the mid- to late nineteenth century, 'Jewishness' which suggested an (increasingly) permanent set of traits was the central concept: 'Jews had been able to escape from Judaism into conversion; from Jewishness there was no escape. A crime, moreover, is met with punishment; a vice can only be eradicated.'[27]

Overall, these developments were expressed in theories which emphasised the biological bases of race and introduced race into the political discourse of mainstream politics. This meant that the older religious anti-Semitism, what Arendt referred to as 'Jew hatred', was replaced by a modern, anti-Christian version embodied eventually and so clearly in Hitler's National Socialism.[28] If to be a Jew was a biological fate, entailing a set of fixed characteristics rather than a tradition and a set of beliefs, then extermination not conversion was the way to rid the world of Jews. Not just Judaism but Jews had to be abolished.[29]

Behind these developments in thinking about race and ethnicity were two important factors. One reason Arendt objected to the 'scapegoat theory' of anti-Semitism was its assumption that the Jews had been passive objects in the entire process. But Arendt contended that the history of post-emancipation Jewry was marked by two quite crucial (mistaken) choices. First, many middle-class Jews had shown an overwhelming desire to join Gentile society (as what she called 'parvenus'). Second, there had been a concomitant neglect by Jews of the importance of politics and the securing of political and civil equality. Indeed, the history of Judaism, she felt, had simply not equipped Jews with the skills to deal with the politicising of anti-Semitism. The decline of the nation-state had been disastrous for European Jewry, since the large financial families (e.g. the Rothschilds) had been identified with, and at times protected by, the state, to which they occasionally extended financial aid and diplomatic advice. The irony was that as Jews were gradually squeezed out of this financial role around the turn of the century, they were identified increasingly with pernicious international financial conspiracies. Though Arendt was criticised when *Origins* appeared for 'blaming' the Jews for their own fate,[30] she was actually trying to identify the factors which had made it easier for Jews to be deprived of their political and then civil rights and, just as importantly, she was trying to make the political point that Jews could no longer afford to remain indifferent to the political realm. Fatefully, anti-Semitism 'had the dubious honor of setting the whole infernal machine in motion', the destination of which was the horrific creation of a 'society of dying' and a 'system in which men are superfluous'.[31]

But unique in Arendt's historical account was the importance she attributed to late nineteenth-century imperialist expansion and overseas colonisation as a kind of warm-up for Nazi 'race imperialism' and totalitarianism generally. In her view, totalitarianism was the European secret sharer of imperial domination, generated by the combination of 'money' and 'the mob', 'surplus capital' and 'surplus men'. Central to that imperialist ethos was an emphasis not just upon making money but upon expansion and domination for their own sake. Indeed, it was this expansion for expansion's sake, the hostility to stability, that Arendt saw as a dominant characteristic of totalitarian movements even before they came to power. Another crucial by-product of the colonial experience was the development of two institutions that were perfected abroad and brought back to Europe: bureaucracy (and with it contempt for political democracy) and the secret police. In other words, the republics and constitutional regimes of Europe signed their own death warrants by establishing regimes against the will of the indigenous populations.

Finally, closest to our theme, what the Europeans learned abroad – and Arendt's focus fell generally upon Africa rather than Asia – was contempt for the people they ruled and exploited. Clearly influenced by Conrad's *Heart of Darkness*, Arendt saw that two crucial things had happened in central and southern Africa. First, Europeans came to believe that they could act like gods in relation to the native population; that, outside Europe, as she would later be fond of saying about the totalitarian ethos, 'everything is possible'. Second, they learned contempt for the native peoples in a 'natural' state, without, as far as Europeans could tell, any recognisable political or social structures or cultural achievement. Humans without specification, outside the context of culture or seemingly lacking roots in a political community, as pure 'species beings', were not only vulnerable, they were close to contemptible. As she summed it up at one point:

> no matter whether racism appears as the natural result of catastrophe or as the conscious instrument for bringing it about, it is always closely tied to contempt for labor, hatred of territorial limitations, general rootlessness and an activist faith in one's divine chosenness.[32]

The chapter in *Origins* entitled 'Race and Bureaucracy' lay at the heart of Arendt's historical analysis; and like Adorno's focus upon the 'mimesis' between civilised and natural, it was both intriguing and frustratingly unclear. First, the main imperial–colonial powers, France and England, did not fall prey to totalitarian movements at home. With Germany, a more compelling case might have been made, but Arendt devoted remarkably little attention to the link between the German experience in South-West Africa or Tanganyika and the development of Nazism. All of which is to say, Arendt made a powerful case in general for the corrupting influence of imperialism, then failed to establish any very convincing causal connection with a specific European experience. What can be salvaged from her analysis, though, is that the whole imperial experience indirectly and subtly corroded the foundation of republican political orders in Europe and the West generally. Indeed, the disciplines of anthropology and racial science were directly rooted in the colonial experience and fed racist ideas and assumptions into the mainstream of European intellectual and academic life. But we might also read Arendt's account of the African experience less as a causal account than as a foreshadowing or prefiguration of the whole ethos of the totalitarian terror culminating in the death camps. There, as in Africa, emerged forms of domination beyond all rational consideration, even self-interest in the conventional sense, and based on infinite contempt for those being ruled. As she wrote in her research notes for *Origins*: 'Conrad's Kurtz inspite [sic] of being a fiction character has become a reality in the Nazi character'.[33]

However, there was a disturbing element in her representation of the initial European encounters with so-called primitive peoples. For, not only did she present a powerful – and plausible – account of the psychology of the European settler-exploiters with their lust for power and contempt for the natives they ruled, she seemed at times to share, not approval of their barbarism, but an identification with the perception that the Africans, all but lacking the 'human artifice' of culture and political order, could only be viewed against 'the dark background of mere givenness'.[34] Her judgment was based not on an idea of racial difference, but on differences in cultural development. Ironically, what comes to mind here is Adorno's suggestion that those who have been forced to settle and to work, to become 'civilised', not only envy but also hold in contempt those who seem closer to nature by virtue of their unsettled existence. It was something like this attitude that Arendt seemed to be expressing in certain passages in *Origins*.

But Arendt did not claim that any or even all of this made the triumph of National Socialism or the death camps inevitable. Perhaps more directly relevant as a bridge to Nazi and Soviet totalitarianism were the so-called 'Pan' movements that emerged in central and eastern Europe in the late nineteenth century as forms of intra-European imperialism. Indeed, Arendt's analysis of them showed interesting similarities to Adorno's mimesis thesis in her emphasis upon the way that ethnic groups (German and Slav particularly) both resembled and envied the Jews: because members of these two groups lived outside what they considered their homeland, Jews reminded them of their political homelessness. Where the Jews held themselves to be chosen, the 'Pan' movements substituted quasi-racial notions of unity to describe themselves.

The final step into the abyss was, as already mentioned, the collapse of the established cultural, political and social structures of Europe after 1918. In what was essentially a 'view from Weimar', she identified the crucial factors as the displacement of millions of people from their homes; massive and debilitating economic dislocations; and the general loss of meaning and purpose or commonality. It was this historical but also spiritual homelessness, superfluousness and worldlessness, categories that took on ontological meaning in her work, that fertilised the soil in which totalitarianism took root. The 'heart of darkness' was *in* Europe and *was* Europe's. The 'natives' there were also expendable.

Finally, Arendt located the heresy of racism right at the heart of European darkness. It signified the 'break' in the spiritual tradition, of which the Holocaust and totalitarianism were both causes and manifestations:

> For no matter what learned scientists may say, race is, politically speaking, not the beginning of humanity but its end, not the origins of peoples but their decay, not the natural birth of man but his unnatural death.[35]

Put another way, the hegemony of ideological racism, in Europe of anti-Semitism, marked the demise of the idea of a unified human community and hence of the tradition of western humanism. With the human race divided internally by insuperable barriers, it was no longer possible to speak of a common human nature, condition or destination of humanity. All that had perished in the Holocaust.

Modernity and reason

The connection Arendt made between ideological racism and the end of western humanism raises many issues, not least among them the relationship between Arendt's thesis about this 'break' in the tradition and the Adorno–Horkheimer 'dialectic of Enlightenment' thesis. For this, two issues need examining: first, the nature of modernity as it contrasted with the (now) problematic tradition; and, second, the nature of Enlightenment reason. In the space remaining I would like to sketch out the differences between Arendt and Adorno on these issues.

The way Adorno characterised modernity was to refer (ambiguously) to the 'dialectic of Enlightenment' itself. Its most salient characteristics were domination of nature and human affairs, combined with '[t]he anger against all that is different'.[36] On this account marginal groups of whatever sort would have either to be assimilated or eradicated. The background assumption in all of Adorno's work – not stressed in *The Authoritarian Personality* but always present in *The Dialectic of Enlightenment* – was that advanced, monopoly capitalism was the engine running the whole process.

Though Arendt's account of modernity in *Origins* bears a certain resemblance to Adorno's position, the 'feel' of her account is quite different. Where he stressed modernity as a process of ordering and rationalising, she identified modernity with the proliferation of disorder and breakdown. Though she was to characterise the modern world in several ways as her thought developed, her general emphasis, as Margaret Canovan has shown, fell upon two dominant traits: the belief that 'everything is possible' and, somewhat contradictorily, the belief that the process of history was irresistible.[37] Put another way, where Adorno saw modernity as the outcome of a continuous process inherent in the tradition itself, Arendt repeatedly drew attention to modernity's difference from what went before, as illustrated by the gap between imperialism and totalitarian expansion, between race-thinking and racism, between a society organised along class lines and a mass society where these and other demarcations had been seriously weakened. This signalled, in retrospect, the unprecedented nature of the Holocaust and totalitarianism generally and thus a 'break' in the tradition.

Indeed, the differences between Adorno and Arendt can be sharpened when we examine where they saw the process of modernity leading. For Arendt, the collapse of the tradition culminated in the totalitarian regime, dominated by terror and empowered by an ideology focusing on class (Marxism) or race (Nazism), and in which the central institution was the concentration–extermination camp. The goal was the creation of a new order, populated by a new sort of men and women and founded on a 'society of the dying' in the camps. The camps would provide the permanent object lesson of what the potential of human nature had become and what might happen to the ideologically condemned. It was truly a vision of hell on earth made into reality.

For Adorno, strangely enough, it was neither the death camps nor the Gulags but the 'culture industry' that illustrated what modernity had in store; Disneyland, as it were, not Auschwitz. But the most glaring omission in Adorno's account of modernity was any discussion of the Soviet Union, whose ideology and the means adopted to implement it were quintessentially products of the Enlightenment. Under the assumption that advanced capitalism was the originating, driving force of modernity, there was no way for Adorno to explain what had gone on – and wrong – in the Soviet experiment. Nor was there any plausible way to connect the horrors of the Holocaust with the depredations of the culture industry. If there really was some subterranean, fugitive logic connecting the two, Adorno failed to identify it.

How Arendt and Adorno saw the nature of the crisis in the tradition was also strikingly different. Adorno's account of what the Enlightenment referred to was ambiguous in the extreme. Often, the definite article is present and the main term is capitalised, indicating that the origins of modernity lay in the eighteenth century, or even earlier, beginning with a figure such as Francis Bacon. At other times, however, the reference was to 'enlightenment' as a kind of metahistorical process, present from the beginning of western history and identifiable as any and all efforts to understand, explain and order the world. In either case, but particularly the second, there was in Adorno's philosophy of history a sense of inevitability about the whole process and the result was a kind of grand, tragic narrative of intellectual and cultural progress combined with barbarism and domination.

Though Arendt's thesis of the break in the tradition sounded more crisis-filled, it was in some respects more modest than Adorno's. By the 'tradition' she seemed to refer to the fund of values and beliefs, derived from canonical works of religion, philosophy, and literature, that constituted the core of western humanism. Her claim was that there was nothing in the intellectual or moral tradition of the West which could be taken to have prefigured or to have sanctioned what had happened, no line running, as Karl Popper suggested, from Plato through Marx and Hegel to modern totalitarian forms of rule. For instance, racial science, she asserted, was a perversion rather than a representative example of what the scientific tradition of the West had produced. The horrors of totalitarianism were fundamentally aberrations.

Yet it was more complicated than that, and Arendt realised it. Ideological murder and total domination did reveal, in her account, some fundamental inadequacies in the traditions of western thought. For instance, the tradition of political thought could scarcely deal with political behaviour that transcended self-interest or with a form of political rule (totalitarianism) that fitted none of the types of rule enumerated by Aristotle and developed by Montesquieu.[38] Nor did the Christian identification of sin with selfishness do justice to the evil manifested in the death camps. Overall, then, the emergence of political order based upon 'ideology and terror' and committed to rendering human beings superfluous constituted not only a break with the tradition: it 'broke' the tradition. It was in light of this she concluded:

> For man, in the sense of the nature of man, is no longer the measure, despite what the new humanists would have us believe . . . we shall have to create – not merely discover – a new foundation for the human community as such.[39]

Thus where Adorno saw modernity and the horrors at its core as the culmination of the tradition of western thought, Arendt saw the Holocaust as a great aberration, as an unprecedented break. At the same time, Arendt did not react with one of those grand reactionary gestures of retreat and retrieval to which intellectual conservatives are prone. Rather, she insisted that everything – politics, society, culture – would have to be rethought and this was both a great burden and a great opportunity. Adorno, on the other hand, displayed little sense of urgency about rethinking things fundamentally.

Finally, the question of rationality was the central issue for Adorno and the Frankfurt School. Indeed, the tradition of modern German philosophy from Hegel and Kant down through Marx to Nietzsche, Weber and Heidegger, and on to the western Marxists, had been concerned to identify some foundational principle which could once again make history and nature explicable and which would be consonant with human flourishing. It was that problematic task which defined modernity philosophically. The work of

Adorno and Horkheimer clearly fell into that tradition negatively by asserting that modern reason, closer to Weber's 'instrumental reason' than to 'substantive reason', itself generated this will to domination of nature and of human beings. Again, all progress in rationality created new forms of domination, all demystification generated new myths.[40]

Though Adorno didn't develop the thought, the emergence in the nineteenth century of what we can call 'scientific racism' was a prime example of the way rationality, in the form of classifying and studying human types and trying to figure out how to order society in response to perceived, allegedly biological differences, was integral to the domination, extrusion and, of course, extermination of whole categories of human beings. Secondly, the crucial role of science and technology in exterminating millions of human beings by, for instance, developing the vast, 'rational' system of supply and delivery through rail 'transport' to the 'east' demonstrated the power and importance of instrumental rationality in the Holocaust itself. In sum, the Holocaust was impossible without, and was a prime example of, the deployment of modern, Enlightenment rationality in the service of horror.

There is much to this thesis that is irrefutable. Still, Arendt indirectly and others, more directly, have suggested problems with it. One common but still powerful objection is that this line of reasoning confuses means and ends, rational processes with (ir)rational goals, the form with the substance.[41] Just because rational or modern or Enlightenment methods were employed (that the three terms are used synonymously in this argument is a problem itself), does not mean that the goals themselves were rational or entailed by Enlightenment values. Nor do we need the 'dialectic of Enlightenment' thesis to tell us that neutral or even benign techniques, e.g. medical science, can be wedded to inhumane and horrible goals. And yet the suspicion remains that the neat separation of means and ends elides too much, as though there were no connection between the nature of the means and the meaning of the ends.

A second objection to Adorno's thesis would be that the Enlightenment as an historical phenomenon was radically more complicated than the dialectic of Enlightenment thesis would have it. Thus Adorno et al. have 'essentialised' the Enlightenment and transformed it into an internally coherent metaphysical concept.

As Jeffrey Herf has suggested (and Arendt makes us aware), Adorno took no cognisance of the emergence of liberalism as a cast of mind or a political ideology, of theories of rights, or even of forms of democratic republicanism as parts of the Enlightenment 'project'. Moreover, according to Herf, Adorno's thesis confused what did or didn't happen in Germany, what the Enlightenment was or was not responsible for there, with the impact of the Enlightenment elsewhere.[42] But though Herf's is an important objection, it also fails to deal with the fact that a classical Enlightenment figure such as Thomas Jefferson accepted theories of white racial superiority at the time. Indeed, Arendt herself placed the emergence of scientific racism as a political force a good deal later than she should have.

The more general conceptual question is whether there is any internal connection between 'scientific' racism and Enlightenment political and social thinking. As John Diggins has suggested, there was a struggle within the Enlightenment ethos between reason and experience, with the former suggesting that all humans are equal and the latter calling that belief into question, particularly when highly educated masters confronted illiterate and oppressed slaves.[43] And there is no doubt that the possession of critical reason came to be taken as a sign of cultural – and by extension, political – superiority over native peoples in North America and elsewhere as well as over African slaves. On the other hand, what may be at issue is a confusion between asserting a causal relationship between, say, racism and Enlightenment liberalism and noting a historical correlation between the two.

The strongest argument against the idea of the essentially repressive nature of modern rationality would be that, as Arendt and Dwight Macdonald emphasised quite early, the relationship between the extermination–concentration camps and the totalitarian project in Germany was not finally rational in any recognisable way.[44] Their argument might be stated as follows. They would agree with Adorno that the relationship between the extermination of Jews, Gypsies, homosexuals, Poles and other groups was not only rationally effected (i.e. it was done with efficiency, with means and ends correlated); it was also rational in terms of what to the Nazis was their substantive goal of a racially pure society. Obviously, to have a racially pure society, 'impure' or inferior races had to be gotten rid of, if not by extrusion (to the 'east' or even to Madagascar) then by extermination.

Finally, however, Arendt saw that the ideology driving the whole Nazi project of creating a racially pure order was immune to reality, out of contact with 'common sense' or 'experience', though even this might still be considered to be a kind of rationality internal to the ideology. But the problem was that if the Nazis wanted to create a new racial order, they had to win the war. And if they wanted to win the war, they had to marshall all their intellectual and material resources towards that end. The final contradiction, the 'break' in rationality of means and ends, came when the resources involving manpower and rolling stock were diverted from the war effort and applied to the process of extermination (or when, for instance, the theoretical physics needed for development of the atomic bomb was branded as 'Jewish'), rather than using all available resources to try to win the war. That was the ultimate irrationality in the process. As historian Christopher Browning has recently asserted:

> ... any attempt to explain the mass-murder policies of the Nazi regime primarily from rational economic calculation ignores the fact that for the Nazis the mass murder of ideological enemies was in their minds already justified ... Racism was not a delusion or myth hiding real economic interests but rather the 'fixed point' of the system.[45]

Whether an analogous judgment about the murder of class enemies or enemies of the Soviet Union applies to the massive violations of Stalinism is another matter. But what is clear is that any straightforward claim that links Enlightenment-derived rationality as allegedly embodied in modern capitalism or in German national interest with racially based extermination of the Jews and other minorities will not stand up to scrutiny.

Coda

Since Adorno and Horkheimer made their original, very general claim about the will to domination embedded in the dialectic of Enlightenment, refinements have been made in the argument. A recent example can be found in the work of Zygmunt Bauman, who groups 'Auschwitz and the Gulag' together as exemplifying the 'suspicion' that such phenomena:

were legitimate products rather than aberrations, of the character-
istically modern practice of 'ordering by decree'; that the other face
of 'universalisation' is divisiveness, oppression and a leap towards
domination, while the allegedly 'universal' foundation all too often
serves as the mask of intolerance to otherness and licence for the
smothering of the alterity of the Other; that, in other words, the
price of the project of humanisation is more inhumanity.[46]

Two arguments are being made in this statement. The first – the
causal relationship between the will to universalise and domination – seems plausible; but the second – the link between a 'universal foundation' and 'the mask of intolerance to otherness' – is
more problematic, at least if an argument about racial and ethnic
intolerance is being made. Nor is Bauman entirely clear on whether
these links are 'legitimate products, rather than aberrations', that
is, inevitable; or whether there is a looser connection ('all too
often') between them. My main point here is that the dialectic of
Enlightenment thesis, expressed in a more tenable and powerful
way here by Bauman, works better for the Soviet case, where the
ethnic–racial dimension was not central, than for the Nazi case,
where it manifestly was. Overall, I would adopt Arendt's position
that nothing should be taken as historically inevitable. To do so
is not only to mistake the nature of human history but to create
a bias towards passivity which is politically dangerous.

Notes

1. Background on Adorno and the Frankfurt School of Social Research
   with which he was associated officially after the mid-1930s is drawn
   from Martin Jay, *The Dialectical Imagination: A History of the Frankfurt School and the Institute of Social Research, 1923–1950* (Boston:
   Little, Brown & Co., 1973), and also his *Permanent Exiles: Essays
   on the Intellectual Migration from Germany to America* (New York:
   Columbia University Press, 1985). See also Rolf Wiggershaus's more
   recent *The Frankfurt School: Its History, Theories and Political Significance*, trans. Michael Robertson (Cambridge, U.K.: Polity Press,
   1994). Hartmut Scheible, *Theodor Adorno* (Hamburg: Rowohlt
   Taschenbuch Verlag, 1989), is also very useful.
       There are many studies of Arendt's work, but most useful bio-
   graphically are Elisabeth Young-Bruehl, *Hannah Arendt: For Love of
   the World* (New Haven and London: Yale University Press, 1982),

and *Hannah Arendt and Karl Jaspers: Briefwechsel, 1926–1969*, ed. Lotte Köhler and Hans Saner (München and Zürich: Piper Verlag, 1985).

2. Theodor Adorno and Max Horkheimer, *The Dialectic of Enlightenment* (New York: Herder and Herder, 1972); and Theodor Adorno, et al., *The Authoritarian Personality* (New York: Harper and Row, 1950). For Arendt, I will be using *The Origins of Totalitarianism*, 2nd edn (Cleveland and New York: Meridian Books, 1958), unless otherwise indicated.

3. I have no evidence indicating that Arendt actually had *The Authoritarian Personality* in mind when she wrote *Eichmann in Jerusalem*.

4. At least from Arendt's side, a series of things over the years turned her against Adorno. These included actions by Adorno involving her first husband, Günther Stern, and Adorno's treatment of Benjamin; revelations that Adorno dropped his Jewish patronymic, Wiesengrund; and, more importantly, wrote a mildly favourable review of a piece of music based on a poem by the Nazi Baldur von Schirach in 1934; and Adorno's strong distaste for the thought not only of Martin Heidegger but also Karl Jaspers.

5. Jürgen Habermas, *Philosophical–Political Profiles* (London: Heinemann, 1985), p. 7; Wiggershaus, *The Frankfurt School*, p. 195.

6. Quoted in Young-Bruehl, *For Love of the World*, p. 104. The charge from Scholem arose in the midst of the controversy over her *Eichmann in Jerusalem*.

7. Translation from Max Horkheimer, 'Die Juden und Europe', *Zeitschrift für Sozialforschung*, 8, 1–2 (1939).

8. '"What Remains? The Language Remains": A Conversation with Gunter Gaus' (1964), in *Essays in Understanding, 1930–1954*, ed. Jerome Kohn (New York: Harcourt Brace and Co., 1994), p. 12.

9. The phrase 'analysis in terms of history' comes from Arendt, 'A Reply to Eric Voegelin' in *Arendt: Essays in Understanding, 1930–1954*, pp. 401–8. The terms 'explanation' and 'origins' are placed in inverted commas since Arendt in fact rejected the desirability of explaining totalitarianism and also was suspicious of any attempt to find its origins.

10. Adorno and Horkheimer, *Dialectic*, p. 3.

11. See Axel Honneth, 'Integrity and Disrespect: Principles of a Conception of Morality Based on the Theory of Recognition', *Political Theory*, 20, 2 (May 1992), 187–201, for an exploration of these two modes of radical analysis.

12. Arendt, *Origins*, pp. 296–8.

13. Hannah Arendt, *Rahel Varnhagen: The Life of a Jewish Woman*, rev. edn (New York and London: Harcourt Brace Jovanovich, 1974), p. xviii.

14. Elisabeth Young-Bruehl, *For Love of the World*, p. 203.

15. Arendt, *Origins*, 306. One objection to the totalitarian line of analysis is that it tends to 'wash out' the specifically anti-Semitic core of National Socialism. See Saul Friedländer, *Reflections of Nazism: An Essay on Kitsch and Death* (Bloomington and Indianapolis, Ind.: Indiana University Press, 1993), pp. 122–3, 126–7.

16. See Wiggershaus, *The Frankfurt School*, p. 416, where he contrasts Adorno with Gunnar Myrdal, who visited the South several times and talked to members of both races, both lay people and scholars, in preparation of his massive *An American Dilemma* (1944).

17. Adorno and Horkheimer, *Dialectic*, p. 303.

18. Adorno, quoted in Wiggershaus, *The Frankfurt School*, pp. 276–7.

19. Adorno and Horkheimer, *Dialectic*, pp. 183, 185.

20. Ibid., p. 185.

21. Adorno et al., *The Authoritarian Personality*, pp. 618–19.

22. Ibid., p. 759.

23. Ibid., pp. 753–71. See Adorno, 'Erziehung nach Auschwitz' in *Stichworte* (Frankfurt-am-Main: Suhrkamp, 1969), pp. 85–101, for the reference to Eichmann.

24. Edward Shils, 'Authoritarianism: "Right" and "Left"' in *Studies in the Scope and Method of 'The Authoritarian Personality'*, ed. Richard Christie and Marie Jahoda (Glencoe, Ill.: The Free Press, 1954), p. 120; Zygmunt Bauman, *Modernity and the Holocaust* (Cambridge, U.K.: Polity Press, 1989), pp. 152–3.

25. The reference to Sartre is in *The Authoritarian Personality*, p. 971. 'Heterophobia' is Bauman's term and refers to our most general sort of undifferentiated fear of that which is different. Bauman denies that it is the crucial ingredient in modern anti-Semitism and racism. See Bauman, *Modernity and the Holocaust*, pp. 62–4, for a discussion of this matter.

26. Arendt, *Origins* (New York: Harcourt, Brace and Company, 1951), p. 431. This is one of the few passages in which Arendt mentions or attributes importance to Hitler or Stalin.

27. Arendt, *Origins*, 2nd edn, p. 87.

28. Ibid., p. 7.

29. See Paul L. Rose, *Revolutionary Anti-Semitism in Germany from Kant to Wagner* (Princeton, N.J.: Princeton University Press, 1990), for an analysis of this particularly German attempt to rid Germany of Judaism. Rose does not deny that there was a shift between religiously and racially ethnic based anti-Semitism but denies, contra Arendt, that it made that much difference. The goal was still ultimately to rid the world of Judaism.

30. For this criticism, see Philip Rieff's review of *Origins* in 'The Theology of Politics', *The Feeling Intellect* (Chicago, Ill.: University of Chicago Press, 1990), pp. 86–97.

31. Ibid., p. 3; *Origins*, 1st edn, pp. 427–8.
32. Arendt, *Origins*, 2nd edn, p. 197.
33. Arendt, Letter to Mary B. Underwood, Container 76 ('Outlines and Research Memoranda File'), Arendt Papers, Library of Congress, Washington, D.C. , p. 4.
34. *Origins*, 2nd edn, p. 157.
35. Ibid.
36. Adorno and Horkheimer, *Dialectic*, p. 207.
37. Margaret Canovan, *Hannah Arendt: A Re-interpretation of her Political Thought* (Cambridge, U.K.: Cambridge University Press, 1992).
38. See Aristotle, *Politics*, chap. 3, and Montesquieu, *The Spirit of the Laws*, chap. 3.
39. Arendt, *Origins*, 1st edn, p. 434.
40. Wiggershaus, *The Frankfurt School*, pp. 332–3, is very good in analysing the difficulties Adorno and Horkheimer landed in with the concept of rationality. Sometimes instrumental or 'subjective' reason is contrasted dualistically with substantive or 'objective' reason; at other times, the former is an aberrant development of the latter; and at still others, the one generates the other dialectically.
41. See Ian Buruma, *Wages of Guilt* (London: Vintage, 1995), p. 89, for the point about confusing the rationality of means with ends.
42. Jeffrey Herf, *Reactionary Modernism: Technology, Culture and Politics in Weimar and the Third Reich* (Cambridge, U.K.: Cambridge University Press, 1986), presents a thorough-going challenge to the Frankfurt School thesis.
43. John Patrick Diggins, 'Slavery, Race and Equality: Jefferson and the Pathos of the Enlightenment', *American Quarterly*, XXVIII, 2 (Summer 1976), 206–28.
44. Dwight Macdonald, 'The Responsibility of Peoples' (1945), in *Memoirs of a Revolutionist* (Cleveland, Ohio: Meridian Books, 1958); see also Arendt, 'Social Science Techniques and the Study of Concentration Camps', in *Essays in Understanding*, p. 233. Macdonald and Arendt were good friends and his essay was clearly influenced by some of her early essays and personal conversations between the two.
45. Christopher Browning, *The Path to Genocide: Essays on Launching the Final Solution* (Cambridge, U.K.: Cambridge University Press, 1995), pp. 75–6. Interestingly, Browning rejects the notion that extermination was carried out because Jews had become somehow economically a burden or superfluous. This would seem on the surface to undercut Arendt's emphasis upon 'superfluousness', but her concept is less an economic than an ontological one.
46. Zygmunt Bauman, 'Morality without Ethics', *Theory, Culture & Society*, vol. 11 (1994), 18.

EXTRACT ONE

From John Locke, *Second Treatise of Government* (1690)

EXTENT AND END OF CIVIL GOVERNMENT.

CHAP. V.

OF PROPERTY.

Sec. 26.   God, who hath given the world to men in common, hath also given them reason to make use of it to the best advantage of life, and convenience. The earth, and all that is therein, is given to men for the support and comfort of their being. And tho' all the fruits it naturally produces, and beasts it feeds, belong to mankind in common, as they are produced by the spontaneous hand of nature; and no body has originally a private dominion, exclusive of the rest of mankind, in any of them, as they are thus in their natural state: yet being given for the use of men, there must of necessity be a means to appropriate them some way or other, before they can be of any use, or at all beneficial to any particular man. The fruit, or venison, which nourishes the wild Indian, who knows no enclosure, and is still a tenant in common, must be his, and so his, i.e. a part of him, that another can no longer have any right to it, before it can do him any good for the support of his life. [...]

Sec. 27.   Though the earth, and all inferior creatures, be common to all men, yet every man has a property in his own person: this no body has any right to but himself. The labour of his body, and the work of his hands, we may say, are properly his. Whatsoever then he removes out of the state that nature hath provided, and left it in, he hath mixed his labour with, and joined to it something that is his own, and thereby makes it his property. It being by him removed from the common state nature hath placed it in, it hath by this labour something annexed to it, that excludes the common right of other men: for this labour being the unquestionable property of the labourer, no man but he can have a right to what that is once joined to, at least where there is enough, and as good, left in common for others. [...]

Sec. 30.   Thus this law of reason makes the deer that Indian's who hath killed it; it is allowed to be his goods, who hath bestowed his labour upon it, though before it was the common right of every one. And amongst those who are counted the civilised part of mankind, who have made and multiplied positive laws to determine property, this original law of nature, for the beginning of property, in what was before common, still takes place. [. . .]

Sec. 32. [. . .] As much land as a man tills, plants, improves, cultivates, and can use the product of, so much is his property. [. . .]

Sec. 34. God gave the world to men in common; but since he gave it them for their benefit, and the greatest conveniencies of life they were capable to draw from it, it cannot be supposed he meant it should always remain common and uncultivated. He gave it to the use of the industrious and rational, (and labour was to be his title to it;) not to the fancy or covetousness of the quarrelsome and contentious. [. . .]

Sec. 37. Before the appropriation of land, he who . . . so imployed his pains about any of the spontaneous products of nature, as any way to alter them from the state which nature put them in, by placing any of his labour on them, did thereby acquire a propriety in them: but if they perished, in his possession, without their due use; if the fruits rotted, or the venison putrified, before he could spend it, he offended against the common law of nature, and was liable to be punished; he invaded his neighbour's share, for he had no right, farther than his use called for any of them, and they might serve to afford him conveniencies of life. [. . .]

Sec. 41. [. . .] several nations of the Americans, who are rich in land, and poor in all the comforts of life; whom nature having furnished as liberally as any other people, with the materials of plenty [. . .] yet for want of improving it by labour, have not one hundredth part of the conveniencies we enjoy: and a king of a large and fruitful territory there, feeds, lodges, and is clad worse than a day-labourer in England. [. . .]

Sec. 43. An acre of land, that bears here twenty bushels of wheat, and another in America, which, with the same husbandry, would do the like, are, without doubt, of the same natural intrinsic value: but yet the benefit mankind receives from the one in a year, is worth 5l. and from the other possibly not worth a penny, if all the profit an Indian received from it were to be valued, and sold here; at least, I may truly say, not one thousandth. It is labour then which puts the greatest part of value upon land, without which it would scarcely be worth any thing: it is to that we owe the greatest part of all its useful products. [. . .]

Sec. 48. And as different degrees of industry were apt to give men possessions in different proportions, so [the] invention of money gave them the opportunity to continue and enlarge them [. . .] I ask, what would a man value ten thousand, or an hundred thousand acres of excellent land, ready cultivated, and well stocked too with cattle, in the middle of the inland parts of America, where he had no hopes of commerce with other parts of the world, to draw money to him by the sale of the product? It would not be worth the enclosing, and we should see him give up again to the wild common of nature, whatever was more than would supply the conveniencies of life to be had there for him and his family.

Sec. 49.   Thus in the beginning all the world was America, and more so than that is now; for no such thing as money was any where known. Find out something that hath the use and value of money amongst his neighbours, you shall see the same man will begin presently to enlarge his possessions.

EXTRACT TWO

Extracts from *The Diario of Christopher Columbus's First Voyage to America 1492–1493*, ed. Oliver Dunn and James E. Kelley (Norman: University of Oklahoma Press, 1989)

Friday 23 November

The Admiral steered all day toward the land to the south [. . .] Beyond this cape [of the land to the south] appeared another higher land or cape which also runs to the east, which those Indians that he was bringing called Bohío, which they said was very large and that there were people on it who had one eye in their foreheads, and others whom they called cannibals, of whom they showed great fear. And when they saw that he was taking this route, he says that they could not talk, because the cannibals eat them, and that they are people very well armed. The Admiral says that well he believes there is something in what they say, but that since they were armed they must be people of intelligence; and he believed that they must have captured some of them and because they did not return to their own lands they would say that they ate them. They believed the same thing about the Christians and about the Admiral when some Indians first saw them.

Saturday 24 November

[. . .] All the people that he has found up to today, he says, have extreme fear of the men of Caniba, or Canima, and they say that they live on this island of Bohío, which must be very large, as it seems to him . . . He says that after they saw him take the route to this land they could not speak, fearing that they would have them to eat; and he could not take away their fear. And they say that they have but one eye and the face of a dog; and the Admiral thought they were lying and felt that those who captured them must have been under the rule of the Grand Khan.

[. . .]

Wednesday 26 December

[. . .] While the Admiral was talking to him [the local king], another canoe came from another place bringing certain pieces of gold which they wished to give for one bell, because they desired nothing else as much as bells [. . .] later a sailor who came from land told the Admiral it was a thing to marvel at, the pieces of gold that the Christians who were ashore traded for a trifle [. . .] The king rejoiced to see the Admiral happy, and he understood that he wanted a lot of gold; and he told him by signs that he knew where, nearby, there was very much, a great quantity of it, and to be of good heart, that he would give him as much gold as he might want. And, about this [gold], the Admiral says that the king gave him a report and, in particular, [said] that there was gold in Cipango, which they call Cybao, in such degree that they hold it in no regard and that he would bring it there; but also that in the island of Hispaniola, which they call Bohío, and in that province of Caribata, there was much more of it [. . .] After they finished [eating], the king took the Admiral to the beach, and the Admiral sent for a Turkish bow and a handful of arrows; and he had one of the men of his company who was familiar with it shoot it; and to the lord, since he did not know what weapons are, because they do not have and do not use them, it appeared a great thing [. . .] The Admiral told him by signs that the sovereigns of Castile would order the Caribs destroyed, and they would order all of them to be brought with hands tied. The Admiral ordered a lombard and a spingard to be fired, and when the king saw the effect of their force and what they penetrated, he was astonished. And when his people heard the shots they all fell to the ground. They brought the Admiral a large mask that had large pieces of gold in the ears and eyes and on other places. The king gave it to him with other gold jewels that he himself had put on the Admiral's head and neck; and to the other Christians who were with him he also gave many things.

EXTRACT THREE

From: Daniel L. Littlefield, ed., *A Sketch of the Life of Okah Tubbee, (called) William Chubbee, Son of the Head Chief, Mosholeh Tubbee, of the Choctaw Nation of Indians, by Laah Ceil Elaah Tubbee, His Wife* (Lincoln: Nebraska University Press, 1988)

NARRATIVE

SKETCH OF THE EVENTFUL LIFE OF
OKAH TUBBEE,
(CALLED) WILLIAM CHUBBEE

*[Here commences a true narrative,
drawn up from his own lips.]*

FIRST RECOLLECTIONS.

The first recollections of my childhood are scenes of sorrow; though I have an imperfect recollection of a kind father, who was a very large man, with dark, red skin, and his head was adorned with feathers of a most beautiful plumage. I seem to have been happy then, and remember the green woods, and that he took me out at night, and taught me to look up to the stars, and said many things to me that made my young heart swell with sweet hope, as it filled with thoughts too large for it to retain. This scene soon changed, for I had a new father, or a man who took me to a new home, which proves to have been Natchez, Mississippi. I have no recollection where this intercourse took place with my own father, but from various circumstances which have since occurred, I am led to believe that it must have been upon the Dancing Rabbit Creek, (Tombigbee) before the Choctaws removed from their old homes. I soon found this was not my own father, neither in appearance nor in action, and began to understand that I could have but one father. This man was white, and a slave woman had the management of his house, she had two children, who were older than myself, a boy and a girl; she was very fond of them, but was never even kind to me, yet they obliged me to call her mother. I was always made to serve the two children, though many times I had to be whipped into obedience. If I had permission to go out an hour to play, I chose to be alone, that I might weep over my situation; but even this consolation was refused me. I was forced to go in company with them, taking with me, many times, a smarting back, after a promise had been extorted from me that I would remain with them and obey them. I soon found myself boxing heartily with the boys, both white and black, because they called me an ill name, and every thing but that which was true, for I could not and would not submit to such gross insults without defending myself, which is so characteristic of the red man. Her children were well dressed and neat; I was not only in rags, but many times my proud heart seemed crushed within me, and my cheek crimsoned with shame because of their filthy condition, and I often left them off in consequence, but soon learned to take them off and wash them myself, such was my abhorrence of filth. I was compelled to go in a naked state to enable me to wash my clothes, and they upbraided me for my nakedness, but I replied, where did you ever see or hear of a child being born with clothes on? I was then a child too young to work, but did errands.

[. . .]

ANOTHER VERSION OF HIS ORIGINS.

[. . .] While I was in prison, a white man came to me, and said he had many things to say to me to which I must listen attentively. He told me that the woman called my mother was a slave, as well as the mother of the two children, but she was set free before the birth of these two children, consequently her two children were free, but I was their slave. This unloosed my tongue, and raised every angry passion of my nature. I loudly asserted that he had brought me from my own home, and had made me a slave; he bade me be quiet until he could tell me all; he then changed his tone, and told me I had a father, probably a white man, but as he did not come to buy me, I was consequently given over as a slave to the children. He said I must never reveal this. I told him I could not and would not make any such promises, for I would be sure to break them, and to spare himself the trouble of trying to console me with such base falsehoods. I told him this woman when angry called me different names; wishing she had never seen the wild savage devils, sometimes even calling me a white woman's child, which, beside her evil treatment, gave me every reason to believe she was not my mother. I told him that some strange mysteries hung over my birth, and I accused him of knowing what it was, and on my knees implored him to unravel it to me if to none other, telling him by so doing he would console me. He turned coldly from me, while I stretched myself on the floor in despair, assuring him my blood was free, and pure. I crawled around where I could look him in the face, telling him he need not fear to rescue me from this place of abuse and disgrace, that every step in after life should be to prove it, and honour him, but he said nothing. I then thought he would do nothing for me; I said, well, I will bear it; it will lay me in my grave, and there I shall be free. He was touched with my earnest importunity; gazed upon me a moment, then stooped, and raised me from the floor with his own hand, and he begged me to be calm, to compose the tumult of my feelings, saying it is a pity you should be wronged for the love of money, for let your skin be what it may, you have a noble heart. [. . .]

[FIRST MEETING WITH INDIANS.]

[. . .] I had just stepped out of a door into the street as they were coming down the street; they were walking slowly, seeming to be looking at the buildings; I appeared nailed to the spot, my heart leaped with joy, yet a choking sensation amounting to pain seized me; confused ideas crowded upon my mind; they were near me, yet I moved not, until the keen eyes of one of them rested upon me; he spoke, the eyes of the whole company turned upon me, and then upon each other, while as it seemed to me they uttered an exclamation of surprise; they came towards me; I was wild with delight, I thought I was their child, that they were seeking for me; I started and held out my hands, tears gushed from my eyes, I addressed them in a language to me unknown before; it was neither English, Spanish, or French; astonished, they spoke kind to me, smoothing my hair with their hands; an explanation now took place, as one could speak English; he said I had asked in Choctaw for my father, saying he had gone and left me, and I was with bad people; that I begged to know if he was not with them. They then asked for my mother. This pained me, I told them she was not my mother; they looked at each other, spoke faster and louder, and looked very angry; there had a crowd of children, and men and women gathered; the Indians loudly asked where and to whom does this child belong? Some one answered to a colored woman. The clouds seemed to grow darker on their wry, yet to me, sweet face, the same one said, to a slave woman, and he is a slave. The Indian held his hands high above his head and said, 'but white man lie, he no good, him no slave no, bad white man steal him, his skin is red'; this was repeated in imperfect English by them all – 'me I love him' the crowd were some smoking, laughing, some mocking, angry and cursing.

EXTRACT FOUR

From: Lorimer Fison and A.W. Howitt, *Kamilaroi and Kurnai: Group Marriage and Elopement. Drawn Chiefly from the Usage of the Australian Aborigines. Also the Kurnai Tribe. Their Customs in Peace and War* (Melbourne, Sydney, Adelaide and Brisbane: George Robertson, 1880).

[. . .] About a week after the boys have run away from their mothers into the bush, the old men go out and make certain wooden instruments called tŭrndūn. The women are not permitted to know anything about this. Three or four of the very old men who cannot hunt remain with the lads to look after them. In the evening after supper time, when it is beginning to be dusk, the other old men come up, each bringing with him a tŭrndūn. Each lad has his head covered up in a 'possum rug, so that he cannot see anything but the ground. An old man puts a throwing stick under the rug, and says, 'Look at the mŭrrawŭn – look where it is going to!' Then he lifts the mŭrrawŭn, pointing upwards, the boy's eyes fixed upon it. Then he points to the old men round, who, in the twilight, are sounding the tŭrndūns, and says, 'See the tŭrndūn'! This has been done to all the boys at the same time. They stare at the strange sight – a wonderful thing, such as they have never seen before. Each boy is held by an old man by the back of the neck with the left hand, while in the right he points a spear to the boy's eye, and says, 'If you tell this to any woman you will die – you will see the ground broken up and like the sea; if you tell this to any woman, or to any child, you will be killed.'
When the time has arrived at which the youth may return, his face is painted with pipeclay and red ochre; feathers are placed in his hair. The mothers are placed in a line – before each one is a bark vessel full of water – before each one stands her son. She stoops to drink – he splashes a little water in her face – she rises up with a mouthful of water, which she squirts over his head; and she repeats this till he is well wetted. The ceremonies are now ended. He is no longer under his mother's control. He is a man. He is no longer wot-wotti, or tūtnŭrrŭng, but jerra-eil. From this time the young men (brewit) are no longer part of the paternal and maternal group, but live in a camp of their own.
All the jerra-eil who have been initiated at the same time are brothers, and in the future address each other's wives as 'wife', and each other's child as 'child'.

It was from Tūlabā that I first obtained particulars of this custom, and who afterwards arranged the rehearsal of the ceremony.

I said jokingly to him, 'I am jerra-eil now.' He replied, 'Yes, now you are my brogan.' Being his brogan, it followed, as I have said, that a peculiar relation was established, and in accordance with the custom, his wife often addressed me as 'brā bittel' (my husband), whilst I spoke to her as 'rūkut bittel' (my wife).

The ceremony which I have described may seem to us but trivial, but to the Kŭrnai it has been an ancient custom of great moment. It formed a bond of peculiar strength, binding together all the contemporaries of the various clans of the Kŭrnai. [. . .] It was a brotherhood including all the descendants of the eponymous male and female ancestors, Yeerŭng and Djeetgŭn.

The young man, or brewit, after his initiation may be said to have commenced a life independent, to some extent, of his parents. He lived with the other young men, and with those who were initiated with him and are his 'brothers'. On the other hand, the girl still lived with her parents. After a while the young man thinks it time to be married. For him a wife might not be within the prohibited degrees of brother and sister, which include all those whom we call cousins. She might not be of his division of the clan – nor, as I shall show later on, at least in some cases, of the division to which his mother belonged. She might even be a 'Brajerak',* could he find one to accept him, or could he acquire such a woman by conquest. But properly she should be a Djeetgŭn as he is a Yeerŭng. [. . .]

The young Kŭrnai could, as a rule, acquire a wife in one way only. He must run away with her. Native marriage might be brought about in various ways. [. . .] But in every such case it was essential for success that the parents of the bride should be utterly ignorant of what was about to take place. It was no use his asking for a wife excepting under most exceptional circumstances, for he could only acquire one in the usual manner, and that was by running off with her.[†]

---

* This word is used to designate any other aboriginal native than one of the Kŭrnai tribe. As Kŭrnai means *man*, so Brajerak means *wild man* from Bra – man, and yeerak or jeerak – angry or savage.

[†] As my friend and correspondent, the Rev. J. Bulmer, of Lake Tyers mission, expressed doubts to me as to the accuracy of my informants' statements on this point, I not only re-examined them, but, in order to obtain a check, I went to the Ramahyŭck mission, and there questioned four women who were most likely to be able to speak positively. They were of the Briakolŭng and Bratauolŭng clans. I questioned them as to the marriage customs of the Kŭrnai *before the white man came*. Of these women, one was young, one middle aged, and two old; and all were, or had been, married. One woman, 'Nanny', is the oldest living Gippsland aborigine, having been a widow, with grey hair, when Angus M'Millan discovered

the country. She stated positively that the rule was that all young women ran off with their husbands; and she could only recollect three cases where girls had been given away. Her own was one of these, and she explained it by saying that she had no parents, but only brothers, who gave her to a friend; and that in such a case there would be no necessity for running away, or for the husband having to fight his wife's relatives. This instance proves the rule and explains the exception, at any rate among the Briakolūng Kūrnai. There are, however, indications that this rule, as also the rules regulating intermarriage between certain divisions, were relaxed among the Brabrolūng and the Kroatūngolūng.

Select bibliography

This bibliography lists principal works referred to by the contributors. For other useful items see the notes to each essay. Not included here are works on race that have not been referenced in any of the essays. The literature on race is enormous.

Adorno, Theodor et al., *The Authoritarian Personality* (New York: Harper and Row, 1950).

Ahmad, Aijaz, *In Theory: Classes, Nations, Literatures* (London: Verso, 1994).

Arendt, Hannah, *The Origins of Totalitarianism*, 2nd edn (Cleveland: Meridian Books, 1958).

Arendt, Hannah, *Essays in Understanding, 1930–1954*, ed. Jerome Kohn (New York: Harcourt Brace and Co., 1994).

Arnold, A. James, *Modernism and Negritude: The Poetry and Poetics of Aimé Césaire* (Massachusetts: Harvard University Press, 1981).

Attwood, Bain, *The Making of the Aborigines* (Sydney: Allen and Unwin, 1992).

Baker, Houston A., Jr, *Modernism and the Harlem Renaissance* (Chicago: Chicago University Press, 1987).

Barnett, Louise K., *The Ignoble Savage: American Literary Racism, 1790–1890* (Westport, Conn.: Greenwood Press, 1975).

Berkhofer, Robert F., Jr, *The White Man's Indian: Images of the American Indian from Columbus to the Present* (New York: Alfred A. Knopf, 1978).

Bernabé, Jean, Chamoiseau, Patrick, and Confiant, Raphael, *In Praise of Creoleness (bilingual edition)*, trans. M.B. Taleb-Khyar (Paris: Gallimard, 1993).

Bhabha, Homi K., *The Location of Culture* (London: Routledge, 1994).

Bleys, Rudi C., *The Geography of Perversion: Male-to-male Sexual Behaviour outside the West and the Ethnographic Imagination 1750–1918* (London: Cassell, 1996).

Blu, Karen I., *The Lumbee Problem: The Making of an American Indian People* (New York: Cambridge University Press, 1980).

Boime, Albert, *The Art of Exclusion: Representing Blacks in the Nine-teenth Century* (Washington, D.C.: Smithsonian Press, 1990).

Brumble, David H., *American Indian Autobiography* (Berkeley: California University Press, 1988).

Burroughs, Edgar Rice, *Tarzan of the Apes*, 5th edn (London: Methuen & Co., Ltd, 1919).

Burton, Richard, *Tales from the Arabian Nights: Selected from the Book of the Thousand Nights and a Night*, ed. David Shumaker (Avenal, New Jersey: Gramercy Books, 1977).

Burton, Richard, *The Thousand Nights and a Night* (London and Benares: Kama Shastra Society, 1885).

Césaire, Aimé, *Notebook of a Return to the Native Land*, trans. Clayton Eshelman and Annette Smith (Berkeley: University of California Press, 1983).

Clifford, James, 'On Ethnographic Allegory', in *Writing Culture: The Poetics and Politics of Ethnography*, pp. 98–121, ed. James Clifford and George E. Marcus (Berkeley: University of California Press, 1986).

Clifton, James A., ed., *Being and Becoming Indian: Biographical Studies of North American Frontiers* (Prospect Heights, Illinois: Waveland Press, Inc., 1989).

Columbus, Christopher, *The Diario of Christopher Columbus' First Voyage to America: 1492–1493*, ed. and trans. Oliver Dunn and James E. Kelley (Norman: Oklahoma University Press, 1989).

Condé, Maryse, *I, Tituba, Black Witch of Salem*, trans. Richard Philcox (New York: Ballantine, 1992).

Darwin, Charles, *The Origin of Species by Means of Natural Selection*, last (6) edn (London: Watts & Co. [n.d.]).

Darwin, Charles, *The Descent of Man, and Selection in Relation to Sex*, Introduction by John Tyler Bonner and Robert May (Princeton: Princeton University Press, 1981).

Davis, Charles T., and Gates, Henry Louis, Jr, eds, *The Slave's Narrative* (Oxford: Oxford University Press, 1985).

Dearborn, Mary V., *Pocahontas's Daughters: Gender and Ethnicity in American Culture* (New York: Oxford University Press, 1986).

Degler, Carl, *Neither White Nor Black: Slavery and Race Relations in Brazil and the United States* (New York: Macmillan, 1971).

Douglass, Frederick, *Narrative of the Life of Frederick Douglass, an American Slave, Written by Himself* (New York: Signet, 1968).

Dove, Mourning, *Cogewea, the Half-Blood* (Lincoln: Nebraska University Press, 1981).

Eastman, Charles, *Indian Boyhood* (New York: Dover, 1971).

Eastman, Charles, *From the Deep Woods to Civilisation: Chapters in the Autobiography of an Indian* (Lincoln: Nebraska University Press, 1977).

Fabian, Johannes, *Time and the Other: How Anthropology Makes its Object* (New York: Columbia University Press, 1983).

Fabre, Geneviève, and O'Meally, Robert, eds, *History and Memory in African-American Culture* (New York: Oxford University Press, 1994).

Fanon, Frantz, *Black Skin, White Masks*, trans. Charles Lam Markmann (London: Pluto, 1986).

Fanon, Frantz, *The Wretched of the Earth* (London: Penguin, 1990).

Fison, Lorimer, and Howitt, A.W., *Kamilaroi and Kurnai: Group Marriages and Relationship, and Marriage by Elopement, Drawn Chiefly from the Usage of the Australian Aborigines. Also the Kurnai Tribe, Their Customs in Peace and War* (Melbourne, Sydney: George Robertson, 1880).

Forbes, Jack D., *Black Africans and Native Americans: Color, Race and Caste in the Evolution of Red-Black Peoples* (Oxford: Basil Blackwell, 1988).

Freud, Sigmund, 'The Uncanny', in *Art and Literature*, pp. 335–76, The Penguin Freud Library, vol. 14, ed. Albert Dickson (London: Penguin, 1990).

Friedman, John Block, *The Monstrous Races in Medieval Art and Thought* (Cambridge, Mass.: Harvard University Press, 1981).

Gates, Henry Louis, Jr, ed., *'Race', Writing and Difference* (Chicago: Chicago University Press, 1986).

Gates, Henry Louis, Jr, *Figures in Black: Words, Signs and the 'Racial' Self* (New York: Oxford University Press, 1987).

Gilroy, Paul, *The Black Atlantic: Modernity and Double Consciousness* (Cambridge, Mass.: Harvard University Press, 1993).

Gissing, George, *The Nether World* (Oxford: Oxford University Press, 1992).

Glissant, Edouard, *Caribbean Discourse: Selected Essays*, trans. J. Michael Dash (Charlottesville: University Press of Virginia, 1989).

Gould, Stephen Jay, *Ever Since Darwin: Reflections in Natural History* (London: Penguin, 1991).

Green, Michael K., ed., *Issues in Native American Cultural Identity* (New York: Peter Lang, 1995).

Hall, Stuart, *The Hard Road to Renewal* (London: Verso, 1988).

Hendricks, Margo, and Parker, Patricia, eds, *Women, 'Race', and Writing in the Early Modern Period* (London: Routledge, 1994).

Howitt, A.W., *The Native Tribes of South-East Australia* (London: Macmillan and Co., Ltd, 1904).

Huet, Marie-Hélène, *Monstrous Imagination* (Cambridge, Mass.: Harvard University Press, 1993).

Hulme, Peter, *Colonial Encounters: Europe and the Native Caribbean, 1492–1979* (London: Methuen, 1986).

Johnson, Susan, and Macintyre, Stuart, eds, *Through White Eyes* (Sydney: Allen and Unwin, 1990).

Kennedy, Liam, 'Memory and Hearsay: Ethnic History and Identity in *Billy Phelan's Greatest Game* and *Ironweed*', *MELUS* 18, 1 (Spring 1993), 71–82.

Kennedy, William, *O, Albany!* (New York: Penguin, 1983).

Kennedy, William, *Ironweed* (Harmondsworth: Penguin, 1986).

Krupat, Arnold, *For Those Who Come After: A Study of Native American Autobiography* (Berkeley: California University Press, 1985).

Krupat, Arnold, ed., *New Voices in Native American Literary Criticism* (Washington, D.C.: Smithsonian Institution Press, 1993).

Kuklick, Henrika, *The Savage Within: The Social History of British Anthropology, 1885–1914* (Cambridge: Cambridge University Press, 1991).

Kuper, Adam, *Anthropologists and Anthropology: The British School, 1922–72* (Harmondsworth: Penguin, 1975).

Kuper, Adam, *The Invention of Primitive Society: Transformations of an Illusion* (London: Routledge, 1991).

Lewis, Diane, 'Anthropology and Colonialism', *Current Anthropology* 14, 5 (December 1973), 581–602.

Littlefield, Daniel L., ed., *A Sketch of the Life of Okah Tubbee (called) William Chubbee, Son of the Head Chief, Mosholeh Tubbee, of the Choctaw Nation of Indians, by Laah Ceil Elaah Tubbee, His Wife* (Lincoln: Nebraska University Press, 1988).

Locke, Alain, *The New Negro: An Interpretation* (New York: Athenaeum, 1968).

London, Jack, *The Cruise of the 'Snark'* (New York: Macmillan, 1911).

London, Jack, *Tales of the Pacific*, Introduction and Afterword by Andrew Sinclair (London: Penguin, 1989).

Long Lance, Chief Buffalo Child, *Long Lance* (London: Transworld Publishers, 1956).

Loomba, Ania, *Gender, Race, Renaissance Drama* (Manchester: Manchester University Press, 1989).

Lorimer, Douglas, *Colour, Class and the Victorians: English Attitudes to the Negro in the mid-nineteenth century* (Leicester: Leicester University Press, 1978).

McLennan, John, *Primitive Marriage: An Inquiry into the Origin of the Form of Capture in Marriage Ceremonies* (Edinburgh: Black & Co., 1865).

Marcus, George E., and Cushman, Dick, 'Ethnographies as Texts', *Annual Review of Anthropology* 11 (1982), 25–69.

Marcus, George E., and Fischer, Michael J., *Anthropology as Cultural Critique: An Experimental Moment in the Human Sciences* (Chicago: Chicago University Press, 1986).

Melville, Herman, *Typee* (Harmondsworth: Penguin, 1938).

Moore, Henrietta L., *Feminism and Anthropology* (Oxford: Polity Press, 1988).

Moore, Henrietta L., *A Passion for Difference: Essays in Anthropology and Gender* (Oxford: Polity Press, 1994).

Morrison, Toni, 'City Limits, Village Values: Concepts of Neighborhood in Black Fiction', in *Literature and the Urban American Experience*, pp. 35–43, ed. Michael C. Jaye and Ann Chalmers Watts (Manchester: Manchester University Press, 1981).

Morrison, Toni, *Beloved* (London: Picador, 1988).

Morrison, Toni, *Playing in the Dark: Whiteness and the Literary Imagination* (Cambridge: Harvard University Press, 1992).

Morrison, Toni, *Jazz* (London: Picador, [1992] 1993).

Nixon, Rob, 'Caribbean and African Appropriations of *The Tempest*', *Critical Inquiry* 13 (1987), 557–78.

Orgel, Stephen, 'Shakespeare and the Cannibals', in *Cannibals, Witches, and Divorce*, pp. 40–66, ed. Marjorie Garber (Baltimore: Johns Hopkins University Press, 1985).

Owens, Louis, *Other Destinies: Understanding the American Indian Novel* (Norman: Oklahoma University Press, 1992).

Parry, Benita, 'Problems in current theories of colonial discourse', *The Oxford Literary Review* 9, 1–2 (1987), 27–58.

Pearce, Roy Harvey, *Savagism and Civilisation: A Study of the Indian and the American Mind* (Baltimore: Johns Hopkins University Press, 1967).

Pieterse, Jan Nederveen, *White on Black: Images of Africa and Blacks in Western Popular Culture* (New Haven: Yale University Press, 1992).

Ralegh, Sir Walter, 'The discoverie of the large, rich, and beautifull Empire of Guiana', in *The Principal Navigations Voyages Traffiques and Discoveries of the English Nation*, vol. 10, ed. Richard Hakluyt, 12 vols (Glasgow: Maclehose, 1904).

Richards, David, *Masks of Difference: Cultural Representations in Literature, Anthropology and Art* (Cambridge: Cambridge University Press, 1994).

Said, Edward W., *Orientalism* (Harmondsworth: Penguin, 1978).

Said, Edward W., 'Representing the Colonized: Anthropology's Interlocutors', *Critical Inquiry* 15, 2 (Winter 1989), 205–25.

Scheik, William J., *The Half-Blood: A Cultural Symbol in 19th-Century American Fiction* (Lexington: Kentucky University Press, 1979).

Shakespeare, William, *The Tempest*, Arden edn, ed. Frank Kermode (London: Methuen, 1985).

Sheehan, Bernard, *Savagism and Civility. Indians and Englishmen in Colonial Virginia* (Cambridge: Cambridge University Press, 1980).

Sider, Gerald M., *Lumbee Indian Histories: Race, Ethnicity and Indian Identity in the Southern United States* (Cambridge: Cambridge University Press, 1993).

Singh, Amritjit, Skerrett, Joseph T., Jr, and Hogan, Robert E., eds, *Memory and Cultural Politics: New Approaches to American Ethnic Literatures* (Boston: Northeastern University Press, 1996).

Smith, Donald B., *Long Lance: The True Story of an Imposter* (Lincoln: Nebraska University Press, 1982).

Smith, Sidonie, *Where I'm Bound: Patterns of Slavery and Freedom in Black American Autobiography* (London: Greenwood Press, 1974).

Sollors, Werner, *Beyond Ethnicity: Consent and Descent in American Culture* (New York: Oxford University Press, 1986).

Sollors, Werner, ed., *The Invention of Ethnicity* (New York: Oxford University Press, 1989).

Spencer, Walter Baldwin, and Gillen, Francis, *The Native Tribes of Central Australia* (London: Macmillan and Co., 1899).

Stepto, Robert B., Jr, *From Behind the Veil: A Study of Afro-American Narrative* (Urbana: Illinois University Press, 1989).

Stevenson, Robert Louis, 'The Strange Case of Dr Jekyll and Mr Hyde', in *Dr Jekyll and Mr Hyde, The Merry Men and Other Tales*, pp. 1–62 (London: Dent, 1925).

Stocking, George W., Jr, *Race, Culture, and Evolution: Essays in the History of Anthropology* (Chicago: The University of Chicago Press, 1982).

Stocking, George W., Jr, *Victorian Anthropology* (New York: The Free Press, 1987).

Street, Brian V., *The Savage in Literature: Representations of 'primitive' society in English fiction 1858–1920* (London: Routledge and Kegan Paul, 1975).

Taussig, Michael, *Shamanism, Colonialism, and the Wild Man: A Study in Terror and Healing* (Chicago: The University of Chicago Press, 1987).

Tedlock, Dennis, 'The Analogical Tradition and the Emergence of a Dialogical Anthropology', *Journal of Anthropological Research* 35, 4 (Winter 1979), 387–400.

Thomas, Nicholas, *Colonialism's Culture: Anthropology, Travel and Government* (Cambridge: Polity Press, 1994).

Toll, Robert C., *Blacking Up: The Minstrel Show in 19th Century America* (New York: Oxford University Press, 1974).

Torgovnick, Marianna, *Gone Primitive: Savage Intellects, Modern Lives* (Chicago: University of Chicago Press, 1990).

Travis, Molly Abel, 'Speaking from the Silence of the Slave Narrative: *Beloved* and African-American Women's History', *The Texas Review* 13 (1992), 69–81.

Trinh, Minh-ha T., *Woman, Native, Other: Writing Postcoloniality and Feminism* (Bloomington: Indiana University Press, 1989).

Turner, Lynnette, 'Feminism, Femininity and Ethnographic Authority', *Women: a cultural review* 2, 3 (1991), 238–54.

Wells, H.G., *The Island of Doctor Moreau* (Harmondsworth: Penguin, 1946).

Wells, H.G., 'The Time Machine', in *Selected Short Stories*, pp. 7–83 (Harmondsworth: Penguin, 1958).

Wilde, Oscar, *The Picture of Dorian Gray* (Oxford: Oxford University Press, 1981).

Young, Robert, *White Mythologies: Writing History and the West* (London: Routledge, 1990).

Young, Robert, *Colonial Desire. Hybridity in Theory, Culture and Race* (London: Routledge, 1995).

Zamir, Shamoon, *Dark Voices: W.E.B. DuBois and American Thought, 1888–1903* (Chicago: University of Chicago Press, 1995).

Index